T0342276

Latecomer State Formation

Latecomer State Formation

Political Geography and Capacity Failure in Latin America

Sebastián Mazzuca

Yale

UNIVERSITY PRESS

New Haven & London

Published with assistance from the foundation established in memory of
Calvin Chapin of the Class of 1788, Yale College.

Yale University Press books may be purchased in quantity for educational, business, or
promotional use. For information, please e-mail sales.press@yale.edu (U.S. office) or
sales@yaleup.co.uk (U.K. office).

Set in Bulmer type by Westchester Publishing Services.
Printed in the United States of America.

Library of Congress Control Number: 2020942447
ISBN 978-0-300-24895-1 (hardcover : alk. paper)

A catalogue record for this book is available from the British Library.

This paper meets the requirements of ANSI/NISO Z39.48-1992 (Permanence of Paper).

10 9 8 7 6 5 4 3 2 1

Contents

Acknowledgments

GERARDO MUNCK AND Ruth Berins Collier helped so much with this book that it would not exist without them. Gerardo read all versions of all chapters. His feedback could easily fill two book-length manuscripts. Yet quality trumped quantity. Each of Gerardo's suggestions was an unambiguous improvement. Gerardo is a true scientist. I hope I have imported into this book some visible outcomes of his constant search for theoretical sophistication, empirical proof, and presentational clarity. Ruth is the gold standard of writing mentors. If I could give my students a fraction of the creative support she has given me, then I would feel accomplished. Ruth is a genuine intellectual. Her brain is a prodigious radar for good ideas. Dozens of times she forced me to pursue insights and rearticulate points that I thought were dead ends. Dozens of times she was right. I found intellectual gold at the end of the road she suggested. Gerardo and Ruth share an endless generosity. The support of both of them was in itself a life lesson. Infinite gratitude is not reserved only for loving parents.

David Collier is on many dimensions the person who most contributed to my scholarship. His encouragement as a mentor is uniquely powerful. Countless times David made me feel that my research and career mattered more to him than his own.

Robert Powell's superior intelligence was directly or indirectly the guardian of all properly microfounded arguments the book has to offer. James Robinson's voracity for understanding politics in unfamiliar places has been an inspiration throughout my graduate school. A curiosity: in the process of helping me, Jim became a better expert on state formation in Latin America than I could ever be. Hillel Soifer is too young to do what he does: he produces creative, serious, and ultrahelpful feedback only. Three colleagues at Johns Hopkins, Nicolas Jabko, Steven Teles, and Adam Sheingate, provided outstanding feedback in a special workshop and superlative advice on almost every issue related to the production of this book. With Ernesto dal Bó, I share an obsession to understand Argentina's economic and political development. Ernesto's support and feedback were as generous as they were smart.

I will never forget my long years of interaction with Guillermo O'Donnell and Tulio Halperín Donghi. Throughout my education in Buenos Aires, Guillermo was the sun in my solar system. I recall vividly the moment I made the decision to study state formation in Latin America. It was when I first read about "brown areas," one of Guillermo's many conceptual innovations that instantly became a classic idea. Meetings with Tulio at the coffee shop at the corner of Center and Oxford in Berkeley were an intellectual feast. A single sentence by Tulio was a thousand lessons in history. I owe him the ability to see nineteenth-century politics in Latin America not as a "foreign language"—as it seemed to me until my late twenties—but as a familiar, inviting, and extremely rewarding place to visit. There is nothing I would have liked more than to give Guillermo and Tulio a copy.

Three colleagues in my department, Steven David, Daniel Deudney, and Robert Lieberman, helped me see bigger questions when I was convinced I had already asked the biggest ones. I find special value in the way they shared their talent with me. They had no reason to do it, other than helping out a junior colleague and a feeling of genuine curiosity about processes beyond their geographic comfort zone.

George Akerlof, Manuel Alcántara Sáez, Robert Bates, Alan Clutterbuck, Jorge Domínguez, Kent Eaton, Tulia Faletti, Robert Fishman, Jordan Gans-Morse, Lucas González, Antonio Hermosa Andújar, Robert Kaufman, Marco Larizza, Steven Levitsky, Juan Pablo Luna, Scott Mainwaring, Andrés Malamud, Christopher Muller, Harris Mylonas, Gabriel Paquette, Aníbal Pérez-Liñán, Eduardo Posada-Carbó, Gérard Roland, María Paula Saffon Sanín, Julio Saguir, Richard Snyder, and Rodrigo Zarazaga gave surgical feedback on critical parts of the manuscript.

The two anonymous reviewers of Yale University Press substantially improved the quality of the book.

The Political Science Department at Hopkins recruits amazing graduate students. Six of them commented on large portions of the book with unique sharpness and originality: Julieta Casas, Nandini Dey, José Luis Rodríguez, Lynsy Smithson-Stanley, Maximiliano Véjares, and Raied Haj Yahya. Lynsy additionally helped to make my written English less nonnative.

Jessie Spruill, who helped me draw the maps in ArcGIS, is a phenomenal asset and a pleasure to work with. Oliver Goodman has been an excellent research assistant.

I thank the good friends I have made since I came to Baltimore for fully supporting my vocation despite not being fully clear what it was about: Charlie and Ruth Cronheim, Anthony Corradetti, Charles and Maureen Platt, Graeme and Leigh Woodworth, Angelo Leto Barone, and Sarah Crowley.

My father, *el flaco Tito*, has been a hero since the day I was born. Medical doctor by profession but intellectual by genetics, he never stopped believing in the value of the book. His consistent enthusiasm was a lovely remedy for my moments of skepticism. Unconditional support from the Mazzuca-Cataldo-Taylor family has been like oxygen for decades—taken for granted yet vital.

This book is dedicated to two women who share a name: M. Magali, the memory and the future.

Tables, Figures, and Maps

xi

Introduction

THE WAVE OF DEMOCRATIZATION that swept across Latin America from the early 1980s to the late 1990s contains a most valuable, if bitter, lesson in political development. Authoritarianism was not the only political evil in the region. *State weakness* was an equally corrosive, although less visible, problem. Most dictatorships are gone, but incapable states persist. State weakness is the single most important source of Latin America's chronic problems, including social inequality, economic stagnation, and poor governance.

Systematic research on state capacities in Latin America began only after the democratization process. Yet weak states predate contemporary democracies in the region by at least a full century. Democracy obviously did not cause state weakness. On the contrary, chronic state weakness caused young democracies to underperform. Most scholarship on Latin America's contemporary, low-capacity democracies looks for causes among recent phenomena, including the form of regime transition, party system dynamics, neoliberal reform, international commodity prices, and policy turns. Research should be purged of this presentist bias and focus instead on the long-term historical sources.

Weakness is a "birth defect" of Latin American states. The process of *state formation* is a true critical juncture in that it creates durable legacies for the development of state capacities. The pioneering modern states of western Europe were created strong, and the formation process endowed them with propensities to upgrade their own capacity. In Latin America, states were born weak, and the formation process in the nineteenth century created tough impediments to building capacity in the twentieth century.

The Latin American state historically has been marked by a distinct combination of territorial stability and capacity failure. Throughout the twentieth century, the risk of territorial losses in Latin America, through either foreign invasion or local secession, was extremely low. Substantial

1

territorial changes have been much more frequent in both western Europe, the region that "invented" modern state capacities, and Tropical Africa, a region of virtual statelessness. Yet resources freed by the absence of territorial threats—the Latin American geopolitical bonus—were not used to build state capacity. Low capacity has resulted in persistent underprovision of public goods.

Latin America succeeded at *state formation*, but it failed at *state building*. This is not an oxymoron. On the contrary. Between 1850 and 1875, most Latin American countries completed state formation, including the twin achievements of territory consolidation and violence monopolization. Yet, in contrast to the cases of western Europe, state formation in Latin America was not a precursor of state building, a process Max Weber characterized as the transition from patrimonial rule to bureaucratic administration. Weberian bureaucratization involves a gradual but steady growth in the quantity, quality, and efficiency of goods and services supplied by the government across the state's territory. Why has so much success at state formation in Latin America—unmatched even by the pioneer European cases—produced such meager results in capacity building?

In early modern western Europe, state formation had multiple linkages to state building. Violence monopolization required great efforts at fiscal extraction, which in turn caused the abolition of the intermediary power of local potentates and incited social demands for new public goods. In Latin America, the obstacles to the development of state capacities were the result of mutually convenient bargains struck by central state-makers and peripheral potentates, who, far from being eliminated during state formation, obtained institutional power to reinforce local bastions.

Alexander Gerschenkron showed that multiple paths to a modern economy exist and that paths are highly consequential for political outcomes. Latecomer industrial economies cannot replicate the trajectory of the industrial pioneers because by the time latecomers initiate the process of development, the world is already populated by industrial economies. Pioneer economies offer opportunities for imitation and create barriers against competition.[1] In the same way, multiple paths to the modern state exist, and each path has massive repercussions for long-term institutional capacity. *Latecomer state formation* cannot replicate pioneer state formation because, at the onset of latecomer state formation, the pioneers have already created a geopolitical and economic order that was absent in the original international context of state formation.

State weakness is not the only legacy of latecomer state formation in Latin America. The other is the emergence of a cluster of countries showing phenomenal variation in the number and diversity of subnational regions amalgamated, which is highly correlated with variation in size. The territory of most western European countries ranges from one-quarter to one-half million square kilometers, and the very process of state formation standardized political institutions across the subnational units of each country. By contrast, Latin American countries range from colossuses like Brazil to microstates like El Salvador. Only two countries in Latin America, Paraguay and Ecuador, fit the European range. Brazil can accommodate two western Europes and combines a substantial number of modern city-ports, several areas endowed with fertile land or valuable mineral resources, and an important number of large backward peripheries. Argentina is the size of five Frances, the largest country in western Europe. On the other hand, El Salvador and seven other Latin American countries fall below the European range. Most of them are based on a single economic region, whose comparative advantage is specialization producing a single commodity.

Both legacies are related. Competitive military pressures made the Westphalian war-maker the leading agent of state formation in western Europe. They also forced states to converge on capacity building, territorial extension, and internal political standardization. In Latin America, the absence of military threats enabled the emergence of a variety of state-formation agents: a *port*, a *party*, or a *lord* led the process. It also allowed agents to form states without Weberian attributes, gave them room to combine and exclude regions on the basis of coalitional calculations rather than geopolitical imperatives, and exempted them from the effort of exerting uniform control throughout the territory.

This book is about comparative state formation. Building on the idea that the timing of state formation in world history is crucial, it develops a theory that is general enough to explain cases of state formation with and without state building—the main contrast between western Europe and Latin America. With a simple extension, based on the type of agent leading the state-formation process, the theory also accounts for variations in territorial composition (and size) of countries, a major source of contrasts within Latin America.

The remainder of the introduction is organized in three sections. The first section lays the groundwork for the study of comparative state formation. It highlights the difference between state formation and smaller-scale political processes, including changes at the level of policy, government, and regime. It provides an overview of the theory of state formation that is able to account for the rise of states with different degrees of capacity (the analytical core of Part 1 of the book). The focus is on the international economic and geopolitical environment and the common response by Latin American state-makers. International conditions shape two opposite macrohistorical paths of state formation: *war-led* versus *trade-led*. The second section introduces the theoretical components required for the comparative analysis of state formation within Latin America (Part 2 of the book). The focus turns to local political agents to delineate variants within the general trade-led path and thereby accounts for major divergences in territorial composition and timing of state formation. The third section previews the empirical studies of each of the two parts of the book and emphasizes the interaction between careful historical reconstruction and effective political analysis.

State Formation and Capacity:
Latin America versus Western Europe
State Formation, Extraordinary Politics,
and Ordinary Motivations

State formation is a fundamentally *political* process. Yet it involves an *extraordinary* form of politics. State formation differs sharply from politics in ordinary times. Political change in ordinary times occurs at the level of policy, of government, or, less frequently, of the political regime (e.g., the rise or fall of a democracy). Changes at all three levels are usually the outcome of a transformation in the composition of the dominant political and social coalition. Even in the case of a regime change—the most fundamental of the three levels—coalition formation and transformation occur within well-defined territorial boundaries and do not challenge the monopoly of violence.

State formation is extraordinary politics in that it defines the *territorial space* enclosing the social and political actors available for subsequent coalition formation in ordinary times. Once the territory of a state is consolidated, coalitions with actors from excluded regions are no longer possible. State formation is also extraordinary politics in that it creates a *monopoly of coercion*. Once coercion is monopolized, the entire range of political strategies relying on violence is physically eliminated. If a political group struggling for a change of policy, government, or regime is willing and able to challenge the monopoly of violence, then ordinary politics becomes extraordinary politics. Under such circumstances, what initially is a policy, a government, or a regime crisis mutates into a much more serious state crisis.

The facts of state formation in western Europe, as stylized by authors working in the Weberian tradition, support a strong division between the politics of state formation and the politics of ordinary times. Warriors, not politicians, led the state-formation effort. They constantly sought to maximize the territory under their control. The main constraint to maximization was the capacity of the neighboring ruler, who was also a warrior. European warriors were too busy preventing invasions or attempting annexations to stop and consider the coalitional implications of incorporating or excluding an additional piece of land.

In Latin America, the distinction between the extraordinary politics of state formation and the ordinary politics of policy, government, and regime transformation remains crucial. Yet state formation in Latin America cannot be understood without considering the ordinary political motivation of coalition formation. Exempted from the geopolitical pressures faced by the western European pioneers, Latin American state-makers made decisions to incorporate or exclude future subnational units on the basis of the expected coalitional consequences of different combinations of regions. Latin American state-makers were willing to incorporate regions that translated into a net coalitional benefit and excluded those regions that were expected to cause a coalitional loss. Latin American state-makers did engage in extraordinary politics, but they did so in pursuit of eminently ordinary goals.

In sum, in Latin American state formation, the demarcation of the "national" territory was a function of expected coalitional outcomes and not vice versa. In contrast to state formation in western Europe, whose leaders maximized the international security of their territories even at the cost of coalitional losses in the national arena, Latin American state-makers, unburdened from international threats, could focus squarely on the coalitional consequences of their territorial decisions. Also, in contrast to ordinary politics everywhere, in which protagonists maneuver to extract as much coalitional support as possible from a *fixed* territorial space, state-formation politics in Latin America allowed its leaders to *adapt* the size of the national political arena so as to engineer the optimal coalition of support. In Latin American state formation, the departure from state formation in western Europe and normal politics everywhere could not be more radical.

State Formation with or without State Capacity

The distinction between state formation and state building is crucial to differentiate outcomes across western Europe and Latin America. If state formation is defined as the process by which a territory is consolidated and the means of coercion within it monopolized, then it becomes conceivable that state formation occurs with or without state building. State building refers to the development of capacity by the central administration to provide public goods in an increasingly efficient and territorially even fashion. The distinction also enables theorizing about the relation between state formation and state building. Depending on the path of state formation, the impact on state building can be positive, neutral, or negative.

Prior research has taken state formation and state building as synonymous, or it has made the assumption that state formation has only positive effects on state building. Yet the best summary of Latin America's long-term political development is "state formation *against* state building." By the time state formation was completed, Latin American states were endowed with strong antibodies against capacity building.

State formation can follow two polar paths: war-led versus trade-led state formation. Both processes are set in motion by a distinct constellation of economic and geopolitical features in the international context. Crucially, only the war-led process has the potential to foster state building, and only the trade-led process carries the risk that the new state will undermine capacity building. In the war-led process, geopolitical pressures are the key input in the decision-making process of would-be state-makers. Their main goal is preparation for war. Political survival depends on the accumulation of resources—land, weapons, taxes, and soldiers—that contribute to the defense and expansion of the emerging state's territory. In the trade-led process, opportunities from international commerce are the key input for state-makers. The main goal is to create a positive business climate for expanding the export sector. Political survival depends on success at generating export-led growth, which in turn unlocks vital flows of fiscal revenue through tariffs on international trade.

The war-led and trade-led processes induce opposite strategies for dealing with patrimonial rulers dominating the peripheries. In the war-led process, the key is to eliminate patrimonialism, which would otherwise compete with central rulers for the control of land, men, and local resources. Central state-makers and peripheral potentates are mortal enemies. In the trade-led process, the elimination of patrimonialism is strictly counterproductive for state formation, at least in the short run. Waging a battle against peripheral notables torpedoes the plan of export-led growth by pulverizing the business climate required for investment and production. The key is to appease peripheral patrimonial rulers through promises of future shares in the expansion of the economy. State-makers in the center and patrimonial rulers in the peripheries become partners. In the war-led process of state formation, the center-periphery relation is a zero-sum game, but it can be a positive-sum negotiation in the trade-led process.

The key technical task of state-makers in the trade-led process of state formation is to supply the key legal and physical infrastructure required to create a dynamic export sector: property rights and a transportation system. In turn, the two technical prerequisites demand a *political* effort: pacification. Pacification is crucial to secure a safe business environment for large merchants and producers in the export sector—primarily landlords and mine owners—and to attract foreign investments in the infrastructure sector.

In nineteenth-century Latin America, a modicum of pacification contained the promise of huge political success for the political elite who was able to achieve it. Pacification would incentivize exports, which in turn would provide hard currency for imports of mass-consumption goods, mostly industrial textiles. Import duties would finally secure a stable stream of government revenues. Enhanced export revenues would fuel the virtuous cycle of trade-led state formation. Revenues would be used to expand the provision of property rights and public transportation and to reinforce pacification, the political prerequisite of the legal and technological projects. Patrimonial rulers in the periphery were potential state-breakers. But they could be bought off with subsidies. The support of patrimonial rulers consolidated pacification. Landlords and mine owners in the export sector benefited from the expansion of infrastructure, including more and better roads to the coast, upgraded port facilities (from larger warehouses to safer harbors), and, starting around 1850, railways and steam navigation of internal rivers. The support of large merchants, landlords, and mine owners enhanced the fiscal prospects of the government, which depended on foreign trade to finance itself. The lion's share of the revenues was contributed by poor or middle-class members of society, who were the largest consumers of European and U.S. imports.

If western European leaders of the state-formation process were warmakers, their Latin American counterparts can be considered *marketmakers*, a historically novel type of state-maker. Their political survival was inextricably tied to the provision of the legal and physical infrastructure required for export-led growth. In contrast to the western European warmakers, the Latin American market-makers neither needed nor wanted a transformation of the patrimonial bastions surrounding the capital, the port, and the export sector. They did not need peripheral transformation because fiscal resources were much more abundant and easier to obtain through import duties, the cost of which was shouldered by a large, disorganized public. The cost was substantial, but, diluted among tens of thousands of consumers, it did not risk retaliatory collective action. Also, the Latin American market-makers did not want to transform the periphery because challenging its patrimonial rulers would require long years of civil war and delay indefinitely the process of trade-led state formation. Patrimonial rulers in the periphery were much more fearsome rivals than the disorganized public. Consumers paid not only for the infrastructure required by the export sector but also for the "peace tax" demanded by patrimonial bastions to remain quiet. The survival, and in some cases revitalization, of patrimonial potentates after the process of state formation was completed has been the chief impediment to state building in Latin America.

Territorial Combination and Timing of Violence Monopolization: Variations within Latin America

The trade-led path of state formation allows for variations in the territorial composition of countries and in the timing of violence monopolization that are inconceivable in the war-led path. Latin America combines territorial colossuses and microstates. In some countries, like Brazil, Chile, and Venezuela, territory consolidation and violence monopolization were achieved at the same time. In others, like Mexico, Colombia, and Uruguay, a gap of decades separated territory consolidation from violence monopolization.

Both the size of the territory and the timing of violence monopolization are important outcomes. Low capacity in the three colossuses, Argentina, Brazil, and Mexico, can be traced to two factors: a chronic lack of fiscal and human resources to broadcast central power throughout the territory and the enduring legacy of negotiations in the state-formation period between central rulers and peripheral oligarchies. State-formation deals allowed peripheral rulers to secure bastions of patrimonial domination, or what Guillermo O'Donnell, referring to more recent phenomena, has called "brown areas."[2] Large physical size is a sufficient condition for weak states in Latin America. A large territory in postcolonial Latin America could only be consolidated through durable patrimonial deals. In contrast, as the cases of Nicaragua, Ecuador, and Paraguay show, small size is not a sufficient condition for capacity. Small size, however, has been a necessary condition for state capacity. Chile, Uruguay, and Costa Rica are the only exceptions to the generalized pattern of capacity weakness. In the period of state formation, a relatively dynamic economic center had virtually no peripheral areas to incorporate. Hence, state-makers in all three countries were able to dispense with concessions to the patrimonial oligarchies that usually dominated peripheries.

A most instructive comparison can be drawn between Uruguay and a counterfactual independent state of Buenos Aires—which was only a few political contingencies away from becoming a permanent reality. Over the course of the nineteenth century, Buenos Aires's economy was much stronger than that of Uruguay. Starting in the mid-1830s, the capacity of the state of Buenos Aires to provide public goods approached that of the countries in the North Atlantic. In the 1850s, Buenos Aires also made the full transition from patrimonial rule to competitive oligarchic politics. Economic prosperity, fiscal strength, and political competition are conventional precursors of state capacity in small states. Armed with all three, Buenos Aires could have created the most capable state in Latin America. In fact, it was an independent state from 1852 to 1861. In the early 1860s, however, Buenos Aires merged with a large periphery subdivided into an array of political bastions dominated by patrimonial lords. Argentina is the territorial outcome of the merger. In Argentina, patrimonial rule in the peripheries not only survived but also propagated, via power-sharing arrangements, through the entire political arena. As a result, the central state became a large-scale patronage machine. Uruguay, currently a high-quality democracy, shows Buenos Aires the kind of state it could have become if in the 1860s it had not unified with the Andean ministates in the West and North of present-day Argentina.

The timing of violence monopolization in relation to territory consolidation can make or break a country's economy. Mexico, Colombia, and Uruguay consolidated their territories three, four, and five decades before they monopolized violence. Colombia and Uruguay experienced an intermediate outcome: pacification through a truce between two partisan armies that had established a 'duopoly of violence.' Before violence monopolization or truce negotiation, civil war was a permanent condition in all three countries. Civil war, in turn, seriously discouraged investments, foreign or domestic, and caused massive destruction of human resources and economic assets, from roads and mines to livestock and farms. By the time the three countries achieved pacification, they had lost, on average, four decades of economic development to civil wars. The loss was particularly acute given the favorable conditions for primary commodity exports in 1850–75. A comparison between Colombia and Brazil provides extraordinary insight. Colombia is endowed with the agronomic resources to produce top-quality coffee, superior even to the coffee grown in the Brazilian Southeast. Yet, by the late 1830s, Brazil became the undisputed world leader of coffee production. Brazilian coffee created extraordinary fortunes in Rio de Janeiro and São Paulo. The hegemony of Brazil's coffee in world markets extended well into the twentieth century. The torrential flows of income could have easily been earned by the coffee farmers of central Colombia. It did not happen because civil wars paralyzed Colombia's economy during the entirety of the first boom in coffee consumption in Continental Europe and the United States.

Brazil fully benefited from the opportunity that civil conflict forced Colombia to miss. Tellingly, the so-called Coffee Republic in Colombia was inaugurated in 1903, a year after Colombia's last major civil war, which persuaded both parties to create power-sharing institutions that would dissuade the opposition from military insurrection.

To account for variations in territory consolidation and timing of violence monopolization, three analytical tools are required. They essentially extend the theory in Part 1 by adding political agency.

From Market-Makers to Polity-Makers

To understand variations in size and timing, the perspective on Latin American state-makers needs to be expanded. They should no longer be seen as only market-makers defending the interests of large merchants and export producers. They also have to be regarded as *polity-makers* centrally interested in advancing their own professional careers. Even after meeting the demands of the economic elites for the physical requirements of trade-led state formation, state-makers have substantial room to maneuver on issues that do not affect profit-making but have a direct impact on power maximization.

As polity-makers, leaders of the state-formation process switch focus from technical decisions (the supply of property rights and transportation infrastructure) to strictly political choices about which regions to include in the territory of the nascent state and which to exclude from it. Latin American state-makers faced highly consequential decisions about territory consolidation. They sought to produce the combination of regions that best served their goal: remaining at the pinnacle of power for as long as possible. Differences in size of Latin American states are rooted in contrasting choices about the optimal combination of regions.

Formula of Territorial Governance

Dominant theoretical visions about the sequence of state formation and regime change explicitly claim that states are created *first* and rules are put in place *subsequently* to limit, divide, or gain access to the power of the state. In the dominant view, rules—like parliamentary supremacy, elections, proportional representation, and federalism—are political institutions created after the process of state formation is completed. A general theory of state formation cannot depend on the "state first" assumption. It must be able to explain the fact that states and lower-level political institutions may be *joint* creations.

The "state first" assumption is simply incompatible with the notion that regions considering whether to join the territory of an emerging state are strategic, forward-looking actors. When regions are the main players in the process of state formation, the key institution is the formula of territorial governance, which can be confederal, federal, or unitarian. When deciding whether to join a state, regions condition entry on their expected position within the institutional hierarchy created by the formula of territorial governance. A region that rejects joining a territory whose leaders embrace a unitarian formula may very well agree to join the same territory if state-making leaders switch to federal (or confederal) institutions of territorial governance, thus granting home rule to the undecided region. The type of formula is then a necessary condition for a set of regions to combine in a single country. The formula is an instrument of territory consolidation.

The leaders of the state-formation process, in their role as polity-makers, see the range of formulas of territorial governance as the menu of options they can offer to the regions they are interested in incorporating into the emerging territory. What offer the state-making center is willing to make and what offer the surrounding regions are willing to accept depend on differentials of economic and military power. No state is born without at least an implicit formula of territorial governance. To the extent that a specific formula of territorial governance can turn a "state-breaking" region into a "state-taking" one, it can be viewed as a proximate cause of state formation, thus reversing the state-first sequence of the dominant vision. The formula of territorial governance is the only variable under full control of the state-making elite. If the elite wants to extend political power beyond its local territory, the formula is its main bargaining chip.

Agents of State Formation: Pathways and Outcomes

Politicians, not warriors, led the processes of state formation in Latin America. Politicians were of three kinds: *port*, *party*, and *lord*. The port is obviously a location, not an actor, but the term is used as a shorthand for a political entrepreneur in close alliance with the commercial interests of an important city-port, like Rio de Janeiro, Buenos Aires, or Valparaíso. The party, in contrast to the port and the lord, is a collective actor. Moreover, the agent of state formation is not a single party; rather, it is the dynamics of competition between two or more parties that sets in motion the process of state formation. Finally, the lord is what in Latin America is known as the *caudillo*, a large landowner at the top of an informal hierarchy of clients that includes smaller landowners and a vast following of rural workers who, in exchange for employment and protection, supply labor in times of peace and become soldiers in times of war. In Part 2, a typology systematizes similarities and contrasts among state-formation agents, including the canonical warrior of western Europe.

Each type of agent defines a distinct pathway of trade-led state formation. The pathways are the main source of differentiation in the number and diversity of regions that form each country (and, thereby, its size) and in the timing of violence monopolization. In the port-driven pathway of state formation, the political entrepreneur shows a propensity to *territorial expansion*, that is, the combination of a dynamic economic center and a number of backward peripheries. The entrepreneur profits from incorporating peripheries that yield coalitional dividends. In incorporating peripheries, the entrepreneur hurts the material prosperity of the port—his original political base—because the peripheries demand a share of the port's wealth. The political entrepreneur persuades the port that economic transfers will appease the peripheries, which if excluded from the emerging state will become a permanent threat of predatory invasion. The lord-driven pathway and the party-driven pathway can usefully be seen as each involving a distinct pair of commonalities and differences in relation to the benchmark. The party-driven pathway shares with the port-driven pathway the expansionary coalitional propensity by which parties are willing to incorporate surrounding regions in order to enlarge the support basis. By contrast, the lord-driven pathway shows a *reductionist propensity* because the lord fears that an expansion of the political arena will undermine the patrimonial hierarchy that forms the basis of his power. Yet the lord-driven and the port-driven pathways have in common the advantage of supremacy: precisely because the lord and the entrepreneur choose the territorial combination that maximizes their power, they rule undisputed in the emerging state. They achieve territory consolidation and violence monopolization at the same time. By contrast, in the party-driven pathway, political supremacy is disputed between two parties that manifestly cannot defeat each other, either in electoral contests or in armed conflict. In the party-driven pathway, a temporal gap separates territory consolidation from violence monopolization.

The port-driven pathway, followed by Argentina and Brazil, produces territorial colossuses that achieve territory consolidation and violence monopolization simultaneously. The party-driven pathway has the potential to create states with large territories combining multiple economic regions, like Mexico and Colombia, but a temporal gap between territory consolidation and violence monopolization causes protracted civil conflict. The lord-driven pathway in Latin America shows some superficial similarities to the warrior-driven path that dominated the experience of early modern Europe. Yet, precisely because it is a specific version of the general trade-led path, lord-driven state formation departs from the warrior-driven state formation in two crucial respects. First, Latin American lords, in contrast to European warriors, are not territory maximizers. They engage in bastion formation rather than in large-scale territorial projects. They are state-breakers in relation to large-scale territorial projects, for instance, Antonio Páez in relation to Bolívar's Gran Colombia (Colombia, Panama, Ecuador, and Venezuela), Rafael Carrera in relation to the Central American Federation, and Ramón Castilla in relation to the Peru-Bolivian Confederation. They are state-makers of smaller states—Venezuela, Guatemala, and Peru—the territory of which is coterminous with the spatial extension of their clientelistic network. Second, Latin American lords, once in power, prioritize commercial opportunities over geopolitical ambitions; they quickly turn from warriors into merchants.

Methods, Cases, and Sources

The persistence of Latin America's modern political geography for almost two centuries is a remarkable phenomenon by the standards of the pioneer cases of state formation in western Europe, which still experienced major border changes in the wake of the two world wars and the Cold War. It is also an extraordinary outcome within Latin America itself. The durability of Latin American national territories since the mid-nineteenth century stands in sharp contrast with the instability of almost everything else, including major changes in political regime and drastic reversals in macroeconomic and social policies during the second half of the twentieth century.

The stability of Latin America's states is most impressive when seen from the perspective of the generalized collapse of state structures in the first half of the nineteenth century, during the periods of Independence (1810–25) and Failure (1825–45), as characterized in Chapter 2. This turning point in the middle of the nineteenth century requires special methodological attention.

No political outcome is ever preordained. Yet, in the formation of Latin American countries, the chain of steps through which small regions combined into national political arenas or made a bid for secession was a particularly open-ended process. History textbooks in every primary and secondary school of Latin America repeat a timeline in which the onset of independence and the birth of the country occur at the same time and through the same process. Until recently, scholarly research has made a similar mistake. Professional historians have admitted the existence of a major temporal gap between political independence and country formation. Yet traditional historiography has largely taken for granted the existence of a unique path linking the declaration of independence and the creation of what the discipline customarily calls "the nation." Most countries around the world craft a national history, together with an anthem, a podium of founding fathers, a flag, and other patriotic symbols. The national history in all Latin American countries is a chronicle of "overconvergence": the entire range of factors in the chronicle, from the most immutable social structures to the volatile choices of different political leaders, intertwined between 1810 and 1850 to produce Mexico, Venezuela, or Chile as the final result.

Few historians believe that social processes have inexorable outcomes. Yet many historiographic traditions have for decades pursued a biased agenda in the research of state formation. They only value findings that establish the antecedent conditions that made a positive contribution to the formation of present-day countries. The loss of theoretical and historical knowledge caused by the bias is enormous. The loss can be divided into two equally pernicious categories: unknown paths and false steps. Unknown paths include processes and events that had a positive impact on the creation of countries that were a different combination of regions from the ones that finally consolidated but have not been recorded. False steps refer to aspects of known processes and events that made a negative contribution to the formation of a present-day country but are ignored at the expense of less important aspects that are assumed to have had a positive impact.

It is historians who warned against the dangers of the *post hoc, ergo propter hoc* fallacy. In the context of the study of large social and political transformations, the sociologist Reinhard Bendix aptly called it the bias of "retrospective determinism."[3] To avoid the fallacy, a typical reaction by contemporary historians has been to forgo notions of causality altogether. However, state formation in Latin America is full of causal processes and viable counterfactuals. Any point in history has multiple futures ahead. At the onset of the state-formation process, a range of territorial combinations is possible.

Borrowing from Charles Tilly's characterization of late medieval western Europe, early independent Latin America is indeed a "cemetery of failed states."[4] Some failed states were "large" in the sense that they combined the territories of various present-day countries, like Gran Colombia, the Central American Federation (all isthmian states minus Panama), and the Peru-Bolivian Confederation. "Small" failed states, which were later absorbed by present-day countries, were much more numerous. A nonexhaustive list includes the Confederation of the Equator (northeast of present-day Brazil), the Republic of Piratini (southern Brazil), the State of Buenos Aires (the largest province of Argentina), the Republic of Tucumán (northern Argentina), Los Altos (eastern Guatemala), the State of Yucatán (southern Mexico), and the Republic of the Sierra Madre (northeastern Mexico). Finally, some failed states combined parts of different countries in today's map, like the Liga de los Pueblos Libres (Uruguay plus the ministates of the Upper Littoral in present-day Argentina).

To avoid the fallacy of retrospective determinism without giving up the search for causal connections, the key methodological premise of the book is to take counterfactual states seriously. Understanding success at state formation is in many ways the flip side of explaining the failure of alternative state projects. The case studies in Part 2 carefully specify the variety of territorial outcomes available before present-day countries consolidated as distinct combinations of regions.

Since the 1990s, a new body of historical research has shown that independence in Latin America resulted in the explosion of *pueblos*, that is, urban and rural municipalities, cities and villages, claiming full sovereignty.[5] The explosion of minisovereignties has been demonstrated in two contexts in which it had been deemed inconceivable, Brazil and Central America. For Brazil, a strong historiographic tradition used to emphasize the exceptional territorial continuity between the colonial state and the independent state. The Brazilian continuity, in turn, had been presented as a sharp contrast with the experience of Spanish America, which "balkanized" its four colonial viceroyalties into almost twenty separate countries. However, since the work by Roderick Barman, it has become increasingly hard to deny not only that independent Brazil faced multiple and serious risks of fragmentation but also that for large intervals various Brazilian provinces were full-blown independent states.[6] On a similar note, Central America, home to the smallest countries in the region, has long been considered a case of "atomization," a level of fragmentation so extreme that units with the minimum viable size became sovereign entities. The work by Jordana Dym has shown that fragmentation in Central America could have gone even further. In Honduras and El Salvador, let alone the larger Guatemala and Nicaragua, interior cities engaged in long struggles for primacy, and the conflict could have resulted in further secessions and microstates.[7]

The example of Central America has a more general theoretical lesson, which also applies to the rest of Latin America, from Mexico to Argentina. Hyperfragmentation was not the only relevant counterfactual scenario for the isthmus. At the same time that small villages were claiming international sovereignty, supraregional political coalitions were attempting to unite all cities, towns, and rural villages within a single country. That was Francisco Morazán's project of a Central American Federation, which was a tangible reality between 1823 and 1839.[8] A "forward-looking" historical approach to the creation of present-day Argentina, Colombia, Peru, and Mexico must show that, like Central America, multiple paths of territory consolidation were possible, some resulting in absorption by a larger territorial unit and others in fragmentation into smaller states.

It is customary in social science work to justify the selection of cases. A major danger for work aspiring to make causal assessments is the lack of cases displaying sufficient variation in the outcome of interest. The selection of cases in this book is ambitious, so the justification can be brief. It will consider all Latin American countries, including the observed outcomes, failed states, and viable counterfactuals.

No work has performed a comparative analysis of Argentina, Brazil, and Mexico, the three largest territories and biggest economies of the region. The comparison is most instructive. Yet, as we will see, key new insights can be derived from comparing less obvious pairs of cases, like Brazil and Central America, and Mexico and Uruguay.

For supporting causal claims about variations in state capacity, the cross-regional comparison between the modal western European process of state formation and the modal Latin American one occupies central stage. Claims about the sources of territory consolidation and violence monopolization in Latin America are based on a comparison across periods within the same region, namely, the failed experiments at state formation in 1810–50 and the successful cases between 1850 and 1880. Finally, the comparative analysis of factual and counterfactual cases within Latin America produces valuable knowledge about variations in the size and composition of national territories and in the propensity for civil war.

A note on sources: a range of concepts and theories in political science, economics, and sociology have been used to frame the largest questions of the book. I used history books in multiple languages to answer them. However, most history books were not written to answer social theory questions. Hence, on multiple occasions, I have had to look for answers in primary sources directly. Fresh archival data have been crucial in the reconstruction of the process of state formation in Brazil, Colombia, Uruguay, and especially Argentina.

Roadmap

The book is divided into two parts. Part 1 explains variations in state capacity across Latin America and western Europe. Part 2 accounts for variations within Latin America with regard to the territorial size and composition of the countries, as well as in the temporal distance between the consolidation of the national territory and the monopolization of violence, which in turn shapes the propensity to civil wars.

Each part is divided into a theoretical section and a series of empirical analyses. The theory in Part 1 builds on Weberian and Marxist insights to produce a general framework for the analysis of state formation (Chapter 1). By transforming the scope conditions implicit in the accounts based on early modern western Europe, the new theory is able to explain cases of state formation with and without state building. The theory offers a template for empirical analysis based on four components: (a) initial international conditions; (b) goals and priorities of the state-making elite; (c) resources for, and resistances against, state formation; and (d) strategies of periphery incorporation. It identifies two polar paths: war-led state formation, which is concomitant with state building, and trade-led state formation, which is inimical to state building. Closely following the template, the empirical chapters of Part 1 analyze failed experiments of state formation in Latin America in 1810–45 (Chapter 2) and the successful process around the mid-nineteenth century (Chapter 3).

In Part 1, political elites that succeeded at state formation in mid-nineteenth-century Latin America are presented as *market-makers*, which highlights the contrast with the *war-makers* of the pioneer cases in early modern western Europe. In Part 2, Latin American state-makers are analyzed from a complementary perspective, as *polity-makers* rather than market-makers.

As market-makers, political elites can initiate export-led economic growth through multiple combinations of economic and political regions. However, as polity-makers, only *a specific combination* of regions creates the political arena in which they can achieve their ultimate goal, that is, *political supremacy* vis-à-vis competing political elites. Once the short-run vitality of the export sector was secured, Latin American polity-makers had a *substantial level of latitude* in decisions that were instrumental to pursue their own political agenda, including which peripheries to include in the emerging state, which ones to exclude, and under what terms. Decisions of inclusion and exclusion were driven by coalitional motives. Polity-makers pursued the combination of regions that was optimal for their political career.

The theory section of Part 2 (Chapter 4) outlines structures and agents of state formation and shows how they shape three distinct pathways, all variants of the trade-led model: port-driven, party-driven, and lord-driven.

The empirical section of Part 2 has six chapters (Chapters 5 to 10). Chapters 5 to 7 examine the two most important cases of port-driven state formation, Argentina and Brazil. Turning to cases of party-driven state formation, Chapter 8 analyzes Mexico, and Chapter 9 focuses on Colombia and Uruguay. Finally, Chapter 10 analyzes the three most informative cases of lord-driven state formation: the collapse of the Central American Federation, Gran Colombia, and the Peru-Bolivian Confederation, followed by the creation of smaller successor states, Guatemala, Venezuela, and Peru.

The Conclusion summarizes the main theoretical and empirical findings and identifies the key contributions to state theory and to the study of long-term political trajectories in Latin America. It also presents a new agenda of research in the political economy of development. It turns from the causes of political geography analyzed in the book to its effects. It closes by sketching a theory of the potential impact of political geography on the growth capacity of countries.

PART ONE

State Formation against State Building
Latin America and Western Europe Compared

A re strong states born or made? In the pioneering experience of early modern Europe, states were born strong and remained strong. In sharp contrast, in nineteenth-century Latin America, a prime example of *latecomer* state formation, states were born weak and stayed weak through the twentieth century. If *state formation* is strictly understood as the monopolization of violence within the borders of a territory, then it can be distinguished from *state building*, the creation of central capacity to tax the population and provide public goods efficiently and evenly throughout the territory.

Variations in state capacity, both across countries and over time, are enormous. Policy innovations and institutional reform can produce *small* changes in state capacity. For *large* differences in state capacity, the main source of variation is the specific *path* taken during the state-formation process. Processes of state formation can be divided into two broad modal paths: *war-led* versus *trade-led*. They produce opposite political outcomes. The war-led path results in *strong* states, in which state formation is coupled with state building. The trade-led path produces *weak* states, in which state formation is *decoupled* from state building and potentially becomes an obstacle to it. Weak states are full members in the category of the modern state: they succeeded at both territory consolidation and violence monopolization. They failed, however, at creating capacity. A universal prerequisite of state capacity is the elimination of local clientelistic powers that can effectively interfere with the national government's ability or willingness to provide public goods in an economically efficient and territorially even fashion.

We lack adequate accounts of the uncoupling of state formation from state building, let alone of state formation becoming an *impediment* for state building. The theoretical deficit has two sources. First, theories of state formation are largely based on the truncated sample of the pioneering western European experience. In the sample, strong geopolitical pressures drove the process of violence monopolization, and international survival required destroying patrimonial rulers in peripheral areas in order to enable the efficient extraction of human and material resources. Yet, in many latecomer experiences, state formation was not achieved under geopolitical pressure. Latecomer state-makers pursued goals other than *war-making*, primarily *market-making* and *coalition-making*. A general theory of state formation must start by acknowledging that war-making is not the only driver of state formation, often it is not the main driver, and sometimes it is not a factor at all.

Second, the literature has largely reduced state formation to violence monopolization. However, state formation also involves *territory consolidation*. Territory consolidation does not refer to diplomatic negotiations between two established countries about marginal changes in their shared frontier. Territory consolidation is the political, sometimes violent, process over the course of which some regions are included within the emerging national political jurisdiction and other regions are excluded from it. In Latin America, state building did not happen because the specific *combination* of regions that constitute most countries placed durable limits to how much capacity could be developed. Other combinations would have facilitated state building. In the two largest Latin American countries, Argentina and Brazil, a central region with the potential to develop a capable local state incorporated large peripheries dominated by patrimonial rulers. In sharp contrast to the pioneer cases of western Europe, patrimonial rulers survived the state-formation process and, indeed, contaminated the entire polity by transforming the emerging central state into a large-scale patronage machine. Latin American states were born with strong antibodies against state capacity. Demarcated in the late nineteenth century, national borders in Latin America have been extremely durable by any standard (compared to borders in

Europe or to other institutions in Latin America). Success at state formation caused failure at state building.

The war-led and the trade-led models are associated with specific world-historical times. War-led state formation took place during the post-Westphalian era of western European history in the wake of the Military Revolution (1550–1650), a radical transformation in the forms and means of *destruction* that was initiated and completed *within* western Europe. Trade-led state formation occurred during the post-Independence era of Latin American history, largely as a response to the First and Second Industrial Revolutions (1760–1890), a seismic range of innovations in the forms and means of *production* that was initiated and completed *outside* Latin America.

World-historical times, such as post-Westphalian Europe or post-Independence Latin America, are defined with proper names. To understand their effects, proper names must be replaced with variables. A critical difference between state formation in the post-Westphalian era of western Europe and the Independence era of Latin America is that whereas western Europe crafted the first generation of modern states, Latin American states formed when the world was already populated by first-generation members, which placed a distinct set of opportunities and constraints for future generations. War-led state formation is the modal pattern among the "pioneer" cases of state formation, whereas trade-led state formation is the modal pattern for "latecomers." Pioneer states do not provide the mirror image of future stages in the trajectory of latecomer states precisely because the very existence of the pioneers encourages adaptation among latecomers.

This part of the book provides the theoretical tools to understand the modal pattern of state formation in Latin America, its origins, process, and final outcome. It is organized into three chapters. The first chapter is theoretical, and the other two empirical. Chapter 1 starts by demarcating the outcome, placing special emphasis on the distinction between state formation and state building, which is crucial for understanding the modal case in Latin America. It then reviews the dominant approaches to state formation in early modern Europe and to state building in nineteenth-century Latin America. The goal is to extract key analytical inputs for a general theory of state formation. The chapter makes explicit the scope conditions implicit in traditional approaches. It claims that the two key scope conditions are whether the international geopolitical context is marked by anarchy or hierarchy and whether the international economic order is dominated by feudalism and mercantilism or capitalism and free trade. The chapter then presents a general theory of state formation based on the construction of two models: trade-led versus war-led state formation. Each model reflects opposite initial conditions: international hierarchy instead of anarchy, and global capitalism instead of autarkic feudalism. Initial conditions trigger distinct causal chains resulting in different outcomes with regard to state capacity. The chapter advances the hypothesis that *under geopolitical hierarchy and global capitalism, trade-led state formation is the optimal path from the perspective of the emerging ruling class, whereas war-led state formation is strictly counterproductive for political survival*. It also specifies *the causal linkages between success at trade-led state formation and failure at state building*.

The empirical chapters offer a new analysis of nineteenth-century Latin American history by applying the theoretical tools introduced in Chapter 1. It divides the modal trajectory of state formation in Latin America into three periods: Independence (1808–25), Failure (1825–45), and State Formation (1845–75). Chapter 2 covers Independence and Failure. Chapter 3 analyzes the State Formation period. Independence can be seen as an aborted attempt at trade-led state formation, which resulted in Failure, the opposite of what independence leaders intended. The Failure period centers on the initiation of a process of war-led state formation that was interrupted by an international economic shock, which created the opportunities for the first boom of primary exports in independent Latin America. Finally, in the period of State Formation, state-making elites employed the resources from the international economic shock to deal with the legacies of the Failure period. The final and durable outcome was state formation without state building.

A Theory of Latecomer State Formation

Outcome: State Formation with and without State Building

State formation includes two processes: territory consolidation and violence monopolization. Territory consolidation refers to the process by which an emerging political center decides which regions to include within its jurisdiction and which to exclude. The importance of state formation qua territory consolidation can hardly be exaggerated. Territory consolidation is the source of a modern country's political geography. Territory consolidation defines the physical and demographic space within which a national polity and a national economy will emerge. From a political point of view, territory consolidation shapes almost every component of subsequent dynamics. It circumscribes the population available for future coalitions, which shape strategies of cleavage activation and political entrepreneurship. Which regions are combined during state formation has massive effects on the prospects for state building.

"State building" is a new phrase for an old concept, which can be traced to Max Weber's original notion of bureaucratization, the transition from patrimonial rule to meritocratic administration.[1] Foundational work by Charles Tilly and Michael Mann on the rise of the modern state in western Europe largely views state building as concomitant with state formation, and because state formation affected almost every corner of early modern western Europe, so did state building. Tilly and Mann complemented Weber's original emphasis on administrative efficiency with a focus on territorial reach. Thus, examining the extractive side of the state, Tilly viewed state formation as including a transition from "indirect rule" to "direct rule," the elimination of intermediary powers by an emerging political center in its efforts to collect revenues from newly acquired territories.[2] Turning to the output side of the state, for Mann, state formation produced a gradual but prodigious rise in "infrastructural power," the capacity of the state to effectively deliver goods and services throughout the territory under its nominal control.[3]

Guillermo O'Donnell's work on Latin America argues that variations in state capacity across contemporary cases are as substantial as the variation over time experienced in the rise of modern western Europe. Latin America has states, but they lack the capacity to fully control their territories, which, according to O'Donnell, are permanent combinations of "brown," "green," and "blue areas."[4] O'Donnell's color scale covers exactly Weber's conceptual range from patrimonial to bureaucratic administration and Mann's continuum from low to high infrastructural power. Research inspired by O'Donnell's observation has reached a strong consensus that only three relatively small countries, Chile, Uruguay, and Costa Rica, are fully blue states, true exceptions within a general pattern of brown and green. O'Donnell focuses on brown areas mainly for their *effects* on the extension and quality of present-day citizenship rights. Yet modern states in Latin America were born with brown areas, which implies that understanding the *historical origins* of brown areas and weak states requires critical scrutiny of theories of state formation based on the western European experience. A more general theory of state formation is needed, and it must account for the emergence and persistence of states with and without bureaucratic, infrastructural capacities.

The theory presented here traces variations in state building to the territory-consolidation component of state formation and *not* to the violence-monopolization one, despite the fact that the literature has tended to see military buildup as a precursor of institutional capacity. During territory consolidation, a political center may choose to form a minisovereignty by excluding all regions other than its immediate hinterland, or it may decide to incorporate one or more surrounding regions. When territorial expansion through incorporation does occur, the new regions can be seen as *peripheries* in relation to the state-formation center. An apt alternative phrase for territory consolidation when the center expands its territory beyond its immediate hinterland would be *periphery incorporation*.

The critical difference between state formation with and without state building is whether periphery incorporation also involves *periphery trans-*

formation, that is, the substitution of local political traditions by a general set of institutions enforced by the center throughout the incorporated territories. In both early modern western Europe and postcolonial Latin America, most peripheries were dominated by local potentates that can be characterized as patrimonial rulers in the Weberian sense. The typical patrimonial ruler in early modern Europe was the old feudal aristocracy, whereas postcolonial Latin America had two rather different types of patrimonial ruler: vestigial colonial oligarchies, to whom the Iberian empires had granted special economic and political privileges, and the new rural warlords mobilized during the independence process, the so-called caudillos. Despite their different origins, vestigial oligarchies and caudillos both controlled the local population through clientelistic linkages, asymmetric exchanges of military protection and subsistence goods for labor services in times of peace and military efforts in times of war.

Figure 1.1 summarizes the key conceptual steps required for the comparative analysis of state development. First, state development is disaggregated into state formation and state building. Then, state formation is disaggregated into violence monopolization and territory consolidation. The dashed line connecting territory consolidation and the tandem bureaucratization/periphery transformation indicates a causal, as opposed to conceptual, relation. Whether the relation is positive or negative depends on conditions that will be analyzed in the next section.

Periphery transformation occurs when periphery incorporation is accompanied by the eradication of the particularistic linkages uniting local potentates and their client population. No bureaucratization, no direct rule, no infrastructural power, and no blue areas will emerge unless patrimonial peripheries are overhauled. Periphery transformation is a true prerequisite both for efficient extraction by the emerging state and for the effective delivery of public goods and the enforcement of citizenship rights. In the process of territory consolidation, western European peripheries were incorporated and transformed at the same time, whereas in Latin America, periphery incorporation occurred without periphery transformation. In this specific sense, state formation was *uncoupled* from state building.

Yet incorporation without transformation is not the most patrimonial outcome. A more patrimonial outcome occurs when the center incorporates peripheries and provides local elites with external support to perpetuate their

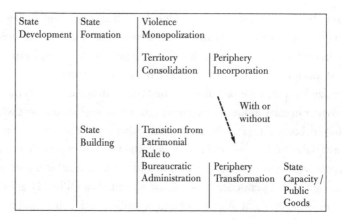

Figure 1.1. Clarifying and disaggregating "state development"

sources of patronage. And the most patrimonial outcome occurs when it is the incorporated periphery that transforms the center in a patrimonial direction, completely reversing the pioneer western European trajectory. In this case, peripheries propagate patrimonialism throughout the national administration and the subnational governments, eventually turning the state into a large-scale patronage machine. In this case, state formation is *inimical* to state building. Only trade-led state formation can produce the latter.

Argentina and Brazil illustrate the modal Latin American pattern of *generalized patrimonialism* resulting from the most perverse form of periphery incorporation. In the mid-nineteenth century, the centers of both countries, Buenos Aires and Rio de Janeiro, were set on a trajectory in which rapid economic growth and sustained enhancement of bureaucratic capacity reinforced each other. Yet they incorporated peripheral regions dominated by patrimonial institutions that not only survived incorporation but also formed a critical mass to place the national state and the subnational units along a durable path of patronage-based politics. Mexico is similar to Argentina and Brazil, except that its center never had the potential for capacity building that Buenos Aires and Rio had. If Chile, Costa Rica, and Uruguay are exceptions to the modal pattern, the main reason is that, in their formation, they incorporated no peripheries and thus escaped the risks of patrimonialization altogether.

The theory presented in this chapter builds on two bodies of research: traditional approaches to state formation in early modern western Europe and recent comparative analyses of state building in nineteenth-century Latin America.[5] The relation between the two bodies of research is quite straightforward. Recent analyses of state building in Latin America largely agree that traditional approaches to state formation in early modern Europe "do not apply" beyond Europe. The problem with the consensus among Latin Americanists is twofold: it has failed to make the conceptual distinction between state *formation* and state *building*, and it has not explored the *scope conditions* of traditional theories of state formation.

The Theory of Pioneer State Formation: The War-Led Path

Work on the rise of the state in early modern western Europe provides one of the strongest examples of progress in the social sciences as a collective enterprise. By the end of the twentieth century, it was already safe to make three impressive claims:

1. The state is a distinctly modern form of political organization. Premodern forms of political organization either were nonterritorial or did not monopolize violence.[6]
2. The state originated in western Europe.
3. The first generation of states was the outcome of war and preparation for war.

All three claims can be found in the work of Max Weber. Yet, for a long time after Weber's work, the "bellicist thesis" (third claim) remained contentious. For scholars working under the assumption that economic conditions have some form of causal primacy over political phenomena, the state was the product of modern capitalism. Marxists had traditionally been the strongest advocates of the rival, "economicist," thesis.

Bellicists and economicists continue to debate about the origins of the state.[7] However, the debate should not eclipse the fact that scholarship after Weber's work—which was motivated by the very same debate—forged a strong consensus on the geopolitical sources of the western European state. Two developments were crucial in the formation of the consensus: historians' research on the origins and repercussions of the so-called Military Revolution and Marxist reinterpretations of the origins of the modern state.

War-Led State Formation and State Building

In his last lecture course, Weber provided the sketch of a theory of war-led state formation, based on one key historical observation: "The mediaeval army of knights made feudal social organization inevitable; then its displacement by mercenary armies and later (beginning with Maurice of Orange) by disciplined troops led to the establishment of the modern state."[8]

Historians' work after Weber has given decisive empirical support to the bellicist thesis. The transition from the "knight" to the "disciplined [standing] army" of Weber's observation is what, since the work of the historian Michael Roberts, has been known as the "Military Revolution."[9] Roberts's work highlighted the impact of more effective forms of military organization, including centrally the so-called linear tactics designed by the Dutch ruler Maurice of Orange and the Swedish king Gustavus Adolphus. Around the time of the Thirty Years' War (1618–48), the new infantry had already proved more effective in the battlefield than the old medieval cavalry. The Thirty Years' War marked the extinction of feudal military organization. Roberts's work in turn inspired an impressive amount of historical research.[10] New accounts show that the range of changes in military tactics and technology in late medieval and early modern Europe was even broader and more radical than Weber and Roberts suggested.

The new research has also assessed the impact of specific military transformations on the emergence of the modern state (an exemplary application of "process tracing" analysis). Historians agree that the introduction of gunpowder, a revolution within the Military Revolution, and the rise of the Trace Italienne were key sequential steps leading to the creation of the standing army. The Trace Italienne was a form of fortification designed to produce effective defense in response to the use of gunpowder by the artillery.[11] Conquering a settlement defended by the Trace Italienne required long months of military siege. Only permanent, professional armies could make the siege successful. Once a professional army is formed, a short step separates it from the rise of the modern state. Among the many paths connecting the permanent army and the modern state, the most prominent one is the "fiscal linkage." Protostates could sustain standing armies only if they also introduced a permanent system of taxation. In the "coercion-extraction cycle," more effective taxation allowed for a more effective army, which in turn allowed the ruler to be more effective at taxation.[12]

The modern state is itself the ultimate innovation of the Military Revolution. In late medieval Europe, geopolitical competition caused the Military Revolution. In early modern Europe, more effective means of destruction, and stronger military pressures resulting from them, forced the extinction of pre-state forms of political organization, including feudal lordships, dynastic empires, mercenary armies, city leagues, and autonomous urban enclaves.[13] They also caused convergence on the modern state, which was a double organizational innovation. The first was the centralization of political authority over a contiguous territory, which was about ten times larger than the medieval kinglets but one-tenth the size of the Roman Empire. The second was the monopolization of violence within the territory, that is, the consolidation of a permanent professional army. Convergence on the state could be voluntary or forced. Forced convergence was a Darwinian process and was the modal case. Rulers who failed to introduce the changes required to create a modern state died at the hands of those who succeeded at producing the required change. Early modern Europe was a cemetery of failed states.

Concomitant with the construction of the modern state, a key innovation was the creation of a permanent system of taxation. This forced rulers competing with each other to open a second, "domestic," front of conflict against local potentates in surrounding areas for the control of the financial and human resources required for war. Success in the domestic arena was key to survival in the international arena. The implacable pressures of Darwinian geopolitical competition that caused convergence on state formation also caused convergence on *state building*. The territories of rulers who failed to eliminate local potentates were absorbed into those of Weberian states, which succeeded at state building. That is, in early modern western Europe, state formation involved not only territory consolidation and violence monopolization but also *periphery transformation*. Through this process, the political center of the emerging state eliminated surrounding local potentates and replaced the variety of preexisting political institutions in the annexed regions with a uniform set of controls, rules, and services geared toward maximizing the quantity and quality of resources extracted. Geopolitical pressures for periphery transformation have been the master driving force behind the creation of state capacity and infrastructural power.

The major difference between early modern western Europe and nineteenth-century Latin America is that territory consolidation and periphery transformation, which had gone hand in hand in western Europe, were *uncoupled* during the process of state formation in Latin America. Uncoupling would have caused state failure in western Europe. It obviously did not in Latin America. Latin American states did not merely avoid periphery transformation during territory consolidation. More seriously, during and after state-formation bargains, patrimonial institutions in the periphery gained new strength through validation from the center, aborted the political modernization of the center itself, and ultimately propagated patrimonialism throughout the entire political arena. In contrast to western Europe, state formation in Latin America became an impediment to state building.

It is not that the bellicist approach is wrong or "not applicable." It is simply that the Latin American cases require that the scope conditions implicit in the approach be made explicit and transformed into proper causal variables. When the implicit scope conditions become explicit causal variables, it is easy to verify that the scores of the causal variables were different in Latin America. The most important scope condition of the bellicist approach is *international anarchy*. Latin American countries were formed not only when the world was already populated by other territorial states—which by definition was not the case of the pioneer cases—but also when the pioneer states had already consolidated a clear international *hierarchy*, topped by Great Britain and, at some distance, France. As we will see, international hierarchy weakened geopolitical pressures during state formation in Latin America and thereby became a key source of the uncoupling between state formation and state building.[14]

Neo-Marxist Approaches

In the debate between bellicists and economicists, Marxism made the most useful contribution for a general theory of state formation. Historians falsified early Marxist approaches to state origins. At the same time, they encouraged the sophistication of Marxism. Based largely on Friedrich Engels's writings, early Marxism had taken too seriously the claim that "the executive of the modern state is but a committee for managing the common affairs of the whole bourgeoisie."[15] The bourgeois-committee thesis was used by early Marxism as a premise of state-formation analysis rather than as one among many possible conclusions of empirical research. As a consequence, early Marxism has repeatedly presented the modern state as the creature of an emerging capitalist class, which builds the state in order to protect property rights, remove internal tariffs, and repress labor unrest.

The basic chronology from systematic historical research dealt a fatal blow to early Marxist theories of state formation. The historical record is conclusive about the fact that the modern state *predated* the emergence of capitalism as a general mode of production—and the formation of the bourgeoisie as a particular economic class—by no less than a century. The Military Revolution occurred about 150 years before the Industrial Revolution. And whereas the modern state was created at some point between the Military and the Industrial Revolutions, the rise of the bourgeoisie occurred only after the Industrial Revolution. The bourgeoisie was not around when the first states emerged. The bourgeoisie could not have produced the modern state. Early Marxist theory of state formation is wrong.

Yet general theories of state formation, which are able to travel outside western Europe and account for Latin America's uncoupling of state building, require the incorporation of key Marxist insights within the Weberian template. The work by the Marxist historian Perry Anderson explicitly deals with the precapitalist nature of the modern state, the bête noire in Marxist social theory. Anderson finds the roots of the modern European state in the transition from early feudalism to mature feudalism. For Anderson, the replacement of "parcellized sovereignty"—the distinctive political mark of Europe after the fall of the Roman Empire—with the modern state was a concerted response by feudal lords to the twin threats of peasant rebellion and the rise of the medieval city. Feudal lords pooled resources to create a political unit with enough coercive military capacity to neutralize the pressures from below and from the sides.[16]

Anderson's work is valuable in three ways. First, it has pushed the debate on state formation between bellicists and economicists to a new level, from which areas of divergence and convergence become both much clearer and more productive for empirical research. Neo-Weberians and neo-Marxists disagree on the *origins* of the impressive surge of war-making activity in early modern Europe, but they fundamentally converge on the long chain of *effects* brought about by modern war.

In relation to origins, neo-Weberians view war as a Hobbesian effect of international anarchy, whereas, after Anderson, neo-Marxists view war as part and parcel of the laws of motion of the feudal mode of production. Under feudalism, economic technologies were stagnant. Without economic innovation, productivity gains—higher levels of economic output using the same levels of inputs—were impossible. The only form of economic expansion under feudalism was to increase the volume of economic inputs, essentially land and labor. Economic expansion required the annexation of new territory and the domination of the population within it. From Anderson's perspective, then, war-making in late medieval Europe derived not from international anarchy but from the economic requirements of the feudal mode of production: "Transnational interaction within feudalism was typically always first at the political, not the economic level, precisely because it was a mode of production founded on extra-economic coercion: conquest, not commerce, was its primary form of expansion."[17]

Disagreement about the origins of war-making should not overshadow the remarkable consensus between neo-Weberians and neo-Marxists regarding its effects, which crucially shaped the priorities of state-making elites. As Anderson put it, "States were machines built overwhelmingly for the battlefield. It is significant that the first regular national tax to be imposed on France, the *taille royale*, was levied to finance the first regular military in Europe—the *compagnies d'ordonnance* of the mid-15th century."[18] Impressive breakthroughs in historical research proved that genuine progress in the social sciences is possible: the most sophisticated Marxist account of the state became indistinguishable from Weber's original observations.

Second, state formation as resource pooling for enhanced *class* domination is a distinctly Marxist insight that is largely absent in bellicist theories but is indispensable for the analysis of Latin America. In contrast to liberal theories that view the emergence of the state as the outcome of rational actors pursuing the creation of "public goods," many nineteenth-century Latin American states were created to provide what can usefully be seen as a *class good*. A class good is similar to a club good in that only members benefit from it.[19] Yet, in contrast to the club good, which is financed by the members/beneficiaries, the class good is financed by the nonmembers of the club/class, typically the general public. The clearest example of a class good is the creation of coercive capacity, using general taxes, to repress forced labor.

Third, Anderson's work, by highlighting that state formation in early modern western Europe was initiated and largely completed in a precapitalist economic context, points to a second set of scope conditions implicit in the bellicist approach, which are geoeconomic instead of geopolitical. The conditions are autarkic feudalism (at the onset of state formation) and mercantilism (the international economic policy adopted by the first generation of fully formed states). In sharp contrast, state formation in Latin America was initiated and completed during the first big global expansion of capitalism and free trade.

In sum, it is safe to claim that the bellicist approach is right. Historical research provides empirical support for it. Marxism, the rival theoretical approach, capitulated to it. Neo-Marxism and neo-Weberianism became indistinguishable for the purposes of building a general theory of state formation. For the bellicist approach to become useful in the construction of a general theory of state formation, the key analytical step is to transform its implicit scope conditions, consisting of the geopolitical and economic environment, into explicit causal variables. Within a general theory, the bellicist approach becomes a *specific path* of state formation, the initial conditions of which are international anarchy, autarkic feudalism, and mercantilism. The specific combination of initial conditions triggers the *war-led path* of state formation, which is concomitant with state building.

When state formation occurs under different values on *both* initial conditions, namely, international hierarchy and free-trade capitalism, state formation becomes an obstacle to state building. International hierarchy and free-trade capitalism set in motion a *trade-led path* of state formation. In the trade-led path, international hierarchy weakens the incentives for state building. As we will see, free-trade capitalism creates incentives for state formation, principally territory consolidation for the provision of class goods. It also makes periphery transformation, a key step toward state building, strictly incompatible with state formation. Trade-led state formation was the modal path in Latin America.

Literature on State Building in Latin America

Studies of state formation and state building began to focus on Latin America only recently, thanks to fundamental work by Miguel Á. Centeno, Marcus Kurtz, Ryan Saylor, and Hillel Soifer.[20] My work builds on this body of research, but it is based on a clear distinction between state formation and capacity building, it covers more cases, and it offers the first comparative and longitudinal analysis of the three largest countries in the region, Argentina, Brazil, and Mexico. Except for Centeno, all works on the Latin American state deal with state building rather than state formation. No work deals with territory consolidation, which is crucial for explaining subsequent success creating state capacity. Quite surprisingly, except for Centeno, none of the works includes an analysis of Brazil. And except for Kurtz, none of the works considers the provision of class goods as a central goal of the state-making elites in nineteenth-century Latin America.

The existing literature analyzes capacity building *after* the country was formed as a distinct combination of regions. Yet, as the next section will show, the combination of regions forged during territory consolidation sets durable limits on how much "state building" can be done after state formation is completed. Additionally, including Brazil in the analysis produces new theoretical lessons that run counter to accepted wisdom about the provision of class goods and the prospects of state formation. Contrary to work inspired by Barrington Moore, slave labor normally *favored* state formation in the trade-led path. Peripheral regions depending on slave work, which would have otherwise preferred secession, agreed to incorporation within a larger territory in order to be able to call on the coercive force of the central state. Prevention and repression of slave revolts was an extreme version of the class good that created incentives for state formation throughout Latin America. Kurtz's work focuses on the creation of class goods in the labor market, but his empirical analysis omits Brazil and Mexico, another case in which threats from below pushed a secessionist periphery to demand incorporation in exchange for help with local repression.

Weak States

Centeno's work is a major contribution toward discerning a modal pattern of state formation in Latin America. Using a rectified version of the bellicist approach, he argues that weak states in Latin America are the result of the "wrong" kind of wars, that is, wars that did not cause the waves of technological, organizational, and ultimately institutional innovations seen in the pioneering cases of Europe. In turn, according to Centeno, wrong wars are accounted for by the existence of "weak states," in a vicious circle in which weak states fight wrong wars, which further debilitate states.[21] The theory presented in the next section departs from Centeno's in three respects. First, even though the vicious cycle of weak states and wrong wars is almost certainly a true fact, it is important to find an exogenous source of variation that specifies what came first, the wrong wars or the weak states. As we will see, international trade, rather than military conflict, was the main source of state formation, and it can be seen as a truly exogenous force. Second, Latin American wars were more frequent in the first decades after independence than in the second half of the nineteenth century, which was the key period of state formation in the region. A war-led path of state formation, no matter how modified, will not account for state formation in Latin America. Given the international geopolitical and geoeconomic context of the mid-nineteenth century, a major change occurred in the priorities of the state-making elites. They switched from a focus on war to a focus on commerce. Most likely, if wars had dragged on for another century in Latin America, as they did in early modern western Europe, strong states would have emerged. Yet successful state-making elites switched from war-making to market-making and coalition-making well before war could have played out its full effects. Finally, Centeno does not explain substantial variations within the modal pattern of state formation in Latin America, which is the focus of the work by Soifer, Kurtz, and Saylor.

A key insight that my analysis borrows from Centeno's work is his observation about the enormous weight of taxes on foreign trade relative to total revenues in the key juncture of state formation in Latin America. My argument endogenizes the observation by pointing to the initial conditions of the trade-led path.

Variations in State Building within
Latin America

My analysis builds on the collective contribution of Soifer, Kurtz, and Saylor in several ways. It relies heavily on Soifer's and Kurtz's observation that state developments in nineteenth-century Latin America have durable repercussions on state capacity in contemporary Latin America. Like all three authors, I am interested in variations in state capacity. Yet, since my argument accounts simultaneously for the modal contrast between Latin America and western Europe and for variations within Latin America, the latter are seen as deviations from a typical pattern characterized by *weak* state capacity. Also, I am interested in capacity variations that are *large*, such as those that separate the Swedish state from the Peruvian state, and I differentiate between state formation and state building. Given the comparison with western Europe, the size of the variation to be explained, and the distinction between state formation and state building, I simplify (dichotomize) differences within Latin America in terms of capacity. I characterize cases as belonging to the modal pattern of weakness or as exceptions to it. The only three clear exceptions to the modal pattern are Chile, Uruguay, and Costa Rica.

Chile, Uruguay, and Costa Rica are obviously interesting cases. Yet, from a theoretical perspective, the cases of Argentina, Brazil, and Mexico are both more informative and more important given their historical leadership in the region. All three cases hide a secret. They were more successful at state formation than were the pioneer cases themselves. The three countries consolidated territories that are far larger than those of the largest western European countries, and, in contrast to France or Germany, their borders have remained immutable for more than a century after demarcation. Yet the very factors that explain their success at state formation also account for their failure at state building.

Kurtz, Saylor, and Soifer rightly dismiss the war-led path and thereby implicitly depart from Centeno's work. At the same time, all three authors miss the role of geopolitical factors. The fact that the war-led path does not explain cross-national variations in Latin America does not mean that geopolitical conditions were not important. Latin American state formation can only be understood in the context of a peculiar geopolitical context, namely, an international hierarchy topped by the European pioneers. Great Britain was a key factor in the independence of Brazil, in the creation of Uruguay, and in the fragmentation of Central America, among many other large-scale developments in the region. Even more important, the *Pax Britannica* provided an external umpire to potential conflicts between Latin American countries. Such a peace-making mechanism would have been unimaginable during state formation in early modern Europe. Given the level of economic investments in the region, Great Britain had a definite interest in the peaceful resolution of conflicts among countries. On many occasions, it became an external supplier of public goods such as defense and protection of property rights.

Saylor aptly places the role of international trade at center stage and views the pursuit of export-enhancing public goods as a major driver of state formation.[22] Two objections to his otherwise brilliant argument are important inputs for a general theory of state formation. First, Saylor's public goods were actually class goods as defined earlier—they benefited a small minority and were paid for by the broader public. Second, economic elites were not the only state-makers; professional politicians, pursuing power rather than profit, were pivotal actors in creating the coalitions that made both state formation and the provision of class goods possible. The path-breaking work by Soifer, in contrast to Saylor's, highlights the autonomy of politics, but it traces political autonomy to ideological convictions (which, in turn, are shaped by patterns of topography and urbanization).[23] I find it more useful, and more consistent with the data, to assume that professional politicians were much more interested in advancing their careers than in implementing programmatic platforms. Naked power maximization must be a central ingredient of state formation.

Finally, Kurtz argues that free labor markets favor state building.[24] If he had included the cases of Mexico and Brazil, the claim would have been drastically modified. The attempts of Yucatán and Pernambuco to form a separate country failed because Mexico and Brazil managed to keep them within their territories. Reincorporation was driven by fear among local white elites that their coercive power was not sufficient to discipline labor and tie it to the land. Yucatán and Pernambuco eventually gave up international sovereignty in exchange for military help from the cities of México and Rio de Janeiro to maintain local peace. Forced labor in peripheral regions helped central elites to succeed at large-scale state formation. The pattern closely resembles Perry Anderson's argument about the origins of absolutism in western Europe, in which the pioneer states originate in a coalition of feudal lords who pool economic and military resources to prevent peasant rebellion.

The theory of state formation advanced in the next section provides a framework to account for one major variation over time and two variations across space. The variation over time is the transition from ill-defined territories in the aftermath of independence to the consolidation of well-demarcated national political arenas in modern Latin America. This transition is the formation of Latin America's modern *political geography*, the most durable legacy of nineteenth-century history. The two variations across space are (a) a contrast between the modal pioneer cases of state formation in early modern Europe and the modal latecomer states in nineteenth-century Latin America, a comparison that "lumps" Latin American countries on the basis of a number of shared attributes, including the stability of national borders and the prevalence of semipatrimonial rule as the typical, but not universal, form of administration; and (b) divergences within Latin America, which "split" countries in the region by the quality of political institutions and highlight the bureaucratic exceptions to the modal patrimonial pattern of administration (Part 2 focuses on an additional set of contrasts among Latin American cases).

A Theory of Latecomer State Formation: The Trade-Led Path

This section presents a theory of state formation that accounts for variations in state building. It borrows from neo-Weberian approaches the implicit template, which can be disaggregated into four components: (a) initial conditions of state formation, which shape (b) goals and priorities of the state-making elites, as well as (c) available resources, and (d) strategies of periphery incorporation. Based on different scores on the initial conditions, the theory presents two paths of state formation: war-led versus trade-led. The paths are polar ideal types. They also fit quite closely the modal cases of early modern Europe and mid-nineteenth-century Latin America. Components (a), (b), and (c) can be seen as increasingly proximate causes of state formation. Component (d) provides the mechanism, or microfoundation, connecting causes and outcomes, which are differentiated by whether state formation favors or impedes state building.

Initial Conditions:
The Origins of Polar Paths

State formation in western Europe occurred under unique geopolitical and international economic conditions: anarchy and feudalism. The context of state formation in Latin America was drastically different: it was marked by a clear international *geopolitical hierarchy*—topped by the pioneer western European states and Great Britain in particular—and by the first wave in the *globalization of capitalism*, which originated in the Industrial Revolution of the United Kingdom, Belgium, the Dutch Republic, and France. In western Europe, even when capitalism replaced feudalism as the dominant mode of production, international economic relations among the emerging states were dominated by mercantilism. The rise of free trade occurred when state formation was already completed in western Europe (with the exception of the German and Italian unifications), and it coincided with the onset of state formation in Latin America.

World-historical times relevant for understanding models of state formation can be transformed into causal variables by building a simple typology based on the intersection of the most fundamental attributes of the international economic and geopolitical context, as shown in Table 1.1. The typology places the western European and the Latin American processes of state formation in opposite quadrants because they differ on *both* sets of variables. The remaining quadrants in the typology are combinations that share at least one initial condition with the pioneer cases and are filled only for the sake of completeness. The analysis of their implications for state formation is outside the scope of this book. The labels (reactive and competing state formation) and cases (eastern Europe, China, Japan, and the United States) attached to the corresponding cells should be taken only as suggestions for exploration of other state-formation paths.

Latin America and Africa share a quadrant. Yet it is instructive to compare the type of international hierarchy of the mid-nineteenth century, when Latin American states formed, and that of the mid-twentieth century,

Table 1.1. Geopolitical and International Economic Environments
of State Formation

		International economy	
		Feudalism/ mercantilism	Capitalism/free trade
Geopolitical context	Anarchy	Pioneer state formation	Competing state formation
		War-led (with military innovation)	Trade + war-led
		Western Europe	United States
	Hierarchy	Reactive state formation	Latecomer state formation
		War-led (with military imitation)	Trade-led
		Eastern Europe, China, Japan	Latin America, Africa

when Africa decolonized. The nineteenth-century hierarchy was topped only by other territorial states, Great Britain and, at considerable distance, France, Prussia, and the United States. Yet the mid-twentieth-century hierarchy included, in addition to two global superpowers (the United States and the Soviet Union), international organizations like the United Nations, which facilitated country creation through multilateral credentialing. If Latin American states formed under an international hierarchy, the African ones formed under a *super*hierarchy, which made state formation qua country creation in Africa easier than in Latin America. At the same time, the very precocity of African state formation made state *building* even harder than in Latin America.[25]

The typology is the first step in the creation of a more general theory of state formation. It transforms scope conditions implicit in the theory of state formation advanced by Weber and his contemporary followers into explicit causal variables. The typology also helps to enrich neo-Weberian approaches to state formation with valuable insights from neo-Marxist alternatives.

The fact that western European state formation was initiated, and in most cases completed, under feudalism is the main reason for preferring neo-Weberian theories of state formation over early Marxist approaches. The fact that Latin American states were created within a global capitalist context requires that special attention be paid to the interests of exporting economic elites and foreign investors. Early Marxist claims portraying the emerging bourgeoisie as the champion of state formation, which are definitely invalid for early modern Europe, may be useful in the analysis of state formation in Latin America. State-making elites in Latin America were *political* elites focusing on power maximization. They pursued interests that in principle differed from those of the economic elites, who by definition focus on profit maximization. However, in the history of Latin America, the interests of the political elites and the economic elites were never more aligned than during the state-formation process.

As a preview of the discussion to come, Table 1.2 summarizes the theory by specifying the four explanatory components and the outcome in each path of state formation.

Shared Goals, Contrasting Priorities: War-Making versus Market-Making

The most fundamental goal of state formation is shared by state-makers on all paths. The goal is always and everywhere the political survival of the rulers who embark on the process. What varies across paths are the immediate priorities, the resources, and the strategy of the state-making elite. International anarchy encourages war-led state formation. It makes political survival depend on the creation of a state that is fundamentally a military machine with which to sustain international sovereignty. The priority in war-led state formation is *war-making*, understood in the broad sense of not just waging wars but also preparing for them by upgrading extractive, military, and organizational capabilities. Otto Hintze claimed that "all state organization was originally military organization, organization for war. . . . This can be regarded as an assured result of comparative history."[26] Hintze's result is "assured" only under conditions of international anarchy prior to the emergence of global capitalism.

On the other hand, the globalization of capitalism fosters trade-led state formation, especially in areas of the world with the potential to derive large benefits from commerce with the industrial pioneers. Global capitalism makes political survival depend on the ability of rulers to secure a commercial

Table 1.2. Models of State Formation: The Five Theoretical Components

Model	Initial conditions	Goal and priorities	Resources	Strategy toward periphery	Outcome
War-led state formation	Geopolitical anarchy + feudalism/ mercantilism	Political survival through war-making	Internal taxation under external military threat	Periphery incorporation with transformation	Strong states
Trade-led state formation	International hierarchy + global capitalism/free trade	Political survival through market-making	Customs revenues due to global trade opportunities	Periphery incorporation without transformation	Weak states

linkage between the leading export sector of the emerging country and the world's most profitable markets. The priority in trade-led state formation is *market-making*, understood in the broad sense of producing the appropriate business environment for local economic elites and foreign investors.

Internal pacification in war-led state formation is achieved as an *unintended by-product* of violence monopolization, which in turn is a direct outcome of geopolitical pressures under international anarchy. Rulers who fail to monopolize violence perish under the attacks of those who succeed. By contrast, in trade-led state formation, peace, both within the emerging country and with foreign neighbors, is the *deliberate policy* of state-making elites. They correctly perceive that pacification is a necessary condition for the production of the proper business environment, the master class good in trade-led state formation.

Feudalism as a dominant mode of production intensifies the incentives for war already created by geopolitical anarchy in the pioneer cases, as noted by Anderson. By contrast, international hierarchy further attenuates military pressures in the context of global capitalism that surrounds latecomer cases. State-makers in Latin America could not realistically aspire to a prominent geopolitical role in an international arena already dominated by the United Kingdom, France, Prussia, and the United States. With competition for international supremacy off the agenda, pressures to catch up to the latest military technology are nonexistent in trade-led state formation. The international geopolitical context favored peace among Latin American emerging countries. Great Britain's role was key. Concerned about disruptions in its trade relations with the region, Great Britain was a virtual referee in disputes between Latin American countries and a decided sponsor of peaceful solutions to them. An informal outside umpire was an unimaginable form of conflict resolution in the original European setting of state formation.

Different Resources:
Internal Taxes versus Tariffs on International Commerce

No state exists without revenue. To form states, rulers must find substantial sources of continuous revenue. Sources of revenue vary depending on the state-formation model, and variations are highly consequential. In war-led state formation, internal taxation produces the revenue, whereas in trade-led state formation, revenue derives from tariffs on international trade. Tariffs in turn may serve as collateral for foreign borrowing, an additional source of state finance. To obtain the physical and human resources required for war, the prevalence of feudalism as a mode of production leaves state-making elites in war-led cases with no option other than to annex surrounding regions and tighten their political and fiscal grip. In the trade-led path, funding state-formation projects requires securing abundant flows of international trade, the consolidation of a small number of international seaports, and the installation of customhouses to collect revenue from import tariffs. The smaller the number of ports, the lower the costs of administering them.

In western Europe, differences in the sources of fiscal income were relatively small, but scholarship has considered them highly consequential. The "inward-looking" cases, best exemplified by France and Prussia, covered 90 percent of the state's expenditures with internal taxes. The "outward-looking" cases, Great Britain and the Dutch Republic, derived only between 15 percent and 30 percent of their revenue from international trade. The small difference has repeatedly been seen as a major source of variation in the emerging political regime, differentiated as absolutist versus constitutional.[27]

Since independence, the modal Latin American country has obtained around three-quarters of its revenues from tariffs on imports. That is, state-makers in Latin America were twice or three times more "outward-looking" than the most outward-looking European cases. Compared to the variations within western Europe, the difference in funding between the trade-led process in Latin America and the war-led process in western Europe is nothing short of astronomical. Paradoxically, the big difference in revenue source did not produce stronger constitutionalism but weaker capacity.

Similar Rivals, Different Strategies: Varieties of Periphery Incorporation

Peripheries largely oppose state formation in both the war-led path and the trade-led path. But they do so for different reasons. In the war-led path, local potentates in peripheral areas correctly view state formation as a threat to their political survival. In a precapitalist context, revenue maximization pushes state-makers into a direct combat against intermediary powers, that is, feudal aristocracies presiding over an expensive hierarchy of local clients. Increased central extraction translates into a more effective army, and a more effective army in turn poses a more serious threat to local potentates. In the trade-led path, peripheral notables also resist incorporation, but they do so largely to secure a bargaining chip in the negotiation with central elites for the size of their share of revenues from international commerce. In the trade-led path, peripheries have special extortion power. It is not peripheral notables who fear for their survival but the political and economic interests of the center who worry that disruption from the peripheries could derail integration into world capitalism. If peripheries neighboring the port and the export sector are left outside the state's territory, local potentates pose a permanent threat of invasion.

Substantial differences in political priorities—war-making versus market-making—and qualitative contrasts in the source of funding—internal taxation versus customs revenues—make rulers in the war-led model and the trade-led model pursue radically different strategies of "periphery incorporation." Whether the periphery is transformed over the course of territory consolidation is a watershed that determines whether the precursors of capacity building are going to take root. Rulers in the war-led model of state formation have no choice but to transform the newly incorporated peripheries, lest they risk international sovereignty. Periphery transformation, and specifically the extermination of intermediate powers interfering with central rule and the rationalization of tax collection, maximizes the security of the emerging state. External geopolitical pressures cause convergence on periphery transformation across the cases engaged in war-led state formation: they either defeat the resistance of peripheries against institutional change, or they fail, only to be absorbed by a neighboring state that is powerful enough to complete the transformation.

By contrast, in the trade-led path of state formation, rulers do not need the peripheries for revenue extraction, as duties collected at the main customhouse are the key source of funding. Moreover, periphery transformation risks provoking military resistance that aborts efforts at pacification, pulverizes the business climate, disrupts foreign trade, and stops foreign investments, placing an indefinite hold on the main source of revenue for state formation. Vital in the war-led process of state formation, periphery transformation is counterproductive in the trade-led process. No periphery transformation, no state building. And without state building, states are weak.

Independence and State Failure, 1808–45

STATE FORMATION IN LATIN AMERICA occurred under extremely auspicious international economic and geopolitical conditions. The century spanning from Napoleon's defeat at Waterloo (1815) to the outbreak of World War I (1914) was the most peaceful period in world history, and it hosted the first global expansion of modern capitalism. Great Britain's centrality throughout the century, as both the undisputed international hegemon and the pioneer industrial economy, gave the period its proper name, the *Pax Britannica*. Britain made a radical departure from policies pursued by the empires of the past. Despite having the capacity to conquer Latin America by force, Britain prioritized free trade between sovereign countries. Free commerce without military conquest would produce large economic rewards while saving on fiscal costs. As designed by Lord Castlereagh and George Canning, British policy toward Latin America deliberately sponsored commerce and peace as mutually strengthening forces.[1]

In the preludes to the independence movements of the 1810s, Latin American and British elites shared the project of creating a new relationship between their economies. The new relation would be based on the exchange of high volumes of Latin American primary products for British manufactured goods and the investment of large amounts of British capital in the region. Latin American leaders expected that partnership with Great Britain would put an end to decades of economic stagnation caused by the mercantilist policies dictated by the Iberian metropolises. A new economy required new politics: it would fundamentally depend on the formation of independent countries with the capacity to provide a specific array of class goods for the economic and political elites of Latin America and Great Britain.[2] The new governments should produce an adequate political environment for international trade and foreign investments, including social peace and property rights, and provide the physical infrastructure required for the expansion of the export sector, like roads, harbors, and warehouses. In a virtuous cycle, new volumes of international trade would provide the resources to fund the creation of new sovereign states, produce the key class goods for the economic elites, and secure the professional survival of the political leaders. Latin American and British leaders of the early nineteenth century did not have a name for it, but they were essentially projecting "trade-led state formation."

The beginnings of the *Pax Britannica* and the onset of Latin America's independence movements roughly coincided in time. Brazil became independent in 1822. Spanish American independence was achieved at the decisive Battle of Ayacucho, Peru, in 1824. However, trade-led state formation both in Brazil and in Spanish America succeeded only three decades *after* the independence was achieved. The temporal gap between the end of Iberian colonial rule and successful state formation was enormously consequential. The decades of virtual statelessness created distinct challenges for state formation, and they required that future generations of state-makers applied special methods of violence monopolization, territory consolidation, and periphery incorporation.

By the mid-1820s, it was clear to all leaders of the independence movement that breaking down colonial rule was different from creating sovereign states. They had expected an easier, more automatic transition from colony to state. In the 1820s and 1830s, large deviations from the original plan of trade-led state formation occurred. Moreover, some of the very actions of the independence leaders had the unintended consequence of creating political and economic conditions that were more propitious for war-led state formation than for any other path of state formation.

The consequences of the wars of independence for state formation were far more detrimental than imagined. Independence was an incubator of warlords, or caudillos. Warlordism became endemic almost everywhere in Spanish America and produced contagion in the southern section of Brazil. Warlords caused statelessness. Some warlords, especially those located in potentially dynamic economic areas, could become state-makers. Yet most warlords were state-breakers who specialized in looting private property and government revenues. Warlord dynamics, at least in early modern western

Europe, was the precursor of war-led state formation. Yet state formation through warlord dynamics is a slow-moving process. It takes centuries rather than decades for it to produce institutional results.

War-led state formation in the 1830s did not make substantial progress in Latin America. Before it began to take any roots, in the mid-1840s, the *Pax Britannica* entered a second phase, which coincided with the transition from the First to the Second Industrial Revolution. The second phase of the *Pax Britannica* made the rewards of trade-led state formation and the opportunity costs of war-led state formation reach unprecedented heights. The spark that ignited the fire was a boom in the price of primary products, which reflected the mechanization of new manufacturing processes, the repeal of the Corn Laws protecting English farmers, the elimination of preferential treatment to imports from British colonies, and a surge of urbanization in northern Europe. Simultaneous improvements in steamship navigation sent transportation costs plummeting, which made the expansion of the export sector in Latin America even more attractive. The invention of the railways, combined with record levels of liquidity in the city of London, made British industrialists and investors eager to find new business opportunities in Latin America. Latin American economic and political elites saw that they could reap the rewards of a new attempt at trade-led state formation within the time span of their own professional lives. Starting in the mid-1840s, a second attempt at trade-led state formation was initiated. It succeeded. But it had to pay the price of failure during the first attempt.

The trajectory of state formation in Latin America can be divided into three periods: Independence (1808–25), State Failure (1825–45), and State Formation (1845–75). This chapter, divided into two sections, analyzes the first two periods. The third period is the subject of Chapter 3. Table 2.1 characterizes each period with regard to the relevant analytical components of the theory of state formation and previews the discussion of the following two sections and Chapter 3.

Independence: Origins and Failure of Trade-Led State Formation, 1808–25

Between 1808 and 1825, plans for trade-led state formation were designed, and important actions were taken to implement them, including centrally the

Table 2.1. Periods of State Formation in Latin America

Period	Initial conditions		Political elites			Outcome
	Geopolitical context	International economic conditions	Priority	Resources	Strategy toward periphery	
Independence, 1810–25	Hierarchy	Moderate international demand for primary products	Independence; free trade	Insufficient customs revenues	Military mobilization in Spanish America only	Failure of trade-led state formation
State Failure, 1825–45	Hierarchy	Stagnation of demand for primary products	Formation of local protection rackets	"Caudillo finance": bankruptcy	Open or latent civil war	Incipient war-led state formation
State Formation, 1845–75	Hierarchy	Boom in demand for primary products + abundant foreign capital	Market-making	Abundant customs revenues and foreign loans	Incorporation without transformation	Success of trade-led state formation; failure at state building

abolition of colonial rule and the opening of Latin American markets to goods and investments from the advanced economies of the North Atlantic, especially Great Britain. Yet the execution of trade-led state formation failed. In Spanish America, the armies that achieved independence failed at state formation. Independence required more military mobilization than expected. The consequence was endemic warlordism. In both Spanish America and Brazil, trade-led state formation required strong economic conditions, but a weak international demand for primary products combined with domestic dislocation of the traditional export sector to cause fiscal bankruptcy. The legacy of failure at state formation was an explosion of minisovereignties in Spanish America and waves of secessionism in Brazil.

International Context:
Support for Sovereignty and Free Trade

The Battle of Trafalgar was the proximate cause of both the *Pax Britannica* and the collapse of the Spanish Empire. In Trafalgar, the Royal Navy destroyed the combined fleets of Spain and France, initiating a long century of British dominion of the seas. Napoleon responded with the "Continental System," a European blockade against English imports. The blockade and the unprecedented growth of manufacturing output caused by the Industrial Revolution forced Britain to search for new economic outlets. Latin America was a prime candidate. In 1807, Lord Castlereagh advocated "the opening to our manufactures of the markets of that great Continent."[3] Castlereagh's "great continent" was Latin America. His priority became a permanent goal of British foreign policy throughout the *Pax Britannica*. British foreign-policy priorities created the geopolitical and economic incentives for trade-led state formation in Latin America.

British statesmen and businessmen saw in Latin America not only a high-potential market for English manufactured goods but also a prime destination for economic investments and a major source of primary products. Latin American consumers could benefit from cheaper and better manufactures, especially cotton textiles, the signature output of the first phase of the Industrial Revolution. Economic elites in Latin America could benefit from new investments to upgrade the export sector and from direct sales to northern European markets.

Latin America's ability to take advantage of the economic opportunity depended on two prior *political* developments. First, Latin America had to abolish Iberian colonial rule because Spain and Portugal monopolized foreign trade and prohibited foreign investment. Second, Latin America had to create sovereign states that provided the necessary political foundations for market transactions, the class goods for the economic elites.

European geopolitics is the single most important cause of Latin America's independence. In 1808, Spain had lost control of the Atlantic Ocean to the Royal Navy. Spain and Portugal were occupied by the army of Napoleon. Imperial weakness in the Iberian Peninsula meant revolutionary opportunity in the Americas.

Britain did not offer direct assistance for Latin America's independence. Great Britain was unwilling to antagonize either Spain or Portugal. Yet Britain's new foreign policy favored the cause of independence in two indirect ways. First, if Iberian colonial rule was a problem, British authorities admitted that military conquest was not a solution. British occupation would simply undermine the political stability required by international commerce and foreign investments by provoking upheaval within Latin America and risking retaliatory measures from France, Prussia, or the United States. Britain did not need military force to achieve its goals in Latin America. It could rely entirely on superior economic capacity. English manufactures outcompeted goods from any other part of the world. Superior technology and financial capacity applied to Mesoamerican and Andean mineral wealth, the backbone of the colonial economy, could supplant the backward techniques used by the declining Spanish Empire. British colonial rule in Latin America was both unnecessary and counterproductive.

Second, British dominion of the seas improved the chances of success of Latin America's bid for independence. In response to Napoleon's invasion of Spain in 1807, Britain decided in 1808 to station warships in the South Atlantic and the Caribbean on a permanent basis. In 1809, warships were sent to the South Pacific to protect trading routes from the ports of Valparaíso and Lima to East Asia and the North Atlantic. Before Latin America began the struggle for independence, the Royal Navy had already surrounded the subcontinent. Britain's purpose was not to replace Spain as a new colonial metropolis but to defend the continent from its closest geopolitical rival, France. Defeating Spain was already a tough challenge for Latin American revolutionaries. British naval measures saved them from having to fight Napoleon's forces as well. A second European enemy would have made Spanish American independence a military chimera.

In late 1824, at the same time Latin American patriots were fighting the decisive Battle of Ayacucho (Peru), Canning famously claimed, "The deed is done, the nail is driven, Spanish America is free, and if we do not mismanage our affairs sadly, she is English."[4] Canning's remark, combining Latin American sovereignty and English hegemony, was a deliberate provocation. Yet it contained no real contradiction. Britain was not interested in transforming Latin America into a colony of the empire—that would be "sad mismanagement." Britain simply wanted Latin America to become a reliable economic partner, albeit naturally a junior one.

Led by Simón Bolívar, all Latin American leaders sought British diplomatic recognition, which they perceived as an entry ticket into international security and economic development. Yet Castlereagh did not want to antagonize Spain or Portugal, and many of his cabinet colleagues opposed the idea of validating rebellion against a monarchy. In a skillful balancing act, Castlereagh abstained from sending consular missions but allowed Latin American vessels to enter British ports, which meant recognition in every sense except on paper. Canning succeeded Castlereagh in 1823. His policies further paved the way for trade-led state formation. In his first year in office, Canning obtained the cabinet's agreement to send consuls to the region. He also had France sign the Polignac Memorandum, by which French authorities committed not to intervene in Latin American politics. A year later, Great Britain gave official recognition to the new Spanish American republics. Between 1825 and 1828, recognition prompted a number of bilateral commercial treaties. In Mexico, Gran Colombia, and the River Plate, Canning obtained free navigation for British ships and "most favored nation" status for British goods, which secured the lowest tariffs vis-à-vis competitors.

British relations with Brazil were even more intimate than with Spanish America. In anticipation of Napoleon's invasion of Portugal, in 1807 the British government arranged the transportation of the entire Braganza House to its American domains. Thanks to British naval protection, the Portuguese Empire was safe in Brazil. As soon as Dom João, the prince regent of the

Table 2.2. Independence: International Conditions, Intervening Local Variables, and Outcome

Initial conditions

Geopolitical context	*International economic conditions*	*Priority*	*Resources*	*Strategy*	*Outcome*
Hierarchy	First Industrial Revolution	Independence	Insufficient customs revenues	Military mobilization in Spanish America	Failure of trade-led state formation
British indirect support for independence	Moderate demand for primary products + blind foreign capital	War against Spain		Independence negotiation through British mediation in Brazil	
		Recognition from UK			
		Free trade			

Portuguese Empire, arrived in Salvador da Bahia, he put an end to mercantilism and opened trade to friendly nations, which essentially meant Great Britain. In exchange for military protection, in 1810 British diplomacy secured large commercial privileges, including a maximum import duty of 15 percent for British goods. After Dom João was forced by the Portuguese congress to return to Lisbon in 1821, his son Dom Pedro declared Brazil's independence. British diplomacy played a pivotal role. Canning did not want to upset Portugal, the oldest English ally, but he also wanted to please Brazil, given that the commercial agreements of 1810 were up for renegotiation within three years. Additionally, if Brazil became more dependent on British military support, Canning could press for the abolition of the slave trade, which made Brazilian sugar and cotton much cheaper than the production in the British colonies. British diplomacy brokered an independence deal by which the Portuguese acknowledged the sovereignty of Brazil in exchange for the latter's payment of reparation of nearly £5 million. British banks provided Brazil with the necessary loan.

As a preview of the discussion to follow, Table 2.2 summarizes initial international conditions, intervening local variables, and final outcomes for the Independence period.

Priorities:
Independence and Economic Development

The international economic and geopolitical context, marked by the global expansion of capitalism, British naval hegemony, and the decline of the Iberian empires, shaped the priorities of Latin America's independence leaders. In 1810, the priorities were two: the abolition of colonial rule and the promotion of economic development through trade-led state formation. Two large armies were responsible for the defeat of Spain in South America, the Ejército Libertador of Bolívar and the Ejército de los Andes of San Martín. In the mid-1820s, their combined forces—one descending by land from Ecuador, the other moving north by sea from Chile—defeated the army of the Viceroyalty of Peru, the last bastion of Spanish rule. The army that liberated Mexico was a gigantic force of fifty thousand men. It resulted from the merger of two former military rivals: the insurgent army under the command of Vicente Guerrero and the royal army under the command of Agustín de Iturbide. Iturbide decided to switch sides—together with most defenders of Spanish colonial rule—after learning that a liberal revolt had succeeded in Spain.

Two types of motivation can be discerned among independence leaders: rejection of colonial economic policies and opposition to the monopoly over government positions held by Iberian officials. A third motivation, republican resentment against monarchic rule, was strong in the River Plate and New Granada, weak in Peru and Brazil, and mixed with the opposite sentiment, monarchic resentment against republican rule, in Mexico. Leaders with the first motivation viewed independence as a means for economic development. Leaders with the second motivation valued independence as an end in itself. The motivation of economic development made independence leaders converge with the interests of British statesmen and businessmen. They agreed that Iberian mercantilism was inimical to material progress. The colonial metropolises siphoned economic resources from the region through excessive taxation. Additionally, Portugal and Spain established commercial monopolies and monopsonies to intensify the transfer of wealth. Monopolies prevented Latin American consumers from gaining direct access to cheaper goods produced outside the Iberian empires. Spanish Americans were forced to buy from merchant monopolies based in Cádiz, which functioned as intermediaries between the colonies and the rest of the world and placed large markups on goods entering the ports of Veracruz, Callao, and Buenos Aires. Official monopsonies prohibited Latin American producers from selling their goods in the best-paying international markets. Entire sectors of economic activity had lain dormant because Iberian restrictions made them unprofitable or illegal.

Revolutionaries who prioritized political goals, like obtaining a share of government power or abolishing absolutism, agreed with those pursuing economic development that the fiscal viability of the newly independent countries would heavily rely on the formation of states based on free trade under the auspices of the *Pax Britannica*. Juan Bautista Alberdi captured in a short sentence an entire constellation of interests. Referring to the revolution in Buenos Aires, he claimed, "the coryphaeus of independence was not a soldier but an *economist*: Dr. [Mariano] Moreno."[5] The meaning of Alberdi's sentence is unambiguous. Either for instrumental reasons or for developmental ones, independence leaders banked on free economic relations with the capitalist world for the success of their political projects.

Resources:
Customs Tariffs and Foreign Loans

Both for achieving independence and for pursuing trade-led state formation, independence leaders relied on new forms of revenue. One of the first measures of the independence movements was to open the ports of the region to foreign trade. Import tariffs began to provide the bulk of governments' revenue. Most colonial taxes, especially the tributes extracted from indigenous communities, the Contribución Indígena, were abolished. They were deemed the most damaging and shameful form of colonial exploitation. From the mid-1810s to the early 1820s, a Latin American mania dominated British private interests. Thousands of English merchants rushed to the Latin American ports the very moment revolutions broke out. Warehouses in Rio de Janeiro, Buenos Aires, Lima, and Valparaíso were constantly refilled with British imports. Sales of British goods in Latin America grew from £1 million in colonial times (mostly contraband) to around £6 million in the early 1820s. In 1825, Latin America absorbed no less than 10 percent of British total exports. An import tariff ranging from 15 percent to 45 percent contributed both to support the independence movement and to set up the rudiments of trade-led state formation.

Customs revenues indirectly opened a second source of government finance. Expecting growing volumes of foreign trade, which would secure fiscal solvency, British financial capital also participated in the Latin American mania. By 1825, British loans to governments amounted to £21 million, a third of which was lent to Mexico, another third to Gran Colombia, a quarter to Brazil, and £1 million to Buenos Aires. As a symptom of the investment fever, speculators managed to float bonds worth £200,000 for a loan to Poyais, a fictional country, which for marketing purposes was described as a developed colony of British settlers somewhere on the Caribbean coast of Central America.

Yet the international commercial relations inaugurated by independence were not sustainable. The key reason was the poor performance of Latin America's export sector. Only four products experienced sustained growth in foreign sales before 1840: Brazil's coffee, Chile's silver, Cuba's sugar, and Buenos Aires's jerked beef and hides. Except for Chile and Cuba, the flood of English imports caused a major deficit in the balance of trade.

In turn, the main reason why the overall level of Latin American exports was disappointing was the relative weakness of the international demand for what the region could produce with the level of capital available. The four exceptions confirm the rule: Cuba and Brazil did not suffer capital destruction due to the absence of independence wars; Chile's early silver boom was based on spectacular discoveries of veins in one single area, Chañarcillo, the exploitation of which demanded relatively modest capital disbursements; and Buenos Aires's cattle-ranching activities were intensive in land, which was abundant, but not in capital, and the main consumers of jerked beef were the slave workers of the coffee and sugar plantations of Brazil and Cuba.

Foreign trade imbalances had deleterious repercussions on government revenues. They were the weakest link within the virtuous circle on which the plans for trade-led state formation had been based. And the link broke. The limited export base of Latin American economies placed a ceiling on the level of imports. British loans to Latin American governments, which helped to cover the trade gaps in the early 1820s, were not allocated to export-enhancing activities. The loans were used to pay debts contracted during the independence process, including primarily arrears of military wages. As a consequence, starting in 1827, only two years after the peak of the Latin American bond fever, one government after another began to default on its debt. Capital markets dried up for all Latin American governments for two decades. Fiscal bankruptcy placed a serious obstacle against the plans for trade-led state formation.

Strategies:
Conflict versus Synergy between Independence and Trade-Led State Formation

The relation between the strategy for achieving independence and the strategy for trade-led state formation was highly dependent on the level of resistance against independence mounted by Spain and Portugal. If resistance was high, the two strategies were incompatible. Independence and integration into world capitalism required opposite types of state. Whereas independence in the face of strong imperial resistance required forming a state that was a war machine, economic development under the *Pax Britannica* required a state that was a trade machine (centered on the provision of the class goods required for the expansion of the export sector). If, on the other hand, Iberian resistance was low, strategies could synergize: independence would be achieved with minimal military effort, incipient commercial relations with Britain would provide sufficient revenue to finish the independence wars promptly, and, once the war was over, political action could be easily redirected from military mobilization to providing the class goods and building the infrastructure required for integration into world capitalism.

A comparison between Spanish America and Brazil offers the most valuable lesson about the conditions under which the strategies for independence and trade-led state formation become synergic or incompatible. Brazil achieved independence largely without war, which meant that in principle it could make a smooth transition from colony to trade-led state formation. In Spanish America, despite the post-Trafalgar balance of geopolitical power, independence was anything but peaceful. Loyalist Spanish military forces within the colonies were still strong, and the restoration of the king of Spain in 1813 was followed by the decision to dispatch reinforcements to the Caribbean and the River Plate. Out of the three major rebellion foci in Spanish America, only one, Buenos Aires, the capital of the Viceroyalty of the River Plate, remained undefeated. In the Viceroyalty of New Spain, the insurgency led by Miguel Hidalgo and José María Morelos was crushed by the royalist army. In the Viceroyalty of New Granada, the rebellions of Simón Bolívar and Francisco de Miranda in 1810 were easily repressed and their leaders imprisoned or exiled. In Peru, the fourth Spanish viceroyalty, no serious revolutionary challenge emerged. Indeed, Peru's strong loyalist army provided support against the revolution in both New Granada and the River Plate. With Peru under control, a large loyal army in Mexico, and fresh soldiers sent from Europe, in the late 1810s Spain had solid reasons to expect continued colonial control. To stand a chance, the independence revolutions required large-scale military mobilization and protracted war-making. The independence revolutions eventually succeeded at war-making. Yet they failed at trade-led state formation.

In Spanish America, revolutions were initiated in the cities, but the war effort demanded sustained mobilization of almost every corner of the rural peripheries.[6] The scale of military mobilization was not as deleterious for the prospects of trade-led state formation as was the *form* of mobilization.[7] Forced to deal with multiple battlefronts at the same time, the military leaders of the Spanish American revolutions had no choice but to improvise armies, delegate decision power to local notables in the peripheries, and furnish them with military equipment. In a radical contrast with war-making in the final stages of modern state formation in western Europe, where kings eliminated local notables to prevent interference with the extraction of human and material resources, independence war-making in Latin America *empowered* local notables.[8] Most of the time, revolutionary leaders pushed local notables to become independence warriors, as they did in the River Plate with Martín Miguel de Güemes, who was charged with defending the northern periphery from attacks by loyalist Peruvian forces.

Few local notables resisted the temptation of becoming autonomous warlords, or caudillos. Independence wars placed them in a position from which they could run profitable protection rackets.[9] Resources supplied by the commanders of the revolution allowed them to expand their prerevolutionary base of clients, which included not only rural workers and peasants but also smaller local notables. Yet independence was not the only source of warlordism in Spanish America. Once a critical mass of warlords was reached, warlordism gained an autonomous dynamic. Warlordism bred warlordism. Several jurisdictions that were not mobilized for war adopted caudillo rule not to fight for independence but as a defense mechanism against neighboring caudillos. In the late 1820s and early 1830s, once the war against Spain was over, new warlords continued mushrooming throughout the region. In the late 1820s, the caudillo Juan Manuel de Rosas began his long rule over the city and state of Buenos Aires. Rosas's rise to power was unrelated to the military imperatives of the wars of independence. It was rooted in the ability to use a rural clientele to protect the city from neighboring caudillos to the north. In Mexico, Peru, and Bolivia, warlordism became even more endemic than in the River Plate.

Outcomes:
Success at Independence and Failure at State Formation

In 1825, all Latin America was free from colonial rule (except for Cuba and Puerto Rico). Yet trade-led state formation was a resounding failure. In 1830, Bolívar drew a bleak balance sheet of the Independence period in Spanish America: "I am ashamed to admit it, but independence is the only benefit we have gained, at the cost of everything else [i.e., political order and economic prosperity]."[10]

The absence of endemic warlordism in Brazil prevented the onset of war-led state formation, but it did not mean that rulers in Rio de Janeiro were able to monopolize violence or consolidate the territory on a definitive basis. Brazil suffered two waves of secessionist challenges, one in the early 1820s and another in the mid-1830s, which were more threatening than any challenge ever experienced by a Spanish American country (except for Mexico). The only two countries that made an almost instant transition from colony to state were Chile and Paraguay, although following opposite paths.

In Spanish America, independence resulted in what several authors have characterized as the "balkanization" of political power.[11] The notion of balkanization combines two distinct processes: the rise of minisovereignties and the proliferation of warlordism. Over the course of the wars of independence, from Mexico to the River Plate, the smallest political units mobilized to claim autonomy, defending their sovereignty not just from Spain but also from the aspiring capitals of the new states.[12] The aspiring capitals were ten midsized to large cities that hosted colonial authorities. They were the seat either of one of the four viceroyalties—México City, Lima, Bogotá, and Buenos Aires—or of lower-level authorities, *capitanías, audiencias,* and *gobernaciones,* which included Guatemala, Caracas, Quito, Charcas (present-day Sucre), Santiago de Chile, and Montevideo. All the aspiring capitals were invariably challenged by the self-proclaimed sovereignty of the pueblos, including small villages of a few hundred inhabitants.

Most pueblos often lacked the economic basis to sustain their autonomy claims. Yet in many cases, it was the very process of military mobilization during independence that provided them with a caudillo who could back up the pueblo's autonomy claims with a loyal clientele and the power of arms.[13] Building on Domingo Sarmiento's writings, the work by Tulio Halperín Donghi described the rise of caudillo power as the unexpected but inevitable "ruralization" and "militarization" of political power caused by the wars of independence.[14]

In Spanish America, the wars of independence created a political arena that, with regard to the physical distribution of military power, was not dissimilar from the scenario of fragmented sovereignty that characterized late medieval western Europe. The independence armies failed to create states.

Yet military mobilization during wars of independence left a legacy of warlordism that could have led to the formation of strong military states through Darwinian competition. Independence created in Spanish America the geopolitical rudiments of the process of war-led state formation that had forged the pioneer cases in western Europe.

Independence wars erected in Spanish America *political* obstacles to state formation that Brazil was largely able to avoid. Yet the unsustainability of international trade relations created an *economic* flaw in the strategy of trade-led state formation both in Spanish America and in Brazil. The economic flaw "overdetermined" state failure in Spanish America and was just enough to prevent territory consolidation in Brazil.

Chile is one of the two exceptions to state failure before 1845. Paraguay is the other one. They both provide evidence of the centrality of a dynamic export sector within the path of trade-led state formation. A prematurely dynamic export sector explains Chile's almost immediate ability to engage in trade-led state formation. The absence of an export sector explains Paraguay's inability to follow trade-led state formation, which resulted in the full adoption of the war-led model. Chile was a unique combination of geographic, political, and economic attributes. Its territory was compact and was separated from its neighbors by the highest mountains in the Andean range.[15] Natural barriers to invasion saved Chile from the need of military defense. Politically, mobilization for independence was the lowest in Spanish America, and no caudillos were created in the process. The bulk of the independence effort was carried out by the Ejército de los Andes led by San Martín and was funded by the states of Buenos Aires, Mendoza, and San Juan in present-day Argentina. The political division between Conservatives and Liberals, a common cleavage throughout Latin America, was precociously solved with a decisive military victory of the Conservatives in the early 1830s. Finally, Chile's economy had two engines, the recently discovered silver mines of Chañarcillo and the port of Valparaíso, which the English transformed into a vibrant entrepôt linking together markets in East Asia, the South Atlantic, and northern Europe. An exceptional combination of circumstances made Chile a precursor of trade-led state formation.

Paraguay, the other exception to state failure, followed the opposite path, war-led state formation. An army led by Gaspar de Francia defeated Buenos Aires's attempts at annexation in the early 1810s. With no products

Table 2.3. Success Rate and Types of State Formation during Independence

		Performance of export sector		
		Poor	*Average*	*Exceptional*
Military mobilization for independence	*Low*		Brazil Failure of trade-led state formation	Chile Early trade-led state formation
	High	Paraguay Early war-led state formation	Modal Spanish America Failure of trade-led state formation overdetermined	

to offer in the international markets, Francia used the power of the army to build a dictatorship and nationalize agricultural farms, the productivity of which was barely above subsistence level. Francia was the undisputed ruler of Paraguay until his death in 1841. His successor, Carlos Antonio López, ruled for another two decades. They both used whatever surplus the Paraguayan economy could produce to purchase military equipment. With only narrow rivers separating Paraguay's territory from Brazil and present-day Argentina, and dependent on those countries' goodwill to reach the sea, Francia and López made international security a national priority. Paraguay was the only state deliberately built as a war machine in the early modern European fashion. Table 2.3 summarizes key variables, outcomes, and cases in the Independence period.

State Failure:
The Short Life of War-Led State Formation, 1825–45

Between 1825 and 1845, most regions in Latin America failed to create a state. New local conditions in Latin America, warlordism and economic weakness, outweighed the international incentives of the *Pax Britannica* and set in motion a process of war-led state formation, the opposite path to the one envisioned by Latin American and British leaders alike. The international incentives and constraints of the *Pax Britannica* had distinct economic and geopolitical effects. The economic incentives were not strong enough to prevent the failure of trade-led state formation, but the geopolitical constraints were strong enough to impede further consolidation of war-led state formation.

International Context:
Economic Stagnation and Suppression of Major Wars

Starting in 1825, the only new element in the international context favorable to state formation in Latin America was the collapse of the Spanish and Portuguese Empires and the consolidation of Great Britain as a global hegemon with no intention to threaten the sovereignty of Latin America's emerging countries. In economic terms, the international context for trade-led state formation had deteriorated, in part because of the string of sovereign-debt defaults in Latin America at the end of the prior period. International financial markets closed the doors for Latin America until the mid-nineteenth century. The demand for primary products stagnated. So did foreign direct investments. The lack of new British investments had two sources: the political instability of most of Spanish America and the meager yields of the English mining ventures in the prior period, which in turn resulted from a combination of longer maturation periods than anticipated, poor adaptation of British technology to Mexican and Andean altitudes, and bad luck with the discoveries.

If international economic conditions in this period did not provide extra incentives for trade-led state formation, the consolidation of Britain as the international hegemon contributed to prevent war-led state formation from making real progress, at least in South America. The warlord dynamics inherited from independence in Spanish America triggered the onset of the war-led path to state formation. Yet steps taken along that path after independence were all undone starting in the mid-1840s. British international policy in 1825-45 was not the main reason why Latin American countries did not form as war machines along Westphalian lines. The main reason was the lack of time. The process was interrupted before it could gather enough momentum, when a combination of international economic and technological changes in the mid-1840s created new incentives for trade-led state formation. Yet the *Pax Britannica* itself played a key, if secondary, role in 1825–45. British interests in the region were strong enough to prevent major conflagrations.

The very year Gran Colombia collapsed (1831), Britain made itself available as a mediator in any future disagreements among successor states Colombia, Ecuador, and Venezuela. Britain's role as an external umpire precluded geopolitical escalation in northern South America. More important was Britain's influence in the Southern Cone and Brazil. In the early 1820s, the territory of present-day Uruguay was claimed by both Brazil and Buenos Aires. They went to war for it in 1824. After four years of conflict, British diplomacy negotiated a peace agreement. Lord Ponsonby proposed the creation of Uruguay as an independent state. Buenos Aires and Rio de Janeiro agreed. The interests and forces behind the solution were transparent to all: Buenos Aires and Brazil saved valuable human and material resources that the continuation of war would have destroyed; British naval supremacy was a sine qua non for Uruguay's survival and thereby the maintenance of regional peace; Montevideo would serve British merchants as an alternative port, heavily dependent on the Royal Navy's protection, in case of turmoil in Buenos Aires. By neutralizing conflict between Buenos Aires and Brazil, Great Britain pacified the two major geopolitical contenders in South America. Chile was a rising power, but geographic barriers, Royal Navy gunboats on the South Pacific, and British merchants well embedded in Valparaíso combined to neutralize Chile's geopolitical ambitions during the critical decades before the mid-nineteenth century. As a preview of the discussion to follow, table 2.4 summarizes initial international conditions, intervening local variables, and final outcomes for the Failure period.

Priorities in Spanish America:
From Continental Armies to Local Security

In early 1822, Iturbide put an end to Spanish rule and became the first Mexican emperor. Only a few months later, San Martín met with Bolívar in Guayaquil, Ecuador's main port. San Martín had liberated the city of Lima, and Bolívar would later defeat the remaining Spanish forces in the Peruvian

Table 2.4. State Failure: International Conditions, Intervening Local Variables, and Outcome

Initial conditions		Priority	Resources	Strategy	Outcome
Geopolitical context	International economic conditions				
Hierarchy	Stagnation of demand	Rural warlords:	Reimposition of	Open or	Failure
British prevention of	for primary products +	protection of	colonial taxes +	latent civil	Interrupted
major conflagrations +	scarcity of foreign capital	clients, extortion of	"caudillo finance"	war	war-led state
protection of waterways		outsiders			formation
		Urban politicians:			
		protection from			
		warlords + party			
		formation			

countryside. In 1822, the three generals were the most powerful men in Spanish America. They were in command of large, victorious armies. Additionally, San Martín and Bolívar were revered as founding heroes throughout Spanish South America. The priorities of the three generals could define the political future of independent Latin America. Victorious armies monopolize violence within the territory under dispute. The armies of Bolívar, San Martín, and Iturbide could in principle become the military core of new states.

Both Iturbide and Bolívar wanted to transition from warriors to statemakers. They could not. San Martín could transition from warrior to statemaker. He would not. The way that the armies of Bolívar and Iturbide were formed made it impossible for them to produce states. In Bolívar's army, a few highly professional marshals, ready to relocate as circumstances required, like Antonio J. Sucre, coexisted with dozens of improvised lieutenants, who were deeply attached to local communities as patrons of large clienteles, that is, caudillos.[16] The state of Gran Colombia, which was coterminous with the former Viceroyalty of New Granada, was Bolívar's largest state-formation project. Instead of focusing on the consolidation of the borders of Gran Colombia and the professionalization of its army, Bolívar extended his military effort to Peru and Bolivia. Overextension demanded further improvisation in military mobilization. Some of Bolívar's own lieutenants became state-breaking caudillos, who boycotted Bolívar's state-formation projects, provoked the collapse of Gran Colombia in the early 1830s, and threatened to destroy Colombia, one of the small successor states, in the early 1840s.

Iturbide's army resulted from the merger of two former military rivals, the royal army under his own command and the insurgent army of Guerrero. The contradictory alliance between conservative counterrevolutionaries and liberal revolutionaries could put an end to Spanish rule but could not form a sovereign state. The two armies had been in a stalemate for almost a decade. Over the course of the stalemate, the insurgent army had become an amalgam of local caudillos. The unified army of independent Mexico was extremely expensive. But it was even more ineffective than it was expensive. Local caudillos escaped central control. Secessionism became endemic. In 1823, liberal forces led the separation of the former Captaincy of Guatemala (present-day Guatemala, Nicaragua, El Salvador, Honduras, Costa Rica, and

Chiapas, although Chiapas decided to remain within Mexico). Iturbide did not last in power longer than a year. And Central America would not be Mexico's only territorial loss.

San Martín's army was a different organization altogether. His Ejército de los Andes was the most professional and effective military force ever created in Latin America. None of San Martín's lieutenants became caudillos. However, during his campaigns in Chile and Peru, the former Viceroyalty of the River Plate fragmented into fifteen minisovereignties. In part because Buenos Aires made overwhelming fiscal efforts to finance San Martín's campaigns, the city was forced to improvise military forces in other battlefronts—the same mobilization strategy of Bolívar in Nueva Granada and Peru and of Guerrero in Mexico. In the territories of present-day Uruguay, military power was delegated to José Gervasio Artigas. Artigas quickly became a bitter enemy of Buenos Aires. In his fight against both Spain and Buenos Aires, Artigas himself had to delegate power to lieutenants. As if following a design in fractal geometry, Artigas's improvised lieutenants turned against their general, and after Artigas was defeated, they began to fight each other. The revolutionary elite of Buenos Aires repeatedly begged San Martín to return from Chile and repress post-Artigas caudillos. Not only did they dominate Uruguay, but they also extended caudillo rule to the minisovereignties of Entre Ríos and Santa Fe north of Buenos Aires. San Martín refused to deviate from his plan. His priority was the elimination of the source of Spanish power in Peru. He viewed the fight against *caudillaje* as a waste of resources and warlordism as rooted in factious divisions unrelated to the cause of independence. If in the mid-1820s San Martín had decided, like George Washington in the United States, to become the president of a new nation, the Ejército de los Andes would have been the kernel of a large independent state, dominating the full territory of the former Viceroyalty of the River Plate (Argentina, Bolivia, Paraguay, and Uruguay) plus Chile.

Structural constraints made it impossible for the armies of Bolívar and Iturbide to pursue the goal of state formation. San Martín's personal decision, rather than structural constraints, disbanded the only army that could have become the core of a large state in the period of Failure.

The inability or unwillingness of the great independence generals to deal with the balkanization of political power in Spanish America prompted the emergence of dozens of poorly connected mini political arenas. Rural arenas were largely dominated by caudillos. Urban arenas were dominated by semiprofessional politicians, *supercaudillos* (caudillos leading an informal hierarchy of smaller caudillos), or a coalition between them. Except for Buenos Aires and Montevideo, an incipient division within the urban oligarchy, between Conservatives and Liberals, began to structure political debate and electoral competition, which often degenerated into open military conflict. Almost everywhere, Conservatives had a vested interest in the defense of corporate privileges granted in colonial times to three institutions: the army, the church, and the *consulado* (the association of monopolistic local merchants, which was especially strong in cities like Lima, México, and Guatemala). Liberals were largely members of the same social class as Conservatives, but their linkages with the networks of colonial privilege were weaker or nonexistent. As a consequence, they pushed for the abolition of corporate privileges.

Within the context of political balkanization in Spanish America, the priorities of urban politicians and rural caudillos became eminently *local*. Most rural caudillos were leaders of protection rackets with limited territorial reach. They specialized in defending their client base, preventing the rise of challengers within their own domain, and raiding neighboring areas. A top priority of the cities was to defend themselves from caudillos. Yet, given collective action problems among urban politicians, protection was usually achieved by accepting the tutelage of a supercaudillo. The supercaudillo provided a praetorian guard in return for control of the modest flow of revenues from taxes on international trade.

Priorities in Brazil:
Empire Building, Slavery Preservation, and Secession

In Brazil, the priority of Pedro I was to preserve the union of the empire's vast territory against a wave of secessionist threats. The priority of provincial oligarchies in the center (Rio de Janeiro and Minas Gerais) and the Northeast (Bahia and Pernambuco) was to preserve slavery against strong British pressure. Pedro I feared the specter of anarchy that swept Spanish America. Provincial slavocrats feared the specter of *Haitianization*, the large-scale slave rebellion that shook the island of Hispaniola in 1791. Pedro I's fears were well founded. The priority of several political oligarchies in the peripheries, from Maranhão in the North to Rio Grande in the South, was to form their own independent states. The motivations for secession were multifold and varied depending on the case. Some rejected the monarchic regime and wanted the splinter state to become a republic; others complained about the level of taxation imposed from Rio de Janeiro; and still others disagreed with the empire's choice of local authorities. The unconfessed but obvious motivation shared by all secessionist movements was the expectation of their leaders to become the supreme authority in the separate country.

Pedro I was the only leader of the Failure period in Latin America with the capacity and the will to carry out clear supralocal priorities. His priority was large-scale state formation. Structural conditions differentiated Pedro I from Bolívar and Iturbide with regard to capacity for state formation, especially the absence in Brazil of a legacy of improvised military mobilization. The emperor's army in Brazil was comparatively strong, cohesive, and professional. At the same time, in contrast to San Martín, Pedro I did not refuse to engage in postindependence politics, which included dealing with conflicts between factions, often for petty prizes, which San Martín detested.

Yet a combination of anti-Portuguese agitation in Rio de Janeiro and political turmoil in Lisbon forced Pedro I to abdicate in 1831 in favor of his five-year-old son. Pedro I returned to Europe to restore the power of the throne of Portugal to his daughter. A regency took power on an interim basis before Pedro II reached adulthood. Starting in 1835, a wave of secession movements put Brazil on the verge of disintegration. The regency lacked both the political capital and the fiscal resources to deal with it.

Resources:
Fiscal Bankruptcy and Caudillo Finance

In Spanish America, none of the governments in the aspiring capital cities had the funds to deal with caudillos. In Mexico, Peru, and Bolivia, demands for manpower by the war effort, combined with high levels of political uncertainty, had caused a sudden paralysis of mining activities, the economic backbone of the region since the Conquest. Left without maintenance, mines suffered massive flooding and subsidence. The rehabilitation of mining required extraordinary amounts of capital and time. None of the three main mining areas would recover colonial levels of output for nearly three decades. In the former territories of the Viceroyalties of the River Plate and New Granada, royal and patriot armies alike had been voracious consumers of cattle.[17] Cattle restocking also made considerable demands for capital. Additionally, starting in 1778, the Spanish Empire in South America had created a zone of free trade among its constituent regions. The customs union had fostered the emergence of various economic networks. The networks were relatively complex supply chains whose end points were the large mining centers, like Potosí, and the capitals of the viceroyalties. They traded locally produced textiles, carts, mules, foodstuffs, and liquor. By paralyzing mining activities and fragmenting the common economic area, independence caused the collapse of the colonial economic networks and the evaporation of the income they used to generate.[18] Finally, the Spaniards who decided to return home, including former high-ranking bureaucrats and large merchants, carried with them incalculable amounts of bullion. The wave of capital flight deprived the emerging countries of the necessary resources to rebuild the economy.

Economic stagnation caused lackluster export performance, which in turn resulted in insufficient hard currency for imports. Imports from Great Britain in all Latin America stagnated through the Failure period at the £6 million level that had been reached in the early 1820s. Due to reliance on customs tariffs, import stagnation caused government bankruptcy. In a clear indication of fiscal desperation, Bolivia, Mexico, and Peru introduced a special tax on indigenous populations, the old Contribución Indígena in all but name, which revolutionary leaders had repudiated as an egregious sign of colonial rule. In the territory of present-day Argentina, every ministate was forced to place tariffs on goods introduced from the other ministates, no matter whether they were produced in the River Plate area or western Europe. In Brazil, the fiscal picture was not as bleak. Yet sugar and cotton exports were in decline, and coffee production had not boomed yet. Besides, Brazil suffered an exceptional restriction on tax capacity. By the independence agreements brokered by Great Britain in the early 1820s, Brazil's import tariffs on British goods could not exceed 15 percent, the lowest in Latin America, which caused serious government underfunding. Brazil would be able to increase import tariffs only in 1844, when the agreement expired. Insufficient fiscal resources partly explain the success of Uruguay's separation from the empire during the first wave of secessionist attempts in the mid-1820s and the protracted nature of many secessionist attempts of the second wave, which began in 1835.

In Spanish America, the combination of fiscal bankruptcy and caudillo power created a vicious cycle of governments unable to deal with caudillo threats, followed by caudillo predation of public treasuries, which deepened the governments' deficits and their inability to deal with caudillo threats. Paul Gootenberg, referring to the Peruvian case, aptly called the phenomenon "caudillo finance," which can be extended with only minor modifications to Mexico, Bolivia, and the minisovereignties of the River Plate.[19]

Strategies in Spanish America: Local Survival

Given the balkanization of Spanish America, the priority of local security in rural and urban settings, together with the lack of fiscal resources in the capital to monopolize violence, induced most actors to pursue military preparation as the dominant political strategy. Even emerging political parties, which provided an incipient form of supraregional structure in the Failure period, were organizations for war, as political debates, campaigns, and elections often degenerated into military confrontation. A small number of warlords, or caudillos, rose to supralocal prominence by taking advantage of temporary moments of vulnerability of neighboring caudillos to subdue them as new members of their client base. They became supercaudillos. In exchange for loyalty, supercaudillos provided vulnerable local caudillos with military protection and occasional subsidies.

The military strategies of caudillos, supercaudillos, and protoparties were inimical to state formation beyond the boundaries of the local community. Large countries became a chimera. In the River Plate area, between the late 1820s and the early 1850s, a dozen caudillo fiefdoms consolidated. Buenos Aires, under the rule of the supercaudillo Juan Manuel de Rosas, emerged as the suzerain at the center of an informal hierarchy of peripheral caudillos. Yet Buenos Aires deliberately blocked large-scale state formation to avoid sharing power and wealth with peripheral caudillos. In Central America and northern South America, two rural caudillos, Rafael Carrera and José Antonio Páez, transitioned from *state-breakers* of a large territorial unit, the Central American Federation and Gran Colombia, to *state-makers* of a smaller territorial unit, Guatemala and Venezuela. Rosas, Páez, and Carrera were in power for at least two decades. During their tenure, they eliminated political instability within their jurisdiction but at the cost of forcing the collapse, or preventing the formation, of states controlling a large territory, similar to the colonial viceroyalties or the projects of independence leaders.

Supraregional alliances of urban politicians and rural caudillos, or protoparties, were fragile phenomena. Protoparties had the ambitious goal of dominating politics in the aspiring capital and setting policies for an area coterminous with the dimensions of a modern country. In Peru and Mexico, attempts at forming such alliances were recurrent, but, once formed, they lacked lasting power to launch and sustain a state-formation project. Nothing approaching a monopoly of violence existed in Peru or Mexico. Additionally, three regions in Mexico—Texas, Zacatecas, and Yucatán—simultaneously pursued secession. They were the only regions to experience some degree of economic prosperity, all three of them were frustrated at the lack of public goods supplied by the central state, and they feared overtaxation from México City.

Like Mexico, the territory of present-day Colombia had multiple cities. The division between Liberals and Conservatives in Bogotá forced each competing protoparty to search for allies in a distant city like Medellín, Cartagena, or Popayán. A protoparty within a city sought allies from outside the city in order to become stronger in the local fight against the rival protoparty. These dynamics of alliance formation centered in Bogotá gradually formed two rival supraregional oligarchic parties that became more stable than any other party organization in Spanish America. They also recruited opportunistic caudillos, who became crucial actors when electoral competition mutated into armed conflict. Yet, in contrast to the cities of Caracas or Buenos Aires, fiscal resources in Bogotá were so anemic that supraregional alliances could not sustain a large-scale state-formation project either. Violence monopolization in Colombia would not occur before the twentieth century.

In postindependence Spanish America, reflecting the relatively low opportunity costs of war, politics was largely dominated by local rural actors, caudillos, driven by security considerations. Supraregional coalitions of protoparties were intermittent, with the partial exceptions of Mexico and Colombia. Isolated pockets of economic prosperity pursued secession in order to remove themselves from political chaos or accepted rule by a super-caudillo in order to shield themselves from predatory attacks. Force, open or latent, marked the interaction among caudillos and between protoparties. The prominence of armed conflict and local priorities—with the concomitant fluidity of political borders—meant statelessness by definition. Militarized local actors were a solid platform for a Westphalian style of war-led state formation.

Strategies in Brazil: A Secession Wave

After Pedro's abdication, Brazil suffered a wave of rebellions. Three occurred in 1835: the Cabanagem revolt in Grão-Pará, which was both a secessionist movement and a social revolution; the Malê revolt in Bahía, a rebellion of almost six hundred Yoruba Islamist slaves; and the Revolução Farroupilha in the southern province of Rio Grande do Sul. Three years later, two rebellions exploded in the North: the Sabinada revolt, which created the Republic of Bahia and promised abolition of slavery, and the Balaiada revolt in Maranhão, where local liberals, allied with fugitive slaves and a contingent of poor free workers, attempted secession against the opposition of provincial conservatives.

Slavery favored territory consolidation in Brazil through the "repression linkage." Local elites in Brazilian regions that initiated separation eventually gave up secessionist aspirations after mobilization for independence got out of control and risked slave rebellion. Secessionist elites acknowledged that only the coercive capacity of the central state was able to prevent slave sedition, repress slave rebellion, and resist foreign pressure against slavery. Separatist provinces agreed to reincorporation in exchange for central assistance in restoring social order.

The Farroupilha, the only rebellion that took place south of the capital, is also the only one that did not involve a slave revolt. It was a purely secessionist movement. It created an independent republic, Piratini, which rejected the empire's political regime, level of taxation, and trade policies. It lasted ten years, longer than any other rebellion in Brazil. No other South American country endured a secessionist challenge of the magnitude of the

Farroupilha. Based on extensive cattle ranching, Rio Grande was the only province in Brazil under caudillo rule. Warlords—or *gaúcho* chiefs, in Rio Grande do Sul's vocabulary—did not originate as delegates of a revolutionary center fighting against colonial rule, as was often the case in Spanish America. The region experienced no independence wars. The power of Rio Grande caudillos derived in part from the diffusion pressures for the organization of protection rackets coming from the neighboring River Plate area and in part from the type of economy, which had a propensity to the formation of informal political hierarchies based on property, courage, and skill at ranching activities.

Although Brazil is customarily regarded as having skipped the balkanization that characterized postindependence South America, it was certainly not exempt from state failure. The fact that secessionist movements were eventually aborted, except in Uruguay, does not mean that Brazil was not under real risk of disintegration. Rio de Janeiro had to make major political, military, and fiscal efforts at state formation. In contrast with Spanish America, Brazil could count on a large and cohesive army and the strength of the "repression linkage" originating in slavery, which made provincial oligarchies that might otherwise aspire to secession hold a stake in the preservation of Brazil's territorial unity. Yet in the region where warlordism prevailed, Rio Grande do Sul, secessionist threats reached maximum strength and could only be dealt with when the *Pax Britannica* entered its second phase.

Outcome: State Failure

Throughout Spanish America, the period produced two complementary outcomes: the decline of large-scale projects of state formation and the consolidation of rural warlords and provincial oligarchies as patrimonial rulers with ultimate authority over small territorial units—usually the size of a village and its immediate hinterland. Supraregional coalitions were intermittent and fragile. The interaction among caudillos and the competition between protoparties were marked by open or latent violence. The dual outcome reflected fiscal bankruptcy and warlord activity. It resulted from the combination of a stagnant international demand for primary products and the aversion of foreign capitals to take new risks in the region with the legacy of emergency military mobilization during the wars of independence (plus San Martín's idiosyncratic decision to eschew state-making efforts).

Mexico, with the three most prosperous regions simultaneously bidding for secession, was the best example of Failure. In Central America, the Federación Centroamericana, which was dominated by a supraregional alliance of Liberal politicians, broke down in 1838 into five separate countries after a tax rebellion in Guatemala led by the rural caudillo Carrera. Carrera rejected the formation of a larger country including the present-day territories of El Salvador, Honduras, and Nicaragua out of fear that the central government in the larger arena would again fall under the control of Liberal politicians and tax Guatemala's wealth to subsidize other regions. The project of Gran Colombia broke down in 1831 due to the secession of Venezuela led by the caudillo Páez. Páez's alliance with Caracas's export elites ensured that Venezuelan secession became irreversible. Reunion with Colombia risked higher taxes in Venezuela to sustain the central government in Bogotá and to subsidize Colombia's poorest regions. As a separate country, Colombia itself was on the verge of disintegration into smaller sovereignties during the Guerra de los Supremos (1839–42), a wave of secessionist attempts led by local caudillos. In the River Plate, Buenos Aires, dominated by the supercaudillo Rosas, resisted any large-scale project of unification with the thirteen minisovereignties to the north and west. A large landowner himself, Rosas and other members of Buenos Aires's landed elites were opposed to sharing their wealth and the revenues collected at the city-port with the other caudillos.

In Brazil, identical international conditions combined with a legacy of negligible military mobilization during independence to provide Pedro I with the incentives and capacity to embrace a large-scale state-formation project. Peripheral oligarchies were torn between opposite forces: the aspiration to form an independent republic and the need of imperial power to keep slaves tied to the plantations. Secession attempts in the northern provinces, where slavery made local elites more dependent on the central state's military capacity, were suppressed through a combination of repression and negotiation. The southern provinces of the empire were dominated by warlords similar to the ones prevailing in South America. Based on extensive cattle ranching, their economies were substantially less dependent on slave labor. Uruguay gained independence with decisive help from Great Britain in 1828.

In 1835, Rio Grande do Sul created a republic that was still independent when the period of Failure in Latin America was coming to a close.

From 1825 to 1840, the fragmentation and ruralization of political power in Spanish America and Brazil were more conducive to war-led state formation than to any other type of state-formation process. Lack of time for the process to gain traction and British diplomatic interventions prevented war-led state formation from producing tangible outcomes. In 1845, the *Pax Britannica* entered a new economic phase, and the winds of trade-led state formation began to blow with irreversible strength for Latin America.

THREE

The Triumph of Trade-Led State
Formation, 1845–75

BETWEEN 1845 AND 1875, the economic stimuli of the *Pax Britannica* boomed. They caused the first period of sustained export-led growth in Latin America. The rewards for trade-led state formation and the opportunity costs of war grew exponentially. Tight coalitions between professional politicians in the city-port and economic elites in the export sector became a widespread phenomenon. By investing in trade-led state formation, they succeeded at political survival and profit maximization. Yet the states they formed had to pay the price of failure in 1825–45. The ruling coalitions succeeded at "periphery incorporation" but avoided "periphery transformation," thereby decoupling state formation from state building.[1]

International Economic Conditions:
A Commercial Revolution

The roots of economic development in mid-nineteenth-century Latin America are found in western Europe. Tulio Halperín Donghi opens his masterful synthesis of the economic history of Latin America since 1850 with a reference to trends and events occurring outside the region: "The middle years of the nineteenth century marked, for the economy of Europe, an impressive wave of expansion destined to last until the Great Depression of 1873."[2] In the transition from the First to the Second Industrial Revolution in the North Atlantic, multiple forces in the international economy, at the level of *prices*, *policies*, and *technology*, combined in a short span to produce seismic effects on Latin America's prospects for development.

The most notable expression of change was a surge in *prices* for most products that Latin America had begun to export only after independence, like sheep wool, coffee, copper, and fertilizers. Higher prices reflected a much stronger international demand. Catching up with Great Britain as industrial powers, France, Germany, and the United States became new large-scale consumers of primary products. In the 1850–70 period, the annual growth rate of imports in the United Kingdom and France was 5 percent and 7 percent, respectively, the largest ever recorded by any economy in the nineteenth century—an unprecedented economic opportunity for Latin America.

Deepening industrialization changed Great Britain's trade *policies*, which became especially favorable for Latin American exports. Rapid migration from the countryside to the cities prompted British rulers to reassess protection for domestic agriculture as well as preferential treatment for the colonies. In 1846, the Corn Laws, which had shielded English farming, were repealed, and the commercial advantages of British colonies began to be dismantled and would disappear by the end of the century. A larger proportion of consumption by the swollen ranks of industrial workers had to be met by imports.

European *technology* caused economic globalization in Latin America in the 1840s and 1850s. Technological innovations altered Latin America's terms of trade. They began to improve in the 1820s, surged in the mid-1840s, and continued to grow for the following three decades. Two innovations explain the improvement. First, productivity gains in modern western European and North American industry caused a large discrete shift in the supply of manufactured goods (a much higher level of industrial output for a given price). Competition among industrial firms meant that benefits, under the form of lower prices, were passed on to world consumers. Since the production of primary goods did not undergo the same level of innovation, price changes were defined by shifts in the demand curve. Higher income in industrial economies translated into higher demand and thereby into better world prices for primary products.[3]

The other source of improvement in the terms of trade was a reduction in the cost of commerce that benefited North Atlantic and Latin American economies alike. In the 1840s, transatlantic trade experienced a transportation revolution with the switch from sail to steam. In the 1840s and 1850s, steamships became more efficient due to a string of innovations, in-

cluding the screw propeller, the compound engine, steel hulls, larger load-
ing capacity, and shorter turn-around time in port. "Before 1869, steam
tonnage had never exceeded sail tonnage in British shipyards. By 1870, steam
tonnage was more than twice as great as sail, and sail tonnage only exceeded
steam tonnage in two years after that date."[4] Starting in 1840, transportation
costs across the Atlantic declined by about 1.5 percent a year; that is, in 1860,
they shrank to roughly 73 percent of the 1840 baseline.[5] The steamship glo-
balized Latin America's economies for the first time in the mid-nineteenth
century.

The economic impact of steam navigation was dwarfed by the potential effect of the invention of the railway. Several areas of the size of Italy remained unproductive in Latin America because of transportation costs
from interior to port. By the mid-1850s, the transportation infrastructure
within Latin America had made no substantial improvements on the system
of roads built in colonial times, most of which had fallen into disrepair after
the wars of independence. Because of endemic political instability during
the period of Failure, Latin America had "largely skipped the turnpike era
of internal improvements."[6]

Adoption of railways in Latin America would then telescope the time
of transition from primitive to modern infrastructure. Before 1850, "a geography highly unfavorable to inland movement was the chief culprit in the high
costs of transport. . . . The steep mountain ranges of Mexico, Brazil, Colombia, and the other Andean regions physically partitioned large expanses."[7] In steep terrains, mules were the dominant form of transportation.
Throughout Mexico and the Andes, some footpaths, which provided key
passages within larger trade routes, were impossible to transform into roads.
A combination of carts, mules, and human porters, or *silleteros*, was required
to move precious metals and members of the elite from core mining regions
to urban centers and seaports in Mexico and Colombia. Mexico lacked navigable rivers. In Colombia, the Magdalena River was the backbone of the
transportation system. Yet the Magdalena was plagued with rapids, and water
levels varied from one season to the next. In northeastern Brazil and Central America, trade still moved along colonial or precolonial trails, only a few
stretches of which were paved with stone for cart traffic. Finally, colonial
roads had been designed for the transportation of traditional exports, including silver from Mexico, Peru, and Bolivia; gold from Antioquia and Minas
Gerais (central Brazil, also rich in diamonds); sugar from the Caribbean, the

Peruvian coast, and northeastern Brazil; and dyestuffs from Central America. For producing the new array of goods demanded by the North Atlantic, Latin America required a transportation infrastructure that could provide an outlet to previously isolated areas with valuable agronomic and mineral endowments for the industrial era.

The railways were an unprecedented promise of material progress. They could cause a massive reduction of transportation costs, both for traditional exports like precious metals and for new exports, including wool, cereals, cattle, and coffee, whose value-to-weight ratio made them prohibitive within the colonial transportation framework. Railways could allow the expansion of the productive frontier by stimulating the production of new tradable goods and thereby integrating vast tracts of previously unworked land into the world economy. William Summerhill computed that, whereas in western Europe the contribution of railways to gross domestic product (GDP) was approximately ten percentage points, in Latin America it approached 25 percent, the largest in the world.[8]

As a preview of the discussion to come, Table 3.1 summarizes initial international conditions, intervening local variables, and final outcomes for the State Formation period.

Political Priorities

Urban Politicians:
Engineering the Export Boom

Given the new international economic context, the priority of urban politicians throughout Latin America in this period was to create a state that could provide an adequate business climate for integration into world capitalism. The leader of the political coalition that could create the conditions for the first sustained boom of commodity exports would generate such a level of material benefits for the economic elites, and produce such an increase in government revenues, that he could legitimately aspire to perpetuation in power. The prize of success at trade-led state formation was political hegemony.

In the mid-nineteenth century, elites throughout Latin America reached a consensus that tighter integration into world markets was the key

Table 3.1. State Formation: International Conditions, Intervening Local Variables, and Outcome

Initial conditions

Geopolitical context	*International economic conditions*	*Priority*	*Resources*	*Strategy*	*Outcome*
Hierarchy	Second Industrial Revolution Boom in demand for primary products + abundant but selective foreign capital	Market-making and coalition-making for virtuous circle of pacification: exports, which lead to foreign investments, which lead to customs revenues, which lead to further pacification	Abundant customs revenues and foreign loans	Incorporation without transformation	Success of trade-led state formation; failure at state building

to material progress in the region. According to the consensus, Latin America should export foodstuffs and raw materials and import manufactured goods and capital. The new consensus had two sources: the new international conditions of prices, technology, and trade policies and the disappointing results of domestic protectionist policies that had been attempted in the 1830s in México City, Lima, Bogotá, and Buenos Aires. By 1850, there was nothing to debate with regard to economic policy. Conflict, as we will see, became purely political.

The economic rewards to free trade were clear, as integration into world capitalism would favor economic elites in the export sector and the vast majority of consumers, who would benefit from better and cheaper manufactured goods. Economic elites and urban consumers would become the social basis of the new ruling coalition. Economic losers would pose a definite political obstacle to free trade. Losers included artisans supplying the cities with simple manufactures based on backward technology and entire indigenous societies holding land in communal property, which were numerous in southern Mexico, Guatemala, and the Andean regions of Peru and Bolivia. The Ricardian division of labor would in principle be implacable with losers in the short run: local artisans would be outcompeted by foreign manufactures, and lands held by communities required the introduction of individual property rights in order to optimize yield.

Dealing with the economic losers of large-scale trade reform is always a delicate *political* task. When modern states have not been established yet, the complications of dealing with economic losers multiply. First, in the 1840s, violence was not monopolized anywhere in Latin America, except for Chile and Paraguay. The option of simply repressing the economic losers of free trade was not available. Second, in contrast to the economic rewards of free trade, which would benefit all members of the economic elites and would be widely distributed among consumers, the political rewards of state formation created conflict among members of the political elite, which, in addition to competing professional politicians in the city-ports, included semiprofessional politicians in the peripheries, supercaudillos, and local warlords. The victory of one political coalition meant defeat of the others. Hence, members of the political elites fearful of being left out of the ruling coalition, although they agreed on the advantages of free trade, had an incentive to boycott the plan for trade-led state formation. Third, borders were ill defined. Entire regions were under the control of rural warlords, who ruled over "subnational jurisdictions" of present-day countries. Urban politicians had to decide whether and how to incorporate regions ruled by rural warlords, who had their own political agenda.

Priorities of Rural Warlords: State-Breaking, State-Making, and State-Taking

Depending on local endowments, size of clientele, and linkages to oligarchies outside their own regions, caudillos can be distinguished into *state-breakers*, *state-makers*, and *state-takers*.[9] They held distinct political priorities. *State-breaking* warlords were the most serious challenge for state formation. If their region had little to offer to world capitalism, state-breaking warlords would specialize in *extortion*, that is, the threat of political upheaval in order to extract a combination of political validation from the center and a share of economic rewards created by the export sector. A good example of state-breaking caudillos are the warlords who ruled the Andean states of the River Plate area from 1830 to 1860, Facundo Quiroga and what one author has called his "children," successor caudillos Chacho Peñaloza and Felipe Varela.[10] If, on the other hand, their regions had valuable resources, including crucially a seaport from which to collect customs duties, state-breaking caudillos would prioritize *secession*, which would make them ultimate rulers within a small territory, isolated from the policies and pressures created by the aspiring capital. A good example of secessionist caudillos are the leaders of the Revolução Farroupilha in the Brazilian province of Rio Grande do Sul, who created the independent Republic of Piratini between 1835 and 1845. This second type of state-breaking caudillo can alternatively be seen as a small-scale *state-making* warlord.

As with state-breaking caudillos, the priorities of *state-taking* caudillos depended on the value of the endowments in their bastions. In contrast to state-breaking caudillos, they had little extortion power, which was a function of a smaller clientele and a more distant location in relation to the export sector or the city-port. The priority of state-taking caudillos was either to become junior *political* partners within the state-making coalition, which occurred when their bastions had little agronomic or mineral value, or to become junior *political and economic* partners if their region could gain from incorporation into world capitalism but needed infrastructural or financial assistance from the capital city in order to ignite local economic activity. Ruling over a poorly endowed region, the Taboada brothers in the North of present-day Argentina are the prototype of state-taking caudillos prioritizing political partnership. In contrast, in Mexico, the Terrazas clan of Chihuahua, a region with high export potential, became the political and economic partners of the so-called Porfiriato (1884–1910). Through the *científicos*, Porfirio Díaz's technocratic advisers, the Terrazas and the Mexican dictator reached a deal by which acceptance of Díaz's hegemony at the national level was rewarded with modernization projects for the province and the informal authorization to convert Chihuahua into a "family undertaking."[11]

Co-optation of caudillos had a price. To generate revenues, statemakers needed to modernize the economy.

Resources: Foreign Loans and Customs Tariffs

Railways, the technological key to unlock development in mid-nineteenth-century Latin America, were enormous investments. In a Catch-22 situation, Latin America could generate the domestic savings required to finance railway construction only if it were able to boost exports to the level that only a full modernization of the transportation system via steam locomotion would make possible.

Fortunately for Latin America, international savings became abundant again in the late 1840s, and foreign capitalists regained the appetite for risky investments. In a classic work, James Rippy notes that "the trickle of British investments of the 1830s and 1840s became a fairly large stream during the next three decades, branching out into at least seventeen countries."[12] After the defaults of the mid-1820s, British investors gradually learned to examine the business climate of Latin America. The loans of the 1820s had been spent on wars against Spain. They could not produce any economic returns. The loans of the 1850s and 1860s largely financed railway construction, which would expand economic activity and thereby improve the creditworthiness of the emerging countries.

At the onset of the period, almost all governments in Latin America were bankrupt. Customs receipts had consistently covered between a half and two-thirds of total government revenues since independence. In the Failure period, foreign trade had stagnated, and so had government revenues.

Given the new international economic context, state-making elites in Latin America made a strong bet that the expansion of international commerce starting in the mid-1840s would allow them to finance large-scale political projects. If they were able to fully integrate their economies into world capitalism, government revenues would grow in both absolute and relative terms. Brazil faced an additional opportunity to increase revenues, for the agreement with the United Kingdom placing a ceiling of 15 percent for duties on British imports was set to expire in 1844. An increase in government revenues derived from a higher level of imports required inflows of hard currency that only sustained export booms could provide. Since export booms in turn required the modernization of the transportation infrastructure, the growth of government revenues indirectly depended on attracting foreign investments. Foreign investors would be attracted by the prospects of expanding economies and increasingly solvent governments, but they demanded a substantial reduction of political risk, that is, a reasonably definitive closure to the period of Failure.

In 1861, Bartolomé Mitre, the leader of the coalition that formed the Argentine state in the 1860s, inaugurated the construction of the Southern Railway, a line connecting the city-port of Buenos Aires with the southern frontier of the hyperfertile lands of the Pampas. In a public speech, he rhetorically asked, "What is the force behind this progress?" to which he replied, "Gentlemen, it is English capital. . . . It is the great anonymous hero of world prosperity." The advantages of a backward economy catching up with the advanced ones and the opportunity to "telescope" developmental time were transparent to Mitre: "England in 1685 was poorer than Buenos Aires today, so my fellow citizens should know that in 185 years they will be more prosperous than the English people are these days, because now we have at our disposal instruments of progress that England did not possess for its own expansion."[13]

Optimism about technological progress and foreign investments did not blind Mitre's political vision. Like several other would-be state-makers in Latin America, Mitre knew that for English capital to be interested in emerging economies, substantial political work had to be completed beforehand. In the mid-1840s, the world made available for Latin America the economic and technological assets required for successful state formation. State-making elites in Latin America needed to produce an adequate *political* response.

Strategies of Periphery Incorporation in Latin America
Co-opting Patrimonial Rulers
through Foreign Trade

State formation was the survival strategy of professional politicians and su-percaudillos in mid-nineteenth-century Latin America. State formation re-quired putting together coalitions that could provide one key public good and one key class good. First, it had to produce pacification, which required turning state-breaking caudillos into state-taking junior partners, forging a power-sharing agreement with competing political elites, and neutralizing economic losers of free trade. Second, it had to provide the class good of a proper physical and financial infrastructure for the expansion of the export sector. Success at providing the public good of pacification enhanced the prospects of success at providing the class good of export infrastructure, and vice versa. Pacification and the expansion of the export sector formed a vir-tuous circle. Pacification was necessary for fresh investments, which would create export infrastructure; in turn, new levels of exports would supply for-eign exchange to increase the level of imports; finally, imports, through cus-toms duties, would create the revenues to deepen pacification and export expansion.

Providing export infrastructure included various engineering, fiscal, and economic measures that by 1850 were no secret to aspiring state-making rulers. Yet achieving a modicum of pacification almost always required ma-jor *political* efforts, and it was largely incompatible with military action. One thing was to keep the virtuous circle of export expansion and pacification functioning; a completely different one was to *launch* it. The former was the work of technocrats. The latter involved the art of politics.

Commodity Lottery, "Political Luck,"
and Political Work

Building on the work of Carlos Díaz Alejandro, the economic historian Vic-tor Bulmer-Thomas has advanced an explanation of variations in economic performance across Latin American countries on the basis of their "luck" at the "commodity lottery" of the mid-nineteenth century.[14] Economically, good luck at the lottery is an exogenous shock given by a substantial growth in the demand for a commodity that an emerging country is well endowed to supply. The notion of a commodity lottery is crucial to provide an exogenous source of variation in the process of state formation in Latin America.

For the analysis of state formation, the commodity lottery requires a political interpretation rather than a purely economic one. State-making elites were *politically* lucky at the commodity lottery if activating the economic sector with boom potential required minimal efforts at producing export infrastructure. Luck would launch the virtuous circle between export expansion and pacification by simply kick-starting exports. Pacification would then follow, unless big political mistakes were made.

Peru is the best example of good *political* luck at the commodity lottery in the State Formation period. Bolivia is the best example of bad luck. Argentina and Brazil are intermediate cases that illustrate the modal pattern.

The political economy of the class good was obvious to all rulers in nineteenth-century Latin America. They knew that the most immediate requisite of a successful state was stable revenues. In turn, the only reliable source of revenue that could be opened within their professional lifetime was import tariffs. Import tariffs would be paid by the general public. Politically disorganized, the general public found it more difficult to mobilize for collective protest than to pay a small increment in the final price tag of the imported good. By contrast, taxes on property or exports would concentrate the cost of government on the economic elites, who had real veto power and could derail the state-formation process in its early stages. To maximize revenues, import tariffs had to be calibrated carefully. They needed to be low enough to allow for large volumes of imports and high enough to cover the bulk of the government's expenditures. Sustained levels of imports in turn required hard currency, which could only be obtained through large volumes of exports. A fully dynamic export sector in turn required foreign investments, in banking institutions, in harbor facilities, in distribution networks, and in railways. The public good of pacification was then the key to unlock the process of state formation.

The political economy of pacification was the true challenge. In contrast to pacification in the pioneer cases of western Europe, which was fundamentally a military process, pacification in the latecomer cases of Latin America had to be an eminently political process. Warlord demobilization required co-optation rather than repression. Repression, or pacification *manu militari*, would create spirals of war, the intensity and duration of which were unpredictable enough to deter foreign investment. Political pacification through co-optation, by contrast, could generate enough revenue to make warlords have direct stakes in state formation. State-making elites had to simultaneously obtain a modicum of pacification to gain the confidence of foreign investors and persuade warlords that a modicum of foreign investments would make military demobilization a good political and private deal.

Argentina and Brazil:
Political and Technical Requirements

Argentina and Brazil are the modal cases of trade-led state formation. Steady export sales required higher levels of technocratic engineering than the guano boom in Peru but were less demanding than the refitting of the mining sector in Mexico. In both cases, export performance and co-optation of local notables marched in lockstep. A modicum of safety in a region with valuable endowments, even if temporary, allowed for a modest surge in exports, which in turn translated into government revenues that could be applied to obtaining the right mix of warlord demobilization and infrastructure construction for a new round of export-led expansion.

Wool and coffee were the commodities that provided state-making elites with the necessary revenues in Argentina and Brazil. Yet, for exports to produce the wherewithal of state formation and economic modernization, elites in Buenos Aires and Rio de Janeiro had to make big political efforts.

The main challenge for wool production in Buenos Aires was pacification, which was constantly threatened by invasions from nomadic aboriginal tribes in the South, state-breaking caudillos in the Andean ministates, and geopolitical pressures from the supercaudillo Justo J. Urquiza in the Upper Littoral of the River Plate (see Map 5.1). In Buenos Aires, members of the economic elites and an important number of political leaders opposed the formation of Argentina. Uniting Buenos Aires with ministates from the Andean region and the Upper Littoral of the River Plate meant becoming a permanent minority in relation to a dozen poorer provinces that expected to obtain a share of Buenos Aires's wealth. In the early 1860s, Mitre was the governor of Buenos Aires, and a ban on reelection meant that his days in power were numbered. He had an incentive to create a larger political arena than Buenos Aires and extend his political life by becoming president of the union. Mitre brokered a deal through which Buenos Aires's economic elites gained pacification in exchange for a federal union, which translated into modernization projects for the Upper Littoral ministates and subsidies for the Andean ministates. With the wool boom, Buenos Aires had reached a level of development such that a modicum of revenue sharing, which was a lifesaver for many peripheral patrimonial rulers, was a small price to pay for permanent peace.

Coffee was the most demanding commodity with regard to infrastructural prerequisites. It had been introduced in Rio de Janeiro only in the late 1800s, it required large initial investments, and it took two decades, from 1810 to 1830, for the bush to spread through the fertile Paraíba Valley.

Coffee growing in Rio de Janeiro faced no geopolitical threats. Local notables in the North and the South of the Brazilian Empire wanted secession, not extortion. Besides, the imperial army was stationed in Rio de Janeiro, which made the Paraíba Valley the safest economic region in Latin America. The security of Rio de Janeiro and the volume of coffee exports prompted the most ambitious project of state formation in Latin America. Secessionist movements from regions that could have formed viable independent countries were defeated through a mix of repression and co-optation. In the North, co-optation was achieved through patronage, nobility titles (a uniquely Brazilian tool), and central help in preventing slave rebellion. In the South, in addition to patronage, local notables received commercial preferences over the imports of salted beef from Buenos Aires and Uruguay and financial backup for infrastructure projects. State-making elites in Rio de Janeiro did not tax property of peripheral oligarchies. They did not interfere with local patron-client networks or master-slave relations.

Peru:
Commodity Exports with No Political Requirements

Independent Peru before 1840 has been repeatedly described as an ungovernable country. It would be more precise to claim that the country did not exist as a political entity, for violence in the "Peruvian" territory was cartelized among rival caudillos. Starting in the mid-1840s, Peru's guano boom

worked like an instant winning lottery ticket for Castilla, the supercaudillo
who happened to be in power at the time. In contrast to Argentina and Brazil,
where export sales required substantial preparatory work, the financial and
infrastructural prerequisites of guano exploitation in Peru were virtually
none. Thanks to the guano boom, the sudden availability of large amounts
of cash in Peru was able to demobilize state-breaking warlords, pacify the territory, and form a state.

Guano exports allowed for a unique fiscal strategy, which nevertheless fell squarely within the general pattern of avoiding efforts at extracting
resources from wealthy urban oligarchies or peripheral patrimonial rulers.
Guano is a potent natural fertilizer formed by bird droppings, which was
found in abundance on a handful of islands off the Peruvian coast.[15] Western European voracious demand and Peru's monopolistic position in world
markets made guano prices skyrocket in the mid-1840s. Extraordinary in
magnitude, the guano boom was unique not only for its extremely low requirements of economic modernization—strong arms and shovels were all
the collection of guano demanded—but also for its "rentier effects" on the
emerging Peruvian state. The Peruvian state was the sole owner of the fields
with guano deposits and obtained torrential flows of revenue by leasing out
their exploitation to private companies. Thanks to the new source of revenue, Peru effectively abolished the Contribución Indígena and reduced import taxes to 20 percent, the lowest in the region.

The modal cases of the State Formation period, Argentina and Brazil, as
well as the extreme case of Peru, are all perfect examples of the trade-led
strategy. The political economy core of the strategy is reliance on import
tariffs, as opposed to taxing the property or income of the urban oligarchies
and rural notables.

Reliance on import tariffs is the common denominator of all successful cases of state formation in this period. It differentiates the modal pattern
of state formation in Latin America from the pioneer cases in western Europe. It reveals the strategy of state-making leaders of forging a tight alliance
with the economic elites in the export sector. Crucially, it also reveals the
reluctance to deploy state capacity in the peripheral bastions of local notables, mostly dominated by warlords, vestigial colonial oligarchies, or a
combination of them. In Brazil, customs duties as a proportion of total revenues grew from 50 percent to 80 percent in the key period of 1835–50,

when the wave of secessionist attempts occurred and the agreement with Great Britain to keep import taxes below 15 percent expired.[16] In Buenos Aires, customs duties represented 90 percent of the ministate's revenues from 1845 to 1861, and when Argentina was formed in 1862, after Buenos Aires united with the other thirteen ministates, customs duties averaged 92 percent of revenues until 1873.

In sharp contrast with the western European experience of war-led state formation, penetration of bastions of local notables in Latin America made neither political nor economic sense. A central state intrudes into patrimonial bastions to recruit manpower for war and to collect money when less contentious sources are not available. Wars in early modern Europe were frequent, and alternative sources of money were virtually nonexistent. In mid-nineteenth-century Latin America, the opportunity costs of penetrating patrimonial bastions became enormous. The emerging center of the state did not need new soldiers. And the little money it could extract from patrimonial bastions would create enough disruption to torpedo the plan to attract foreign investments, expand the export base, and collect revenues at the customhouse. The potential flow of money from incorporation into world capitalism was orders of magnitude larger than any potential surplus produced in patrimonial bastions.

Mexico: The Acid Test

Mexico is the least likely case of trade-led state formation in Latin America. A big geopolitical phenomenon separated Mexico from South America. Mexico suffered the expansionism of the United States, which peaked under the presidency of James K. Polk (1845-49). The United States' pressure eventually led to the annexation of about half the territory of postindependence Mexico. Mexico is the only case for which an international geopolitical hierarchy might have created incentives for war-led state formation. Whereas the *Pax Britannica* was a benevolent force in South America, proximity to the United States was in principle a negative influence on Mexico's state formation.

Paradoxically, proximity to the United States, which directly caused major territorial losses, indirectly favored state formation in Mexico. The large portion of land sold under military threat to the United States gave Mexico the financial resources to retain some of its present-day peripheries.

It is well known how and why Mexico lost territory to the United States. However, it is an enigma why and how Mexico did not fragment further, as did Central America, a much smaller independent state that nevertheless divided into five minirepublics.

Secessionism was a permanent threat for Mexico since independence. In the 1830s, Mexico teetered on the brink of disappearance. Around 1835, secessionism was most determined in two border areas, Texas (then part of the state of Coahuila) and Yucatán, and in one interior state, Zacatecas, which expected to be joined by Jalisco and thereby obtain a Pacific port (see Map 8.2). In Texas, the secessionist movement had been growing for years, resulting from a combination of aggressive U.S. migration and the opposition to antislavery laws passed by the Mexican congress, which directly hurt the interests of the U.S. settlers, largely white slavocrats from Louisiana.

The military response by the Mexican government can be described, at the risk of numerical overprecision, as only 33 percent successful. It crushed the rebellion in Zacatecas before secessionism was able to spread to neighboring states. Yet Yucatán was considered lost because of lack of fiscal resources. Finally, the actions against Texas, led by General Antonio López de Santa Anna, were a boomerang. Santa Anna was captured by Texan soldiers, sent to Washington, and in the process made the expansionist ambitions of the United States substantially larger. United States finally annexed Texas, Arizona, New Mexico, and California.

The reannexation of Zacatecas was the only successful action of "military incorporation" ever taken by Mexico. Zacatecas was worth it. It was the only region in which new investments in the mining sector produced tangible results before the mid-nineteenth century. Zacatecas provided hard currency to finance imports, the fiscal basis of trade-led state formation. Crucially, if Zacatecas had managed to become an independent country, Mexico's fragmentation would have been unstoppable. Permanent secession of Zacatecas would have erected a territorial cordon separating Mexico's heartland from the states in the North—present-day Durango, Sinaloa, Sonora, and Baja California.

Yucatán became a separate republic in 1835, the same year of Texas's secession. Yucatán was a prosperous but highly unequal society. In the early 1830s, Yucatán experienced a boom in the production of henequen, the agave cactus that is the source of sisal fiber. A few years later, Yucatecan sugar experienced another boom. Trade relations of Yucatán were substantially closer with New Orleans than with Veracruz, Mexico's main port. For Yucatán, Mexico was a perfectly dispensable entity. The Yucatán government ran a small fiscal surplus based on revenues from international trade and taxes on the Mayan communities, which made up three-quarters of the peninsula's population. Union with Mexico would have made Yucatán a fiscal loser. Yucatán defended its independence by force. In 1843, the Yucatecan elite recruited and armed eleven thousand Mayan soldiers to reject an invasion from Mexico. Invaders were forced to surrender and withdraw.

Yet mobilization of the lower classes for independence got out of control for the leaders of the secession. The white elites had expanded their plantations by encroaching on Mayan communal lands and secured Mayan labor through debt peonage and strict vagrancy laws. When the Mayan communities that had been mobilized for secession from Mexico decided to also attack exploitation, the local elite panicked.

In 1846, Yucatán's president requested military help from the governor of Cuba, the admiral of Jamaica, and the ambassador of the United Kingdom. He offered Yucatán's sovereignty in exchange. None of them found the offer appealing enough. In desperation, a Yucatecan delegation was sent to Washington to make a formal offer of annexation to the United States. Polk welcomed the offer, but the "Yucatán Bill" was rejected by the Senate, whose members did not want to risk prior annexations of Mexican territory in a second war.

In 1847, at the same time that Mexico received cash compensation for the loss of the Far North to the United States, the white elite in Yucatán reversed more than a decade of separatism and created a demand for incorporation into Mexico. In 1848, it formally requested federal help with the "Caste War." Given Yucatán's relative prosperity, Mexico was more than willing to supply it. A gift of 150,000 pesos, a small fraction of the U.S. compensation, and some ammunition sufficed to put down the Mayan rebellion. To recover local social control, the chief priority of the elite in the peninsula, Yucatán became Mexican again.

Income from land sales was a uniquely Mexican ingredient within a general strategy of revenue collection that emphatically avoided the politically contentious method of taxing the property or income of the upper class. Taxation of the upper class would have provided the rudiments of state building, the path not taken in Mexico and in any other Latin American case. As in the rest of the Latin American countries, except for Chile and Paraguay, the trade-led process finally prevailed in Mexico in the mid-nineteenth century. The only difference is that mid-nineteenth-century Mexico did not sell *flows* of primary products as much as it sold *stocks* of assets (land).

Mexico's adoption of the trade-led path of state formation despite being the most vulnerable country to geopolitical threats provides the acid test proving the weakness throughout Latin America of the incentives for war-led state formation relative to those of trade-led state formation. If Mexico discarded the war-led path of state formation, then for the much less exposed emerging states of South America, the opportunity costs of war-led state formation were much higher. If Mexico did not build a Westphalian state, no other Latin America country could possibly have a reason to do so.

Outcomes: State Formation without State Building

Economic booms fueled by exports of agricultural commodities are the most glittering outcome of the 1845–75 period. They occupy a prominent place in all history books, which repeatedly portray the export booms as some kind of inflection point. Yet the booms were only *symptoms* of a less glittering but more fundamental outcome: the formation of states.[17] States were not automatic products of the independence process, as most national histories have assumed. Most countries in Latin America stabilized the borders of their territories (a process that involved the key political decision of which regions to include and which ones to exclude) and monopolized violence (or, short of monopolization, achieved pacification) only in the period of 1845–75, on average three decades after independence. Brazil has been repeatedly differentiated from Spanish America for its political stability in the nineteenth century. Yet Brazilian political stability is only a superficial impression given by continuity at the level of *government*—members of the Braganza House making decisions from Rio de Janeiro. At the level of the *state*, which involves deeper issues of violence monopolization, periphery incorporation, and territory consolidation, Brazil faced challenges at least as serious as in the most turbulent Spanish American cases. Brazilian state-making elites found a solution to the challenges only in the period 1845–75, through a trade-led strategy.

State formation was a precondition of economic growth. Except for Peru, a case in which state formation clearly followed an unexpected export boom, all emerging countries in Latin America required a modicum of stateness before they could produce economic expansion. The key task to produce an export boom was to reverse the political legacy of the Failure period (1825–45), that is, to put an end to warlordism and fragmented sovereignty in Spanish America and to secessionism in Brazil. When world capitalism created unprecedented commercial opportunities for exporters of primary commodities in the mid-1840s, Latin America, far from being a tabula rasa, was plagued with political obstacles to economic activity. State formation in Latin America was fundamentally about removing obstacles to growth.

Before 1873, Mexico traded a portion of its territory to be able to keep the rest of it. It achieved territory consolidation. It was a special adaptation of the trade-led strategy, in which the trade of a stock gained precedence over the trade of flows of exports.

Export booms caused state formation only in the sense that the international economy presented state-making elites with a distinct set of incentives and potential resources. A yet to be achieved economic bonanza became a priority motivating state-making elites, but their ultimate goal was political survival rather than economic prosperity. They delivered economic prosperity to a social class that had veto power over their professional careers in the specific context of mid-nineteenth-century Latin America. They also benefited from the fiscal resources created by prosperity. But prosperity could not be obtained by decree. It demanded the completion of sustained efforts at state formation, including mainly pacification within a territory large enough and for a period long enough to encourage foreign investment. The international economy pushed political elites to embrace a strategy of trade-led state formation as their best chance at professional survival.

If the formation of states was the less glittering side of the export boom, the absence of state building was the decidedly dark side of trade-led state formation. The modal cases in Latin America avoided state building in order to achieve state formation within the window of opportunity opened by world capitalism in the mid-nineteenth century. Peripheries were incorporated but not transformed. They were a target of appeasement and concessions rather than of extraction and transformation. In early modern Europe, peripheries had been mobilized for war. In mid-nineteenth-century Latin

America, they were *de*mobilized to attract trade and capital. Political leaders pursuing trade-led state formation did not have the time or the incentives even to initiate state building. Instead of eradicating patrimonialism in the peripheries, state-making elites in Latin America deepened it by distributing patronage among peripheral rulers who were thus able to perpetuate their political power. Peripheral patrimonialism was instrumental to state-making elites. Co-optation was a mutually beneficial deal for political elites at the center and patrimonial rulers in the periphery.

If Chile, Uruguay, and Costa Rica are exceptions to state weakness, it is precisely because they incorporated no patrimonial peripheries. Chile and especially Uruguay provide a mirror image of what Buenos Aires could have been if it had remained a separate country. But Buenos Aires became Argentina by incorporating multiple patrimonial peripheries and thereby placed a durable ceiling on how much state building could be achieved after territory consolidation. In Latin America, small, relatively prosperous countries rapidly created a two-party system. In the absence of patrimonial peripheries, electoral competition escaped the temptation of forming large-scale patronage coalitions and instead fostered state building. Three enclaves of state strength do not alter continent-wide state weakness.

Conclusions

In Tolstoy's short tale "How Much Land Does a Man Need?," Pakhom, the protagonist, claims, "If I had plenty of land, I'd fear no one—not even the Devil himself!" Pakhom's claim is meant to reflect a special sense of protection derived from land acquisition. The motivation of Tolstoy's fictional character is identical to the motivation of the very real protagonists of the state-formation process in early modern western Europe. In the pioneer cases of state formation, for good geopolitical reasons, both the winner (the center) and the losers (the incorporated peripheries) made territorial expansion and border defense a top political priority. The western European experience has been so influential in our understanding of state formation that territorial maximization seems to be inscribed in the DNA of every modern state.

In sharp contrast to Pakhom and the western European pioneers, state-making elites in Latin America were not obsessed with land and were not engaged in territorial maximization. In 1909, Roque Sáenz Peña, a notable Argentine statesman who became an expert in international relations, gave a speech on the constant features of Argentina's foreign policy: "War caused by Argentina: Against whom? For what purpose? Commercial supremacy? Nothing would be more incompatible with the fruits of economic endeavor, which demands peace, not war!" Like many other Latin American leaders, Sáenz Peña was the anti-Pakhom: "War for territorial expansion perhaps? We do not need it. We have land to spare, we are surrounded by unexploited natural assets, and we suffer from a scarcity of men to work on them. The Argentine instinct is a permanent lack of interest in expanding its territory. . . . That is our legacy and our tradition."[18]

In the mid-nineteenth century, state-making elites in Buenos Aires, Rio de Janeiro, Lima, Bogotá, and México City had much more important challenges than territorial expansion. Territorial expansion required war. Economic development, a much more profitable political project, required peace. Trade-led state formation prevailed over war-led state formation in Latin America.

Quite paradoxically, pursuing trade-led state formation, Brazil state-making elites created a territory that is twice as large as all western European countries combined. Argentina, the outcome of the same state-formation strategy, can accommodate five Frances, the largest country in western Europe. Neither the state-making elites of Rio de Janeiro nor those of Buenos Aires ever displayed anything remotely resembling the ambition for territorial expansion of the French kings or Napoleon.

The trade-led path followed by Argentina, Brazil, and Mexico explains what, by Pakhomian/Napoleonic standards, is an incredible success at state formation. It also explains the durable failure at state building.

PART TWO

Ports, Parties, and Lords

Pathways to the Political Geography of Latin America

Just before the Commercial Revolution of the mid-nineteenth century, a multitude of Latin American regions claimed sovereignty. The size of a city or a rural village and its immediate hinterland, regions had distinct economic endowments and political institutions. Combining regions, pacifying them, and concentrating the means of violence within the joint territory required Herculean efforts. What types of agent rose to the challenge? What were the incentives? The state-formation agent in Latin America was a *politician*. It was not a professional *army*, it was not a *nation*, and it was not a dominant *economic class*. The politician is the key piece to complete the theory of trade-led formation presented in Part 1. Striving to find the combination of regions that best suited his professional ambitions, the politician produced the *political geography* of modern Latin America, by far the most durable legacy from the nineteenth century.

Part 2 advances a "politician-centered approach" to state formation. It focuses on the political mechanisms in the process of territory consolidation, which explain why each country in Latin America stabilized into a distinct combination of regions from a spectrum of possible alternatives. In Part 1, the Latin American political elites who succeeded at state formation were presented as *market-makers*. The characterization highlighted the contrast with the *war-makers* of the pioneer cases in early modern western Europe. Latin American rulers had the choice of prioritizing international trade or geopolitical competition. Given global conditions, they chose international trade. As market-makers, they formed a tight alliance with economic elites of a booming export sector and co-opted patrimonial potentates in the peripheries. Co-optation of patrimonial potentates was the key to the creation of the class goods—property rights and transportation infrastructure—required for export-led growth.

In Part 2, Latin American state-makers will be analyzed from a complementary perspective, as *polity-makers* in addition to market-makers. As market-makers, political elites can ignite export-led economic growth through *multiple combinations* of economic and political regions. However, as polity-makers, only *a specific combination* of regions creates the political arena in which they can achieve their ultimate goal, that is, *political supremacy* vis-à-vis competing political elites. Once the short-run vitality of the export sector is secured, polity-makers have a substantial level of latitude in decisions that are instrumental to pursue their own political agenda, including which peripheries to include in the emerging state and which ones to exclude. Coalitional motivations drive decisions of inclusion and exclusion. Polity-makers pursue the combination of regions that maximizes their power. They unite the center with the selection of peripheries that provides the greatest chances to move up in the hierarchy of power or to prolong their political career for as long as possible. As market-makers, political elites in Latin America *initiated* trade-led state formation. As polity-makers, they *closed* the state-formation process by structuring the final composition of the new political arena.

The process of state formation in Latin America was led by three kinds of polity-makers: an urban political entrepreneur based in a major city-port; rival oligarchic parties linking together an aspiring capital and a number of secondary cities and rural villages; or a rural lord in command of a large contingent of clients. Each type created a distinct variant of trade-led state formation: *port-driven, party-driven,* or *lord-driven.*

State-formation outcomes in Latin America show unprecedented variation along two key dimensions: (a) the number and diversity of regions included in each state (which are highly correlated with country size) and (b) the timing of violence monopolization relative to territory consolidation. The three pathways explain these variations. The port-driven pathway produces *large* countries, including colossuses combining city-ports, several regions endowed with fertile land or mineral deposits, and a vast number of backward peripheries. In the port-driven pathway, territory consolidation and violence monopolization occur simultaneously. The party-driven pathway also creates large, multiregion countries, but it invariably generates a substantial temporal gap between territory consolidation and violence monopolization. The gap is the source of protracted civil wars. Finally, the lord-driven pathway differs from the other two in that it is inimical to the creation of multiregion countries. The lord prefers to consolidate a small country demarcated by the borders of his clientelistic network, which he protects either by seceding from a larger state or by resisting merger with neighboring regions. Like the port-driven pathway, the lord-driven pathway achieves territory consolidation and violence monopolization at the same time.

A Politician-Centered Approach to State Formation

STATE-FORMATION ACTIVITY IN LATIN AMERICA reached its zenith in the mid-nineteenth century. It produced two contrasting outcomes of territorial aggregation and territorial fragmentation, which gave the region its definitive political geography. On the one hand, three of the largest countries in the world, Brazil (fifth), Argentina (eighth), and Mexico (thirteenth), consolidated their territories. The three colossuses combined multiple regions, some of which had struggled for decades to become sovereign units. A political settlement prevented the secession of major portions of their current territories. The areas that had sought secession were well-defined economic regions endowed with the fiscal rudiments to become viable independent countries. In fact, for substantial periods, they had been separate states. The three longest living independent states that were later absorbed into Argentina, Brazil, and Mexico were Buenos Aires (1830–62); Rio Grande do Sul, known as República de Piratini (1835–45); and the Yucatán Peninsula, or República de Yucatán (1841–48).

On the other hand, three other large states suffered irreversible collapse because they failed to stop secessions: Gran Colombia (present-day Colombia, Panama, Venezuela, and Ecuador), the Peru-Bolivian Confederation, and the United Provinces of Central America (the small states in the isthmus minus Panama, which then belonged to Colombia).[1] Gran Colombia and the Peru-Bolivian Confederation would have been territorial colossuses similar in size to Argentina, and the United Provinces of Central America would have been 20 percent larger than Paraguay. The extinction of the three states resulted in the emergence of ten small to medium-sized countries. The territorial consolidation of three colossuses and the simultaneous collapse of three large states account for the creation of thirteen countries in Latin America—out of a total of twenty.[2]

It is a true enigma why Brazil, Argentina, and Mexico succeeded at territory consolidation while Gran Colombia, the Peru-Bolivian Confederation, and the United Provinces of Central America failed. To add to the puzzle, some of the regions incorporated within Argentina, Brazil, and Mexico were more viable countries than were the breakaway states that resulted from the disintegration of the three failed states. For instance, Buenos Aires did not secede from Argentina, but it would have had a stronger government and a stronger economy than any of the ten splinters that replaced the three failed countries.

Wealthy regions within present-day Argentina, Brazil, and Mexico agreed to be part of a union that offered no direct economic benefit. At the same time, poorer economic regions of United Central America, Gran Colombia, and Peru-Bolivia broke apart despite the economic benefits that union could have produced with regard to commercial complementarities and material savings in the provision of public goods.

We lack a theory of why some sets of regions merge into a single country while others form separate countries. The theoretical void is a serious deficit in the social sciences because territory consolidation, understood as the sovereign combination or separation of regions, is largely equivalent to "country creation." Since countries are the most common unit of analysis, the theoretical void forces scientists to deal with objects whose origins remain obscure but have decisive repercussions on the processes taking place within them.

In general, the decision of a region to merge with another region or form a separate country depends on both the region's structural wherewithal for state formation and the type of political leadership. Independence requires a regular flow of revenues and the ability to prevent disruptions to such flow. In the context of mid-nineteenth-century Latin America, disruptions included labor unrest (slave or peasant rebellion) and looting raids by neighboring regions. A region with sustained fiscal capacity is the precursor of a state. Regions that lack the fiscal capacity or are threatened by disruptive attacks will seek merger with other regions in order to pool resources to face economic, social, and military challenges.

Who provides political leadership in the region is critically important for its state-formation propensities. Three agents of state formation can be distinguished: a political entrepreneur, competing oligarchic parties, or a rural lord. All three agent types can emerge in any region. In a region with the potential to make or break a state, the key issue is who is in control at the onset of the Commercial Revolution. The types of state-formation agent differ from one another in their constituencies, which in turn shape their territorial ambitions. Different surrounding regions generate distinct sets of opportunities and constraints, and each type of agent designs its political plan accordingly.

To preview the impact of agency, it is useful to contrast the plan of action of a rural lord and an urban political entrepreneur—who offer opposite kinds of leadership on several dimensions—within the same type of economic region. If a highly productive area endowed with its own seaport is ruled by a rural lord, it will make a systematic effort, generally successful, to become an independent country. Within the region, the rural lord has hegemonic power based on the clientelistic control of a large contingent of workers. The port provides the necessary revenues. An expanded political arena stretching beyond the lord's clientelistic network will definitely generate political contenders. Contenders will not only create a larger structure of power, in which the lord occupies a secondary position, but also may challenge the hegemony of the lord in his own political fiefdom. To preserve hegemonic rule within his fiefdom, the rural lord pursues secession and opposes expansion. By contrast, if an urban political entrepreneur dominates the same region, then it will become a center of territorial aggregation. The leadership of the entrepreneur within his regional basis is much less secure than that of the lord. He cannot count on the permanent loyalty of rural clients, and his career depends on mobilizing public opinion, which is inherently volatile. The entrepreneur then wants to subsume his region within a selection of regions that maximizes his chances at political survival. The political entrepreneur makes deals with leaders from other regions in order to hedge against the political risks of his own region.

Roadmap

This chapter presents a theory of varieties of territory consolidation. The most important dimensions of variation in territory consolidation are two:

1. The number and diversity of regions combined within a state,
   which is strongly correlated with country size. Outcomes
   in Latin America range from small, highly homogeneous

countries based on a single agronomic region to gigantic, radically heterogeneous countries that include active city-ports dominated by an urban oligarchy, a handful of areas with abundant fertile land or valuable minerals, and a number of backward peripheries ruled by rural lords.

2. The timing of violence monopolization. Outcomes range from simultaneity of territory consolidation and violence monopolization to a decades-long gap between the two fundamental components of state formation.

The theory presented in this chapter combines domestic structural antecedent conditions and political agency into an explanation based on three distinct pathways of trade-led state formation: *port-driven*, *party-driven*, and *lord-driven*. The correlation between pathways and outcomes is straightforward. Pathways are marked by either an "expansionary" or a "separatist" drive toward territory consolidation, and they account for whether violence monopolization is simultaneous with territory consolidation.

The port-driven pathway, illustrated by Argentina and Brazil, is marked by an expansionary drive provided by a central port willing and able to incorporate a vast array of peripheries. The pathway leads to simultaneity in territory consolidation and violence monopolization. The party-driven pathway shares the expansionary drive, as reflected in the political networks built from the capitals of Mexico and Colombia, but it fails to achieve simultaneity of territory consolidation and violence monopolization. The gap accounts for decades of civil war (and lost economic opportunities) after the nominal jurisdiction of the state was settled. Finally, in contrast to the other two pathways, the lord-driven pathway is based on a patrimonial ruler's decision to separate his fiefdom from a larger political unit. The separatist drive explains the collapse of three large-scale projects of state formation: the United Provinces of Central America, Gran Colombia, and the Peru-Bolivian Confederation. A dominant lord in Guatemala, Venezuela, and Peru opted for secession. Like the port-driven pathway but in contrast to the party-driven one, the lord-driven pathway achieves territory consolidation and violence monopolization at roughly the same time. Table 4.1 presents the three pathways, their territorial propensities, and their outcomes with regard to violence monopolization. The microfoundations of each pathway are the subject of this chapter.

Table 4.1. Pathways, Propensities, and Outcomes of State Formation

	Expansionary drive	Simultaneity of territory consolidation and violence monopolization
Port-driven	Yes	Yes
Party-driven	Yes	No
Lord-driven	No	Yes

This chapter is organized into three sections. The first section is based on structures, or fundamental causes; the second section is based on political agency, or proximate causes; the third section focuses on the combinations of structures and agents.

Three Structural Accounts of Territory Consolidation

The analysis of economic, social, and military structures allows crafting three distinct but complementary accounts of state formation qua territorial combination. The theories focus on a key set of region-level attributes that generate mechanisms of state formation. According to the first account, the decision of two regions to merge or remain separate entities depends on their factor endowment, in particular, the existence of commercial complementarities or economies of scale.[3] The second account centers on a Marxist type of incentive: the reason for state formation is the creation of repressive capabilities to secure labor exploitation by owners of the means of production.[4] The third account centers on a Weberian motivation, which views state formation as the creation of a large-scale extortion venture: those who have achieved an overriding control of the means of violence force a territorially circumscribed population to buy their protection (including protection from damage caused by the sellers themselves, as Tilly claimed).[5] All three explanations are structural and materialist in that they are rooted in the overall distribution of tangible assets—factor endowments, means of production, and means of destruction. Each of them is associated with a distinct set of mechanisms.

Table 4.2. Structural Accounts of Territorial Combinations

	Source of differentiation	*Types of region*	*Mechanisms*
Economic structure	Factor endowments	Backward interiors; entrepôts; dynamic interiors; rudimentary port states	Mergers (or secessions) occur when economies of scale and commercial complementarities are present (or absent)
Social structure	Dependence on slave labor or the privatization of communal land	Threatened by slave or peasant rebellion vs. appeased by social hegemony	Peripheries demand incorporation into a larger political unit to borrow additional repressive capacity from the center
Military structure	Warlords' relative capacity	State-takers vs. state-breakers vs. state-makers	A caudillo ruling a rudimentary port state has the full set of incentives and capabilities to form a separate state; capitals of territorial colossuses incorporate poorer peripheries to prevent looting raids

If "pure politics" is seen as the actions that seek to reach, and keep, the top positions in government—primarily coalitional operations—then it is useful to regard the three structural explanations as providing "prepolitical" incentives for state formation. They all generate valuable insights to further develop the theory of trade-led state formation presented in Part 1, but they are all incomplete. They share a theoretical blind spot, which has important empirical repercussions. They all miss the purely political motivation of achieving coalitional supremacy.

As a preview of the discussion to follow, Table 4.2 presents the key elements of each structural account, the associated types of region derived from the structural dimensions, and the key set of mechanisms driving merger or separation between regions.

The Economic Account:
Factor Endowments, Complementarities, and Savings

A useful typology of economic regions in nineteenth-century Latin America is based on two criteria: whether the region possessed a high-traffic seaport and whether it could profitably produce commodities for the international market. Table 4.3 presents a four-category typology of economic regions.

A characterization of regions based on factor endowments supports three key claims:

1. A *Rudimentary Port State*—a region that has both an important port and substantial agronomic value—pushes to become an independent minicountry. It rejects union with backward interiors out of fear that merger will raise taxes to subsidize poorer areas. For the same reason, unless economies of scale or strong complementarities exist, the rudimentary port state also rejects union with other rudimentary port states or dynamic interiors. The preferences about state formation of rudimentary port states are the polar opposite of those of the backward interiors.

2. The *Backward Interiors*—regions producing subsistence levels of income because of the lack of agronomic and mineral assets or because the distance from a major port makes overland transportation costs prohibitive—want to join wealthier regions in order to obtain subsidies and thereby improve their economic outlook.

3. *Dynamic Interiors* and *Entrepôts* are regions whose economic value depends on territorial mergers that can produce a durable commercial partnership. If distance does not create prohibitive overland transportation costs, the dynamic interior and the entrepôt are perfectly complementary economies. A dynamic interior needs a maritime outlet, which the entrepôt can provide, and, in turn, the entrepôt requires that a dynamic interior provide its output in order to generate revenue through foreign trade.

Table 4.3. A Typology of Economic Regions

		Seaport	
		No	Yes
Profitable	No	Backward interior	Entrepôt
exports	Yes	Dynamic interior	Rudimentary port state

Empirical Insight. The economic account generates two valuable empirical insights. First, the typology makes it possible to map the great economic divergence across regions created by the Commercial Revolution of the mid-nineteenth century. The rudimentary port states were the undisputed winners, about a dozen city-ports surrounded by fertile land able to produce large volumes of agricultural surpluses. Key examples of rudimentary port states are the city of Buenos Aires and the surrounding Pampas, the Chilean Central Valley around Santiago and the neighboring Valparaíso port, Rio de Janeiro and the Paraíba Valley, and the Yucatán Peninsula. They sharply differentiated themselves from most other regions in Latin America, which were backward interiors. Prominent dynamic interiors were the cattle-ranching areas in northern Mexico and Entre Ríos (north of Buenos Aires) and regions with large and easily accessible deposits of precious metals, like Zacatecas (central Mexico) and Antioquia (south-central Colombia). The number of entrepôts was enormous, but only a handful, such as Cartagena (connected to Bogotá through the Magdalena River) and Veracruz (linked to México City by high-quality roads built during the colonial era), became major outlets for dynamic interiors.

Second, the theory succeeds at explaining the collapse of three projects of state formation combining multiple regions: Gran Colombia, the United Provinces of Central America, and the Peru-Bolivian Confederation. Because of their factor endowments, the elites of the rudimentary port states of Venezuela (Caracas and its vast rural hinterland), Peru (centered on the Lima-Callao combination), and Guatemala preferred independence. Similarly, the theory accounts for the strong secessionist currents in the formation of Latin America's three colossuses: Argentina, Brazil, and Mexico. In Brazil, at least three regions struggled to become separate countries because they had the necessary endowments to follow their own trade-led path of state formation and saw a union centered on Rio de Janeiro as a liability (see Map 7.1). In present-day Argentina, it was the very center, Buenos Aires, that rejected merging with the states in the Andean region in the Northwest and the Upper Littoral in the North (Map 5.1). In Mexico, the successful secession of Texas was followed by similar attempts in three regions that would have also benefited from separate statehood. In the Yucatán Peninsula (South), for instance, the local oligarchy controlled an international seaport and did not need the intermediary role of México City to ship sisal fiber and sugar to Louisiana, its main export market (see Map 8.2).

Critical Assessment. The economic theory fundamentally *fails* to explain why secessionism was eventually abandoned. It is the failure of the theory to explain the creation of Argentina, Brazil, and Mexico that highlights how deeply puzzling the formation of territorial colossuses is. No economic motive can be found for their creation. The most fortunate economic regions in South America, especially Buenos Aires and Rio de Janeiro, were surrounded by stagnant areas of little or no agronomic value. If the interests of the economic elites had been the only drivers of state formation, the fortunate regions would have never merged with stagnant areas. The economic oligarchies of each fortunate region would have formed a ministate because they were reluctant to share revenues with backward areas that provided no productive complementarities or economies of scale.

More generally, the theory predicts the emergence of a much larger number of (smaller) countries than actually formed. According to the theory, Mexico and South America should have fragmented into a multiplicity of minicountries, as Central America did. The expected outcome of the theory is the creation of about a dozen minicountries based on rudimentary port states; the formation of an additional small set of countries based on the merger of dynamic interiors and entrepôts, especially along the Pacific coast of South America; and the subdivision of the rest of Latin America (about four-fifths of the total area) into two dozen countries, one per each backward interior that should have been rejected by rudimentary port states. Precisely because the economic theory can explain the breakdown of large state projects like Gran Colombia, United Central America, and the Peru-Bolivian Confederation, it cannot explain the emergence of states that were even larger, like Argentina, Brazil, and Mexico.

In sum, if the general trade-led theory of state formation in Part 1 predicts "no port, no state," the special theory of state formation based on factor endowments makes the dual prediction of "one rudimentary port state, one state" and "one backward interior, one state." The prediction of the general theory is essentially right; the predictions of the special theory are fundamentally wrong.

A theoretical gap in the economic account creates its empirical failures. The theory defines *preferences* about state formation, but it is silent regarding the *power* to execute them. Several secessionist regions—which became subnational units in present-day Argentina, Brazil, and Mexico—actually lacked the power to make independence irreversible. Political independence required the capacity to deal effectively with two types of threat: threats from below, which were rooted in the fundamentals of the social structure of the region—including the reliance on slave labor and the encroachment of land held communally by indigenous groups—and predatory threats from neighboring regions.

The two remaining structural theories of state formation build on the economic theory by adding social threats from below and military threats from outside. They help explain why regions whose factor endowments created a strong secessionist drive eventually pursued incorporation into a broader political unit.

The Social Account:
Slave Labor, Communal Land, and Threats from Below

The Commercial Revolution had multiple social repercussions. Particularly consequential was the extent to which the region's antecedent social structure provided fertile ground for threats from below against the local oligarchy's property rights. In some regions of Latin America, the local elites responded to the commodity boom by deepening repressive labor relations, especially slavery in Cuba and northern Brazil. In others, they privatized communal land under control of indigenous populations, a frequent pattern in the former domains of the Mayas (Mesoamerica) and the Incas and Quechuas (Peru and Bolivia). From an economic point of view, the two responses were standard solutions to the increased level of inputs required to meet the demand of the foreign markets.

What matters for state formation is that both responses had similar social repercussions, as illustrated by Bahia and Pernambuco in northeastern Brazil (deepening of slavery for sugar and cotton production) and in Yucatán in southern Mexico (privatization of communal land for sisal and sugar production). The three regions were rudimentary port states, which, according to the baseline economic theory, implanted strong secessionist preferences in their economic elites. Economic elites did make a bid for independence, but the ensuing military mobilization got out of control. Once mobilized for independence, slave labor and communal peasants turned against the local secessionist elite who had armed them. In Bahia, Pernambuco, and Yucatán, the local elite faced a stark choice: gain independence at the risk of social revolt against private property, or forfeit sovereignty in exchange for central assistance repressing labor. They chose private property rights over political independence.

If the economic classification of regions is expanded to include key elements of the social structure, in particular, the propensity to social revolt, an important theoretical claim can be advanced: *a rudimentary port state's secessionist drive, as determined by its factor endowment, is reversed if secessionism induces social unrest and threats to property rights.*

The root cause of social unrest is not secessionism but exploitation or expropriation. Yet the secessionist bid by the local elite provides labor the opportunity for mobilization and the means to challenge social order. The motivation of the formerly secessionist region to join a larger political unit is squarely Marxist: to defeat labor, the region needs an army it cannot afford on its own and therefore becomes willing to join a larger political unit with enough repressive capacity. This form of merger is the best example of state formation as a creation of a class good, according to the definition in Part 1.

Critical Assessment. Even though the social theory of state formation solves the puzzle of the end of secessionism in some regions within the colossuses, including Yucatán and Bahia, it does not solve all of them. Rio Grande do Sul in southern Brazil and the regions of Zacatecas and Sierra Madre in Mexico (center and north, respectively) were fiercely secessionist and did not incite threats from below. Yet they eventually abandoned secessionism. In sum, the social theory of state formation explains only a fraction of cases of aborted secessionism.

More important, the social theory fails to answer why the emerging centers of the colossuses, Buenos Aires, Rio de Janeiro, and México City-Veracruz (rudimentary port states themselves) were willing to incorporate other rudimentary port states as future peripheries. Absent geopolitical pressures, territorial expansion is a low-priority goal, if it is a goal at all. Given the need to ignite the export boom, efforts at incorporating peripheries—which divert resources from the export sector toward military campaigns in the peripheries or economic transfers to poorer regions—are strictly counterproductive.

Despite the defects of the purely economic theory, it had a fundamental insight: emerging centers, especially those holding the ticket with the major prizes of the commodity lottery—for example, Buenos Aires and Rio de Janeiro—should systematically reject merging with poorer regions. None of the potential benefits of the territorial merger could possibly outweigh the benefits of forming a separate country completely unburdened by fiscal responsibilities toward less fortunate regions.

The expansionary drive of the emerging capital cities of the Latin American colossuses is a genuine enigma. It has never been presented as such only because, extrapolating the goals of the small sample of the western European pioneers to the rest of the world, state formation has been seen, uncritically, as synonymous with territorial expansion. The assumption is wrong theoretically, and Buenos Aires provides a drastic empirical counterexample: for three decades after 1830, it was a center that deliberately rejected union with the poor peripheries of present-day Argentina. A center that does not want peripheries is only a puzzling fact in the context of war-led state formation. In the context of trade-led state formation, given the strong predictions of the economic theory, the puzzle is why wealthy centers incorporate poor peripheries. The willingness of a rudimentary port state to incorporate peripheries can be understood only when military structures are brought into the analysis.

The Military Account:
State-Taking, State-Breaking, and State-Making Caudillos

In most parts of Latin America, the legacy of independence was not states but warlords, or caudillos. Dozens of caudillos dominated Latin American politics between 1815 and 1845.

Warlords typically ruled a single region—a rural village and its immediate hinterland. Few regions were exempt. Chile, Antioquia and Bogotá in Colombia, and Costa Rica were notable exceptions in South America. Brazil experienced virtually no warlordism, except in the southernmost regions of Cisplatina (present-day Uruguay) and Rio Grande do Sul. Warlordism had two sources. The wars of independence mobilized rural lords and placed them in control of substantial contingents of men and arsenals. The other, more durable source was contagion, that is, rural lords forming private armies to defend themselves against neighboring caudillos. Their typical environment was a relatively large cattle-ranching area (e.g., the Venezuelan Llanos and the vast Pampas in the Southern Cone). There, the necessary inputs for the production process, peons and horses, were easily turned into private armies when the local potentate sensed an invasion or perceived an opportunity for expansion.

Even before the Commercial Revolution hit the continent, caudillos differentiated themselves between poor and wealthy, depending on the value of the land under their control. When the Commercial Revolution hit the continent, and the winning economic regions began a process of state formation, warlords fell into three well-defined categories: state-takers, state-breakers, and state-makers (see Figure 4.1).

By definition, state-*taking* lords could not produce their own states. They ruled a backward interior. They had a modicum of military power—that is what made them caudillos—but economic backwardness caused fiscal scarcity, which in turn made any state-formation project unviable. The highest aspiration of a state-taking caudillo was to contribute his contingent of followers to the winning side of a state-formation project initiated

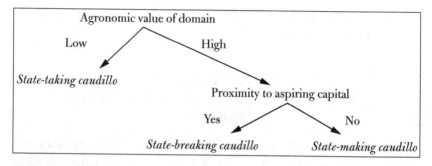

Figure 4.1. A taxonomy of warlords

elsewhere. Hoping to receive economic subsidies from the center, caudillos were ready to incorporate their fiefdom as a subnational unit within a larger territorial conglomerate. In exchange, they provided coalitional support or, if circumstances required, a small contingent of soldiers.

From a military perspective, the state-*making* caudillos were initially indistinguishable from all other caudillos. Yet, economically, they became lucky; the Commercial Revolution transformed their region into a rudimentary port state. As a consequence, their private economic ventures grew, as did the number of dependent peons and horses. They could combine increased military power and an extraordinary flow of taxes from foreign trade to form their separate domain, excluding most surrounding regions (except for those that were ruled by a satellite, state-taking caudillo).

State-taking caudillos and state-making caudillos drastically simplified the politics of state formation. The state-takers were cheap political support for state-makers. They had little to offer and demanded little in exchange. On the other hand, the state-making caudillos single-handedly created countries. They avoided the complications of electoral politics and coalition building by carving a territorial state out of the extension of their vast clientelistic network. Latin America had three successful state-making caudillos—Carrera, Castilla, and Páez—who created Guatemala, Peru, and Venezuela. They made states after causing the implosion of a larger political unit—Central America, the Peru-Bolivian Confederation, and Gran Colombia. In the larger unit, they could only aspire to a secondary position because the broad structure of power rewarded coalition building and partisan juggling rather than clientelistic favors and military force.

Finally, the state-*breaking* type of caudillo differs from the other warlords on two dimensions. First, in contrast to the state-taking caudillo, the land of the state-breaking caudillo possesses substantial agronomic value. He rules either a dynamic interior or a rudimentary port state. Second, in contrast to the state-making caudillo, his domain is physically proximate to that of a wealthier region, like the aspiring capital of a colossus (Buenos Aires, México City, and Rio de Janeiro) or of a multiregion country (Bogotá). Location expands the range of actions available to the state-breaking caudillo: in addition to making his own state or taking a state formed elsewhere, the state-breaking caudillo can plunder a more fortunate neighbor.

The state-breaking caudillo is an inherently unstable, self-liquidating political character. He can bid for the independence of his fiefdom and, if successful, become a state-making caudillo; alternatively, he can specialize in threatening the wealthier neighboring region with looting raids, a form of extortion in exchange for which he turns into a state-taking caudillo. Concessions range from a substantial subsidy to cover the extortion tax to a real share of political power in the larger unit centered in the neighboring capital region.

The military extension of the theory of trade-led state formation builds on the baseline economic theory to produce two key claims. The first is that *rudimentary port states, when dominated by a warlord, become stable, irreversible states.*

The caudillo provides military muscle and clientelistic obedience; the port and its valuable hinterland provide the economic wherewithal. The process may involve the breakdown of a large-scale state-formation project. The state-making caudillo goes through a phase of state-breaking in relation to a political unit that is populated by a number of real contenders ruling neighboring regions. The caudillo creates a state out of the territorial domain he fully controls using clientelism and, secondarily, force.

The military account also provides a convincing answer to the great enigma of colossus formation in Latin America, namely, why their capitals incorporated less valuable peripheries. The military answer is straightforward: *the center incorporates peripheries in order to prevent invasions from state-breaking caudillos ruling neighboring regions that were less fortunate at the commodity lottery.*

When faced with the option of producing a mild export boom or threatening a predatory attack against a wealthy rudimentary port state, the state-breaking caudillo choses to threaten. To appease the state-breaking caudillo, the rudimentary port state incorporates his region into the emerging state and secures him a share of political power, which is the key to making economic transfers from the center to the periphery credible.

Critical Assessment. Although plausible at the theoretical level, the military account does not fit the historical record. An analysis of the political possibilities of the capital of the two largest colossuses is most instructive: for Buenos Aires and especially Rio de Janeiro, the permanent exclusion of state-breaking peripheries was a viable course of action. Caudillos never threatened Rio de Janeiro. Caudillos in southern Brazil wanted secession from Rio de Janeiro rather than supremacy over it. Buenos Aires repeatedly faced the threat from peripheral caudillos, and they invaded twice before 1860. Yet, by 1860, Buenos Aires could afford a military cordon that made invasion unviable—not a Chinese Great Wall but a line of perimeter forts sufficiently armed to dissuade looting raids. Rio de Janeiro incorporated peripheries that were no threat, and Buenos Aires incorporated peripheries that were a threat but could have been deactivated with a relatively small defense investment.

The extortion argument is logically sound—it is the best explanation available for mergers between economically asymmetric regions. Military rationality explains an economically irrational process of state formation. But it does not explain why three rudimentary port states formed the colossuses of Argentina, Brazil, and Mexico, which incorporated the largest number of peripheries in Latin America. Argentina and Brazil are particularly puzzling because, in the long run, the incorporation of peripheries exhausted the economic potential of central regions that could have otherwise become major engines of growth for the entire continent—the Pampa Húmeda and the Paraíba Valley.

Structural Explanations:
The Balance Sheet

The three structural approaches contribute valuable theoretical claims that explain a substantial number of empirical state-formation outcomes in Latin America. Part 1 highlighted the "international" antecedent conditions that

Table 4.4. Structural Explanations Compared: Empirical Successes
and Failures

	Empirical assessment	
Theory	Explains	Fails to explain
Economic	Formation of minicountries (Central American republics) and secessionism in colossuses	Peripheral secessionism abandoned
Social	Reversal of secessionism in Yucatán (Mexico) and Pernambuco and Bahia (Brazil)	Center's incentive to incorporate threatened peripheries (in Mexico and northern Brazil)
Military	Collapse of large-scale state-formation projects (Central America, Peru-Bolivia, Gran Colombia) at the hand of state-breaking caudillos and emergence of small successor states (Guatemala, Peru, Venezuela) led by state-making caudillos	Center's incentive (in Buenos Aires and Rio de Janeiro) to incorporate poorer peripheries (Andean states in Argentina and the northeast and south in Brazil)

sent all Latin American countries along the trade-led path of state formation. In a funnel strategy of explanation, the three prior subsections each contributed a new layer of "domestic" antecedent conditions—economic, social, and military—that had a critical impact in narrowing down the range of possible mergers and separations.

Yet structural explanations share a weakness. They overlook the ordinary ambition of building winning political coalitions. In the extraordinary context of state formation, the ambition is to demarcate the territory that, through the inclusion of some regions and the exclusion of others, optimizes the state-formation agent's chances for political survival. Table 4.4 summarizes the facts that the structural theories succeed at explaining and those they fail to explain.

To overcome the limitations of the structural theories of state formation, pure politics—the ordinary ambition of politicians in extraordinary
times—needs to be brought into the analysis. Political agency is crucial to
understanding the formation of the three Latin American colossuses as well
as Colombia and Uruguay. The next section combines the three types of
structures—economic, social, and military—with three types of political agent
to produce a "politician-centered" approach to trade-led state formation.

State-Formation Agents: Ports, Parties, and Lords

This section identifies agents of state formation in Latin America: the port,
the party, and the lord. It systematizes commonalities and differences among
them. It also differentiates state-formation agents in Latin America from the
late medieval European warrior, who at least since Tilly's work has been
seen as the canonical agent of state formation. A key takeaway is that not all
states are produced by warriors. When other agents produce states, the final outcome is substantially different. The typology of state-formation
agents is the key building block for completing the theory of trade-led state
formation presented in Part 1. The central mechanism of the theory is the
coalitional propensities of each type of agent.

Ports, Parties, Lords

Three types of political agent were responsible for territory consolidation: a
political entrepreneur in a city-port (or port, for short); competing political
parties emerging from networks connecting primary cities, secondary cities, and rural villages; or a powerful rural lord, known in Latin America as
a supercaudillo. Each agent generated a specific territory-consolidation pathway: port-driven, party-driven, and lord-driven.

Agents had geographic roots, but the relation between agents and regions is not one-to-one. The political entrepreneur and the supercaudillo
could each dominate a rudimentary port state. The entrepreneur emerged
in the main city of the rudimentary port state, whereas the lord came from
the immediate rural hinterland (the supercaudillo is the state-making type
of rural lord). Political parties originated either in a rudimentary port state
or a dynamic interior. Backward interiors and entrepôts produced no state-

formation leaders. A political entrepreneur could have been born in an entrepôt or an interior region. Yet he had to launch and develop his career in a rudimentary port state because it provided the means to accumulate political capital and was the source of the economic means for state formation. Backward peripheries were largely ruled by the state-taking type of caudillo.

Admittedly, the trio of possible agents of territory consolidation is an inductive inventory based on who the most prominent political actors were at the critical time of state formation, when the Commercial Revolution hit the subcontinent in the mid-nineteenth century. A more systematic approach, based on a typological exercise, confirms the utility of the inventory and helps develop comparative insight. Two dimensions of variation, the means and goals of political action, generate a typology of agents of state formation.

The general means of state formation were the revenues derived from international trade. Because each agent-driven pathway is a variant of trade-led state formation, all three share a reliance on international commerce. In addition to the flow of revenues (economic capital), a would-be state-maker also requires a modicum of noneconomic capital. It is the noneconomic capital that empowers the state-formation agent to gain supremacy over political rivals. Human and social capital may help, but state-formation agents gain a real edge over rivals by amassing either *political* or *military* capabilities. Political capital includes support from the public, trust from fellow politicians, and deal-making abilities. Military capacity includes troops, weapons, and discipline. By the 1850s, some political entrepreneurs and protoparties managed to accumulate abundant political capital. On the other hand, a few warlords had become supercaudillos with formidable military capabilities, including a loyal clientele of rural workers readily available for military action, a number of satellite caudillos, a considerable stock of horses to put together a cavalry—the supercaudillo's distinctive military force—and an arsenal of lances and rifles.

Along the second dimension of variation—the goals of the state-formation agent—territory consolidation can be either the result of a *deliberate plan* or the *unintended by-product* of pursuing other goals. The political entrepreneur and the supercaudillo differed from the political party in that they made explicit plans about which regions to include and which ones to exclude in the emerging political arena. Both saw in the commercial boom a political opportunity to maximize power by creating a political arena that aggregated the regions that were the most worthwhile from a coalitional perspective. Political entrepreneurs and supercaudillos produced combinations of regions by design. Countries are their creatures. By contrast, parties originated in strictly *local* political clubs. At some point in their struggle for supremacy within the confines of their city, clubs decided to build an alliance with a similar club in a neighboring region. They exchanged mutual support for their respective contests against the rival local club. Members of rival clubs came from the same educated minorities, including lawyers, physicians, and journalists. Ostensibly, they engaged in competing campaigns to either block or advance reforms to the legacy of colonial institutions, which in most cases activated the Conservative-versus-Liberal cleavage (Uruguay is the exception). In practice, they were fighting for control over municipal government.

When parties are the agents of state formation, party formation precedes and inadvertently produces territory consolidation—an inconceivable sequence among pioneer states. Because a state had not been formed yet, alliances between protoparties in different cities and villages were the first rudiment of interest aggregation across regions. The deepening division along partisan lines gradually erased divisions along regional lines, thereby consolidating a "national" political arena. Also, in contrast to political entrepreneurs and supercaudillos, who initiated and completed territory consolidation within the time span of their political careers, it took the protoparties generations to create permanent supraregional coalitions. Only along this second dimension is party formation in Latin America similar to war-making in western Europe. Regions are combined as the unintended by-product of local fights carried out by several generations of rival factions— educated oligarchies in the Latin American cases versus feudal armies in the western European ones.

Table 4.5 presents the typology of state-formation agents that provides the conceptual space to distinguish the three agents of state formation in Latin America as well as the late medieval European warrior. Scholarship views the warrior as the most influential actor in shaping western Europe between the fall of the Roman Empire and the Industrial Revolution. The typology highlights that the political entrepreneur is the most different agent of state formation in relation to the original European warrior. Warriors and entrepreneurs share neither the means nor the goals of state formation.

Table 4.5. A Typology of State-Formation Agents

		Territory consolidation (goal)	
		Unintended by-product	Deliberate plan
Kind of noneconomic capital (means)	Military	Warriors (Europe)	Rural lord (Venezuela, Peru, Guatemala)
	Political	Political parties (Mexico, Colombia, Uruguay)	Political entrepreneur / city-port (Brazil, Argentina, Chile)

Significantly, the two largest countries in Latin America, Brazil and Argentina, were formed by political entrepreneurs. Mexico, the third largest, was formed by competing political parties. That is, Latin American and western European state formation differed sharply not only with regard to the international economic and geopolitical conditions (Part 1) but also, crucially, with regard to the agents leading the processes.

The rural lord is the Latin American agent of state formation that most closely resembles the European warrior. But the Latin American rural lord was a very "soft" version of the Westphalian warrior. He might have come to power through military action. Once in power, however, his focus was on profit-making through economic expansion rather than on territorial expansion through war-making. Responding to the international context, the rural lord privileged trade over security. The commercial motive led the rural lord to dismiss the European warrior's agenda of periphery penetration and transformation. The rural lord was rapidly tamed by the promising rewards of the *doux-commerce*. The sole exception to the soft rural lord that dominated Latin America was José Gaspar de Francia and his successors Carlos Antonio López and son Francisco Solano López, who ruled Paraguay unchallenged for six decades after independence. They did not become traders only because Paraguay had no commodity to offer to world capitalism (the only Latin American country fully formed out of a backward interior). They focused instead on military buildup and perhaps after several generations could have produced an effective "Prussian enclave" within South America.

Political parties as agents of state formation are a complete novelty in relation to the European antecedent. In every tradition of analysis, the state forms first, and then parties emerge to compete for control.[6] Yet, in some cases of Latin America, party formation preceded state formation. A paradoxical feature of party-driven state formation is that key aspects of the process can be seen as indications of state failure. The distinction between territory consolidation and violence monopolization is crucial to understand the opposite effects of party-driven state formation. On the one hand, Latin American parties were inimical to state formation because party competition, especially in Mexico, Colombia, and Uruguay, often escalated into full-blown civil war, which by definition is antithetical to the monopoly of violence. On the other hand, any form of party struggle, even if violent, has the unintended consequence of producing territory consolidation by defining the spatial reach of interparty competition. Interparty conflict propagates through a political arena with increasingly clearer physical contours.

Coalitional Propensities

Although the three agents of state formation adapted their political strategies to the surrounding environment, each type of agent has specific propensities regarding territory consolidation and violence monopolization.

In the port-driven pathway of state formation, the political entrepreneur shows a propensity to "territorial expansion," that is, the combination of a dynamic economic center and a number of less dynamic peripheries. The entrepreneur profits from incorporating peripheries that yield coalitional dividends. In incorporating peripheries, the entrepreneur hurts the material prosperity of the port—his original political base—because the peripheries demand a share of the port's wealth. The political entrepreneur persuades the port that economic transfers will prevent the "voracity" of peripheries that would become a permanent threat of predatory invasion if excluded from the emerging state.

Party-driven state formation is not carried out by a single party but is an unintended by-product of the formation of two rival parties as competing political networks connecting several regions. Like the entrepreneur, parties favor territorial expansion for political reasons (as opposed to economic or military motivations). In contrast to the entrepreneur, the goal of territorial expansion in the party-driven path is primarily local—securing municipal control. Yet the exchange of mutual support between two clubs in different regions inadvertently creates supraregional alliances and thereby enlarges the physical dimension of the political arena. The territory of the state—the set of regions included—is coterminous with the spatial extension of the partisan networks built by municipal political clubs.

Finally, the lord-driven pathway is marked by a propensity toward "territorial reduction." Reduction manifests itself either as secession from a larger unit or as rejection of merger with distant peripheries. The lord is averse to the incorporation of his fiefdom into a larger political unit that may place him in a subordinate position. He may welcome new clients if they are caudillos who unambiguously belong to the state-taking type and come from regions proximate enough to make monitoring costs negligible. The lord definitely rejects mergers with distant areas ruled by less predictable types of caudillo. The lord knows that they will be on the lookout for an opportunity to dispute his position at the peak of the patrimonial pyramid. The supercaudillo's clientelistic fiefdom in effect becomes the consolidated territory of the emerging state.

If the port-driven pathway is taken as the benchmark process of state formation in Latin America, then the lord- and party-driven pathways can be seen as each involving a distinct pair of commonalities and differences. The party-driven pathway shares with the port-driven pathway an "expansionary" coalitional propensity by which parties are willing to incorporate surrounding regions in order to enlarge their bases of support. By contrast, the lord-driven pathway shows a "reductionist" propensity because the lord fears that an expansion of the political arena will risk the patrimonial hierarchy that sustains his power. The lord- and port-driven pathways have in common the advantage of "supremacy": precisely because the lord and the entrepreneur choose the territorial combination that maximizes their power, they rule the nascent state undisputed. By contrast, in the party-driven pathway, political supremacy is disputed between two parties that manifestly cannot defeat each other, in either electoral contests or armed conflict.

Combining Structural Attributes and Political Agency:
Varieties of Territory Consolidation
The Distinct Political Dynamics of the Pathways

Each of the three "politician-centered" pathways of state formation is a distinct mix of structural constraints and political actions.

The Port-Driven Pathway. This pathway combines the structural constraints of multiple regions, including the main rudimentary port state, with a highly sophisticated strategy of territory consolidation by the political entrepreneur. The entrepreneur's strategy involves a multilateral bargaining with the main port and its productive hinterland and a number of surrounding peripheries that the entrepreneur selects based on the professional motivation of political survival. The port and its hinterland are the entrepreneur's own geographic base, and each of the selected peripheries makes a distinct set of demands derived from its economic, social, and military structure.

If the same wealthy rudimentary port state were instead dominated by a rural lord, then the political strategy of territory consolidation would be massively simplified. The strategy would consist of secession followed by the reduction of the political arena to the physical area occupied by the lord's patrimonial hierarchy. That the political entrepreneur rules the rudimentary port state makes all the difference. His professional goals turn the region from an exclusionary sovereign unit into a center of territorial expansion through political brokerage.

The rural lord's strategy does not work for the entrepreneur because he cannot count on the clientelist loyalty of rural workers and satellite caudillos. To build a solid coalition, he needs to expand the political arena. Expansion requires negotiating with economic elites in the main port, with social oligarchies and state-breaking caudillos from prosperous but less dynamic areas (secondary rudimentary port states or dynamic interiors), and with state-taking caudillos in backward interiors.

The entrepreneur builds his career—and forms a state—by taking full advantage of the opportunities and resources available within the arena formed by the expected merger of the main rudimentary port state and the peripheries he selected to maximize his chances at political survival. For the entrepreneur, a fundamental asset is the fiscal resources of the main rudimentary port state. Hence, an ineliminable structural constraint for the entrepreneur's political action is to protect the export boom. Yet, to obtain the support of the main rudimentary port state, the entrepreneur must make deals with peripheries and must make those deals appear beneficial to the economic elites in the main city-port. The entrepreneur finds political opportunity in the socioeconomic and military needs of peripheral elites. He provides solutions in exchange for political backing.

The entrepreneur generates political capital from two types of deal with peripheries. The first is rooted in the social structural conditions highlighted by the Marxist explanation; the second, in the military structures emphasized by the Weberian explanation.

Peripheral economic regions that depend on slave labor or the forceful privatization of communal land provide the political entrepreneur a key opportunity at career enhancement and territory consolidation. If secondary rudimentary port states are under the threat of slave revolt or peasant uprising, the entrepreneur can gather the support of their economic elites by promising central assistance to restore social order. The economic elites in the main rudimentary port state go along with the commitment made by the entrepreneur because of the economies of scale generated by the consolidation of a single army within a larger territory. The costs of delivering the class good, labor repression, to secondary rudimentary port states are more than compensated by the extra revenue their foreign trade generates. The social structure of the rudimentary port states under threat does not by itself produce the political effort required for territory consolidation. It is the initiative of the entrepreneur, his commitment to provide a solution to slave or peasant rebellion, that transforms the structural threat into an effective agreement of territorial merger between center and periphery.

State-breaking and state-taking caudillos provide the entrepreneur the other opportunity at career enhancement and territory consolidation. The political entrepreneur publicly deplores the political methods of the caudillos. Yet it is fundamental for his survival plan to build a tacit alliance with state-breaking caudillos. Such alliance helps the entrepreneur display political connections and negotiation skills that are extremely valuable to the main rudimentary port state. Thanks to the political capital built in the peripheries, the entrepreneur can prevent looting invasions of the center. It is in exchange for that preventive political service that the economic elites in the main rudimentary port state throw their support behind the entrepreneur. The entrepreneur thereby gets resources from the center to subsidize the incorporated peripheries. Regional lords use subsidies to consolidate personal rule at the local level. The entrepreneur in turn minimizes the economic cost of buying peripheral support in two ways. First, he obtains the support of the state-taking caudillos in backward peripheries, which helps him show to the state-breaking caudillos of secondary rudimentary port states that they are not the only source of peripheral support. Second, the entrepreneur persuades caudillos that generosity has limits because excessive subsidies will strangle the economy of the main port and result in general bankruptcy. In sum, the military structures of the surrounding regions alone do not produce direct effects. It is the entrepreneur's leveraging them that drives territory consolidation. He manipulates the fears of the economic elites in the center by exploiting the military capabilities of state-breaking caudillos in the peripheries. He obtains money from the port to transform state-breaking warlords into state-taking local oligarchies. Through brokerage, the entrepreneur gains the support of multiple regionally defined constituencies. He consolidates them to create a large political arena in which he can rule unchallenged.

The two types of deal highlight the entrepreneur's expertise in taking advantage of the dangers created by the social and military structures that characterize the surrounding regions. If surrounding regions open structures of opportunity, the entrepreneur supplies closure to territory consolidation through political brokerage. In crafting an agreement between a prosperous port and a selected set of less dynamic or fully stagnant areas and in balancing out their interests, the entrepreneur gains autonomy from both the center and the peripheries. He thus becomes a strictly political creature who prioritizes his career goals over the economic interests of any particular region or class. The entrepreneur promises all the territorial components of his coalitional combination that unification will deliver important material rewards. But he does so as a means to his ultimate ends, maximizing political power.

Argentina and Brazil followed the port-driven pathway to territory consolidation. The impact of the entrepreneur, Bartolomé Mitre in Argentina and the Saquarema bloc in Brazil, can hardly be overstated. In fact, it is no exaggeration to claim that in both colossuses, the entrepreneur reversed the outcome expected from the distribution of economic factors across the regions incorporated. In present-day Brazil, the factor endowments of Pernambuco, Bahia, and Rio Grande do Sul made them strongly secessionist regions. More important, in both present-day Argentina and Brazil, the very centers, Buenos Aires and Rio de Janeiro, had every economic reason to avoid periphery incorporation. Merger with poorer peripheries could only mean lost income. Hence, the formation of Argentina and Brazil ran counter to the preferences shaped by economic structures.

The leaders of the Argentine and Brazilian centers incorporated peripheries of dubious economic value because they pursued an expanded political arena in which their rule was more secure than within the confines of the city-port. Yet what made periphery incorporation palatable to the economic elites of the Argentine and Brazilian centers were the noneconomic attributes of the peripheries themselves. In Brazil, two of the incorporated peripheries, Bahia and Pernambuco, changed their initial attitude toward secessionism—which was firmly rooted in their factor endowments—because of their social structure, the extensive use of slave labor, the preservation of which required central help. Slavery in the northern Brazilian peripheries created a demand for incorporation into a state centered in Rio de Janeiro, thereby lowering the cost of creating a territorial colossus. In both Argentina and Brazil, the dominance of state-breaking caudillos in peripheries closer to the capital (Entre Rios and Rio Grande do Sul, respectively) helped the political entrepreneur of the port persuade the cattle ranchers of Buenos Aires and the coffee planters of Rio de Janeiro to foot the bill of incorporating economically less dynamic but militarily challenging peripheries. Subsidies from the center to regions ruled by state-breaking caudillos were a small price for generating a political climate that was friendly for foreign investors.

In sum, economic, social, and military structures in the peripheries pushed local notables to demand incorporation within a larger sovereign unit centered on an extraordinarily wealthy city-port, Buenos Aires and Rio de Janeiro. A structure-based demand of incorporation by peripheral oligarchies is one thing—the willingness of the center to grant incorporation is another entirely. Buenos Aires and Rio de Janeiro had no economic motive to merge with poorer areas. The entrepreneur's political ambition and action created the incentives for otherwise reluctant centers to sustain the consolidation of an expanded territorial arena. Driven by professional ambition, the political entrepreneur exploited the social and military structures in the peripheries to form territorial colossuses that made no sense from an economic point of view.

The Party-Driven Pathway. Whereas the entrepreneur aims to rule a multiregion, "national" political arena, the party-driven pathway involves eminently local political goals. The lowered ambitions of the politicians in the party-driven pathways are rooted in fiscal incapacity. Their own rudimentary port state or dynamic interior cannot provide subsidies to poorer regions (a key instrument available to the entrepreneur). In the party-driven pathway, a multiregion territory does consolidate but only as the unintended by-product of the political networks formed by municipal politicians. The networks are built in the process of exchanging mutual favors to secure local supremacy. Municipal politicians can borrow from one another supporters, programs, and slogans for campaigns. The deals are based on the exchange of political capital as opposed to economic transfers.

Politicians with strictly municipal goals originate in a special subset of rudimentary port states and dynamic interiors. The regions must be wealthy enough to produce a competitive oligarchic arena (multiple newspapers, social clubs, and revenues that can finance different packages of local public goods and thereby become a source of political conflict) but not so wealthy to afford economic transfers to poorer regions. The unavailability of central subsidies prevents the emergence of a politician with the ambition of an entrepreneur, whose very career depends on extracting money from his city-port to buy support in surrounding regions. In other words, the economic structure of the regions within the political network in the party-driven pathway is incompatible with the existence of a political entrepreneur.

Networks of municipal politicians can expand to include a number of state-taking caudillos ruling backward peripheries. A caudillo in a distant periphery can help an urban politician by turning his clients into the politician's supporters and into gangs to intimidate rivals in times of elections. The allied caudillo can also contribute essential manpower when electoral competition morphs into armed conflict. In exchange, the caudillo gets public validation of his local patrimonial methods. By joining a partisan network, he also obtains programmatic cover and favors from the friendly press.

Networks of municipal politicians are fragile objects, especially in their formative phase. They link together otherwise autarkic regions, but, in contrast to the political entrepreneur, they cannot prevent the secession of a rudimentary port state ruled by a state-breaking caudillo. Two reasons make it unlikely for the party-driven pathway to retain a rudimentary port state determined to secede. First, the regions in the partisan network cannot afford the economic compensation that would make union appealing to the seceding rulers. Second, the politicians in the network only care about local supremacy, so the secession of one region is not an important loss (especially if the seceding region is distant).

Colombia, Mexico, and Uruguay followed the party-driven pathway. Liberal and Conservative networks centered in Bogotá and Antioquia united the regions of present-day Colombia, but they could not prevent the disintegration of Gran Colombia, which included the rudimentary port states of Venezuela and Ecuador. Similar partisan networks centered in México City and Veracruz were responsible for holding together the large number of regions of present-day Mexico, but they could not prevent the secession of Texas, which, with the intervention of the United States, led to the loss of almost half of the colonial territory. Uruguay is a small state *despite* the expansionary propensity of its partisan networks. Powerful external actors, including Brazil, Argentina, and especially the United Kingdom, set clear limits to the territorial scope of the networks of the Colorado and Blanco parties.

The Lord-Driven Pathway. The lord-driven form of territory consolidation is the simplest one. It is based on only two components: (a) a single region that is a rudimentary port state from an economic perspective and the bastion of a rural lord from a military perspective; (b) the political strategy of the rural lord, a state-breaking caudillo in relation to a large territorial project who morphed into a state-making caudillo in relation to a breakaway political unit. The rudimentary port state and a dominant rural lord are individually necessary and collectively sufficient conditions for country creation. The rudimentary port state provides resources to the lord in the form of revenues from international trade. It also creates constraints on the lord, as he must secure an adequate business climate for export-led growth. Political action in the lord-driven pathways is, as in the other two pathways, crucial to territory consolidation. Yet, in contrast to the other two pathways,

political action in the lord-driven pathway is a minimalist intervention: all
the rural lord needs to do is to secede from a larger territorial unit and then
dominate the breakaway territory through his clientelistic hierarchy. In rare
circumstances, it requires an exemplary dose of force. A rural lord dominating a rudimentary port state has no incentives to expand or shrink the
territory of the state, and he possesses all the fiscal and military capacity to
sustain the sovereignty of his country. Venezuela, Peru, and Guatemala followed the lord-driven pathway to territory consolidation.

Colossuses and the Formula of Territorial Governance

In the two expansionary pathways, the port- and party-driven ones, the outcome is the emergence of a multiregion country—and potentially a colossus. A key bargaining tool for the center in relation to the other regions is
the *formula of territorial governance*, which formalizes the terms of the
agreement with the incorporated peripheries. The formula can be confederal,
federal, or unitarian. Each is a distinct distribution of political and fiscal resources both among subnational units and between the central government
and lower-level governments (states or provinces). The formula is by far the
most significant institution to accommodate the interests of the center and
the other regions of an emerging state.

The number of peripheries incorporated—which is strongly correlated
with country size—and the terms of incorporation are components of the
same political negotiation between central elites and peripheral notables.
Territory consolidation and the formula of territorial governance are *joint*
creations of the state-formation process. Peripheries will resist incorporation
unless they find the terms favorable. They may form a small independent
country, or they may be incorporated in a subsequent round of state formation under more convenient terms.

By way of illustration, before the Commercial Revolution created the
potential for a positive-sum bargaining between an aspiring capital and surrounding peripheries, a unitarian formula of territorial governance wrestling
political power from local potentates provoked civil war in the territory of
present-day Argentina in 1819 and again in 1826. Unacceptable terms of incorporation caused state failure, from which myriad ministates emerged.

After the Commercial Revolution, which benefited the economy of Buenos Aires as it did few other regions, peripheries in present-day Argentina became interested in merger with the main city-port. The peripheral ministates that had rejected unification in 1819 and 1826 agreed to merge under a federal formula in 1853. Yet the formula was so generous to peripheral ministates that the economic elites in Buenos Aires vetoed it. A deal brokered by an entrepreneur in the city-port was necessary to form present-day Argentina.

Analysis of center-periphery interaction requires a systematic approach to the formula of territorial governance. Small sovereignties considering unification into a larger territorial unit compare the option of continued *separation* with the three broad categories of territorial formulas: a *confederation*, a *federal system*, and a *unitary state*. The four possible outcomes differ with regard to territorial unification, violence monopolization, the existence of a higher level of government, and the degree of autonomy of the small sovereignties. When small sovereignties fear becoming losers in the new distribution of power and wealth induced by the formula of territorial governance, projects to form multiregion states will fail.

Separation and confederation differ in that the confederation provides an element of territorial unification that is absent under separation. The confederation is an arrangement in which fully independent states agree to adopt the same policy in a selected set of policy realms. The shared policies—which can range from the elimination of import tariffs among the confederate units to the coordination of diplomatic affairs—provide the element of territorial unification in confederations. Policies outside the shared set are decided autonomously by the independent states. A confederation shares with separation the attribute that no monopoly of violence exists within the joint territory of the relevant states. Under both separation and a confederation, small sovereignties maintain their own armies. The lack of a monopolistic concentration of violence is the Achilles' heel of every confederation because policies agreed among constituent states depend on noncoercive mechanisms of enforcement. Hence, a confederation's common policies are less credible than in formulas of territorial governance where a monopoly of violence exists.

In contrast to both separation and the confederation, a federal system and a unitary state are *full* states in a large territory: small sovereignties merge their territories into a new, larger one, and violence becomes monopolized

Table 4.6. Formula of Territorial Governance: Separation and
Three Types Compared

	Territorial unification	Common policies	Monopoly of violence (small units without armies)	Political subordination of small units
Separation	✗	✗	✗	✗
Confederation	✓	✓	✗	✗
Federal system	✓	✓	✓	✗
Unitary state	✓	✓	✓	✓

within its borders. Under both a federal system and a unitary state, small sovereignties are either forcefully expropriated of their armies or they voluntarily relinquish them. In the federal system, as in the confederation, a limited set of policies is shared across all constituent units, while the individual constituent units autonomously define the policies outside the set. Unlike the confederation, the federal system has a superior level of government that directly controls the monopoly of violence within the territory in order to enforce the policies that affect all constituent units. The difference between the federal system and the unitary state is the autonomy of the subnational units. In the latter, subnational units have no political autonomy, including the ability to choose local authorities, whereas in the former, they autonomously select the authorities who design the policies outside the set of national ones. Table 4.6 summarizes the analysis of different formulas of territorial governance.

Every modern state has a formula of territorial governance. In fact, territorial consolidation and the emergence of institutions of territorial governance are *co-originating* factors of modern states. Unification between previously sovereign units can occur via military conquest, political agreement, or, most frequently, a combination of both. Even in the extreme case of pure military conquest, a formula of territorial governance exists: most likely, the victorious sovereignty would impose a unitary formula to minimize the political autonomy of the conquered territory and maximize the extraction of physical and human resources. In all cases where some degree of agreement is required, which was the modal case in Latin America, unification crucially depends on the specific terms included in the formula for territorial governance. A region's decision to accept or resist incorporation into a broader territory is a function of its expected position within the political and economic hierarchies established by the emerging state. Expected losers will derail the project if they have the means to do it.

As we will see in the case studies, the formula of territorial governance was a decisive institution in the formation of Argentina, Brazil, Colombia, and Mexico and in the failure of Gran Colombia and the Central American Federation.

Recapitulation

By way of recapitulation, this section contrasts each of the three pathways of state formation in Latin America with the war-led pathway of pioneers in western Europe.

In all three trade-led variants of territory consolidation in Latin America, the state-formation agent had a level of political autonomy that was unimaginable in the pioneer experience of western Europe. Geopolitical pressures in the pioneer cases left the state-formation agent with only two options: expansion or extinction. Moreover, expansion had to be coupled with the effort to transform the annexed territories in order to maximize military capacity. By contrast, agents of state formation in Latin America had an expanded menu of political strategies because the international environment was marked by the absence of serious geopolitical threats and a strong demand for primary products. They faced only one real restriction. They had to produce an adequate business climate for foreign investments and export-led growth. State-formation agents in Latin America could fulfill the economic requirements and still maintain substantial levels of freedom in decisions about territorial expansion or contraction and about transformation or preservation of institutions in the peripheries. Without risking international survival, Latin American state-formation agents could merge with distant political bastions, exclude all surrounding regions, or secede from larger units. The very lack of Darwinian pressures for administrative efficiency allowed eminently ordinary political motivations to drive the state-formation process. State-formation agents in Latin America made decisions about territory consolidation with an eye on coalitional returns. If the state-formation agent found it politically profitable to expand, the annexed territories did not need to be transformed. Thus, instead of extracting resources from them, he could offer generous packages of concessions.

Both in western Europe and in Latin America, the center-periphery interaction lies at the core of the territory-consolidation process. The greater level of freedom of Latin American state-formation agents had crucial repercussions for the relation between the emerging center and its peripheries. The zero-sum game of the pioneer cases could become a positive-sum game in the latecomer cases.

In early modern western Europe, the emerging center, generally an *interior* kinglet, sought territorial expansion by incorporating surrounding rings of land. Conquering increasingly larger rings provided the central kingdom with additional manpower, fiscal resources, and buffer space from rival kingdoms. In turn, peripheries in the surrounding rings resisted incorporation because it would invariably result in military, political, and fiscal subordination. The recalcitrant element in the peripheries was not the rural serfdom. Peripheral patrimonial lords led the resistance, as incorporation caused political, if not biological, extinction. Gains for the emerging center were losses for the regions that became peripheries.

The port-driven variant of state formation in Latin America sharply departed from the pioneering experience. State-formation agents in the ports of Latin America launched their political projects from a *coastal* city. Peripheries were not seen as reservoirs of military capability but as sources of potential political support for trade-led state-formation or, if dominated by state-breaking caudillos, as potential threats to export-led growth. Peripheral territories had political or economic value, but they were not a military asset. Crucially, success at trade-led state formation increased the overall level of revenues of the emerging country. Hence, the interaction between center and periphery could be negotiated to generate mutual benefits. Peripheries could receive a share of the economic prosperity generated by the center in exchange for abstaining from causing political disruption of the general business climate or for providing coalitional support to the political entrepreneur at the port. When peripheries were dominated by patrimonial lords, the center's concessions expanded the political arsenal available to the lord to reproduce his local clientelistic hegemony. Even if the central city-port had begun a process of administrative modernization, the bargains involved in periphery incorporation created a political arena based on *enclosing patrimonialism*. Through institutions like federalism, the senate, and the electoral college, periphery incorporation gradually propagated patrimonialism through all levels of government. Peripheries "patrimonializing" the center was a 180-degree change in relation to the trajectory followed by the pioneer cases of western Europe, where the center bureaucratized the peripheries.

The lord-driven variant of state formation in Latin America also departed from the pioneering experience but in a distinct way. The lord avoided the incorporation of peripheries. The key reason was that periphery incorporation was costly and provided no benefits. In contrast to the Latin American entrepreneur, the lord did not need to expand his political coalition because his power was already hegemonic in his clientelistic fiefdom. A larger political arena would jeopardize his hegemony. In contrast to the western European warrior, the Latin American lord did not need additional manpower because he faced negligible threats of invasion. Since the lord is the pinnacle of a patrimonial pyramid, lord-driven state formation is based on *top-down patrimonialism*.

In the party-led variant, no master plan existed for the incorporation or exclusion of peripheries. The center incorporated peripheries as a by-product of rival local partisan clubs competing to create extensive political networks. Party leaders in the center did not demand transformation of the peripheries. When peripheries were dominated by patrimonial lords, the needs of the party were better served by the preservation of the lord's local position. Preservation secured contingents of clients who were mobilized as voters in times of elections and as soldiers when partisan competition escalated into armed conflict. Party-driven state formation fuels *network patrimonialism*.

In sum, the commercial environment of state formation in Latin America supplied ports, parties, and lords—the agents of territory consolidation—with a level of freedom and resources to create territorial units that had no antecedent in modern times. Peripheries were militarily expendable. Political leaders in the emerging capitals of Latin America could afford the luxury of making decisions about peripheral incorporation or exclusion on the basis of the coalitional dividends associated with them. If peripheries did not serve a coalitional purpose, they were excluded. If they served a coalitional purpose, they were incorporated via mutually convenient arrangements, a central clause of which was the preservation of patrimonial institutions.

Before Argentina

Four Failed States

ARGENTINA IS A TERRITORIAL NOVELTY. Although Buenos Aires, Argentina's capital, began the fight for independence in 1810, only fifty years later did the territories of Buenos Aires and those of the rest of what today is Argentina merge as a single political unit. By 1820, the area corresponding to present-day Argentina had exploded into a dozen small sovereignties. A common thread in Argentine national historiography is to "read history backward" by assuming that the dynamics across the postcolonial minisovereignties were leading to the creation of the Argentine state. However, in the political geography of South America before the 1860s, Argentina was never an inevitable outcome, and most of the times, it was not even a likely one. The "pre-Argentina" political space had no special propensities to become Argentina. Argentina is the result of a distinct combination of long-term antecedent conditions and short-term political struggles and negotiations. Struggles and negotiations could at different points have taken different turns from the ones they actually did, and they could have either produced a large number of smaller countries than Argentina or made portions of present-day Argentina join neighboring countries, like Uruguay.

In the fifty years after independence, the territory of Argentina hosted four failed states. Since only the fifth attempt at state formation succeeded, Argentina's nineteenth-century trajectory could be summarized as "Four Funerals and a Wedding," in a slight but crucial permutation of the title of the British comedy. Before 1862, only two periods were marked by a relatively stable political geography. They are what historiography customarily calls *Pax Rosista* (1829-52) and "Divided Country" (1853-61).

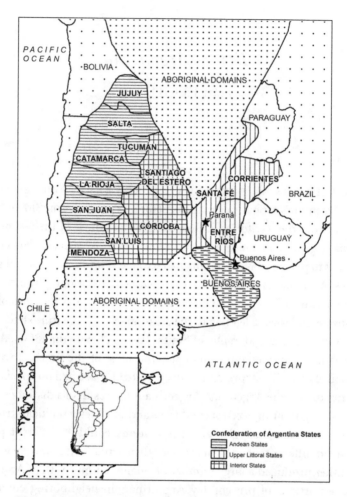

Map 5.1. Ministates before unification, 1830–50

    Yet the political geography of the two periods was radically different
from that of present-day Argentina. The *Pax Rosista* was, rather than a single sovereign country, a loose confederation of fourteen independent states,
each with its own army and tax-collection system (Map 5.1). Buenos Aires
was becoming the most powerful rudimentary port state in Spanish America and was dominated by a rural lord, Juan Manuel de Rosas (who gave the
period its name). As expected by the theory presented in Chapter 4, Buenos

Aires fully embraced a lord-driven pathway of state formation. Rural lord Rosas systematically resisted union with poorer regions because it would have induced some form of power and wealth sharing. Sharing was not in Rosas's plans because both his political power and his private fortune depended on the continued separation of Buenos Aires.

During the *Pax Rosista*, Buenos Aires was economically ahead of the other thirteen states in part because location allowed its port to hold the monopoly of taxation over international maritime trade. Three other potential rudimentary port states in present-day Argentina, in the so-called Upper Littoral region, were endowed with rivers leading to the sea. However, following a funnel pattern, all those rivers led to the River Plate, at the mouth of which Buenos Aires had built its port. Hence, ships had to cross the port of Buenos Aires before connecting the other rudimentary port states and the Atlantic markets. The Upper Littoral rudimentary port states depended on the goodwill of Rosas to gain direct access to international trade and to collect revenues from import tariffs. Rosas never granted free passage, thereby downgrading the three states from rudimentary port states to dynamic interiors that lacked the necessary fiscal resources for independent state formation. That is, state formation in Buenos Aires impeded state formation in neighboring regions. Conflicts around the privileges of the port of Buenos Aires became the core obstacle to the formation of Argentina.

The Divided Country (1853–61) was the other period of a stable political geography. Yet, in the period, two separate states coexisted in the territory of present-day Argentina: the state of Buenos Aires and the Confederación of thirteen provinces (former ministates; see Map 5.2). The notion of the Divided Country is one example of reading history backward, for at least one of the states, Buenos Aires, could have become a separate country on a permanent basis. The country was not "divided" because the "country" had not been formed in the first place. The creation of the confederation was led by the most important rural lord outside Buenos Aires, Justo José de Urquiza. His goal was unambiguous: to destroy Rosas's navigation and fiscal monopoly. The monopoly was hurting Entre Ríos, Urquiza's state, more than any other region. Located in the Upper Littoral, Entre Ríos had the potential to become as dynamic an economy as Buenos Aires or Uruguay, but it needed free navigation of the rivers connecting it to the Atlantic markets. Urquiza took the lead in fighting Buenos Aires because he

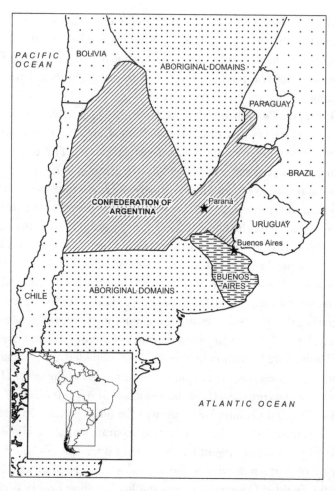

Map 5.2. Duopoly of violence, 1852–61

was comfortably the main landowner in Entre Ríos, and whatever was good for Entre Ríos's economy would be extremely profitable for Urquiza himself.

Argentina was created only in 1862, after Buenos Aires's leadership changed hands. In the early 1850s, Urquiza and his coalition destroyed the power of Buenos Aires's lord, Rosas, and control of the main rudimentary port state was taken by Bartolome Mitre, the epitome of a political entrepreneur.

Argentina illustrates the role of the political entrepreneur better than any other case precisely because the same region that had been staunchly separatist under the rule of a rural lord became expansionary when an entrepreneur became its leader.

The driver for the formation of Argentina was the entrepreneur's political ambition, the need to create a political arena larger than Buenos Aires itself. Argentina became an aggregation of regions in which the coalitional support for the founding entrepreneur was more secure than within the limits of Buenos Aires.

The purpose of this chapter and Chapter 6 is to account for the formation of the Argentine state. This chapter focuses on four failed states before 1860, and Chapter 6 focuses on successful state formation in the early 1860s. The comparative analysis of the failed states is valuable in two ways. First, it helps to identify causes of state failure and, *a contrario*, the conditions of potential success at state formation. Second, it contributes to a historical understanding of the 1860–62 process that resulted in the creation of the Argentine state. Over the course of the rise and fall of every failed state, a set of legacies was created that decisively shaped the range of options available to the political leaders who did succeed at state formation. The legacies of the four failed states were the antecedent conditions that entrepreneur Mitre had to deal with in the early 1860s.

A common thread running through the analysis of this chapter is the critical importance of the formula of territorial governance, as defined in Chapter 4. This formula is the set of institutions that distribute power and wealth both across the constituent states that will become subnational units of the new, larger state and between the subnational units and the national authorities. Typically, small sovereignties considering unification into a larger territorial unit compare the option of (1) continued separation and three broad categories of territorial formulas of unification: (2) a confederation, (3) a federal system, and (4) a unitary state.

Projects to form a state by combining small sovereignties before 1862 failed because some of the small sovereignties feared becoming losers in the new distribution of power and wealth induced by the formula of territorial governance that was part of the project. In the territory of Argentina before 1862, no individual minisovereignty was ever able or willing to fully conquer the rest. Even the weakest states and regions were able to demand a modicum of political autonomy and a share of the wealth generated in the most dynamic regions.[1]

Failed State 1: The Revolutionary State, 1810-20
Overview

Buenos Aires began the struggle against Spanish colonial rule in 1810. Defeating Spanish imperial forces, a formidable achievement, proved much easier than effectively controlling the newly independent territories. The patriot forces of Buenos Aires did try to create a state. The "Revolutionary State" would exert power throughout the territories that the revolutionary armies managed to liberate from Spain, which roughly corresponded to present-day Argentina and Uruguay. However, the revolutionary effort had demanded the improvised transformation of rural notables into warlords, or caudillos. Caudillos in turn provoked the failure of the Revolutionary State.

The 1810s were a paradoxical decade. On the one hand, Buenos Aires succeeded at causing irreparable damage to Spanish rule in South America. Buenos Aires organized and funded two large military forces, the Ejército del Norte and the Ejército de los Andes, under the commands of Manuel Belgrano and José de San Martín, Argentina's national heroes. The Ejército del Norte liberated about half the territory of the Viceroyalty of the River Plate (Spanish forces stopped it at what today is the border between Argentina and Bolivia). The Ejército de los Andes freed the Captaincy of Chile in 1818, and three years later, it successfully invaded Lima, the stronghold of Spanish power in South America. On the other hand, by 1820, the territorial dominion of the Revolutionary State was confined to the limits of a minirepublic composed of the city of Buenos Aires and its immediate rural hinterland. After liberating a territory larger than western Europe, Buenos Aires was reduced by internal rival forces to an area smaller than Portugal.

The Source of Caudillo Power

The main rivals of Buenos Aires's revolutionary elite were a product of their own creation, the caudillos, rural notables turned into warlords.[2] Several regions, to the north and the east of Buenos Aires, remained loyal to Spain, which created multiple battlefronts. The combination of multiple battlefronts and limited resources forced the revolutionary elite to improvise methods of army formation. Caudillos are children of revolutionary improvisation. The first generation of caudillos emerged in the course of military mobilization against imperial enemies to the east of the River Plate and then in the course of the redeployment of the Ejército del Norte. Buenos Aires decided to face Spanish resistance to the east, which was based in Montevideo, by delegating the bulk of the military effort to José Gervasio Artigas, a local potentate and former chief of rural militias under colonial rule who pledged allegiance to the cause of independence. Artigas, Uruguay's national hero, was the first caudillo in the River Plate area. He excelled at military mobilization and managed to gain control of Uruguay's entire rural hinterland, but he was unable to subdue the city of Montevideo, which remained a bastion of Spanish resistance.

Challenges to State Formation

After only two years of joint military efforts against Spain, the revolutionary elite in Buenos Aires and Artigas had the first clash of a series of confrontations that would eventually cause the destruction of both. Artigas not only pursued liberation from Spanish imperial rule but also headed the resistance against Buenos Aires's plan to centralize authority. Artigas and the Buenos Aires elite agreed in principle to unite the newly liberated territories of the former viceroyalty. Yet they had opposite preferences for the formula of territorial governance. Artigas wanted a loose confederation of small states, whereas Buenos Aires's revolutionary elite strove for a unitary state ruling over a large territory.

Artigas's military mobilization did not confine itself to Uruguay but spread westward into the northern sections of Buenos Aires, provoking the separation of what would become the Upper Littoral states. Artigas's influence even reached Córdoba in the geographical center of present-day Argentina. The same way that Buenos Aires had delegated military power to Artigas, Artigas selected local potentates in the Upper Littoral states of present-day Argentina to enlarge his army, a military tactic that would help him both in his fight against imperial powers and in his aim to strengthen his position vis-à-vis Buenos Aires. In turn, the same way that Artigas got out

Map 5.3. Liga de los Pueblos Libres, 1815–20

from under the control of his recruiters in Buenos Aires, his lieutenants in the Upper Littoral states would eventually escape Artigas's control.

Artigas's tactics caused the political subdivision of a natural economic region into multiple informal military jurisdictions. The subdivision became permanent and was the root cause of many of the state-formation challenges that the River Plate would recurrently face.

Between 1814 and 1815, under Artigas's so-called Protectorship, a new state was formed, the Liga de los Pueblos Libres, which was independent both from Spain and from Buenos Aires (see Map 5.3). The league was a loose confederation of five newly created minisovereignties: Uruguay, Entre Ríos, Santa Fe, Corrientes, and Córdoba. With the formation of the Liga, Artigas had enough power to make an attempt at conquering Buenos Aires.

To confront the threat posed by the Liga, the revolutionary government of Buenos Aires made a bold decision: it agreed in 1816 to the invasion of Uruguay by Brazil. Buenos Aires's decision reflects how fearful it was of Artigas's Liga. Buenos Aires essentially exchanged a substantial section of the former viceroyalty—and the purity with which it had embraced the principles of emancipation—for a small geopolitical relief provided by the partition of Artigas's confederation. In 1820, the Luso-Brazilian Empire annexed Uruguay (renamed Cisplatina province) and provoked the extinction of the Liga. The governors of the other states in the Liga, Francisco Ramírez and Estanislao López, caudillo rulers of Entre Ríos and Santa Fe—originally Artigas's lieutenants—profited from the Uruguayan hero's defeat to release themselves from his tutelary power. By not allowing Artigas to enter Entre Ríos, Ramírez forced Artigas into exile in Paraguay, from which he never returned.

Failure

The political neutralization of Artigas, however, was not enough to prevent the collapse of Buenos Aires. In 1819, the revolutionary elite from Buenos Aires made an attempt to place a range of neighboring regions under its full control by sponsoring a constitution with a unitary formula. States in the Andes, the Interior, and the Upper Littoral would become provinces of a larger country, and their political autonomy, including the right to choose their governors, would be eliminated. Authorities in the provinces would be delegates from the center, designated by Buenos Aires. The bid for centralization backfired. Caudillos in the Upper Littoral correctly viewed the 1819 constitution as their death sentence and got ready for armed conflict.

The Revolutionary State in Buenos Aires ordered the redeployment of the professional armies, the Ejército de los Andes and the Ejército del Norte, to repress recalcitrant caudillos. San Martín refused. After liberating Chile in 1817, his plan was to sail the Pacific northward and fight the Spanish forces at the very source of their power, Lima. San Martín's priority was to lead an independence movement of a truly continental scale, so he dismissed Buenos Aires's duel with the Upper Littoral caudillos as a myopic quarrel that would only distract valuable resources from the battle against the real enemy. Belgrano did respond to the request, but his Ejército del

Norte, under the command of General Juan Bautista Bustos, mutinied in the staging post of Arequito, in Santa Fe. Allegedly, Bustos preferred fighting Spaniards in Upper Peru rather than caudillos in the Upper Littoral. However, on his way back to the battlefront, Bustos chose to station his battalions in Córdoba and used it to capture the government of the ministate. Bustos became just another caudillo. In early 1820, the Upper Littoral caudillos, with a decisive contribution of the cavalry, easily defeated the small army in Buenos Aires in the Battle of Cepeda (the "ten-minute battle").

Legacy

The Revolutionary State made war, but war "unmade" the Revolutionary State. The revolution taught cruel lessons to the leaders of Buenos Aires. Buenos Aires had funded the finest army of the wars of independence in Latin America, the Ejército de los Andes, which was truly continental both in ambition and in achievement. The fiscal effort was so taxing that some battlefronts were taken care of by an improvised delegation of military responsibilities to local notables in rural areas. Rural mobilization proved effective at army building but disastrous for state formation, as it was the cradle for caudillos who fragmented the territory that the Revolutionary State was meant to consolidate. Particularly consequential for the long term was the subdivision of the Great Pampas—an economic region with unique productive potential—into multiple fiefdoms, whose future relations would be marked by fiscal competition and political conflict rather than economic cooperation.

Failed State 2: The Unitary State, 1820–28
Overview

After the 1820 collapse, the constituent units of the Revolutionary State gained full sovereignty. The pre-Argentina political space was fully atomized in the sense that every city or rural village and its immediate hinterland became a ministate. All minisovereignties lived under full separation. In 1824, former revolutionary leaders revived the attempt to build a unitary state. It failed again. This time the key opponent was Buenos Aires itself. Elites in

Buenos Aires were not unitary anymore. They embraced separation or confederation, a change of preference that had strong economic roots: Buenos
Aires was becoming a rudimentary port state and did not want to share its
wealth with laggard neighbors.

Trade-Led State Formation in
Buenos Aires

In 1820, elites of Buenos Aires abandoned their project of dominating the
territory of the former Viceroyalty of the River Plate. Instead, they focused
on strengthening political order within the much more limited space of
the city of Buenos Aires and its rural hinterland, under the conviction
that local political order would create substantial economic prosperity.
The defeat of Buenos Aires at Cepeda in 1820 had opened a period of
chaos in Buenos Aires. Large sections of the rural working class and the
urban poor remained mobilized and willing to follow rival leaders to settle
political differences by military methods. However, chaos was brief. The
well-organized rural militias under the command of Martín Rodríguez and
Juan Manuel de Rosas managed to control the situation and reimpose political order by 1821. Rodríguez became governor of Buenos Aires, and Rosas
returned to private life.

Rodríguez led a sociopolitical coalition that focused on developing the
economy of Buenos Aires. Independence had broken down the commercial
restrictions imposed by Spanish imperial mercantilism and thereby created
unprecedented economic opportunities. Buenos Aires was abundant in fertile lands and wild cattle. Rodríguez and his allies expected that securing
cattle ranchers an adequate business climate would create a boom based on
the production of hides, tallow, and especially jerked beef, for which the slave
economies of Brazil and Cuba created an endless demand. The wars of independence and the ensuing conflict with Artigas and his lieutenants had
diverted massive amounts of human and material resources from productive
use and had thereby blocked economic progress. To ignite growth, Rodríguez and his right-hand collaborator, Bernardino Rivadavia, under the newly
formed Party of Order, implemented three key policies: the transfer of large
tracts of public lands to private hands, which eventually created a landowning class with kingdom-size estates; the expansion and fortification of the

southern frontier of Buenos Aires, beyond which a vast array of hostile seminomadic tribes were always ready for looting raids called *malones* (big evils); and the creation of a disciplined supply of rural workers—as scarce a resource in the Pampas as land was abundant—through the implementation of vagrancy laws.

Economic results of the policies by Rodríguez and Rivadavia far exceeded even the most optimistic expectations. In a few years, Buenos Aires became a rudimentary port state. The growth of exports had indirect but crucial fiscal effects. By inaugurating a substantial and stable inflow of hard currency, export-led growth allowed for an expansion of imports, which in turn became the main source of government revenue. The taxation structure of Buenos Aires relied heavily on import tariffs, which were low—they pursued fiscal purposes, not protectionist ones—and minimized taxes on exports (property taxes were negligible). The tax structure clearly reflected the close ties uniting the political and economic elites of Buenos Aires. A substantial section of Buenos Aires's landowning class was being created during this very period. For the next half a century, the new landowning class came to have a considerable influence in Buenos Aires's politics.

Rodríguez, Rivadavia, and their Party of Order inaugurated, within the confines of Buenos Aires, what in Part 1 was called "trade-led state formation" as opposed to "war-led state formation." In effect, in the early 1820s, Buenos Aires created the rudiments of an independent state by betting that a modicum of political pacification would create a virtuous circle in which enhanced export opportunities would produce a higher level of fiscal resources, which in turn could finance a new array of pro-growth class goods, including an even more secure business environment. By pursuing trade-led state formation, Rodríguez and Rivadavia broke off with the canonical form of war-led state formation experienced in early modern Europe. More important, they switched the state-formation path that the very Revolutionary State had set in motion. The atomization of present-day Argentina into thirteen minisovereignties by the end of the 1810s had created a political scenario in which it is easy to imagine that reciprocal military pressures among rulers would have fostered geopolitical competition. In turn, such competition would have gradually resulted in the emergence of a reduced number of fully bureaucratic states (perhaps only one) by selecting out the minisovereignties that retained patrimonial forms of rule. By pursuing trade-led state formation, Rodríguez and Rivadavia removed Buenos Aires from that environment.

The Geographic Basis of the Conflict over State Formation

Buenos Aires's new private wealth was the result of the combination of local peace, natural endowments, and international prices. Yet Buenos Aires's *public* (fiscal) wealth was in part rooted in the exploitation of the other minisovereignties. Buenos Aires's revenues derived from import taxes, and its location at the mouth of the River Plate allowed its port to control navigation over the entire River Plate basin, which was vital to connect consumers in the Upper Littoral, the Andes, and the Interior with markets abroad. A monopolistic port enabled Buenos Aires to collect taxes from goods consumed by all the minisovereignties of the former viceroyalty and spend the proceeds only within the limits of the city and its immediate rural jurisdiction. Consumers of all minisovereignties thus partially funded the local class goods that allowed the takeoff of Buenos Aires's economy.

The political economy of state formation in Buenos Aires hurt the prospects of state formation in the other minisovereignties. But the negative effect worked differently in the states of the Upper Littoral and those in the Andes and the Interior. In colonial times, many of the economies of the Andes and the Interior had specialized in the production of goods required by the silver economy of Potosí, from primary products like mules, timber, and fruits to simple manufactures like carts, liquor, and woolen textiles. The separation of Upper Peru (present-day Bolivia) during the wars of independence and the subsequent decline of the Potosí mines extinguished the most important source of demand for the Interior's products. In turn, free-trade policies embraced by Buenos Aires deliberately encouraged the importation of European textiles, implements, and foodstuffs that were cheaper and better than those of the Interior. Some economies of the Interior would never recover from foreign competition.

For the Upper Littoral provinces, especially Santa Fe and Entre Ríos, the problem was not that Buenos Aires imposed too much free trade but that it granted too little. In effect, Buenos Aires's control of the entire River Plate basin, based on its physical ability to block navigation of the tributary Uruguay and Paraná Rivers, prevented direct contact between the economies of Entre Ríos and Santa Fe and markets overseas. The customhouses in these states received products that had already been taxed in Buenos Aires and thus took away from their rulers a substantial source of revenue for state formation. Entre Ríos and Santa Fe were almost replicas of Buenos Aires with regard to the quality and abundance of land.

Minisovereignties other than Buenos Aires also funded themselves by resorting to tariffs. However, the volume of commerce between them was small, and tariffs shrunk it even further. From their very inception, most minisovereignties lived in bankruptcy. The only solution to their fiscal precariousness was to force Buenos Aires to share its wealth. The solution would prove extremely elusive for two reasons. First, throughout the 1820s, all the minisovereignties other than Buenos Aires were torn between mutually incompatible formulas of territorial governance. On the one hand, they all wanted political autonomy, for which only separation or confederation would be suitable institutions. On the other, they needed either a federation or a unitary state in order to create a central government that was strong enough to force Buenos Aires to share its wealth. Second, states in the Interior and the Upper Littoral, although aligned on the same side with regard to their interest in forcing Buenos Aires to share its wealth, had opposite preferences with regard to trade policies: the Upper Littoral states preferred free trade, whereas Interior and Andean states wanted to shield their primitive industries under protectionist tariffs.

In sum, the fundamental fiscal problem of state formation in Argentina was the ability of Buenos Aires to extract surplus from consumers in other states. One solution to that problem was the formation of an alliance among the other twelve provinces, but they were divided into blocs, Andes/Interior versus Upper Littoral, with different preferences about economic policy.

The Rise of the Unitary State

By the mid-1820s, the unexpected benefits of isolation created a division within the political elites of Buenos Aires. Some considered that the new prosperity should translate into political power and prompt a new attempt at unifying the minisovereignties, whereas others wanted to preserve local autonomy indefinitely under the fear that unification would either involve renewed armed conflict or create institutions of wealth transfer from Buenos Aires to the rest of the states. Starting in 1824, two external factors temporarily tipped the balance in favor of the pro-unification political elites: the economic incentive from Great Britain, which would recognize independence and extend commercial agreements if the minisovereignties became a single country, and the geopolitical threat from the Brazilian Empire, which, after annexing Uruguay in 1821, was forced to block several attempts by Uruguayan leaders to rejoin a union of River Plate states.

For the new attempt at unification, Buenos Aires invited minisovereignties to form a constituent assembly. Immediately after, an agreement was signed with Great Britain, in which sovereignty was recognized and commercial advantages were exchanged. At the same time, fueled by an increasingly bellicose public opinion in Buenos Aires, the assembly also decided to accept the request of incorporation by Uruguay, which was an informal but unambiguous declaration of war against Brazil. Most Uruguayan leaders wanted independence from Brazil; but they needed an outside ally, and Buenos Aires was the obvious choice.

In 1826, in preparation for a new war effort, the assembly created the "United Provinces of the River Plate" and appointed Rivadavia as president— the first one ruling over a territory roughly equivalent to present-day Argentina. The Party of Order, which had made such a big effort to create and strengthen an independent state in Buenos Aires, split itself and provoked the polarization of Buenos Aires's politics. As new president, Rivadavia revealed himself a direct heir of the Revolutionary State when he began to mobilize political support within the assembly to relaunch the project to unite all minisovereignties under a unitary formula. On the other hand, Gregorio Las Heras, who succeeded Rodríguez as governor of Buenos Aires, was reluctant to support Rivadavia, given both the catastrophic antecedent of 1819–20 and the new constellation of interests among Buenos Aires's landowners, who embraced separation.

As the first step in his state-formation project, Rivadavia presented the "Bill of Capitalization," which separated the city of Buenos Aires from its rural hinterland and made it a "national" jurisdiction under the control of the president. The bill precipitated events. The original split in the Party of

Order became full-blown rivalry. Dissidents within the Party of Order joined the opposition, which in turn was backed by large landowners of Buenos Aires, especially the tight-knit network centered on the Anchorena, Rosas, and Terrero families. They saw the loss of the city and, most important, the port, which generated the revenue to enhance the functioning of the cattle-ranching economy, as an existential threat.

Despite the opposition of Buenos Aires, Rivadavia and the assembly decided to move forward with a unitarian formula. The other states also opposed the project. With the lessons of the failed 1819 constitution in mind, and after learning about the economic potential of Buenos Aires, they now preferred a federation formula, which preserved their autonomy at the same time that it created a central government that could force Buenos Aires to share its wealth. Against the interests of the minisovereignties, the assembly, which included representatives from all of them, approved a unitary constitution. The paradoxical mismatch between the assembly's decision and the provinces' preferences has a simple explanation: provincial representatives betrayed the rulers in their provinces. Whereas provincial rulers were caudillos, the representatives were members of the educated elites whom the caudillos had marginalized from political life. The 1826 constitution was a death sentence for provincial governors, and several representatives in the assembly, coming from displaced minorities in their own provinces, were more than willing to sign it.

Backlash and Collapse

The unitary state collapsed because it could not face three battlefronts at the same time: the veto of Buenos Aires's landowning class, the war against Brazil, and the federalist reaction of key caudillos in the interior against the unitary constitution.

The unitary state created a big loser: the emerging landowning class of Buenos Aires, which preferred port revenues to be spent in local class goods, like the protection and expansion of the southern frontier or the improvement of the roads between the *estancia* (large rural estate) and the *saladero* (beef-salting plant) and between the *saladero* and the port.

After Rivadavia agreed to the annexation of Uruguay, the Brazilian navy blocked navigation of the River Plate. The army of the Provincias Unidas won the biggest battle of the war at Ituzaingó in February 1827. However, Ituzaingó's victory neither won the war nor broke the blockade of the River Plate. English merchants began to lose business, got impatient with the prolongation of conflict, and pressured British diplomats to find a solution.

The war against Brazil and the resistance against the 1826 constitution got intertwined in the Andean states. Rivadavia had sent General Gregorio Aráoz de Lamadrid to the northwestern provinces to recruit manpower for the war. Facundo Quiroga, the caudillo of La Rioja, led his rural militias to resist Lamadrid's efforts. In the process, he gained control over three provinces, Catamarca, Tucumán, and San Juan. Facundo not only blocked Rivadavia's efforts but also persuaded the provinces of Córdoba and Santiago del Estero—also dominated by caudillos—to derail the unitary state-formation project. Irreversibly weakened by caudillo resistance, the Rivadavia government was barely able to continue the war against Brazil. The solution to the conflict over Uruguay was provided by English diplomacy, in particular, Lord Ponsonby's Solomonic proposal that Uruguay should belong to none of the rival powers but become an independent country. In June 1827, Rivadavia tendered his resignation as president, the assembly dissolved, and provinces regained full power as minisovereignties. Argentina and its president lasted one year.

Rivadavia left the political scene for good, but his unitary project would have a brief revival led by an unexpected successor: the demobilized army of the war against Brazil. Two generals of the war, Juan Lavalle and José María Paz, used the forces under their command to gain control of the cities of Buenos Aires and Córdoba, respectively. To repel Lavalle's forces, Rosas returned from private life in command of large rural militias. Rosas was the leader of the new constellation of economic interests and political actors created over the course of Buenos Aires's first export boom. Although they called themselves federals, like some caudillos in the Interior and the Upper Littoral, they rejected any form of unification—either under a federal or a unitary formula—that created a national power that could force Buenos Aires to share its wealth. In truth, they wanted either separation or a loose confederation that did not produce any special commitments between Buenos Aires and the other minisovereignties. Overpowered by Rosas, Lavalle's rule over Buenos Aires lasted five months. Rosas inaugurated a long dictatorship in Buenos Aires. As expected by the theory of Chapter 4, as a rural lord, he pursued trade-led state formation of a rudimentary port state.

General Paz's endeavor was initially more successful than Lavalle's. In early 1829, Paz displaced Bustos from power in Córdoba and then defeated Facundo, the most prominent rural lord in the Interior. In a few months, Paz gained control of Córdoba, San Juan, La Rioja, Mendoza, San Luis, and Catamarca, with which he formed a "Unitary League," an incipient state, parallel to Buenos Aires. Paz's league faced two fundamental challenges: the power of the rural lords, who abhorred the unitarian formula, and the lack of fiscal resources to defeat them.

Legacy

An irreversible legacy of the Rivadavian state was the rise of the landowning elite of Buenos Aires. Buenos Aires's exports of jerked beef and hides provided the initial profits of what would become the wealthiest social class in Latin America in the second half of the nineteenth century. With Rosas in power, the landowning class of Buenos Aires had an obvious source of "instrumental" influence in politics. Rosas was himself one of the ten wealthiest landowners in Buenos Aires and had family ties with the Anchorena clan, the largest landowner in South America. Direct control of political power secured an undistorted translation of the class's economic interests into public policies. Yet the landowning class also had a key source of "structural" power. Their exports provided the hard currency to sustain high levels of imports, and imports, through customs tariffs, were the fiscal basis of the emerging state of Buenos Aires. Structural fiscal dependence of Buenos Aires on the health of cattle-ranching activities secured landowning elites a less direct but far more permanent source of political power.

The other ministates of the River Plate region, from La Rioja to Entre Ríos, were economically stagnant. No new economic class emerged within them. Yet they developed a distinct type of local ruling class, the patrimonial caudillos. Moreover, the backlash against Rivadavia's ephemeral unitary state made caudillos extremely protective of their bastions, and through clientelistic networks, they acquired the power to veto any form of unification under a formula that was not federal.

The economic interests of the landowning class in Buenos Aires were incompatible with union under a federal formula. Federalism involved a level of power sharing with peripheral ruling classes that risked the redistribution of wealth from Buenos Aires to the Interior and the Upper Littoral. The combination of the ability of peripheral caudillos to veto unification under a unitary formula, on the one hand, and the power of the landowning interests of Buenos Aires to veto unification under a federal formula, on the other, created a permanent stalemate between state-formation projects and a durable obstacle to the formation of Argentina. It provided the background for the emergence of the *Pax Rosista*.

Failed State 3: *Pax Rosista*, 1829–52
Overview

The 1830s and 1840s are the time of Rosas's rule. The period began as a hybrid between separation and a very loose confederation of minisovereignties. In the late 1830s, it began to morph into a specific type of confederation, namely, a suzerainty, under which small sovereignties formed an international system of states on key dimensions, including the preservation of local armies and the enforcement of interstate tariffs. Yet Buenos Aires had become a regional hegemon. Buenos Aires took advantage of an initial superiority in economic and military resources in order to make such superiority more substantial and permanent. The new superiority, however, was not secure enough to prevent rebellion and collapse. In 1851, the Upper Littoral ministate of Entre Ríos formed a military alliance with the ministate of Corrientes, Brazil, and Argentine exiles in Montevideo to force Rosas out of power. The fall of Rosas was the breakdown of the suzerainty.

Buenos Aires's Separation

Rosas became governor of Buenos Aires in 1829 after defeating Lavalle's brief attempt at reviving the unitary project. Given the chaos resulting from the clash between unitarians and federalists, the legislature of Buenos Aires endowed Rosas with extraordinary powers to restore peace. Rosas's new order involved substantial degrees of censorship against the unitarian press and prompted the first of several waves of political émigrés. Although the original power basis of Rosas was the rural militia he had led since 1820, by the late 1820s his constituency expanded to include the urban lower classes that had been mobilized in the intervening years by antiunitarian leaders. Large landowners of Buenos Aires linked to Rosas through family or commercial ties were his natural political partners. The rural potentates lacking private ties to Rosas knew that his power was unparalleled and were quick to accept his political leadership as the most effective approach to resume trade-led state formation within the confines of Buenos Aires.

The threat from General Paz's Liga del Interior, whose ambition was to use the Interior as the territorial basis to relaunch a large-scale unitary project, forced Rosas to engage in politics *beyond* Buenos Aires. Rosas looked for allies in the Upper Littoral, which since Artigas's times was a bastion of antiunitarian forces. In early 1830, the states of Buenos Aires, Santa Fe, and Entre Ríos signed the Pacto Federal (Federal pact). From Rosas's perspective, the purpose of the agreement was to pool military forces and repel Paz's league. For the governors of the other states, the agreement also contained the promise of future unification under a federal formula, which in turn was a means to get a share of the material prosperity of Buenos Aires. Unification also contained the promise of the end of Buenos Aires's monopolistic control over the navigation of the River Plate basin.

In the early 1830s, then, two blocs of ministates competed for supremacy within the territory of what today is Argentina. The political banners of the blocs would have been unimaginable only fifteen years earlier. The Interior, a traditional bastion of federalism, was united in a Unitary League, whereas Buenos Aires, the birthplace of unitarianism, was the leader of the federal bloc.

Paz was an expert military tactician, but a careless mistake allowed federal soldiers to capture him when Paz walked unarmed into a military camp under the wrong impression that it belonged to his army. After Paz's capture, the Unitary League quickly unraveled. Although Paz's accidental fall invites counterfactual speculation, it was impossible for Paz's occupation of the Interior to last. His project had no economic basis. The Interior states he controlled were poor, and both their local oligarchies and popular classes repudiated his project. In the early 1830s, a unitarian project of state formation required military conquest of recalcitrant provinces, and conquest required a volume of fiscal resources that only the customhouse of Buenos Aires could produce. Yet, after experiencing the economic boom of the 1820s, Buenos Aires had more profitable ways of using its money than embarking on military conquest.

After the Pacto Federal defeated the Liga del Interior, the ministates were purged of unitarian influences. Andean and Interior provinces joined the Pacto Federal. It seemed that an opportunity was opened to transform the Pacto into a project of large-scale state formation uniting all the minisovereignties under a federal system. A "Representative Commission" created by the Pacto Federal decided to convoke a constituent assembly in early 1832. Representatives of Corrientes and Córdoba drafted a unification plan. According to letters that were supposed to be confidential, the plan of Corrientes and Córdoba was that the "provinces work against Buenos Aires" to "deprive it from the control of national revenues." They complained about the fact that "rivers and revenues monopolized by one province [i.e., Buenos Aires]" made the "whole country poor and miserable."[3] The letters were intercepted by Facundo and transmitted to Rosas, who reacted by recalling Buenos Aires's delegate. Under pressure from Rosas, the governor of Santa Fe, Estanislao López, pointed out that, after defeating the Liga, the Representative Commission had no political purpose and induced it to vote its own dissolution. Rosas had co-opted López and Facundo.

An informal triumvirate of caudillos, topped by Rosas and including López and Facundo, ruled the minisovereignties, subdivided into three blocs: Buenos Aires, Upper Littoral, and Andes/Interior. The triumvirate was a serious obstacle against the creation of Argentina. Rosas opposed it because Buenos Aires did not want to share power and wealth. López and Facundo could have joined forces to defeat Rosas and Buenos Aires. Yet an alliance between the two secondary caudillos was unlikely. Although the personal misgivings between López and Facundo are well documented, what made coordination fail was the deeper incompatibility between a pro-free-trade Upper Littoral and a protectionist Interior.

In late 1832, Rosas stepped down from Buenos Aires's government because the legislature refused to extend him extraordinary powers. Rosas's de facto power, based on his leadership of rural militias and a central position in the network of Buenos Aires's landlords, allowed him to retain decisive influence over policy even without a formal position in government. Two actions of Rosas out of power, the "Desert Campaign" and the "Facundo Mission," reveal how committed the coalition of interests he represented was to the cattle-ranching economy of Buenos Aires. Commitment to local interests translated into sabotage of projects to form Argentina.

The Desert Campaign was a military action against hostile native tribes on the other side of Buenos Aires's southern frontier. The campaign was funded by the government and by private landowners who had suffered the looting raids. As a result of Rosas's campaign, Buenos Aires's southern frontier reached the limits of the Patagonia region, which meant a formidable annexation of productive lands. The campaign revealed that, for Rosas and his partners, stepping down from a formal position of power was motivated not by constitutional limitations but by a distinct interest in economic expansion, which had priority over political ambitions. After Paz's defeat, the purge of unitarians across most minisovereignties, and the co-optation of Facundo and López, Rosas could return to what Buenos Aires's landlords considered at the time the raison d'être of their collective efforts, that is, the expansion and increased security of cattle-ranching activities.

The years out of power taught Rosas a key lesson. Given the rapidly growing economic disparity between Buenos Aires and the other states, and given that such disparity was in part rooted in Buenos Aires's monopoly of taxation over international trade, states in the Upper Littoral and the Interior would be an increasingly fertile ground for the incubation of threats against Buenos Aires's position. The threats ranged from looting raids led by small caudillos to formal leagues of ministates advocating a project of unification in which a central government, relatively independent of Buenos Aires, secured a more even distribution of the benefits derived from international commerce. Some political groups in the Interior and Andean states became willing to put aside their disagreements about trade policy with the Upper Littoral in order to form a unified front against Rosas. While still leading the Desert Campaign, Rosas had to make enormous political efforts to block unification projects.

The Facundo Mission was designed by Rosas to prevent a second attempt at the creation of Argentina. In 1834, Rosas ordered Facundo to travel across the northern provinces and campaign against projects of unification under a federal rule. Rosas wrote to Facundo the famous "Carta de la Hacienda de Figueroa," in which he made the case about the "inconvenience" of creating a central government. In his justification, Rosas claimed that the provinces were too poor to form a union. Rosas was putting the horse behind the cart because it was the lack of union that had made the provinces poor. But Rosas cared about power, not about truth. Rosas believed that his explicit disapproval of the creation of a central government, even if based on dubious logic, would suffice to abort the project.

Confederation and Suzerainty

In 1835, Rosas returned to power as governor of Buenos Aires. The legislature granted him, in addition to "extraordinary faculties" as in his 1829–32 term, the "Summation of Public Powers" on an indefinite basis. It was the formalization of a dictatorship, in which elections were celebrated on a regular basis but only one party was allowed to participate, voting became a plebiscitary demonstration of support for Rosas, independent media were forbidden, and other branches of government had no meaningful power.

The return of Rosas to power had a double origin. First, Facundo was assassinated during his mission to the northern states, which Rosas was quick to exploit politically by claiming the continued existence of anarchical forces and unitarian conspiracies. Second, the Federal Party of Buenos Aires split into two factions. Dissident federalists wanted a federal union and thereby were a threat to the economic privileges that Buenos Aires's landowning elites had recently discovered in both free trade and the revenues from the port. Rosas accused them of being "savage unitarians"—a ritual characterization of every force opposing Rosas, genuinely unitarian or not. Rosas's fear was that dissidents would look for federalist allies in the other ministates in order to defeat him and in the process make concessions that would eventually lead to the kind of large-scale state-formation project that Rosista federalists abhorred. Against this background, Rosista attacks against the opposition became systematic, and a second wave of political emigration took place.

As in his first government, Rosas's priority in his second government was the development of Buenos Aires's rural economy. However, in contrast to his first government, this time Rosas's goals required a substantially larger political effort to appease the other twelve states (which became thirteen in

1835 after Jujuy's secession from Salta). Rosas had to find a solution to two countervailing forces: the caudillos' defense of the political autonomy of their states and the expectation of the states to unify with Buenos Aires in order to get a share of its wealth. Rosas's solution was inherently fragile.

In order to preserve Buenos Aires's fiscal privileges and to appease the advocates of unification projects, the Rosista coalition chose a formula of territorial governance that involved a minimalist form of territorial consolidation, a loose confederation of the ministates, legally based on the 1831 Pacto Federal. The confederation was sustained by an implicit but clear deal between Buenos Aires and the other states: caudillos would preserve their political autonomy—including the ability to form a permanent army and raise taxes on goods entering and leaving their territories—while Buenos Aires, absent a federal state, would be exempt from any obligation of financing public goods that would benefit the entire confederation. Yet the economic grievances created by the lack of revenue sharing prompted several ministates to exploit the room left by the very permissiveness of the confederation in relation to the formation of local armies. Some states could at some point challenge Buenos Aires's position, on their own, in combination with other ministates, or allied with foreign powers.

Rosas's original plan in relation to the other ministates was to prevent conflict through a repertoire of strategies—including co-optation, concessions, and repression—that nevertheless should ideally have been much less costly than forming a full federal state that eliminated Buenos Aires's fiscal privileges. Despite the fact that the Rosista coalition had traditionally been a strong advocate of free trade, in 1836 Rosas's government passed a new tariff law that afforded a tenuous protection to some manufacturing and agricultural activities in the interior. At the time, Rosas thought that the combination of political autonomy afforded by the confederal organization and the economic concessions of the tariff law were enough to dissuade governors of the Interior and Upper Littoral provinces from projects of unification containing revenue- and power-sharing agreements.

A relatively exogenous event, the French blockade of the River Plate (1838–40), threatened Rosas's plan of maintaining a loose confederal arrangement on an indefinite basis and forced a mutation of Rosas's original design into a more costly formula of territorial governance, a suzerainty, a deviant form of confederation, which included higher doses of control and coercion.

France decided to block the port of Buenos Aires for two reasons: it wanted to obtain the same kind of preferential treatment that Rivadavia had granted Great Britain in 1822 (tariff concessions and the exemption of British citizens from military service) and to repeal the import duties that the port of Buenos Aires charged on French goods that were first unloaded in Montevideo (Montevideo was the beachhead of French merchants). The extra import tariffs that Rosas placed on goods transshipped from Montevideo was a piece of his overall strategy of giving the port of Buenos Aires a commercial and fiscal stranglehold on the entire River Plate basin. Rosas already controlled navigation of the Uruguay and Paraná Rivers by physically patrolling the mouth of the River Plate, but the Montevideo port, far away from the River Plate's mouth, could only be subdued through economic penalties.

The French blockade, which seriously weakened Buenos Aires's revenues, was taken as an opportunity by Rosas's enemies to challenge his rule. Key enemies of course were the old unitarians, some of them exiled in Montevideo, but they also included a number of federal forces throughout the confederation, which revealed that Rosas's appeasement strategies, even if carefully designed, were far from securing an indefinite peace with the ministates that resented Buenos Aires's fiscal monopoly. Corrientes, a federal bastion, and Lavalle, the old unitarian leader, joined forces in the Upper Littoral to invade Buenos Aires. At the same time, a number of cattle ranchers in the South of the very province of Buenos Aires rebelled in protest because of the impossibility of exporting their output due to the blockade. Finally, an alliance of northern ministates, the Coalición del Norte, including Tucumán, Salta, La Rioja and Catamarca, also rebelled under the expectation of coordinating military movements with the forces led by Lavalle.

Rosas decisively defeated his enemies on all battlefronts. He was helped by Lavalle's poor tactical decisions, which failed to coordinate the opposition foci. Rosas's repression was exemplary. Most rebellion leaders were executed. Punishment caused the extinction of rebellions in the Interior. Only Corrientes, in isolation, would continue to produce rebellions against Rosas, but General Justo José de Urquiza, Rosas's lieutenant and governor of Entre Ríos, repeatedly defeated them.

To prevent a repeat of the 1838–40 crisis, Rosas's politics changed drastically. He resorted to terror and executions in Buenos Aires and to increased intervention in the internal affairs of the other states. In 1835, Rosas had already intervened in the election of Córdoba's governor (the former governor was accused of plotting the assassination of Facundo and was executed). In 1838, after the death of Estanislao López (by natural causes, a rare ending among caudillos), Rosas again exerted pressure to place a protégé as governor of Santa Fe.[4] However, after the rebellion and collapse of the Coalición del Norte, Rosas openly dictated who the ruler of defeated states would be. In the early 1840s, a transition from unruly caudillos, like Facundo and López, to "tamed" (*mansos*) caudillos was completed.

In the terms of Chapter 4, Rosas single-handedly transformed all *state-breaking* rural lords in the Andes and the Interior into *state-taking* rural lords. Rosas himself was not willing to create a state beyond Buenos Aires, but any future state-formation venture that planned to unite Buenos Aires and the other states could benefit from the transformation of the provincial rural lords produced by Rosas. The tamed caudillos were also patrons of large blocs of rural clients. Yet, given that they owed their position to Rosas's blessing, they never raised the issue of forming a national state in which the provinces could have a meaningful stake. They knew Rosas hated large-scale state formation, and they offered full loyalty and utmost passivity in exchange for Rosas's blessing. Moreover, the French blockade provoked a scarcity of various types of good in Buenos Aires, which in turn prompted its governor to virtually repeal the 1836 tariff law. Not only had Rosas survived the blockade, but he emerged stronger from it.

In the mid-1840s, then, Rosas had established a deviant type of confederation. Among the standard attributes, it included the absence of a central state that overpowered the leading member of the confederation, that is, Buenos Aires; no institutions of revenue sharing among members existed; member states were able to raise tariffs against goods introduced from other states; they could also recruit their own militias; and the set of policies agreed on were reduced to "foreign affairs," the management of which were delegated to Rosas himself. However, Rosas's fiscal and trade policies had enormous externalities for the provinces, as Buenos Aires's tariffs affected private ventures, and the monopolization of revenues weakened the fiscal standing of the other states. The truly deviant attribute was the use of Rosas's de facto power to select friendly governors in a number of states, which is actually an attribute of unitary systems. The combination of various confederal attributes—all of which were meant to preserve Buenos Aires's economic privileges while respecting the local autonomy claimed by all the minisovereignties since Artigas's time—with some de facto unitary attributes built by Rosas in order to protect Buenos Aires's position made the so-called Confederación Rosista a suzerainty.

Rosas's suzerainty after the French blockade was put to a test with a new blockade of the Buenos Aires port (1845–48). It was jointly sustained by French and British forces in protest of Rosas's prohibition on navigating the River Plate tributaries, the Paraná and Uruguay Rivers, without paying taxes in the Buenos Aires port. The new blockade showed how successful Rosas's repression and interventions in the Interior and Andean states had been five years earlier. State caudillos, all of the state-taking type, were no material for new rebellions. This time, no one saw the blockade as opening a window of opportunity to confront Rosas's power. Given Buenos Aires's natural assets, food supply was not a major problem for Rosas, which allowed resisting the blockade for long periods. Eventually, the British decided to lift the blockade out of self-interest, as it meant a serious loss of business for English producers and merchants.

The Achilles' heel of Rosas's suzerainty was the Upper Littoral, which had long felt the economic exploitation resulting from Buenos Aires's navigation and fiscal monopolies. In 1851, General Urquiza, governor of Entre Ríos since 1841, who had been a loyal collaborator of Rosas for years, revolted against Buenos Aires. Commanding an army of twenty thousand men, Urquiza decisively defeated Rosas's forces in the Battle of Caseros in February 1852. Urquiza's move was the culmination of a silent economic process in the state of Entre Ríos. Over the course of the 1840s, the economy of Entre Ríos experienced the kind of economic growth that Buenos Aires had seen since the early 1820s.[5] The economy of Entre Ríos had been devastated by the war of independence. Under Urquiza's rule, Entre Ríos gained political stability, and political stability—combined with land policies similar to those of Buenos Aires in the 1820s—fostered the sustained development of cattle-ranching and *saladero* activities. A small but powerful landowning elite emerged in Entre Rios, at the center of which was Urquiza himself. The landowning elite of Entre Rios benefited from the exports of salted beef to Brazil and from international commerce through the Montevideo port during the blockades of Buenos Aires. The navigation and fiscal monopoly imposed by Rosas seriously hurt its economic interests.

Why did Urquiza switch from ally to foe of Rosas? The change was a reflection of how fragile and simulated the loyalty to Rosas was among rural lords. They deeply desired to see Rosas's suzerainty break down, but they were just not powerful enough to challenge it. Urquiza had always been willing to challenge Rosas, but only in the late 1840s did he finally accumulate the means to do it. Urquiza's power in the early 1850s did not derive only from the new economic prosperity of his province. Despite having gained control over a large clientele of rural workers throughout the 1840s, Urquiza still needed allies to defeat Rosas. He found them in three places: Corrientes, the only consistent challenger of Rosas; Brazil, which also wanted free navigation of the Paraná River so as to be able to access its own Matto Grosso region (overland passage from Rio was impossible); and Montevideo, the informal capital of Argentina's political émigrés, who, rather than resenting Rosas's suzerainty in relation to the other states, opposed Rosas's dictatorial methods within Buenos Aires.

Rosas's fall cannot be explained solely as a geopolitical defeat caused by forces outside Buenos Aires. The superior military capacity of Urquiza's army, especially the strength of Entre Rios's cavalry, played a key role. Yet, at some point in the mid-1840s, support toward the *Pax Rosista* gradually began to erode within Buenos Aires itself. The economic elites of Buenos Aires, the very social class whose interests Rosas was supposed to defend, started to desert Rosas. Declining support reflected the mutation of the *Pax Rosista* itself. Rosas began his political career as a direct representative of Buenos Aires's landowners. In the early 1830s, he delivered to his social class exactly what it needed for the cattle-ranching business to prosper: military protection from Interior and Upper Littoral caudillos and the annihilation of unitary projects within Buenos Aires, which would risk power and wealth sharing with the other minisovereignties. Yet, during his long tenure in power, Rosas developed autonomous political interests. By the early 1840s, it became clear that Rosas's government had stopped being just the "central committee" of the landowning elites of Buenos Aires. It was also a political machine designed to secure Rosas's perpetuation in power. In the mid-1840s, landowners perceived that the priority of political perpetuation had gained precedence over the advancement of cattle-ranching interests. Too many resources were being spent on propaganda, on co-optation of Upper Littoral caudillos, and on unnecessary wars. Rosas's mutation into an eminently political actor fighting for his own survival undermined the support from the chief economic class. Rosas's politics diverted resources that could have been used in the modernization of Buenos Aires. In the late 1840s, the *Pax Rosista* became a source of long-term backwardness for the economic sector that Rosas himself had pioneered and protected in the early 1830s. Urquiza's invasion from Entre Ríos accelerated the death of Rosas's suzerainty. Without Urquiza's invasion, the agony would have been much longer. Yet Urquiza's victory revealed how advanced the deterioration of the support of Buenos Aires's landowners for Rosas was. None of them offered material support in the preludes to the battle. Landowners of Buenos Aires were confident that any new government, even if led by Urquiza, would be forced to pay careful attention to the evolving requirements of the modernization of the River Plate's key export sector.

Legacy

The legacy of the Rosas's suzerainty was twofold: the transition of caudillos in the Interior and the Andes from the state-breaking type to the state-taking type (the "taming") and the unintended creation of a unified front against Buenos Aires's navigation and fiscal monopoly.

The decades-old prosperity of Buenos Aires, the new prosperity of Entre Ríos, and the military repression in the Andes and the Interior created such a power differential between the Pampas and all other regions that no rural lord outside Buenos Aires or Entre Ríos could aspire to reach the position that Facundo once enjoyed. Rosas had left the interior militarily and economically exhausted. Facundo's successors could at best become a junior partner of one of the coalitions that would fight for supremacy within the Pampas.

Rosas's suzerainty drastically simplified political conflict in the post-Rosas era. Entre Ríos and Buenos Aires became the main contenders for political power. One implication was that protectionist policies, abhorred by both Buenos Aires and Entre Ríos alike, completely disappeared from the political agenda. Contention would be focused on the free navigation of the River Plate basin and the redistribution of the revenues collected at the port of Buenos Aires, which Rosas had monopolized. Urquiza could use his temporary victory over Buenos Aires to extract from the ministate the promise of free navigation and revenue sharing. Yet the promises were inherently non-credible. As soon as Buenos Aires translated its economic strength into military recovery, it would renege on promises to Urquiza.

Urquiza's victory created its own legacy. It reduced the conflict over formulas of territorial governance to only two options: federalism or separation. The fall of the Rosista state showed that the confederal formula was not sustainable, and the victory of Urquiza made the unitary formula unviable. Aware of the credibility problem of Buenos Aires's promises, Urquiza sought a permanent redistribution of political power by promoting union under a federal formula. The formula would create a national government more powerful than the government of Buenos Aires. Buenos Aires was left with the choice of accepting a federal union under Urquiza's control or regrouping and fighting for separation.

Failed State 4: The Duopoly, 1852–61
Overview

Between 1852 and 1861, the territory of present-day Argentina was divided into two states: the republic of Buenos Aires and the Confederación Argentina—which despite its misleading name was a federation of thirteen provinces under a strong central government. The creation of this duopoly of violence was an unintended consequence of Urquiza's victory over Rosas. Urquiza had thought that Rosas's government was the main, and perhaps the only, obstacle against the formation of a federal system composed of all fourteen states, including Buenos Aires. Reality would soon prove Urquiza wrong. The removal of Rosas did not change the deepest preferences of Buenos Aires's political and economic elites. With or without Rosas, Buenos Aires's elites refused to share wealth and power with the other states. As soon as Urquiza's plans of power and wealth sharing were revealed, Buenos Aires revolted and formed a separate state (Map 5.2). The Confederación and Buenos Aires engaged in a cold war throughout most of the decade. By 1861, only eight years after its creation, the Confederación was financially exhausted and politically divided. A short battle provoked its collapse and gave elites in Buenos Aires the opportunity to create a new state under a range of options for formulas of territorial governance. Mitre, the first political entrepreneur, found himself in a position to broker a durable settlement that unified Argentina. However, for the settlement to work, he chose a formula that in the long run proved to be the most damaging for Buenos Aires's economic interests.

Origins

Urquiza's political plan for the day after the collapse of Rosas's rule pursued the twin political goals of creating a federal state—funded by the revenues collected by Buenos Aires's customhouse—and of becoming the president of the new country. Urquiza, the largest landowner outside Buenos Aires, also had an economic interest in mind. He wanted to free the navigation of the Uruguay and Paraná Rivers, which Buenos Aires had blocked in order to extract revenues from the traffic of goods between the other states and the markets overseas. Export duties had especially hurt the cattle-ranching business of the other states in the Upper Littoral. Rosas's navigation policies had also prevented the states of Entre Ríos and Santa Fe from collecting import duties themselves, thus impeding the formation of strong governments outside Buenos Aires. Urquiza's challenge against Rosas, for instance, was in part privately funded. Legions of Entre Ríos's soldiers were recruited from the clientele of rural workers employed by a tight-knit network of Upper Littoral landowners led by Urquiza himself.

Urquiza's goals were reflected in the Acuerdo de San Nicolás of May 1852, an agreement among state governors to create a constituent assembly, which in turn had the specific mandate to form a federal union. Crucially, the constituent assembly would be composed of twenty-eight representatives, two per state, a form of representation that was obviously meant to undercut the influence of Buenos Aires. By far the most populated state, Buenos Aires would have preferred that the number of representatives be proportional to the number of citizens in each state. The agreement also created a provisional president and granted the position to Urquiza himself, who would rule the country until a new constitution was crafted and general elections were held. Finally, the agreement provisionally established the free navigation of rivers and "nationalized" the revenues from all customhouses, including those of Buenos Aires.

In June, Buenos Aires's political elites and public opinion almost unanimously voiced a strong rejection of the agreement. In a clear indication of

Buenos Aires's permanent economic and political interests, the reaction against the agreement sponsored by Urquiza unified old foes: former Rosistas and liberal politicians whom Rosas had forced into exile. On September 11, just two days after Urquiza had inaugurated the constituent assembly, Buenos Aires's political forces took up arms against the puppet government that Urquiza had left in charge of the state. The "September Revolution" triumphed and forced Urquiza to form a federation of thirteen provinces without Buenos Aires. The revolution was a true inflection point in the trajectory of state formation in Argentina. It created the rudiments of the political movement that, almost ten years later, would finally succeed at the creation of the Argentine state.

Winners and Losers

Under the assumption that Buenos Aires would be incorporated into the territory of the new state, the 1853 constitution produced clear winners and losers. The new constitution was a radical innovation with regard to formulas of territorial governance. It departed from the brief unitary experiments of the 1810s and 1820s at the same time that it broke off with the longer tradition of confederal arrangements of the 1830s and 1840s. The 1853 constitution created a federation in which national authorities, the president and a bicameral congress, were invested with considerable powers. A senate was created in which minisovereignties, converted into provinces, had equal institutional weight. Assuming that Buenos Aires would be part of the federation, the senate was meant to curb the leading province's influence. The 1853 constitution afforded the provinces important levels of institutional autonomy, including centrally the election of their own authorities, which was certainly a sine qua non incentive for local oligarchies in the minisovereignties to support Urquiza's plan. With the abolition of internal tariffs and local armies, the minisovereignties were to lose the traditional fiscal rights and military capacities that, under the Confederación Rosista, had been the basis of their autonomy vis-à-vis the other minisovereignties. However, by subordinating local armies to the command of national authorities, the federal state would create the Hobbesian public good par excellence, thereby relieving minisovereignties from old security threats, which would in turn allow for substantial savings. Also, income lost from the elimination of provincial tariffs would be more than compensated by the share that provinces would obtain after the nationalization of Buenos Aires's revenues, in the form of either subsidies or centrally funded public goods. The new federal state was supposed to draw most of its fiscal resources from Buenos Aires and its military capacities from both Buenos Aires and Entre Ríos, the only two states with substantial armies. Urquiza, governor of Entre Ríos, did not need to worry about a potential loss of political power for he was certain to become the president of the new federation. In sum, most, if not all, of the economic and political gains that the 1853 constitution granted to the peripheral provinces, the net winners in the new institutional design, would be paid by Buenos Aires, the only loser. By creating a higher level of government and transferring Buenos Aires's revenues to the federal state, the 1853 constitution was meant to downgrade Buenos Aires's leaders to the status of ordinary provincial rulers.

However, without the incorporation of Buenos Aires, Urquiza's plans and the 1853 constitution had a completely different meaning. When he was elected president of the Confederación in 1854, Urquiza found himself ruling over a state whose financial sustainability was far from certain. He had chosen to create a federation with the participation of provinces that were much less productive than his own Entre Ríos only to be able to defeat Buenos Aires and force its incorporation. As years passed and Buenos Aires remained a separate republic, Urquiza realized that keeping the federation afloat was a punishing cost both to Entre Ríos's finances and to his personal fortune, the pillars of the Confederación's economic survival. The free navigation of the Paraná and Uruguay Rivers was a substantial improvement both to public revenues and to private businesses in Upper Littoral provinces, but it failed to compensate for the extra cost of maintaining a federal state and attending to the financial needs of the Interior and Andean provinces. To alleviate the economic burden, in 1856 the Confederación initiated an economic war against Buenos Aires by imposing "differential tariffs" at the port of Rosario, the most active one in the Confederación. Differential tariffs charged higher taxes on foreign goods that, instead of arriving directly in Rosario, had previously been unloaded in the port of Buenos Aires and then reshipped to the Confederación. Differential tariffs might have allowed the Confederación to become a fiscally sustainable state within a reasonable time frame.[6] However, the main obstacle against solvency was the cost of the

Confederación's army, which was much larger than needed just because of the separation of Buenos Aires. Urquiza wanted to be militarily prepared both for an opportunity to attack Buenos Aires or for the need to defend himself from Buenos Aires.

The State of Buenos Aires: The Professional Politician and the Wool Boom

As an independent state, Buenos Aires experienced in the 1850s two novelties that would have a major impact both on the failure of the Confederación in the early 1860s and on the subsequent success of a new federal state. One novelty was political, the other economic. The political change was a direct consequence of the regime transition from Rosas's dictatorship to a meaningful form of competitive politics. The new regime restored fundamental political and civil liberties that had been suppressed for two decades. In turn, within a competitive political environment, a key figure was born: the *professional politician*. The economic novelty was a direct repercussion of the acceleration of economic growth and technical change in northern Europe and the United States. The mechanization of wool mills coincided with the availability of more efficient means of transportation based on steam power—railways and steamships—to incentivize the introduction of sheep rearing in Buenos Aires, which was much more profitable than the traditional production of jerked beef and hides and encouraged a much wider spectrum of Hirschmanian "backward linkages" (investments and innovations required for sheep rearing to succeed).[7]

In the new context of competitive politics, two professional politicians stood out: Bartolomé Mitre and Adolfo Alsina. They led cliques, or protoparties, that set in motion a fierce competition for the vote of the public. Competition was fierce because positions in government were scarce rather than because they had substantial ideological differences. Most new professional politicians had been political émigrés under Rosas who returned from their exiles in Montevideo and Santiago de Chile. Mitre, Alsina, and most other politicians in Buenos Aires defined themselves as liberals in the standard mid-nineteenth-century European sense, and they formed a unified front every time Urquiza made an attempt to damage Buenos Aires through economic sanctions or military conquest.[8]

Differences between factions within Buenos Aires allegedly revolved around diverse strategies for dealing with the Confederación. Alsina led the "Autonomist" faction of liberalism, which defended permanent separation of Buenos Aires from the Confederación, whereas Mitre was the leader of the "Nationalist" faction, which advocated unification under conditions that he deliberately avoided to define with any precision. Professional politicians of Buenos Aires represented a big break from the rural caudillo that had dominated Buenos Aires only a few months before and still dominated most provinces in the Confederación. The key source of power of the caudillo was his *estancia* and the constituency of peons who worked for him and for satellite landowners. By contrast, Mitre's main constituency was made up of anonymous urban citizens attracted by his political expressions in the press, legislative debates, and campaign speeches. Mitre's breakthrough as a political leader occurred in the June 1852 debates when the legislature of Buenos Aires rejected the San Nicolás Agreement sponsored by Urquiza. Mitre's followers were swayed by a captivating oratory exalting Buenos Aires's civic traditions, which would allegedly prevent the return of caudillo rule and usher in a new era of material progress.

Mitre had a competitive advantage over his fellow politicians. He did not shy away from adapting programs and allies if doing so yielded electoral dividends. Mitre was not a permanent "nationalist" in the sense of always advocating the union between Buenos Aires and the other states. Before his presidential term (1862–68), which coincided with the peak of his nationalist vocation, Mitre adopted unambiguously secessionist postures. In 1856, he published what is a small political masterpiece defending the creation of the República del Plata, the new name he proposed for a completely sovereign state of Buenos Aires. Similarly, in the 1850s, Mitre repeatedly assumed the role of a dogmatic enemy of caudillo rule. Like many other émigrés under Rosas, Mitre insistently reminded his public that *caudillaje*, which dominated so many provinces in the interior and even the Confederación's national government, was incompatible with the rule of law. However, when he became president in 1862, he incorporated into his governing coalition three of the most powerful caudillos in the country, Urquiza from Entre Ríos and the Taboada brothers, Manuel and Antonino, from Santiago del Estero. Ideological and coalitional flexibility set Mitre apart from other professional politicians as a true political entrepreneur.

The mechanization of the wool mill produced an unprecedented boom in the economy of Buenos Aires—hitherto mechanization had been limited to the production of cotton cloth. Demand from western Europe and the United States grew exponentially in the 1850s, and wool replaced leather as the main export from Buenos Aires. The stock of sheep grew by a factor of ten in a single decade. Given the potential scale of wool production in Buenos Aires, the introduction of railways could create massive economies in transportation costs.

The wool boom was as much an economic opportunity for the landowning class of Buenos Aires as it was a political opportunity for the new professional politicians. Maximizing the profits made possible by the new wool prices required railways; railways demanded large-scale foreign investments; and foreign investments required peace between Buenos Aires and the Confederación in order to make sure that the underlying economy would produce enough profits. Indirectly through the demand for capital, then, pacification itself was the ultimate "backward linkage" of the wool boom. The professional politician who delivered peace could rightly aspire to perpetuation in power. The entrepreneur, as defined in Chapter 4, found a window of opportunity to engage in large-scale state formation.

Failure

The Confederación was a dead state by late 1861. Paradoxically, failure was preceded by a promising military victory of the Confederación against Buenos Aires at the Battle of Cepeda two years earlier (October 23, 1859). Victory at Cepeda forced Buenos Aires to accept unification under the federal formula. Urquiza had decided to go to battle in 1859 because the Confederación had proven financially unviable without the revenues collected in Buenos Aires's customhouse and because all nonmilitary strategies that attempted to produce Buenos Aires's incorporation had not worked. The Confederación was essentially a union of a few economically dynamic provinces with a large number of backward regions that could not sustain their own governments, let alone contribute to funding the federal state. The financial weakness of the Confederación was a constant drain on the resources of Entre Ríos.

The Battle of Cepeda was the first military attempt to annex Buenos Aires. The battlefield was located close to the border between the provinces of Santa Fe and Buenos Aires. The rapid acknowledgment of defeat by Buenos Aires's forces led both to military demobilization and to a unification agreement, the Pacto de Unión (also known as Pacto de San José de Flores). Signed in November, the Pacto was unusually generous with the defeated party. It allowed Buenos Aires to examine the 1853 constitution, propose amendments provided it kept intact the federal formula, and only gradually transfer its financial and military resources to the Confederación. The generosity of the terms indicated how desperate the Confederación was to achieve Buenos Aires's incorporation. However, it probably also reflected Urquiza's belief that invading the city of Buenos Aires—which would have given immediate control of the customhouse—was potentially counterproductive. Urquiza speculated that granting Buenos Aires the opportunity to revise the constitution would make unification more solid.

An apparently trivial event, the constitutional succession of Urquiza by Santiago Derqui—then a relatively minor political figure—as president of the Confederación in May 1860 had enormous unexpected repercussions. It granted Buenos Aires the opportunity to transform the military defeat at Cepeda into a political victory. Given Urquiza's unparalleled political and military power within the Confederación, the political community took for granted that Derqui would be Urquiza's puppet. That is precisely why, once inaugurated, Derqui wasted no time before he started to look for allies who could provide him with autonomy from the supercaudillo. Under most circumstances, Derqui's attempt would have failed. However, while Buenos Aires was still transitioning toward unification, it was possible for Derqui and Buenos Aires's politicians to negotiate a deal under which better terms of incorporation for Buenos Aires would be exchanged for support toward Derqui's position vis-à-vis Urquiza. At around the same time that Derqui became president of the Confederación, Mitre became governor of Buenos Aires. Only three weeks after Mitre's inauguration, Derqui began to exchange letters with the new governor of Buenos Aires with the unambiguous goal of forming an alliance that would undermine Urquiza's power. Derqui promised Mitre that he wanted "to rule with the Liberal Party [of Buenos Aires], which hosts all clever people and ideas": "therefore I have to work in order to secure that it will gain a majority in the legislatures. . . . I am certain I will be able to do it."[9]

Derqui began to deliver. He started by appointing conspicuous members of the political and economic elites of Buenos Aires to top positions in his cabinet, including Norberto de la Riestra, a staunch defender of Buenos Aires's autonomy, as finance minister. Also, Derqui partnered with Mitre in campaigning for the Liberal Party in the provinces of Córdoba, Tucumán, and Salta, with the purpose of preparing, for the time of Buenos Aires's incorporation, a legislative alliance that would be strong enough to outpower the bloc of representatives controlled by Urquiza.

The incipient alliance between Mitre and Derqui was sabotaged both by Urquiza, who naturally sensed he was losing control of the Confederación, and by the most extremist elements of the Liberal Party in Buenos Aires, especially those who still aspired to form a unitary state under Buenos Aires's control. In mid-November, extremist Liberals sponsored a revolution in the province of San Juan, which caused the death of its governor, Colonel José Antonio Virasoro, a close ally of Urquiza. Urquiza took advantage of the situation to regain control over Derqui. Urquiza urged the federal government to intervene in San Juan. Two months later, Antonino Aberastain, the Liberal governor of San Juan who had replaced Virasoro, was captured and killed by the president's military envoy. It was the first serious blow to the Mitre-Derqui alliance. Mitre understood that Derqui had been cornered by Urquiza. Derqui realized that the assassination of Aberastain alienated even the moderate elements of Buenos Aires's Liberal Party, which would in turn force Mitre to demand greater concessions from the president. Derqui tried to resuscitate the alliance by gaining the congress's approval for the incorporation of Buenos Aires's representatives, who had been chosen according to provincial laws instead of the national constitution. That is when Urquiza mounted a systematic attack against the alliance between Derqui and Mitre. In May 1861, he worked behind the scenes to make the congress reject the representatives from Buenos Aires. The provincial electoral laws, which took Buenos Aires as a single district, had produced uniformly Liberal representatives. Urquiza argued that if the representatives had been chosen according to the national constitution, which required the subdivision of Buenos Aires into smaller single-member districts, his Federal Party would have gained an important share of the seats. The rejection of Buenos Aires's representatives was the coup de grâce for the Derqui-Mitre alliance, as it showed that Derqui could not deliver any longer. More seriously, it also led to war. Buenos Aires and the Confederación clashed in the Battle of Pavón. The battle itself produced no clear winner, but it caused Urquiza to retreat to Entre Ríos and stop supporting the Confederación. Without Urquiza's support, the Confederación collapsed.

Legacy

The main economic legacy of Urquiza's rule was the free navigation of rivers, which was backed up by three factors: Urquiza's military might, international treaties signed with the leading world powers, and the fact that Buenos Aires's economy in the 1850s had become so dynamic and its port so naturally attractive that letting a fraction of international trade skip Buenos Aires's customhouse became a relatively minor fiscal loss. Free navigation of rivers further clarified the conflict between the Upper Littoral and Buenos Aires. Urquiza had opposed Rosas because Rosas banned free navigation and did not share revenues from the port of Buenos Aires. Urquiza and his supporters seemed to have assumed that free navigation alone would generate the fiscal resources required in the Upper Littoral to create a state that outpowered Buenos Aires. A key lesson that Urquiza learned in the 1850s was that free navigation was not enough. Contention between Buenos Aires and Entre Ríos then got further reduced to a single issue, namely, the creation of a mechanism for sharing the revenues collected by Buenos Aires, that is, fiscal federalism—which to become credible required a state with a federal formula of territorial governance.

The main political legacy of the period was the (re)birth of competitive politics in Buenos Aires after the long Rosista dictatorship. Competitive politics in Buenos Aires in turn prompted twin developments that would prove crucial for the formation of Argentina: the rise of professional politicians and the creation of purely political divisions within the leading mini-state. Competition, professionalization, and division in Buenos Aires's politics set in motion a process of large-scale state formation that no actor in the Upper Littoral or the Interior had ever been able to launch. As we will see in Chapter 6, divisions in Buenos Aires and the residual military power of Urquiza combined to create a state that favored a minuscule group of

Buenos Aires professional politicians in the short run but in the long run became an irreversible concession to patrimonial rulers in the peripheries.

Conclusions

The aggregate legacy of the four failed states was the *incompatibility* between the postrevolutionary distribution of military power, fragmented into multiple caudillo bastions, and the unitary formula of territorial governance as the method of unification of the regions liberated by Buenos Aires. Half a century after independence, for the unitary formula to prevail, caudillos had to be annihilated. If caudillo power persisted, unification could only occur under a federal formula.

Table 5.1 summarizes the case studies of failed state formation, with a special emphasis on their permanent legacies, which provide the contextual conditions surrounding the critical juncture of the formation of the Argentine state.

Two other legacies made caudillo annihilation impossible. One was the rise of the landowners of Buenos Aires as an economic class that could generate extremely high levels of income by any standards, Latin American or international. In the mid-1840s, incentivized by the wool boom, Buenos Aires landowners experimented with a first round of technological innovation. Incipient modernization yielded exorbitant profits, which indicated that further modernization would create enormous fortunes. Pacification was a backward *political* linkage of the wool boom: deepening modernization in Buenos Aires required peace. Caudillo annihilation demanded war—a long, costly, and uncertain venture, which Buenos Aires's landowners were not willing to risk.

The other legacy was the rise of Entre Ríos's rural economy, a slightly less dynamic replica of Buenos Aires. The rise of Entre Ríos was associated with the emergence of the supercaudillo Urquiza, who could not compete with Buenos Aires's landowners in economic capacity but could defeat Buenos Aires in the battlefield. Urquiza was an effective veto power against projects of state formation under a unitary formula.

In 1860, Buenos Aires faced an impossible trilemma, resulting from the accumulation of legacies since 1810. Given that caudillo annihilation was unfeasible, unification under the unitary formula was unviable. Unification under the federal formula was acceptable for the Interior, the Andes, and the Upper Littoral, but it would translate into the loss of major political and fiscal privileges. Finally, separation would preserve privileges, but it would risk military invasion by Urquiza.

It is exactly in this context that Bartolomé Mitre, an exemplary *political entrepreneur*, himself a creature of the birth of competitive politics in Buenos Aires, offered a political solution. His solution was compatible with the interests of Buenos Aires's economic elites. Crucially, it maximized Mitre's professional goals. Mitre's solution secured pacification, the core component of the trade-led state-formation strategy, by creating a union under a federal formula, which was Urquiza's preferred option. In the 1860s, the economic elites of Buenos Aires were more than able to afford a small short-term fiscal cost. In the expanded political arena, Mitre was able to reach political supremacy.

One sad legacy of the four failed states is one particular path not taken along the many forks in the road faced after independence. Warlordism in the 1810s caused the political division of what was a natural economic region, the Pampas of the River Plate basin. The Pampas include Buenos Aires, Entre Ríos, Santa Fe, and southern Córdoba in present-day Argentina, Uruguay, and Rio Grande do Sul in present-day Brazil. Delegation of military power to Artigas, an emergency measure in 1811, created a first territorial cleavage within the economic region, which was divided into a western and eastern shore. The political division created competition between two ports, Buenos Aires and Montevideo, which, had they remained within the same political jurisdiction, could have cooperated to create an efficient division of labor and extract better terms in the negotiations with foreign merchants and international powers. In turn, Artigas's improvised delegation of power to Ramírez in the mid-1810s further subdivided the western shore of the River Plate between Entre Ríos and Buenos Aires. The inability of Artigas, Ramírez, and the various governors of Buenos Aires to find a reasonable power-sharing agreement prevented the emergence of what would have been the Australia of South America. In the late 1810s, San Martín still had the power to extinguish post-Artigas caudillos, but he refused to do so. Peru was more important for San Martín. Political divisions within the River Plate basin—into different countries and into different provinces within the same country—precluded the creation of a united economic powerhouse. The

Table 5.1. Four Failed States: Territorial Formulas, Number of States, Causes of Failure, and Legacies

	Formula of territorial governance	Number of states	Cause of failure	Legacies
Revolutionary State (1810–20)	Unitary for Revolutionary State (1810–20) Confederal for Liga Pueblos Libres (1815–19)	1 (1810–15) 2 (1815–19) 13 (1820)	Military overextension Upper Littoral's caudillos' resistance against territorial formula	Rise of caudillos Political division of Littoral: Lower Littoral (Buenos Aires) versus Upper Littoral (Entre Ríos, Santa Fe, Corrientes) Separation of present-day Uruguay Path closed for formation of "United States of River Plate" as economic powerhouse
Unitary State (1820–28)	Separation (1820–24) Unitary (1824–27)	13 (1820–24) 1 (1824–27)	War with Brazil over Uruguay Caudillos' resistance against territorial formula in Interior, Upper Littoral, and Buenos Aires	Rise of Buenos Aires's landowning class as the most powerful economic actor, which develops permanent structural (fiscal) power and intermittent instrumental power Unviability of unitarian formula

Pax Rosista (1829–52)	Confederal (1829–35) Suzerainty (1835–52)	14	Rejection by Entre Ríos's supercaudillo of Buenos Aires's fiscal and navigation policies Autonomization of Rosas's political agenda Attenuation of landowners' support	Rise of Buenos Aires's raison d'état: preference for separation and small-scale trade-led state formation Rise of Entre Ríos's rural economy Taming of Interior caudillos Conflict reduced to free navigation of the River Plate basin and to revenue sharing Buenos Aires and Entre Ríos only serious contenders for power; Interior actors serve as junior partners
Duopoly (1852–61)	Federal in Confederación Unitary in Buenos Aires	2	Bankruptcy of Entre Ríos–based Confederación	Free navigation of rivers Conflict further reduced to revenue sharing Rise of professional politician in Buenos Aires Export boom with backward linkages in Buenos Aires

United States of the River Plate, a country coterminous with the basin's Pampas, was only a few contingent decisions away from being born in the 1810s. By 1850, it became a structural impossibility. In the United States of the River Plate, neither Rosas nor Urquiza would have existed. In the 1850s, the economy of the United States of the River Plate would have been too modern to make room for super patrimonial rulers. And without them, Mitre would not have had the opportunity to become a political entrepreneur as late as 1861.

Port-Driven State Formation in Argentina

THE BATTLE OF PAVÓN on September 17, 1861, was a founding episode in Argentina's state formation. In the battle, the army of Buenos Aires clashed against the military forces of the Confederación. Buenos Aires and the Confederación had been separate states for almost a decade. The battle itself was an indecisive military event. However, it set in motion a four-month bargaining process between Bartolomé Mitre, the leader of Buenos Aires, and Justo José de Urquiza, the leader of the Confederación, that resulted in the merger of the two states and the birth of Argentina.

The negotiation was a true critical juncture. A laborious agreement found a solution to conflicts that had swept the River Plate area for decades, taking thousands of lives, destroying large amounts of material resources, and causing the failure of four projects of state formation based on Buenos Aires.[1] Negotiations produced an irreversible change in the process of state formation. The territory of Argentina would never again experiment with the loose confederations of minisovereignties that characterized the 1830s and 1840s (Map 5.1) or the duopoly Confederación versus Buenos Aires of the 1850s (Map 5.2). All prior forms of state would be replaced by a single country uniting fourteen provinces under a federal formula. The territory of the new state, as well as the formula of territorial governance, has remained intact until today. Few legacies in Argentine history have been more durable.

The federation formula institutionalized the existence of provinces that varied immensely with regard to economic performance and political institutions. No less than six of them were financially unviable backward interiors, whereas two, Entre Ríos and especially Buenos Aires, were rudimentary port states with income levels comparable to the most dynamic rural economies of the world, like the U.S. Midwest or Australia. Prior to the formation of Argentina, most individual minisovereignties, from poor San Luis to wealthy Entre Ríos, had for decades been dominated by a specific form of patrimonial rule, the rural lord or caudillo. Buenos Aires was the only ministate that, after the fall of Rosas, had a competitive political arena dominated by professional politicians.

The Argentine state has proximate and distant causes. The proximate cause is the leadership of a political entrepreneur, Bartolomé Mitre, who emerged as the main winner of the negotiation process. In addition to Mitre, the founding settlement included the rural lord Urquiza, the political and economic elites of Buenos Aires, and minor state-taking caudillos and pro-Mitre minorities in the interior. The distant causes are the set of antecedent conditions that shaped the goals of, and provided resources and constraints to, the actors involved in the negotiation. Antecedent conditions were structural factors that placed a heavy weight on the actions during the critical juncture. Nevertheless, in the interaction among Mitre, Urquiza, and other political leaders, a dose of free agency and political creativity, within clear structural parameters, was undeniable. Such range of freedom allowed for marginal deviations from the course of actions actually taken. Small deviations could have produced large variations in the final outcome.

This chapter has three sections. The first section introduces Bartolomé Mitre as a political entrepreneur, the key agent of the port-driven pathway of state formation. A distinctive feature of Mitre's entrepreneurship was his autonomy from the economic interests of Buenos Aires, a sine qua non in the creation of Argentina. The second section analyzes antecedent conditions, the set of challenges, resources, and constraints faced by Mitre, as they emerged from the combination of international economic forces and the domestic trajectory of state failures from independence until 1861. Following the template presented in Chapter 4, two broad sets of antecedent conditions are crucial: the distribution of economic power across regions, which was decisively shaped by the wool boom—the specific version of the Commercial Revolution in the River Plate—and the distribution of political capabilities across regions, which distinguished states other than Buenos Aires depending on whether they were ruled by state-taking, state-breaking, or state-making caudillos. The third section analyzes the critical juncture, the arduous negotiation between Mitre and Urquiza amidst strong pressures against a peaceful settlement, and its outcome, the creation of Argentina.

The Political Entrepreneur

Around 1860, a major novelty occurred in the politics of Buenos Aires: the rise of a political entrepreneur, Bartolome Mitre. For decades before 1860, the two most powerful men had been patrimonial rural lords, Rosas and Urquiza. Their source of power was ownership of immense tracts of land and a tall pyramid of clients, which included rural workers, some of whom were their direct employees, and minor local notables, who contributed additional contingents of rural workers. Given the type of economic activity prevailing at the time, extensive cattle ranching, it was easy for rural lords to transform workers and horses, key economic inputs, into a military force, especially cavalries. The rural lord was respected as a patron within his fiefdom and was feared for his military might outside it. Mitre's basis of power was completely different. It was purely political, based on the ability to mobilize voters through programmatic appeals, to build trust among fellow politicians, and to cut deals with central economic elites and peripheral oligarchies.

An associated novelty was that, for the first time in history, the governor of Buenos Aires, Mitre, and the economic elites of Buenos Aires developed different interests regarding union with the Confederación. Mitre began to defend union against the traditional attitude of Buenos Aires's political rulers and landowners, who advocated either secession (the consolidation of Buenos Aires as separate country) or union under a unitarian formula (the power of Buenos Aires to eliminate provincial caudillos and appoint subnational authorities). They all unanimously abhorred Urquiza. In 1861, Mitre became the only political leader of Buenos Aires willing to achieve unification via negotiation with Urquiza and accept the federal formula of territorial governance. Mitre's differentiation from the economic and political elites of Buenos Aires was his inaugural action in political entrepreneurship.

Mitre himself had played a key role in building a strong antiunification consensus in Buenos Aires during the prior decade. This would seem to be a paradox if Mitre is not seen as a political entrepreneur who adapted his program to ambition and circumstances. Five years before the Battle of

Pavón, in an influential newspaper article, suggestively titled "La República del Río de la Plata" (Republic of the River Plate), Mitre had advocated the consolidation of Buenos Aires, under the new name, as a sovereign country. With an eye on electoral dividends, Mitre carefully chose a prophetic tone: "A silent yet powerful and irreversible trend is under way. It is a secret that everybody knows. It shines like the sun. It is the consolidation of Buenos Aires as a national state." Mixing unashamed demagoguery praising Buenos Aires's civic attributes and a good deal of common sense, Mitre gave the rationale for his antiunification position: "Some people repeat like parrots that we should join Urquiza's Confederación. They do not realize that Buenos Aires and the Confederación are based on incompatible principles. It is not possible that an organization centered on the virtues of the public opinion [i.e., Buenos Aires] joins another one dominated by a caudillo [the Confederación], unless of course one of them is willing to commit suicide."[2]

In late 1861, Mitre individually broke away from the consensus he had helped to build. Mitre learned from Pavón that unification by military conquest would require substantially more resources and time than those involved in a single battle. Mitre's willingness to achieve unification via negotiation broke a taboo in Buenos Aires. Mitre's plan of unification via negotiation required concessions to the Andean and Upper Littoral provinces, the most important of which was the federal formula, the institution forbidden by the taboo.

The formation of Argentina can be seen as the "Mitre effect" on politics. The Mitre effect is not a contingent event, resulting from idiosyncratic attributes in Mitre's private or public personality, such as a special set of civic virtues, ideological convictions, extraordinary skills, or psychological strengths.[3] The effect simply derived from Mitre's position as a political entrepreneur facing a critical juncture in which the formation of Argentina was, among the several alternatives opened up by Pavón, the most compatible one with his power-maximization goals.

The Mitre effect introduces political agency in state formation, through which professional ambition and leadership become key drivers of the process. It is not possible to understand the creation of Argentina without the political autonomy of Mitre in relation to the dominant economic interests of Buenos Aires. The most important manifestation of Mitre's independence was his willingness to extract from Buenos Aires the resources needed to attract outside support and form a supraregional coalition that included at least a subset of the other minisovereignties.

Yet Mitre's agency had clear structural roots. His agenda reflected with remarkable precision the set of resources and constraints he was facing in the wake of the Battle of Pavón. Mitre was both a market-maker and a polity-maker. As a market-maker, he had to deliver the class goods required for export-led growth, which would keep Buenos Aires's economic elites invested in Mitre's project and would also provide the fundamental fiscal resources for state formation. As a polity-maker, Mitre would form Argentina only if doing so contributed to his professional career. The structural incentives faced by Mitre as a polity-maker were different from those he faced as a market-maker.

The incentives that made Mitre a market-maker derived from international economic conditions. They subsume his plan of action under the broad class of the trade-led path that characterized all Latin America. The incentives that made Mitre a polity-maker were largely rooted in local political conditions. They made him the leader of the specific port-driven variant of trade-led state formation. Both types of antecedent conditions are distant causes of the formation of the Argentine state. The following two sections move from the international economic structures to the local political structures, following a funnel strategy of explanation, by which the former account for the generic impulse toward state formation and the latter explain the specific direction the impulse took with regard to the regions consolidated within a single state and the formula of territorial governance adopted.

Antecedent Conditions

International Economic Conditions: The Revolution in Atlantic Trade

Mitre's political strategy in the early 1860s can be seen as a case of latecomer, trade-led state formation. The boom in wool exports experienced by Buenos Aires starting in the mid-1850s created a sudden availability of economic resources for coalition-making that Mitre could use for a large-scale state-formation project.

Around the time of Pavón, a true revolution in Atlantic trade was taking place, which in Buenos Aires was expressed as a combination of a boom in the price of wool, the introduction of steamboats for transatlantic transportation, and a renewed appetite for foreign investments among British businessmen. British investors were especially interested in railways, for they could benefit not only as owners of the new transportation system but also as suppliers of the machinery, iron, and coal required for their construction, functioning, and maintenance.

In the three decades spanning from the early 1820s to the early 1850s, the economy of Buenos Aires had specialized in extensive cattle ranching, in particular, in the production of hides for western European markets and jerked beef for the slave economies of Brazil and Cuba. The economy was characterized by technological backwardness. Animal stocks remained unrefined, grazing lands unfenced, and transportation systems primitive—the cattle moved from the pastureland to the slaughterhouse by their own means.[4]

Everything changed with a specific technological innovation within the broader Industrial Revolution: the mechanization of the wool mill. In the late 1840s, international demand for wool suddenly skyrocketed. The United Kingdom, France, Belgium, Germany, and even the United States became large importers. Given the quality of grass in the Pampas, Buenos Aires, together with Australia, was uniquely endowed to meet the new demand.

Starting in the early 1850s, wool replaced leather as Buenos Aires's main export. Changes were immense on almost every dimension: the stock of sheep grew from three million head in the mid-1840s to ten million in 1850 to twenty million in 1855 and reached fifty million during Mitre's presidency (1862–68). During the era of leather, which roughly coincided with Rosas's rule, the value of exports had grown at an annual rate of 3.5 percent; during the era of wool, which preceded the formation of the Argentine state by roughly five years and lasted almost two decades, the value of exports grew at an annual rate of 7 percent, probably the highest in the world.[5] Moreover, the wool boom induced the first systematic wave of economic modernization in rural Buenos Aires. The stock of sheep had to be refined. The quality of the wool produced by the initial endowment was extremely poor. Exemplars of Merino and Rambouillet were introduced for crossbreeding. Pasturelands were fenced. The Pampas region had historically been characterized by the abundance of land and the scarcity of labor and capital. For the first time, land became relatively scarce in Buenos Aires. The intensity of the expansion of sheep farming convinced several landowners in the northern region of Buenos Aires to acquire or rent land in the southern sections of the Confederación's provinces of Santa Fe and Córdoba, near the border with Buenos Aires. Finally, the impact on the labor market was immediately felt. Much more vulnerable to bad weather and small predators than cattle, sheep demanded year-round attention. The seasons of shearing (September–November) and lambing (April–May and July–August) required a special skillset, which was initially provided by Basque and Irish immigrants. For the first time, women, especially dexterous in the use of scissors during shearing, were incorporated into the rural labor market.

The production of wool had large synergies with the innovations in transportation. Compared to sailboats, steamboats cut in half the duration of the trip between Europe and the South Atlantic and carried three times the volume of goods. Larger ships were crucial for the production of wool, which had a lower volume-to-price ratio than hides. Wool could also benefit from railways. In contrast to cattle, the sheep remained in the pasturelands after the shearing, so the animals would not transport their own output. Given the potential scale of wool production in Buenos Aires, the replacement of the traditional oxcart—a vestige from colonial times—for the train would massively reduce transportations costs.

Three Wool-State Linkages. The impact of the wool boom in Buenos Aires on state formation in Argentina is undeniable. However, what were the specific channels of causation? Since the effect of the wool boom on the Argentine state is a case-specific expression of a more general causal relation between economic development and state formation, it is useful to review three prominent channels: the Marxist *instrumental* channel, the *fiscal* channel, and the *backward-linkage* channel.

The premise of the Marxist instrumental channel is that the economic interests of the Buenos Aires landowning class expanded into the territories of the Confederación in search of additional pasturelands, especially in Córdoba and Santa Fe.[6] The territorial expansion of the wool economy created an incentive for unification. Unification would generate the economic benefit of removing tariffs on goods that had to cross the borders of the Confederación in Córdoba and Santa Fe before reaching the port of Buenos

Aires to be shipped to western Europe and the United States. Presumably, then, a group of Buenos Aires landowners—those with establishments near the borders with Santa Fe and Córdoba—lobbied Mitre for unification. Evidence on the lobby does *not* exist. Yet the argument can work if reframed in strategic political terms. Landowners at the northern border of Buenos Aires did not lobby Mitre, but Mitre knew they would benefit from unification and that economic benefit would eventually produce political support. As a true political entrepreneur, Mitre had an acute forward-looking vision. It was part of his survival instinct. He generated economic value for landowners in anticipation that it would translate into political dividends. Yet the instrumental linkage does not explain why Mitre was interested in generating political dividends beyond Buenos Aires, Córdoba, or Santa Fe—the wool production area. Mitre also sought to build political capital in Entre Ríos and in the Andean and Interior states. Mitre did not want to form "Merinoland." He wanted Argentina.[7]

The fiscal channel is built on the fact that an economic boom generates an extraordinary flow of financial resources with which to fund the formation of a new state. As in most Latin American countries, in the Argentine case, the fiscal channel was indirect. Taxes on exports were negligible, but a higher level of exports made new volumes of hard currency available for purchasing foreign goods. Import tariffs were in fact the main source of revenue. The wool boom was indirectly a fiscal boom for Buenos Aires. The fiscal channel, however, is about the *capacity* of Buenos Aires to form Argentine but not about the *willingness*. The difference between the availability of means for the creation of Argentina and the desirability of the goal is the reason why international economic causes leave the final territorial outcome undetermined and need to be supplemented with political motivations. With the extra fiscal resources, the economic elites of Buenos Aires could have demanded, rather than unification with the Confederación, the provision of more and better local public goods, including improvements in the infrastructure of transportation and communication, which would further accelerate the wool boom and prepare the rural economy of Buenos Aires for other business opportunities to come. At the same time, the political elites of Buenos Aires could have demanded an upgrade of the military defense against the Confederación, which would reinforce separation rather than promote unification. The fiscal channel, then, cannot provide a full account of state formation in Argentina, for it clearly requires political leadership to direct the new resources toward unification despite potential pressures for alternative paths.

Finally, the backward-linkage channel is based on the fact that making the wool boom sustainable over time required pacification. In the context of the post-Pavón juncture, pacification amounted to an end to the conflict between Buenos Aires and the Confederación—battles like Cepeda and Pavón should not recur. A protracted war would ruin the opportunities from the boom in wool prices. The wool boom created two sources of peace demands. First, compared to cattle ranching, sheep farming was much more labor intensive. Manpower had always been scarce in rural Buenos Aires. The recruitment of soldiers in preparation for war transformed a labor shortage into a supply catastrophe. Second, the onset of the wool boom preceded the modernization of the transportation infrastructure by almost a decade. Exports of large volumes of wool began when train tracks were nonexistent and oxcarts still dominated the routes between the hinterland and the port. Increasing export capabilities required more efficient transportation. The wool boom created a strong demand for the construction of railways—a backward linkage. Railways in turn demanded large investments of capital, which, like labor, was characteristically scarce in mid-nineteenth-century Buenos Aires. Fortunately, the timing of the wool boom coincided with a renewed appetite for foreign investments among British businessmen. However, the demand and the supply of capital would not meet unless the proper political conditions were in place. Large-scale capital investments required peace to make sure that the underlying economy would produce enough profits to repay the British investor. Indirectly through the demand of labor and the demand of capital, then, pacification can be seen as the ultimate backward linkage of the wool boom, or of economic modernization more generally. The backward linkage had proper political microfoundations: Mitre wanted pacification to deliver a key growth-enhancing class good for Buenos Aires landowners, who would in turn reward him with coalitional support.

Two Territorial Options for Pacification. The Commercial Revolution presented economic and political elites in Buenos Aires with special resources but also with unique constraints. At the juncture of Pavón, the wool boom was not incipient but was still far from reaching its full potential. Given the need for a proper physical infrastructure and an adequate business climate for taking full advantage of the boom, all prominent political leaders of Buenos Aires were perfectly aware that, if they were able to achieve a durable peace with the Confederación, they would be able to attract large-scale investments and release manpower for productive work. Peace would generate direct dividends for private businesses, but political leaders prioritized the indirect electoral rewards they could obtain from it. The search for the "peace dividend" made political leaders market-makers as much as it made them state-makers. Buenos Aires's political leaders envisioned the virtuous circle that marks the initiation of successful latecomer, trade-led state formation: a modicum of peace would foment economic progress via foreign investments, export-led growth, and increased revenue via import tariffs, which in turn would further consolidate peace.

The latecomer strategy of state formation is in principle agnostic regarding the combination of regions that will form the state and the formula of territorial governance. In Buenos Aires in the early 1860s, the strategy could be employed either for the consolidation of Buenos Aires as a sovereign ministate or for unification with the Confederación under a variety of territorial formulas. Most members of the economic elites were in favor of continued separation and the reinvestment of profits from the wool boom within the jurisdiction. Some members of the political class, especially those with close ties to the traditional cattle-ranching interests, like Adolfo Alsina and Pastor Obligado, joined the economic elites in their goal of consolidating Buenos Aires as a sovereign state. Norberto de la Riestra, a precursor of the modern economic technocrat and a vocal advocate of the need for foreign investments, preferred unification under the unitary formula but often conceded that separation was more viable. Unitarian by vocation, de la Riestra and many other Liberals in Buenos Aires were secessionist on tactical grounds.

Mitre's distinct contribution was a strategy of state formation based on the negotiated unification with the Confederación and the acceptance of the federal formula. Capturing the peace dividend required for Mitre not merely a negotiated truce but the formation of a political coalition spanning a physical arena much broader than the jurisdiction of Buenos Aires. Mitre wanted to allocate a portion of the peace dividend to fund such a supraregional coalition.

Mitre's goal not only gave the latecomer strategy of state formation a distinct territorial scope but also generated a specific temporal horizon. Mitre cared less about the material welfare of generations in the distant future than about his short-run presidential project—a dark but powerful side of political entrepreneurship. In the early 1860s, Mitre had to capitalize the peace dividend in a few years, if not months. To make the specific port-driven pathway adopted by entrepreneur Mitre intelligible, attention must turn to local political conditions.

Local Antecedent Conditions:
Competitive Politics in Buenos Aires and Caudillo
Politics in the Interior

The Rise of Competitive Politics in Buenos Aires. Mitre's political agenda in 1861 largely derived from the maturation of competitive politics and the consolidation of politics as a professional career in Buenos Aires after the fall of Rosas's dictatorship. Mitre sponsored the union of Buenos Aires and the Confederación mainly because the prospects of his political career were better served in such an expanded political arena than in the smaller political arena of the separate state of Buenos Aires.

The combination of regions, and thereby the size of the territory of the Argentine state, was a function of *coalitional calculations*, as opposed to geopolitical imperatives, as had occurred in early modern Europe, or economic considerations, as is the case of many contemporary rich member regions that strive for secession from a less wealthy union. At the time of Pavón, Mitre had already been occupying the position of governor of Buenos Aires, the state's top political office, for a year and a half, and the constitution provided for three-year terms and no reelection. Additionally, in the late 1850s, Mitre began to face stiff competition from rival politicians. For Buenos Aires's powerful landowning class, Mitre was not as reliable a protector of the state's economic privileges as politicians like Alsina or Obligado. Mitre's days as a leader of Buenos Aires were numbered, both constitutionally and politically. His political survival at the top of the political game required the creation of a new political arena, considerably larger in territorial scope, in which he could extend his career. How could Mitre *not* change his position about unification? Precisely because he continued to be a power-maximizing entrepreneur, in 1861 he was willing to unite Buenos Aires and the Confederación, even if unification involved important economic costs for the state he was representing.[8]

In theoretical terms, the Mitre effect can be presented as a paradox: under some conditions, a *local* division causes *national* unification. Division within Buenos Aires, between Mitre and the rest of the *porteño* elite, drove Mitre's search for allies outside Buenos Aires and the construction of a supraregional alliance, which achieved success by creating an expanded political arena, that is, the territory of Argentina.[9]

For a local division to cause national unification, three conditions must hold, two referring to the factions into which the small territory is divided and the other referring to forces outside the territory. First, the faction within the small territory advocating unification expects a reward in the expanded territory that is more important than whatever benefits it already enjoys within the smaller territory. Second, the faction within the smaller territory opposed to unification must lack veto power over the unification process. Finally, forces outside the divided territory must get concessions that make unification with the small territory attractive. All three conditions were met in the post-Pavón juncture. It was precisely Mitre's political entrepreneurship that made it happen.

What neither Mitre's agenda, as derived from the competitive pressures of Buenos Aires's politics, nor his adoption of a trade-led strategy of state formation, based on the international conditions that created the wool boom, are able to explain is the prevalence of federalism as the territorial formula of governance. To account for federalism, the key element is the distribution of political power outside Buenos Aires.

State-takers and State-breakers in the Peripheries. Whereas the fall of Rosas caused the end of caudillo rule and the rise to competitive civilian politics in Buenos Aires, the provinces of the Interior, the Andes, and the Upper Littoral experienced little political change. Throughout the 1850s, most of them continued being dominated by patrimonial rural caudillos. However, by the late 1850s, caudillo domination outside Buenos Aires was far from uniform. Important differences with regard to the caudillos' ability to project their power outside their local domain separated *state-makers* from *state-breakers* and *state-takers.*

Urquiza was the only *state-making* caudillo. Very much like the professional politicians who ruled Buenos Aires, Urquiza commanded sufficient human and economic resources to sponsor a large-scale state-formation project uniting several minisovereignties. The difference between the state-maker rural lord and the state-maker political entrepreneur was that the power of the caudillo derived from *private* sources, including centrally his position as a large landowner who was able to provide useful occupation to his clients in times of peace and demand military services in times of war. Around 1860, Urquiza had been the largest landowner in Entre Ríos for more than a decade, and his domains continued expanding. By contrast, *state-breaking* caudillos could only extend their power to a few districts beyond their own minisovereignty, which usually consisted in the ability to install or overthrow governors in neighboring provinces. They could not lead large-scale state-formation projects, but they possessed "extortion power" in their dealings with state-makers. They could launch attacks against provincial governments, ranging from rebellions to looting raids, and thereby damage the prospects of pacification that were vital for trade-led state-formation projects. An example of a state-breaking caudillo was Ángel Vicente "Chacho" Peñaloza, who dominated vast contingents of clients in the states of La Rioja and Catamarca and could extend his influence into the provinces in the Northwest and Cuyo subregions. In addition to Peñaloza from La Rioja, caudillos with state-breaking power included Juan Saá from San Luis and the brothers Antonino and Manuel Taboada from Santiago del Estero. Finally, *state-taking* caudillos did not have enough power to project their influence beyond their province. Usually, their own local position depended in part on the favor of superior caudillos. State-taking caudillos were clients of the other two types of caudillo. They received political protection, military support, or economic subsidies in return for loyalty, which usually meant a modest contribution—a small contingent of informal soldiers—to the army of their patrons.

Except for Entre Ríos, La Rioja, San Luis, and Santiago del Estero, all states were governed by state-taking patrimonial rulers, or *caudillaje manso*. The simplification of the caudillo landscape was the legacy of Rosas's response to the challenge of the Coalición del Norte in the late 1830s, which largely destroyed the military capabilities of the states that took part in it. It was also an effect of the rise of Entre Ríos's economy in the 1840s, which made Urquiza the only ruler who could mobilize enough financial and human resources to match those of Buenos Aires. By the late 1850s, state-makers, either political entrepreneurs or caudillos, needed an army of at least eight thousand men, which in turn required no less than $2 million in annual military expenditures. Given the increasing economic gap between the states of Buenos Aires and Entre Ríos and all other states, only the former could afford a state-making role. To qualify as state-breakers by the mid-1850s, caudillos had to be able to mobilize around one thousand men, but mobilization for state-breakers was much less onerous. To obtain obedience from their followers, state-breaking rural lords relied on a mix of military charisma, clientelism, rewards from looting raids, and a shared sense of local identity.

As an entrepreneur planning to unite several regions ruled by caudillos, within a general trade-led state-formation path, the key task for Mitre was to provide concessions within a range: concessions had to be large enough to obtain the caudillos' support but not so large that they threatened the prospects of export-led growth. Big economic concessions diverted resources from productive investments. Also, big economic concessions helped local political rivals of Mitre to mount a negative political campaign that could undermine the entrepreneur's plans.

The biggest challenge for Mitre was to deal with Urquiza, the state-making rural lord. A war of extermination was out of the question because it risked derailing the trade-led path to state formation, and its duration and outcome were fundamentally uncertain. A long war could devour Mitre's political capital. Mitre had to offer Urquiza sufficient elements of power sharing, which could range from alternation in power to central support for securing Urquiza's local hegemony. Power alternation between Mitre and Urquiza could secure the presidency for the former and the passivity of the latter, who could otherwise become a state-breaking actor. As we will see, Urquiza's military power was the single most important reason why Mitre agreed to the federal formula of territorial governance, despite the recalcitrant opposition of Mitre's own allies in Buenos Aires.

Through modest economic concessions, the entrepreneur could buy the loyalty of state-taking caudillos, the cheapest form of support available. Incorporating state-taking caudillos could help Mitre balance the power of the state-breaking and state-making lords and thus reduce the cost of building a large multiregion coalition. The entrepreneur could occasionally use a modicum of violence to deal with state-breaking caudillos if a military campaign was less expensive than the concessions they demanded. Yet the trade-led path of state formation required strong economies in the use of violence. A peaceful political environment is the precondition for sustained export-led growth.

Liberal Minorities in the Interior. If Mitre was the political leader of Buenos Aires's Liberal Party, Urquiza was the leader of the Federal Party. In contrast to Liberalism, which was a typical oligarchic party, the Federal Party was a loose league of provincial caudillos united by their personal loyalty to Urquiza, the supercaudillo, and by a common interest in forcing Buenos Aires to share its wealth. The Liberal Party was divided into two, and sometimes three, factions within Buenos Aires, whereas most governors in the Confederación—who formed the skeleton of the Federal Party—did not suffer internal dissension. Each federal governor was a hegemon in his own province. In some interior provinces, however, such as Córdoba, Tucumán, and San Juan, educated minorities resented the domination of local politics by patrimonial rulers, whose source of power was not superior capabilities as administrators but the physical force derived from the control over large rural clienteles.[10] Educated minorities did not have the slimmest chance of disputing the power of the federal governor on their own, but they could aspire to strengthen their position if, in the context of a unified Argentina, they received the support of the Liberal Party of Buenos Aires.

Striving for individual political survival, Mitre's strategy of state formation took into account opportunities and constraints derived from the revolution in Atlantic trade of the mid-1850s, the varieties of caudillo domination in the interior, and the competition between the Liberal and Federal protoparties in the early 1860s. Mitre was a protagonist and final victor of the post-Pavón negotiations. Yet constraints forced Mitre to make concessions, including the adoption of the federal formula to make unification agreeable to Urquiza, who was thus able to capture a share of the gains generated by the creation of Argentina. The final section of the chapter analyzes the settlement that formed the Argentine state.

The Settlement That Created Argentina
Players

The critical juncture opened by the Battle of Pavón created multiple developmental paths. The resolution of the critical juncture was the unification of

Buenos Aires and the Confederación under the federal formula. However, over the course of the post-Pavón negotiation, both Mitre and Urquiza experienced strong pressures from members of their own political movements to pursue courses of action that, had they been taken, would have led to radically different final outcomes. In the four months between the Battle of Pavón and the closure of the critical juncture, unification—let alone federal unification—was sometimes the least likely outcome.

Mitre and Urquiza led the military actions in Pavón, and after the battle, they also led the peace negotiations. Both Mitre and Urquiza were willing to make mutual concessions in order to achieve peace and unification—which they implicitly agreed were a precondition for extending and stabilizing their political careers. Both Mitre and Urquiza were surrounded by actors within their own political movements, usually referred to as *elementos exaltados* (hardliners), who did not want to compromise and preferred a continuation of war to making concessions. On Mitre's side, all his fellow Liberals in Buenos Aires were against even negotiating with Urquiza. They demanded the complete destruction of Urquiza's power basis and in some cases the exile or execution of the Confederación's leader. Liberals also had institutional demands. Some Liberals advocated the consolidation of Buenos Aires as a separate state. Others preferred unification between Buenos Aires and the Confederación through the imposition of a unitary formula à la Rivadavia, which would have eliminated altogether the political autonomy of the provinces. Mitre could have pursued any of those options and in the process gain more support from Buenos Aires than by agreeing to the path that was finally taken.

Mitre's post-Pavón position was fragile in many respects. He was the only voice in Buenos Aires advocating for unification under the federal formula. In Buenos Aires, the range of rivals of the federal solution was intimidating. They included a wide group of prestigious politicians and all elements of a powerful landowning class. The day after the Battle of Pavón, Mitre could count on only two advantages over his rivals in Buenos Aires: he had direct control of Buenos Aires's army, and the other political leaders in Buenos Aires faced serious collective-action problems. Despite sharing a long-standing animosity toward provincial caudillos and a deep-seated opposition to spending the resources of Buenos Aires's customhouse outside their jurisdiction, Mitre's rivals in Buenos Aires did not always agree on the method for solving the critical juncture. Mitre could take advantage of the disorganization and disagreement among his fellow Liberals.

On Urquiza's side, except for an intimate circle of five people, all his traditional allies, lieutenants, and clients urged him to continue the war to its conclusion. Most of them were convinced of the Confederación's military superiority. However, given the radial nature of their loyalty toward Urquiza, Urquiza's continued leadership was the only method of solving their collective-action problem. Without the protection of Urquiza's leadership, provincial governors in the Confederación feared for their political life and sometimes for their biological life as well. Given the historical preference of many members of Buenos Aires's elites for a unitary formula of territorial governance, if Mitre's army was not destroyed, provincial autonomy would be under constant risk. Moreover, Urquiza himself considered the option of forming a separate republic composed of Entre Ríos and the satellite province of Corrientes.[11]

The field of conflicting forces and interests created by the Battle of Pavón had multiple viable solutions. Argentina was only one among many. Based on the analysis of antecedent conditions, Table 6.1 identifies actors, preferred outcomes, resources, and constraints.

Stakes

The naked facts of the Battle of Pavón and its aftermath are a concatenation of five events that resulted in the rise of Mitre to the presidency of a unified Argentina: in September 1861, Urquiza withdrew from the battlefield of Pavón; in October, the army of Buenos Aires advanced into the key province of Santa Fe; in early November, the allies of Mitre in the province of Santiago del Estero, the Taboada brothers, helped Buenos Aires dominate the entire Northwest region; in mid-November, Córdoba, another key province, joined Buenos Aires's movement; and finally, by the end of the year, a wave of government changes in the other provinces completed the support required by Mitre to become the first president of a unified Argentina (1862–68).

In conventional historiographic interpretations, Pavón is customarily regarded as a "victory" for Buenos Aires. Conventional interpretations are wrong. Buenos Aires was the loser. Conventional accounts focus only on who captured the presidency. Since Mitre, the governor of Buenos Aires, became

Table 6.1. Actors, Preferences, Resources, and Constraints

Actor	Preferred territorial outcome	Preferred formula of territorial governance	Resources	Constraints
Mitre	Unification	Federalism	Promise of "peace dividend" Intermittent support of Buenos Aires's public opinion Potential allies in the Interior Formidable army	Time 1: Expiration of economic opportunities Time 2: End of tenure as governor Resources: Caudillo power in Upper Littoral and interior
Hardline Liberals 1 (Separatists)	Buenos Aires, sovereign country	Not applicable	Support of economic elites	Collective-action problems
Hardline Liberals 2 (Unitarians)	Unification	Unitary, after military conquest of the interior	Support of political elites	Collective-action problems
Urquiza	Unification or secession (Entre Ríos + Corrientes)	Federalism	Formidable provincial and private army Loyalty from lower-level caudillos	Semibankruptcy of Confederación's interior provinces
Confederación's governors	Unification	Federalism, after military defeat of Buenos Aires	Support of Urquiza	Fiscal unviability
Liberal minorities in the interior	Unification	Federal or unitary	Support from Buenos Aires's Liberal Party	Small number

the president, it is assumed that Buenos Aires was the winner. Yet the notion that what was good for Mitre in the short run was also good for Buenos Aires in the long run has no basis. Moreover, the presidency was not the only issue at stake. It was not even the most important one from the perspective of state-formation analysis. Two more important issues were unification (whether Buenos Aires and the Confederación would merge) and the territorial formula (whether it would be unitarian or federal).

Mitre obtained the presidency, the goal he pursued. Yet the state he formed made Buenos Aires a long-term loser. Only a few years after Mitre ended his presidency, the Argentine state got captured by a coalition of Interior and Upper Littoral provinces that deliberately excluded the province of Buenos Aires.[12] Domination by Interior and Upper Littoral provinces in turn set in motion a process through which Buenos Aires gradually lost its political and economic power at the hands of both the central government and the other subnational units in the federation. Hence, from the perspective of conventional accounts, Pavón creates the "paradox" that Buenos Aires, the alleged victor, actually embraced unification under the formula of territorial governance that hurt its long-term political and economic interests.

To solve the "paradox" of Buenos Aires's long-term defeat, it is crucial to see Mitre as a political entrepreneur, whose professional ambition, at a critical point in his career, clashed with the interests of the province of Buenos Aires. The differentiation between the preferences of Mitre and those of the local elites of Buenos Aires was in fact a necessary condition for the formation of supraregional alliances that overcame the territorial conflicts that had dominated politics since independence and had prevented the formation of a durable state. If Buenos Aires's political elites had not been split by the ambition of a political entrepreneur, Argentina would not exist.

The Negotiation Process, Part 1: Urquiza's Opening Strategy (September–October 1861)

The battle that opened the state-formation critical juncture took place near the banks of the Pavón stream, in the southernmost section of the Santa Fe province, close to the border with Buenos Aires, on September 17, 1861. The battlefield was located about 25 miles south of Rosario, the Confederación's main port, and 160 miles north of Buenos Aires city. Both the armies of Buenos Aires and the Confederación were around seventeen thousand men strong, each including cavalry, infantry, and artillery divisions. The battle lasted two and a half hours, from the moment when the artilleries opened fire until the moment when the bulk of Buenos Aires's infantry found refuge at the Palacio estate—a private cattle-raising establishment—surrounded by the Confederación's cavalry. The cavalry of the Confederación defeated the cavalry of Buenos Aires, which was completely disbanded. If not killed, wounded, or captured, Buenos Aires's horsemen were forced to cross back over the Arroyo del Medio, the border between Santa Fe and Buenos Aires. On the other hand, the artillery of Buenos Aires, better equipped, defeated the artillery of the Confederación.

Mitre left the battlefield persuaded that his forces had been defeated. Mitre retreated to San Nicolás, the closest village to the battlefield within Buenos Aires. In a clear sign of pessimism, he ordered that the arsenal be buried or destroyed.[13] However, while his orders were being executed, Mitre learned that Urquiza, the commander in chief of the Confederación, had withdrawn from the battle, taking four thousand horsemen from Entre Ríos with him. Although the causes of Urquiza's withdrawal were uncertain at the time, its potential consequences were clear. It gave Buenos Aires a chance to regroup, fight back, and eventually win the war.

The army of the Confederación, for its part, split into three groups. The bulk retreated to Rosario, the closest village to the battlefield within the province of Santa Fe. A few cavalry divisions, some under the command of Urquiza's loyal lieutenants, remained in the battlefield, looking for their leader. Finally, Urquiza returned with his cavalry divisions to a point that was much more distant from the battlefield. After a short stop in Diamante, a small port by the Paraná River on the western border of Entre Ríos, he moved his battalions to his San José palace, a king's castle near the village of Concepción, by the Uruguay River, on the eastern border of the province. The distance traveled by Urquiza indicates that—in contrast to the forces of Buenos Aires in San Nicolás and those of the Confederación in Rosario— his forces had not retreated to regroup. Urquiza had abandoned the war, at least temporarily.

Urquiza's Opening Move. Urquiza's withdrawal from the Battle of Pavón might be a mystery from a military point of view, as many historians have claimed.[14] Yet, from a *political* point of view, it was certainly a sophisticated plan of action. It closed a battle, but it initiated a bargaining process. Crucially, Urquiza's withdrawal from the battlefield was a *strategic* decision: he did so *in anticipation* of future negotiations with Buenos Aires's leaders. Urquiza's plan took into account two possible scenarios. In the negative scenario, the rest of the Confederación's army would surrender, but Urquiza would have secured that at least his province, Entre Ríos, and satellite Corrientes would become true military bastions, immune to invasion by Buenos Aires. When Urquiza left Pavón, he took with him a cavalry force that had not had an active participation in the battle. A fresh military force was a clear indication that he wanted to fortify Entre Ríos. In the positive scenario, the rest of the Confederación's army would continue the fight and would manage to inflict severe damage to Buenos Aires's forces, which in turn would clearly improve Urquiza's future negotiation position vis-à-vis Mitre. Ideally, the rival armies would destroy each other, and in the process, the power of Derqui, the Confederación's president, and Mitre, Buenos Aires's governor, would vanish. Urquiza would then emerge as the only reasonable candidate to occupy the presidency of a unified Argentina. That was certainly Urquiza's top aspiration.

Urquiza wanted President Derqui out of power because he found Derqui completely unreliable. In 1859, Urquiza had selected Derqui as his successor because he met all the requirements of a political dauphin. As often happens with dauphins, Derqui started to seek autonomy from Urquiza the moment he was inaugurated. Derqui made a secret agreement with politicians from Córdoba, his native province, and the caudillo Juan Saá, the governor of San Luis. Derqui's conspiracy had two legs. Politicians from Córdoba would coordinate with colleagues from other provinces in order to form a bloc in the congress that excluded legislators who were loyal to Urquiza and would move the national capital outside the province of Entre Ríos, Urquiza's fiefdom, either to Rosario (province of Santa Fe) or the city of Córdoba (the capital of the province with the same name). In turn, Saá would supply the military force that would gradually replace the role of Entre Ríos's army. In the preparations for the Battle of Pavón, Urquiza learned about Derqui's machinations through a mixture of espionage and good luck (Urquiza found correspondence revealing the conspiracy in a coat that Derqui accidently forgot in Urquiza's palace).

The first few weeks after the battle were dominated by Urquiza's duplicity toward Derqui and other key leaders of the Confederación. Urquiza's postbattle duplicity was a political complement to the military withdrawal the day of the battle. Urquiza wanted Derqui to continue the war against Buenos Aires without risking any of his own military capital. Urquiza systematically nurtured the false expectation that he would return to the war.

Three days after the war, Urquiza reported to President Derqui that, after the cavalry under his command had defeated the corresponding divisions of Buenos Aires, he left the battlefield because he was physically exhausted after days of poor health. However, Urquiza crucially added, "I promise you that I will immediately contribute to the definitive resolution [of the war] by gathering all elements of power I am able to mobilize."[15]

For Derqui, Urquiza's absence in the war was a "hole" that he would "never be able to fill," but the war was not lost.[16] Derqui took a battery of bold measures during his first week in Rosario, indicating that he was optimistic about the prospects of the war even without Urquiza's intervention. Derqui worked in tandem with Pascual Rosas, the governor of Santa Fe, the most vulnerable province if Buenos Aires decided to attack the Confederación. Derqui had the port of Rosario barricaded. He promoted Juan Saá to general and named General Benjamín Virasoro as commander in chief in substitution for Urquiza. He energetically harangued the soldiers gathered in Rosario and shared his plans with foreign diplomats. The English representative reported that "[Derqui] thought that it would not be long before General Mitre would be forced by his countrymen to resign and insisted that he would be able to produce a revolution in the town of Buenos Aires by laying siege to it."[17]

For Derqui, the most immediate danger was not Mitre's attack. Rather, he feared that, in light of Urquiza's return to Entre Ríos, the Confederación's troops would desert en masse. To prevent desertions, he issued a decree ordering that all soldiers join him in Rosario under the threat of formal discharge from the army.

Derqui was right in fearing desertions, but he did not expect that Urquiza would actively sabotage his attempts to strengthen the Confederación's army. Communications between second-level authorities and troops in Entre Ríos reveal that Urquiza neutralized Derqui's decree. Colonel Manuel Navarro, appointed mayor of the Nogoyá county and one of Urquiza's many political clients, told military officers in his jurisdiction, "[Derqui's] decree applies only to soldiers in the National Army, but not to us, who belong to the Army of Entre Ríos. We have our Governor [Urquiza] to obey. Laugh at all that talk [from Derqui's circle], dismiss what you see [in Rosario], and just know that General Urquiza is today as strong as he was after Caseros and Cepeda."[18]

The Impact of Urquiza's Plan. The effects of Urquiza's sabotage were rapidly felt. Derqui was never able to put together a sizable army in Rosario. In only ten days, Derqui's initial optimism turned into desperation. Derqui realized that Urquiza's return to the war was the only chance for his survival, but he was completely blind as to what it would take to regain Urquiza's trust, if anything.

All secondary leaders of the Confederación were quick to perceive the risks that Urquiza's abstention was placing on the state's military capacity and their individual careers. The governor of Santa Fe could not have been plainer in his correspondence with Urquiza: "Your presence at the head of the army is indispensable to free the Nation from the threat of chaos. I beg your cooperation to achieve a definitive victory. Without you, everything unravels. . . . What a disaster it will be for the rest of the army when they learn what is happening right now [i.e., Urquiza keeping his cavalry in Entre Ríos]! I simply cannot believe you will be capable of exposing us to total devastation. . . . Your glory demands that you come here."[19]

Representatives from Córdoba joined the plea: "We see the resolve of everyone to fight for the cause of the Confederación. It is only your absence that at some point may cause despair. . . . We hope you will not give us the right to reproach you [that you had abandoned the cause]."[20]

Urquiza's sabotage against Derqui proved too effective even for Urquiza's own purposes. The military leaders of Entre Ríos and Corrientes who remained in Rosario under the command of Derqui grew increasingly anxious at the lack of news from Urquiza.

Derqui, desperate for his political survival, sent Colonel Ricardo López Jordán, Urquiza's right hand, to the San José palace. It was an attempt to obtain Urquiza's forgiveness for prior political sins and at least a modicum of military assistance. However, López Jordán's direct contact with his leader further debilitated Derqui. In the last days of September, a lethal sentence from a conversation between Urquiza and Nicanor Molinas, the Confederación's minister of foreign affairs, became a political maxim that summarized the political climate at the San José palace. After Urquiza assured Molinas that he had been betrayed by President Derqui, he added, "It is better to be defeated by the enemy than to fall in the hands of treasonous friends."[21]

Back in Rosario, López Jordán shared the climate of opinion in San José with fellow officers. Desertions spread like wildfire. The first week of October, Derqui sent a mission to Corrientes, requesting troops from Governor José María Rolón. Urquiza responded by sending his own mission, which aborted Derqui's orders. Rolón was just another client of Urquiza. Over the course of the first three weeks after Pavón, Derqui's forces in Rosario shrank from six thousand men to less than two thousand, approximately a tenth the size of the Confederación's army in Pavón.

Urquiza's Plan Revealed. Urquiza's full political plan needed to remain secret to be effective. The British chargé d'affaires in Paraná, however, got very close to discovering it: "I have been lately led to believe that General Urquiza is playing a deeper game. It is well known that he has sent private messages to the officers devoted to him, recommending them to leave the army. His object seems to be to weaken the action of the President, . . . to induce by intrigues the inhabitants of the Confederación to call upon him to take direction of the affairs of the country."[22]

Urquiza's "deeper game" was actually deeper than the British diplomat's reconstruction of it. Urquiza wanted Derqui to inflict substantial losses on Buenos Aires's army before the Confederación had to "call upon him to take direction." The only mention of Urquiza's full plan can be found in the reports of the Spanish chargé d'affaires in Montevideo, Carlos Creus. In his late-September report, after describing the delicate situation of Derqui's army, "which has shrunk to half its size due to dispersion and discouragement," Creus emphasized that "Urquiza, in the important province of Entre Ríos, keeps a solid influence over many military chieftains." Creus made an informed guess about Urquiza's plan: "fearful that a complete triumph of [Derqui's army] will be followed by vengeance against him, Urquiza might want to take a position that forces both parties [i.e., Derqui's and Mitre's armies] to destroy each other [*desangrarse*] in order to dominate them down the road."[23] Creus was right in that Urquiza was counting on the mutual destruction of Derqui and Mitre. Creus was wrong about Urquiza's motivation. Urquiza did not fear the military power of Derqui or Saá. His forces in Entre Ríos and satellite Corrientes were much stronger than the forces of the other eleven provinces of the Confederación combined. Urquiza was far more worried about Buenos Aires's military capabilities, and he expected that Derqui would undermine them.

By the end of the first week of October, two facts combined to break the resistance of Derqui. At the same time that he realized that Urquiza's sabotage had extended to virtually all the battalions in the Confederación's army, Mitre, aware of Derqui's increasing weakness, decided to advance toward Rosario with Buenos Aires's troops, some six thousand men, including a new cavalry force. Simple military arithmetic induced Derqui to abandon the city of Rosario on October 7. Buenos Aires's forces occupied the city four days later. Urquiza's plan became transparent to everyone, and a balance of achievements and failures could be made. Urquiza's goals were fulfilled only partially: Derqui had fallen, but he had not been able to inflict any damage to Mitre's forces.

Derqui remained as the nominal president of the Confederación for another month and left an unadorned record of his last days in power. In late October, in a letter to Juan Saá, Derqui complained, "I had already been informed by reliable sources that General Urquiza maintained clandestine communications with the enemy. But now he has taken away his mask and communications with the enemy are transmitted by warships under truce flags sailing between Diamante and Buenos Aires. . . . You and I are his principal victims. You, because you had the courage to triumph on the battlefield from which he fled, and myself because I am a legal obstacle to his dictatorship."[24]

Derqui was right. The same week he abandoned Rosario, Mitre and Urquiza began to negotiate a peace agreement, inaugurating the master bargaining of the critical juncture.

The British diplomat was quick to perceive the convergence of interests between Mitre and Urquiza: "The first object of these two [Mitre and Urquiza] is evidently to bring about the downfall of Sr. Derqui. The former of them desires it, I believe, that he may afterward be able to come to terms with General Urquiza, and the principal object of the latter is to get rid of his rival, Sr. Derqui, with the intention perhaps of subsequently coming to an arrangement with General Mitre."[25]

The alliance between Mitre and Urquiza was, in principle, partial and transitory. With Derqui out of their way, the terms of a new arrangement between Mitre and Urquiza were far from obvious because both leaders held the same ambition: to reach the presidency of a unified Argentina.

The Negotiation Process, Part 2:
Mitre's Closing Strategy (October–December 1861)

A Change of Contenders: The Entrance of Hardline Liberals. Throughout the critical juncture of state formation, Mitre and Urquiza were key leaders of the process. If in the first half, Derqui was a third center of power, in the second half it was the hardline Liberals of Buenos Aires who gained enough prominence to affect Mitre's and Urquiza's actions.

Immediately after the occupation of Rosario, Mitre and Urquiza were willing not only to negotiate a peace agreement but also to form a lasting alliance. The terms of the alliance were straightforward: Mitre would become president of a unified Argentina in exchange for Urquiza's survival as ruler of Entre Rios. Urquiza's survival depended on the preservation of his provincial army and the federal formula of territorial governance he had sponsored since 1853. The provincial army of Entre Ríos was the material basis that made the preservation of the federal formula credible. The dissolution of Urquiza's army would have led Mitre and his fellow Liberals to impose the unitarian formula. Since the constitution banned reelection, Mitre could implicitly promise Urquiza alternation in power. In the foreseeable future, Urquiza was the only leader besides Mitre who was able to put together an electoral coalition at the scale required to succeed in the territory of unified Argentina. Urquiza had more than a fair chance of becoming Mitre's successor in 1868.

Yet, in contrast to Urquiza's position in Entre Ríos, Mitre did not concentrate political power in Buenos Aires. He was surrounded by hardline Liberals, who had been historically opposed to any deal with Urquiza. Mitre was the governor of Buenos Aires, but he had delegated executive authority to Manuel Ocampo in order to be able to lead military operations at the border with Santa Fe. Ocampo formed a triumvirate with ministers Pastor Obligado (government) and de la Riestra (finance), who collectively analyzed Mitre's reports and before replying to Mitre agreed on a shared vision of the way war operations or peace negotiations should proceed. Mitre had to ne-gotiate decisions with the triumvirate and the minister of war, Juan Andrés Gelly y Obes, all of whom in turn had to keep in mind the opinions in Bue-nos Aires's legislature, which had the last word on the vital issue of how many resources should be allocated to Mitre's military campaign and under what conditions. Also influential were political commentators in the press. Leg-islators paid close attention to the press for it was seen as an echo chamber of the voters' preferences.

The triumvirate, the minister of war, the legislatures, the press, and other notables in Buenos Aires were all strong advocates for Buenos Aires's political and economic interests. For hardline Liberals, the unitarian state was the ideal formula of territorial governance, and federalism was the worst one—even worse than separation. Hardliners were willing to give up unifi-cation if it required the federal formula. For hardliners, the federal formula would induce transfers of power and wealth to the other provinces and the national government that no member of the elites of Buenos Aires was will-ing to tolerate.

The Public Arguments and the Private Interests. Mitre and hardline Lib-erals accused each other of political and economic myopia. They both had good arguments. For Mitre, the elites of Buenos Aires were unable to see that unification was beneficial for most Argentines. A peace agreement with Urquiza had the potential to drastically reduce military expenditures both in Buenos Aires and in Entre Ríos, which in addition to channeling new re-sources into productive activities would attract foreign investors who had hitherto been dissuaded from participating in the Argentine economy because of its chronic political instability. For Mitre, unification was only possible under the federal formula because the introduction of the unitarian formula would cause a war against Entre Ríos, which under the banner of resistance against central domination would have little trouble in recruiting the support of the other provinces. The political results of a war over the formula of territo-rial governance were largely uncertain. The only certainty was that the war would be a long and expensive one—which would force Argentina to miss the unique opportunity created by the revolution in Atlantic trade.

On the other hand, the elites of Buenos Aires did not care about the welfare of "Argentine" citizens because no such thing as an Argentine nationality existed. The elites of Buenos Aires were interested in the power and wealth of their ministate. Unification under the federal formula would make Buenos Aires's citizens net economic losers, for they would have to pay for the expenditures of the central government and the transfers to the other provinces.

Mitre was the only member of the elite of Buenos Aires who refused to acknowledge the perverse effects of unification under the federal formula, because for him the prize of winning the presidency dwarfed the costs that he would have to pay as an individual citizen of Buenos Aires. Mitre's presidential ambitions made him willing to extend concessions to Urquiza and other potentates in the interior that the hardliners found unacceptable.

Divergence in Buenos Aires. Mitre and the hardliners had been in perfect agreement until the occupation of Rosario. Once Rosario was occupied, Mitre and hardline Liberals grew increasingly distant. For hardline Liberals, the priority was to call for a new constituent assembly, which should introduce the unitarian formula and thereby remove caudillo rulers from the provinces. If Urquiza opposed, the hardliners were willing to invade Entre Ríos and destroy his power. Two days after the occupation of Rosario, the triumvirate of Buenos Aires suggested that Mitre should "invite provinces to a constituent assembly, and if they do not want to come, then Buenos Aires will have to consider what is most convenient for itself [i.e., continue as a separate country]." The same letter also focused on Urquiza: "We have to deal with the most important issue: Entre Ríos and General Urquiza. . . . We believe he will soon try to approach us with a pro-peace proposal that requests that we allow him to stay in Entre Ríos. Such a deal is obviously not beneficial to the Liberal Party. . . . The best thing for us would be his voluntary retirement from public life . . . but that would be like expecting pears from the elm tree."[26]

Mitre wanted a deal to become president in the short run. The political path suggested by hardline Liberals might have been the right one for the safety of Buenos Aires's interests in the long run. Yet the time to maturation of the alternative path was incompatible with the small window of opportunity that had just been opened for Mitre's presidential ambitions. Mitre's prestige reached a peak after the capture of Rosario. A reform of the constitution would be a long process, and before it was concluded, Mitre's prestige might lose momentum. Mitre's presidential aspirations made him too impatient for constitutional negotiations and too averse to the risks attached to them.

To become president, Mitre was willing not only to preserve the federal formula but also to extend the deal with Urquiza to other caudillos, especially the Taboada brothers, whom he expected to transform from state-breaking warlords into state-takers under his government.

Mitre did not want to fight against the army of Entre Ríos for three reasons. First, he feared defeat. Mitre never revealed to the triumvirate his belief that Urquiza's army—his dreaded horsemen—was probably stronger than that of Buenos Aires. Had he done so, advocates of the unitarian formula would have accused him of cowardice, which would have ruined his political career. Also, advocates of separation would have demanded that his military campaign be terminated to avoid further expenses, which would have aborted Mitre's plans for unifying Argentina.

Second, fighting Entre Ríos would have diverted resources from the much more profitable venture of turning key provinces like Córdoba, Mendoza, and Tucumán into allies for Mitre's presidential project. Provinces in the interior hosted Liberal minorities that needed Buenos Aires's economic and military support to replace authorities who were loyal to Urquiza or Derqui. Given the enormous disparity between the military capabilities of Entre Ríos and those of the interior provinces, Mitre preferred to direct Buenos Aires's efforts toward the interior. Interior provinces were much easier to conquer individually, and collectively they provided a much greater volume of electoral support than the single province of Entre Ríos. A fight with Entre Ríos would require an army of fifteen thousand men, whereas supporting Liberal revolutions in the provinces of the interior would normally demand one thousand soldiers and never more than three thousand.

Finally, if Mitre gave in to the belligerent pressure of hardliners and went to war against Urquiza, a victory would possibly enhance his public reputation in Buenos Aires. However, it would most likely make Mitre more dispensable for his fellow Liberals rather than more prestigious among the public. The elimination of Urquiza would strengthen the political position of Liberals who wanted separation or unification under the unitarian formula. Circumstances made Mitre and Urquiza partial allies again. This time, it was hardline Liberals, rather than Derqui, who united them. The success of Mitre's presidential bid required that Urquiza's power remain within a narrow range. It had to be strong enough to justify Mitre's campaign in the interior and to defend the adoption of the federal formula but not so strong as to encourage Urquiza to interfere with Mitre's plans.

Mitre's Original Plan. Given his presidential ambitions and his assessment of the constraints placed by Urquiza, by the hardline Liberals, and by the capacity of his own army, Mitre devised an eminently political plan. Persuasion campaigns and coalition-making would play a much more substantial role than military conquest. Mitre's original plan had two parts: to achieve control of key provinces in the interior and to make a lasting deal with Urquiza.

In the interior, Mitre's few military targets were subordinated to his political aspirations. He had captured Rosario to obtain a basis from which to extend his influence into a critical number of provinces, including primarily Córdoba. He planned to invite all of them to "disavow" the authority of President Derqui and choose the president for a unified Argentina. The campaign in the interior would require some military efforts: outside Rosario, the province of Santa Fe still hosted the residual army of the Confederación, which would need to be disbanded; in Córdoba, Mitre planned the fall of the provincial government (occupied by old Derquistas), but the Liberal political minority would need military support from Mitre to stay in power. Mitre also pursued the elimination of the state-breaker caudillo Juan Saá from the province of San Luis. Mitre and other Liberals feared that Saá would join Urquiza (they did not know that Urquiza and Saá hated each other).

Hence, in tandem with his military efforts, Mitre invested most of his political energy in obtaining support from the government of Buenos Aires for a plan that was presented as a strategy to replace federal caudillos with Liberal politicians as governors of key provinces. The change would allegedly help to protect the economy of Buenos Aires from political instability, looting raids, and irrational redistributive demands. In reality, Mitre wanted to place governors that secured him a winning coalition in the election of the first president of a unified Argentina.

In Mitre's plan, Urquiza was a different story altogether. Mitre decided to ignore Buenos Aires's hate toward the supercaudillo and initiated informal negotiations with him. Mitre speculated that if he could obtain some form of capitulation from Urquiza, the hardliners would be appeased. Around the same time that Mitre occupied Rosario, he sent an emissary to the San José palace, Juan Cruz Ortíz. Ortíz was a mutually reliable diplomatic agent. Mitre let Urquiza know that Buenos Aires was open to peace negotiations.

In mid-October, Mitre and Urquiza reached a virtual agreement through the emissary. Mitre committed to sustain the federal formula and not to invade Entre Ríos, whereas Urquiza committed the province of Entre Ríos to disavow Derqui's government. A new government would be formed after inviting all provinces to a new congress. However, before making decisions official, Mitre drafted a peace agreement and sent it to the government of Buenos Aires for approval.

Mitre under Pressure: The Veto of the Hardliners and the Loss of Political Power. Mitre miscalculated the reaction of the hardliners. The triumvirate of Buenos Aires vetoed the agreement with Urquiza. In a collective letter to Mitre, Ocampo, Obligado, and de la Riestra argued that the peace proposal was detrimental to Buenos Aires's interests: "We oppose . . . the formation of a new congress on the basis of the 'equality' of representation for the provinces. That 'equality' is for us a 'leonine' equality. If we had to accept it with repulsion because we were powerless to reject it after being defeated in '59 and '60, nothing would today, when we are the victors, justify that we accept it. If we should not accept it, much less ground is there to propose it spontaneously [as Mitre had done]." For the triumvirate, the federal formula was the worst ("leonine") deal for Buenos Aires. It was the old legacy of Buenos Aires's past defeats. Given that the occupation of Rosario made Buenos Aires the new winner, the constitution had to change and introduce a formula of territorial governance that reflected the new balance of power. The triumvirate did not make a specific mention of the unitarian formula, but the elimination of political autonomy in the provinces seemed the obvious next step: "The idea of not installing or overthrowing governors, especially when we are dealing with people like Saá [the caudillo/governor of San Luis], Nazar [Mendoza], and Rolón [Corrientes], . . . is incompatible with our rights and our safety."[27]

Obligado wanted a war to finish against Urquiza. "It is neither convenient nor honorable to seek an alliance [with Urquiza]."[28] De la Riestra seconded Obligado: "I think that the idea of [unification] through an amalgam with the elements of *caudillaje* that are still in power, and that dominate in most provinces, is incompatible with the principles, the interests, and the safety of Buenos Aires." De la Riestra's choice was the unitarian formula, but he conceded that it would require military imposition, which would simply be too expensive for Buenos Aires: "The only safe basis for a stable and truly beneficial unification is the unitarian system. . . . But that would only be possible by conquest. I am not sure whether we can obtain it by force, unless we are prepared for a long war, which would destroy Buenos Aires's force and credit."[29]

Mitre's conciliatory attitude toward Urquiza began to undermine his political capital in his own Buenos Aires. On October 23, the newspaper *Tribuna* offered the most incisive version of the hardline vision: "The alliance between Urquiza and Mitre is a revolution against the authorities [of Buenos Aires]. War was not made for Mitre to become president. If Mitre becomes president without reorganization [i.e., a change in the formula of territorial governance and the replacement of governors from the Federal Party], it would take our leader and give him to the Confederación."[30]

In late October, the triumvirate requested that Mitre demand that Urquiza surrender the naval squadron stationed in Diamante and dismantle the batteries protecting it from the coast. The triumvirate would consider the disarmament of Diamante, a bastion in Entre Ríos, as a reliable sign of Urquiza's peaceful intentions.

Mitre vented his frustration in a letter to Domingo Sarmiento: "Unitarians see the world and the country through the keyhole of their own house, and they do so from the side of the door facing the street."[31] Mitre was right about unitarians, but he did not admit that he in turn was seeing the world through another keyhole, that of his presidential ambition.

Mitre Updates His Plan. Being flanked by hardline Liberals on one side and the power of Urquiza on the other was both a problem and an opportunity for Mitre. The problem was that the concessions required by Urquiza were incompatible with the agenda demanded by the hardliners. The opportunity originated in the fact that Mitre, in his dealings with the hardliners, could refer to his superior knowledge of the military capacity of Buenos Aires and Entre Ríos in order to gain autonomy from them; and vice versa, in his negotiations with Urquiza, Mitre could point to restrictions imposed by hardliners in order to reduce the number of concessions he had to grant to the supercaudillo.

In order to keep the negotiations with Urquiza alive, Mitre asked Ortíz to return to the San José palace and communicate to Urquiza that the draft of a peace agreement had been vetoed by the government of Buenos Aires. It was a clear message that Urquiza would have to consider further concessions.

Mitre's new challenge was to overcome the veto of the hardliners, especially those who wanted war. Precisely because Mitre's political plans were ambitious and had to be carried out in a matter of months, lest they lose momentum, his military plans were necessarily cautious, given resource constraints that he knew better than anyone. Mitre's approach to the veto of the hardliners was persuasion. He had to obtain their support for limited military goals outside Entre Rios and at the same time hide the fact that he did not want to go to war against Urquiza because he feared defeat.

Instead of highlighting the limitations of Buenos Aires's military power, Mitre placed an emphasis on the magnitude of the challenge involved in turning interior provinces into supporters of the Liberal Party. A better understanding of such a challenge, Mitre thought, would make hardline Liberals see that Entre Ríos and the interior were two different political fronts and that it was too risky to attack both at the same time. Mitre made his greatest pedagogic effort in a letter to the triumvirate in late October: "What we need to accomplish may be *superior to the forces of Buenos Aires*. We have to be pragmatic. We have to take the Argentine Republic as was made by God and men, and accept it as it is, until men, with the help of God, improve it." Mitre's call for pragmatism and the acceptance of the men available at the time was an unambiguous declaration that compromises with at least some caudillos ("Argentina as it is") would be necessary. The opposite of pragmatism was for Mitre "Quixotic politics": "We do not need Quixotic politics. It will jeopardize any success and prolong the fight. Once Santa Fe is completely dominated, I will do the same with Córdoba, and only then will we have a basis for 'political and military' operations, aiming at San Luis as our next target. . . . Quixotic politics is very imprudent, because it would want us to attack two challenges at the same time, forgetting that Rome, which was a warrior nation, never had two enemies at the same time, and that is why it always triumphed."[32]

Mitre achieved a key political victory after gaining the full support of Gelly y Obes to his conciliatory position toward Urquiza. A week after the occupation of Rosario, Gelly y Obes visited Mitre at his new military base.

In his report to the Buenos Aires government, Gelly y Obes started with the good news: "Pacification of Santa Fe is proceeding very well." But he immediately exempted Mitre for the responsibility of not invading Entre Ríos: "It is the fear in all chieftains of our army [toward the cavalry of Entre Ríos] . . . that is preventing the General [Mitre] from giving a resolute order so that the sun rises in Antequera [i.e., the war against Urquiza begins]. I think he is right. . . . Our army wants to go home; they are tired, angry at the bad weather, and bored."[33]

In order to secure a deal with Urquiza that at least a fraction of hardliners would find viable, in early November, Mitre sent Urquiza a new proposal. He repeated his commitment to sustain the 1853 constitution, that is, the federal formula—a concession to Urquiza—but he demanded the dismantling of the batteries in Diamante and the surrender of the Confederación's navy, a concession to hardliners who wanted to secure Buenos Aires's control of the River Plate basin. Additionally, Mitre openly told Urquiza his plans to overthrow Saá. Mitre wanted to keep Urquiza informed about his military plans for two reasons. First, he feared that surprises would trigger Urquiza's wrath. Second, by sharing his plan to deploy military resources in the West, Mitre implicitly promised Urquiza that he would withdraw troops from the Upper Littoral, the most credible commitment that Entre Ríos would not be invaded.

The conditions for a peace agreement seemed ready. If Urquiza acceded to the disarmament of Diamante, an important number of hardliners would view it as a sufficient concession to accept peace with Entre Ríos.

However, only three days after Mitre's letter, Derqui, who was still formally the president of the Confederación, tendered his resignation. Urquiza decided to up the ante in his negotiations with Buenos Aires. Was it too late for Urquiza to replace Derqui and face Mitre's challenge from a new position? Now he was again president of the Confederación and not just governor of Entre Ríos.

Urquiza's Bluff and Mitre's Opportunity. In mid-November, Urquiza wrote back to Mitre trying to persuade him that, as representative of all thirteen provinces, he would be better able to contribute to unification and pacification than as governor of a single province. In addition, Urquiza significantly changed the terms of the agreement. Diamante would be disarmed only if Buenos Aires withdrew its forces from Santa Fe. Urquiza also claimed that he would not allow governors in the interior to be changed. He requested the service of the British and French diplomats as mediators, instructing them that the new proposal was the limit of Urquiza's generosity. The foreign diplomats communicated that if Buenos Aires rejected the new terms, Urquiza was able to mobilize twenty thousand men and resume the war.[34]

The reaction to Urquiza's new terms by hardline Liberals was as incendiary as could be expected. Obligado started the reproach to Mitre: "now Urquiza obtained the delegation [of the Confederación's presidency] . . . you see how everything changes. . . . A new infidelity by Urquiza, . . . and that is why we have to keep our guard up." Obligado pressured Mitre to change his military plans: "Anxiety here is enormous. . . . In general, the opinion is that the expedition to Córdoba should be suspended, and instead launch all our forces against Entre Ríos with maximum speed."[35] Governor Ocampo found negotiations with Urquiza futile: "[Urquiza's new terms show] that we cannot trust him, no matter how powerful your wishes are of making an agreement with him. . . . He is going to be so demanding that we will never be able to meet his requests."[36]

Mitre became less worried about Urquiza's attempt to renegotiate from an allegedly stronger position than about the effects that Urquiza's new proposal produced on his fellow Liberals and the opinion in Buenos Aires. Mitre was perfectly aware of the political costs of his negotiations with Urquiza: "I would not be surprised if, upon my return to Buenos Aires, people throw stones at me instead of flowers."[37]

Urquiza's new attitude created serious limits on Mitre's room to maneuver within Buenos Aires's circles. Given the reaction of the triumvirate, Mitre could not agree to any new concessions to Urquiza. Yet Mitre was almost certain that Urquiza was more concerned about preserving his Entre Ríos bastion than about saving the Confederación. He was ready to call Urquiza's bluff.

Urquiza's defense of the Confederación was not credible because the Confederación was absolutely bankrupt. The day after the Battle of Pavón, the congress had authorized Derqui to obtain a loan for eight million silver pesos. It was impossible to find a lender. In late September, voluntary loans were requested among the merchants of Rosario, Corrientes, and Paraná. The funds collected were less than 10 percent of the intended amount. In early October, Derqui decided to issue treasury notes, which could be used to pay for import taxes. In three days, they were traded in the market with a 50 percent discount. The loss of Rosario in the first week of October was a lethal blow for the Confederación's finances, for its customhouse was the main source of revenue. By November, public employees of the Confederación had not received pay for seven months. Critical for any kind of military operation was the fact that the machinists of the Confederación's naval squadron were ready to abandon their positions for lack of pay and provisions.

If Urquiza dared to refloat the Confederación as a power bloc under his leadership, he must have had reasons other than its financial health. Urquiza was not relying on the Confederación's power but on Mitre's political weakness. He speculated that Mitre's attempt to instigate and sustain Liberal revolutions in the provinces of the interior was doomed to failure. The British diplomat reported that Urquiza had candidly admitted that his new proposal was the best offer he would make *provided* that Mitre was not able to gain control over the interior.[38] Urquiza, as sophisticated a political actor as Mitre, let the fate of his final attempt to revive the Confederación be decided by the balance of power between Mitre's allies and Federal rulers in the interior.

Mitre's Ultimatum, Urquiza's Capitulation, and Hardliners' Pressure. Four days in November pulverized Urquiza's last illusions of getting from Mitre a better deal than the preservation of the federal formula and his Entre Ríos bastion. On November 18, the Liberal minority in Córdoba revolted. A change in the political wind in Córdoba could not be sustained without the military assistance of Buenos Aires. Mitre sent troops under the command of his "proconsul" in the interior, General Wenceslao Paunero. Events in Córdoba helped Mitre not only to intimidate Urquiza but also to relax the pressure from Buenos Aires's hardliners. Even if hardliners could not understand it, Paunero's military mission actually weakened Mitre's military position in the Upper Littoral. With three thousand soldiers dispatched to Córdoba, Mitre needed *porteño* opinion to acquiesce to peace negotiations with Urquiza more than ever. He astutely reintroduced the motion for peace talks: "[With the revolution in Córdoba], we now have a new argument in the negotiation, which was not in their books [i.e., in Urquiza's forecast]."[39] At the same time, the instructions to Paunero could not be more revealing: "Detain or establish your forces in the place that you consider most convenient to accomplish two things: first, cover Córdoba against any attack from San Luis, and second, remain as close as possible to your base of operations, that is, the Upper Littoral, not advancing inland more than absolutely necessary."[40] Mitre wanted Paunero's contingent to remain close to his position in Rosario because he clearly feared an attack from Urquiza.

Encouraged by the events in Córdoba, pressed by hardline Liberals, and aware of the financial irrationality of reviving the Confederación, on November 19 Mitre gave Urquiza an ultimatum. Buenos Aires would go to war against Entre Ríos unless Urquiza stopped protecting the government of the Confederación and surrendered the navy. Mitre suggested that Urquiza should abandon his political career, but he never questioned the federal formula.

On November 25, Urquiza capitulated. He accepted all demands from Mitre, except for his resignation of the governorship of Entre Ríos. Urquiza knew that Mitre's ultimatum was not a bluff. After Córdoba, Mitre had also secured two crucial military victories, one in Santiago del Estero, the other in Santa Fe. In Santiago del Estero, the Taboada brothers, Manuel and Antonino, recovered executive power after overthrowing one of the few loyal Derquistas. Santiago del Estero is located just north of Córdoba. With Córdoba under Mitrista control, Buenos Aires could enter into direct communication with Santiago and provide the Taboadas with military assistance. The Taboada brothers were state-breaking caudillos. Their power derived from a large clientele of Quechua aboriginals who were distributed into half a dozen agro-military colonies along the northern frontier. Some of the colonies were located on land owned by a third Taboada brother, Gaspar. The Taboadas held enough military power to extend their influence into neighboring provinces like Salta, Tucumán, and Catamarca. The Taboadas, especially Antonino, became Mitristas after learning that the Confederación was too poor to offer them any material assistance—only "empty projects," as they pejoratively referred to Urquiza's support, that is, flattering words and military honors with no money attached to them. An alliance with wealthy Buenos Aires, by contrast, promised real rewards that would help them consolidate local power. The creation of a Buenos Aires–Córdoba–Santiago axis meant that a Liberal column separated Entre Ríos and Corrientes from Federal allies in Cuyo and the Andean West (Catamarca and La Rioja).

On November 22, Mitre's army obtained its only clear military victory in the entire war. A contingent of 350 soldiers led by General Venancio Flores attacked what was left of the Confederación's army in Santa Fe. Flores surprised the army during their sleep in Cañada de Gómez. Out of thirteen hundred troops, around a third were butchered in their improvised beds, another third were made prisoner, and the rest disbanded. Gelly y Obes, not a particularly sentimental soul, informed the government in Buenos Aires that "the event of the Cañada de Gómez is one of those military facts that, once their outcomes are known, horrify the victor himself."[41] Cañada de Gómez secured the entire province of Santa Fe for Mitre and crushed any remaining hopes in the ability of the Confederación to stay alive.

Capitulation was the only rational decision for Urquiza. The last week of November, Urquiza explained to his provincial lieutenants and legislators that in order to save Entre Ríos from a war against Buenos Aires, it was necessary to stop defending the Confederación. On December 1, the legislature of Entre Ríos did exactly what Mitre wanted. It disavowed the Confederación's government and authorized Mitre to invite the provinces to a congress that would create a new national government, at a place and time to be defined by Mitre. It was the virtual recognition of Mitre as the first president of a unified Argentina.

The capitulation of Urquiza and the deployment of small military contingents at Córdoba's border with San Luis provoked a wave of replacements of Federal governors with Liberal ones. With no military effort from Buenos Aires, Saá abandoned San Luis and left for Chile. The Federal governors of the other two provinces in Cuyo followed Saá's example.

Hardliners Neutralized. Some hardline Liberals were insatiable. Urquiza's capitulation was big news, but political forces in Buenos Aires who favored either separation or unification under a unitarian formula—a prerequisite of which was the elimination of Urquiza—would not stop putting pressure on Mitre. Mitre finally found a solution to the problem: he would split the hardliners. Given that the elimination of Urquiza was incompatible with his presidential aspirations, Mitre decided to ignore the unitarians and court the separatists.

Separatists feared that Mitre's plan was too expensive. For them, Buenos Aires's assets were sacred resources, which under no circumstances should be shared with poorer provinces: "The army and the customhouse of Buenos Aires shall not be given to anyone, not even if the future president is an angel [i.e., not even if he is a fellow Liberal like Mitre].["][42]

To overcome the resistance of separatists, Mitre constantly looked for methods of saving money. The port of Rosario and the Taboada brothers provided two substantial sources of economic support. Mitre had to be and to appear austere. On December 3, to placate the Liberals' worries about military expenses, Mitre informed Ocampo, "We can count on the resources of the customhouse of Rosario, which can produce, according to very precise estimations, between eighty and one hundred thousand silver pesos per month, with which we can at least pay for the war in the interior, if it lasts longer."[43]

The Taboadas provided the military muscle to extend Mitre's domination in the Northwest and substantially reduced the costs of the campaign. From early December to mid-January, Manuel and Antonino Taboada, recruiting soldiers from Santiago del Estero's small forts in the northern frontier, launched a number of military operations against Catamarca, Salta, and Tucumán that resulted in the fall of pro-Urquiza governors. Since the connection between the Taboadas and the health of Buenos Aires's economy was clear only to Mitre, he had to make it explicit. A document from late December reveals the political economy of Mitre's path toward the presidency of a unified Argentina and the role of the Taboadas in it: "I want to focus only on the resources required to place friendly provinces in a situation that will allow them to collaborate effectively to peace and to the definitive organization of the Republic. You will remember that . . . we committed ourselves to help the provinces of Corrientes, Córdoba, and Santiago del Estero with one thousand ounces of gold." To appease separatists, Mitre highlighted the savings made possible by the alliance with the Taboadas: "Santiago del Estero, using only very moderately that authorization, has requested only two hundred ounces, which will for now be *covered by the customhouse of Rosario*. Only later on shall we send them the remaining eight hundred ounces, which is still very little for what this courageous province deserves, which has so effectively, and using its own resources or—to be perfectly precise—having no resources at all, contributed to the victory of our cause in the interior. *It has saved millions of Buenos Aires's treasury*."[44]

The Taboadas provided the same military capability of Buenos Aires's professional army at a substantially lower price. The higher military

efficiency of the Taboadas was rooted in the caudillo subtype of patrimonial domination that they exerted in Santiago. Thomas Hutchinson, an
Anglo-Irish explorer, revealed the secret of the Taboadas' military efficiency: "All these forts [in Santiago] constitute a species of Agricola-
military establishments. The most curious fact about them is that *the soldiers receive no pay and yet their fidelity to the general* [Antonino] *is very
remarkable.* Each man has a 'chacra' or plot of ground for the cultivation
of wheat, maize, melons and so forth but of these he is not allowed to sell
any until he can prove to his commanding officer that he has enough for
his family's winter store."[45]

Mitre was perfectly aware of how cost-effective an alliance with the
Taboadas was. The role of the Taboadas in Argentina's state formation illustrates both the challenge of juggling the contradictory political and economic demands of Buenos Aires's elites and the ability of Mitre as a political
entrepreneur to deal with them. Buenos Aires's elites abhorred rural caudillos. However, Mitre had little choice but to resort to their services in order
to save Buenos Aires's revenues. If there was something that *porteño* elites
disliked more than caudillos, it was spending money outside their jurisdiction. The military capacity of the Taboadas and the customhouse of Rosario gradually neutralized the objections of separatists.

If Mitre's success in the interior and the Andes appeased the separatists, it had the opposite effect on the unitarians. The unitarians thought that
control of the interior left Mitre with no excuse to continue avoiding a war
against Entre Ríos. Unitarians were not satisfied with Urquiza's capitulation.
They strove for his elimination, which was a stepping-stone for the substitution of the federal formula by the unitarian one.

The unitarians apparently did not know that Liberal control of some
parts of the interior was too dependent on the military backup of Buenos
Aires's forces. Therefore, they did not understand the risks of redeploying
Buenos Aires's army to Entre Ríos.

Mitre was certain that an open conflict with Urquiza would derail his
presidential project, no matter what the result of the war was. If he lost, his
political career would end. If he won, the struggle would take too long, and
victory would only open a new period of constitutional design in which
unitarian *porteños* would have the opportunity to change the formula of territorial governance, producing another substantial delay.

Mitre tried to appease unitarians by requesting that Urquiza step down from power in Entre Ríos. Yet Urquiza drew a line. He decided to mobilize his province. If Urquiza's proposal in November was a bluff, the military mobilization in December was tangible proof of the limits of his tolerance. Urquiza had given up on the Confederación, but he would risk everything to defend his hegemony in Entre Ríos. He issued a decree calling every man between the ages of fifteen and sixty to military service in defense of the province. Urquiza's lieutenants were exultant.

Mitre understood that Urquiza had run out of patience. Mitre must have welcomed Urquiza's military reaction. In January, the only element separating Mitre from his presidential prize was the attitude of the unitarians against Urquiza. The mobilization of Urquiza's cavalries certainly instilled enough fear among *porteños* to dissuade at least some unitarians from war. Mitre resumed his political campaign, which ostensibly was a rational call for peace, but it could not hide either his alliance with Urquiza or his impatience to become president: "Irrespective of the benefits we can obtain through war, we cannot, and we should not ignore the serious problems that war would bring about. Controlling our bellicose passion, we must subordinate our political march to the fundamental idea of getting peace as soon as possible. . . . We should not jeopardize the advantages we have obtained by making this situation last any longer. In a country like ours, the smallest incident can ruin all our efforts."[46] Gelly y Obes agreed with Mitre: a war against Urquiza will "bring a complication of all demons."[47]

By mid-January, the pressure of the unitarians finally began to fade. Many separatists had already become Mitristas after learning about Mitre's efforts to save money. A substantial portion of the unitarians realized that Urquiza was still a real threat against Buenos Aires and accepted that only Mitre had the political capital to prevent Urquiza from turning into a statebreaker. When the ranks of active unitarians were significantly thinned, Mitre simply stopped paying attention to them.

Although Mitre was born to political life as a hardline Liberal, he would not sacrifice his presidential ambitions to the hatred of residual unitarians for Urquiza. Mitre knew, however, that the hatred for Urquiza was not irrational. By forming an alliance with Urquiza, Mitre was also letting the federal formula survive. Mitre would be president for six years, but he sacrificed Buenos Aires's power and wealth forever. On January 23, Mitre "assured"

Urquiza "in the most formal and solemn manner that the province of Entre
Rios can rest in peace."[48] Because of Urquiza's recent demonstration of force
and Mitre's decision to marginalize remaining unitarians, the peace agreed
between the last supercaudillo and the first political entrepreneur was not
vetoed. The war was over. Argentina was born.

Recapitulation

Argentina is the outcome of a four-month critical juncture. The juncture was
inaugurated by the Battle of Pavón, but the key process was the postbattle
negotiation between the political entrepreneur Mitre and the rural lord
Urquiza. The first half of the juncture was shaped by Urquiza's strategic decision to abandon the battle. Urquiza achieved only two of his three goals:
the fall of the Confederación's president, Derqui, and the preservation of the
military capabilities of his rudimentary port state, Entre Ríos. Urquiza hoped
that Derqui would inflict substantial damage on Buenos Aires's army, but
Urquiza's sabotage against Derqui was so strong that Derqui fell from power
before the expected clash with Mitre.

The second half of the critical juncture was marked by Mitre's campaign to become president, which was an operation on multiple political and
military fronts. The campaign included two central components: the exchange of mutual concessions with Urquiza in the Upper Littoral and the
neutralization of hardline Liberals in Buenos Aires. Both Urquiza and the
hardline Liberals supported Mitre's presidential ambitions. Yet, in exchange
for their respective support, they demanded concessions from Mitre that
were mutually incompatible. It was impossible to please Urquiza and the
hardliners at the same time.

Mitre produced a Machiavellian solution, not a Solomonic one. He was
more responsive to Urquiza than to hardline Liberals. Only by betraying the
interests of his former fellow political colleagues and the economic elites of
Buenos Aires could Mitre capture the presidency. Mitre carefully manipulated the threat that Urquiza created for Buenos Aires to extract from Buenos
Aires key concessions for his campaign. He also manipulated the animosity
of Buenos Aires's elites toward Urquiza in order to reduce the cost of obtaining Urquiza's support for his presidential aspirations.

A key step in Mitre's campaign was the creation of a split within the hardliners, which weakened their position. Mitre managed to split the hardliners by "economizing" the cost of his campaign, which he achieved by forming alliances with state-taking caudillos.

Mitre won the presidency. Political ambition led him to create a territorial colossus. The cost of Mitre's victory was a state founded on the preservation of patrimonial bastions, for which the adoption of the federal formula was the institutional cover.

SEVEN

Port-Driven State Formation in Brazil

THE MOST PROMINENT OUTCOME of state formation in Brazil is a physical colossus, which its founders aptly called an empire. Brazil is the fifth-largest country in the world and the largest contiguous territory in the Americas. A hidden facet in the process of Brazilian state formation, known only to a few historians, is even more remarkable: in the 1830s, an intense wave of secessionism swept across the country and put Brazil at serious risk of disintegration. To keep the country alive, Rio de Janeiro, the capital at the time, made great efforts to extinguish separation attempts from three large outlying regions, Pernambuco and Bahia in the Northeast and Rio Grande do Sul in the South. All three regions could have formed perfectly viable countries. The acute experience of failure in the 1830s makes the (re)birth of a colossus in the 1840s an impressive achievement. Brazil's size was not manna from heaven. Both the extraordinary wealth created by a coffee boom and a carefully designed emergency plan by a triumvirate of political entrepreneurs were required to consolidate Brazil's territory.

The consolidation of the Brazilian territory was achieved despite a marked scarcity of elements of union. "Soft" linkages uniting peripheral regions and the national capital, like a shared sense of national identity or a regular system of communications, did not exist. By contrast, "hard" economic assets furnished secessionist regions with the fundamental means for attaining international sovereignty: in all of them, fiscal resources were more abundant than those that at the time were sustaining Uruguay, which Brazil had annexed in 1821 but which successfully seceded in 1828. For the northeastern provinces, commerce with Europe was orders of magnitude more important than commerce with Rio de Janeiro.

The period in which Uruguay was a province of Brazil, which the empire renamed "Cisplatina," produced an archival gem that gives a clear sense of the magnitude of the success by Rio de Janeiro. Since independence, Brazil collected data on revenues for each of its nineteen provinces. In 1822–28, the revenues of Bahia and Pernambuco, the wealthiest provinces after Rio de Janeiro, were four and three times larger than those of Cisplatina. Those of Rio Grande do Sul were 20 percent larger. Revenues of the future Uruguay, although above average, were smaller than those of Maranhão, which at the time was the northernmost productive frontier of Brazil.[1] If Uruguay broke away from Brazil, why not Bahia, Pernambuco, and Rio Grande do Sul?

The data on imperial revenues in the 1820s reveal that all three of the secessionist provinces of the 1830s were rudimentary port states, deeply integrated into the world economy and highly developed by Latin American standards of the time. Additionally, one of them, Rio Grande do Sul, was dominated by rural lords. As theorized in the lord-driven pathway of Chapter 4, rudimentary port states dominated by rural lords are a simple and highly effective precursor of country creation. Paraguay seceded from the future Argentina, Ecuador from Colombia, and Central America from Mexico on the basis of much-weaker economies than those of Bahia, Pernambuco, and Rio Grande. In comparative perspective, Brazilian achievements at state formation are outstanding not only with regard to country size but also with regard to the economic strength of the regions incorporated.

This chapter analyzes state formation in Brazil in three sections. The first section provides an empirical overview of state formation in Brazil and introduces two key theoretical puzzles: (a) What were the motivations and the resources of Brazil's emerging center, Rio de Janeiro, to (re)annex outlying regions? (b) Given that annexation did not occur *manu military*, what were the incentives of Bahia, Pernambuco, and Rio Grande do Sul, the provinces with the capacity to secede, to agree to reincorporation within Brazil? The second section accounts for the failure of the Brazilian state in the 1830s. The roots of the failure were eminently political, for failure coincided with economic expansion, a phenomenon that would actually contribute to state formation a decade later. The third section analyzes success at state formation in Brazil in 1835–50. The key factor of success was the rise of a triumvirate of political entrepreneurs, the founding fathers of the so-called Saquarema group. The Saquaremas were truly amphibious creatures: they were a central component of the coffee oligarchy of Rio de Janeiro, and at the same time, they developed a political agenda that was autonomous from Rio de Janeiro's narrow economic interests. Professional ambition made them willing to sacrifice a portion of Rio's wealth to consolidate a territorial colossus that only they were competent enough to manage. The rise of the political entrepreneurs can only be understood in historical terms, in particular, as a response to a prior period of political crisis and realignment.[2]

State Formation in Brazil: Overview and Puzzle

If the western European states made war, and war made the European states, then it is no exaggeration to claim that the Brazilian state made coffee, and coffee made the Brazilian state. The analogy between Brazilian coffee and European wars is useful, but it can be made more precise in two ways. First, the coffee was not Brazilian but *fluminense*; that is, its production was confined to the rural hinterland of the city-port of Rio de Janeiro and the Paraíba Valley in particular (which runs almost parallel to Rio's Atlantic seashore at an approximate distance of 150 kilometers).[3] The northeastern provinces of Bahia and Pernambuco, which until 1750 had been the most prosperous regions of Portuguese America, were unsuitable for the production of coffee. After independence, they continued specializing in sugar and cotton, which by 1820 had initiated a gradual relative decline. By contrast, coffee boomed in the 1830s and became the mainstay of Brazilian economic activity in the mid-nineteenth century. Coffee gradually spread out from Rio de Janeiro, but it covered only neighboring provinces, Minas Gerais and São Paulo, endowed with highly fertile land for growing coffee bushes ("terra roxa," cherry-red soil).

Second, whereas in western Europe it is hard to disentangle what came first—whether war or the state—in Brazil, coffee has causal primacy. It was a change outside Brazil, namely, a substantial increase in the international demand for the beans—and therefore of their price—that both generated the means and shaped the goals of state formation. Like all states, the Brazilian state required revenues for survival. Stable and abundant revenues are especially critical in the formative period, when funds are needed to co-opt or repress recalcitrant regions. Coffee provided the revenues, but, as in the rest of Latin America, it did so indirectly. Coffee exports were not taxed. Yet they secured the level of hard currency needed to sustain a considerable volume of imports, mainly textiles from Britain, slaves from Angola, and jerked beef from the River Plate area to feed slave labor. It was import duties that sustained the treasury of the budding Brazilian state.

A panoramic vision of Brazilian state formation can then be summarized in a two-part statement: *coffee made Rio de Janeiro*, and then *Rio de Janeiro made the Brazilian state*. Whereas the first part of the statement focuses on economic drivers, the second one relies on political actions.

The focus on economic drivers subsumes Brazilian state formation under the general model of *trade-led* state formation, which Brazil shared with all other Latin American countries (except Paraguay), in a radical departure from the war-led path followed by the western European pioneers. The focus on political action underscores that Brazilian state formation followed the *port-driven* variant within the general trade-led path, which Brazil shared only with Argentina and Chile.

Both the trade-led model and the specific port-driven variant of state formation are required to explain the emergence of the Brazilian state. The trade-led model accounts for two generic attributes. First, it explains the rise of a territorial center that, given its economic endowments, was willing to carry out the formation of a state that was designed to become a machine for foreign commerce rather than international war. The center was the city-port of Rio de Janeiro. Second, the trade-led model also explains why co-optation, instead of transformation, was the preferred strategy for dealing with recalcitrant peripheral regions, which eventually resulted in the creation of a state that was a large-scale patronage machine, arguably the largest in the Western world at the time.[4] The trade-led path explains why Brazilian state formation was inimical to state building.

Yet the trade-led path does *not* explain the specific set of regions included in and excluded from the Brazilian state and the resulting size of the territory under Brazilian control. That is the task of the theory of the port-driven variant. The port-driven approach specifies and completes the trade-led explanation.

This chapter solves two enigmas of Brazilian territory consolidation. First, what was the source of the expansionist motivation of the center, which in the Brazilian context is the imperial drive of Rio de Janeiro? The distinction between motivation and capacity is crucial. Even if Rio de Janeiro had the capacity to form a colossus, it is not at all clear what its incentives were. Would not the revenues derived from coffee exports yield better economic results if reinvested in Rio de Janeiro rather than spent in the peripheries? Second, precisely because Rio de Janeiro was pursuing the peaceful, trade-led path of state formation, what were the motivations of Bahia, Pernambuco, and Rio Grande do Sul to rejoin the empire given that military conquest by Rio de Janeiro was not a credible threat? The secessionist regions did not fear war against Rio, so union with Brazil must have had some other appeal to them.

State Failure: Coffee Boom and Liberal Mismanagement

The 1830s is the most paradoxical decade in the history of Brazil. At the same time that the state collapsed both in the capacity to preserve the union among the constituent regions and in the capacity to hold the monopoly of violence, the economy of Rio de Janeiro embarked on the most powerful expansion experienced by any Latin American country before the mid-nineteenth century: the boom of coffee production and exports.

The Coffee Boom

Coffee was an economic novelty in independent Brazil. If the Brazilian economy in the nineteenth century was coffee, in colonial times it had been sugar. A common denominator in both periods was slave labor. Plantations of sugar and coffee were highly profitable. The commerce of African captives, although a subsidiary activity, was even more profitable. Together with fertile lands, slave labor was the main input of the plantations. In colonial times, sugar was cultivated in the lowlands of three areas: the northeastern provinces of Bahia and Pernambuco and the Center-South province of Rio de Janeiro. Cane plantations and sugar mills were much more numerous and productive in the Northeast than in the Center-South. Higher economic output throughout the seventeenth century made the city of Salvador (da Bahia) the original capital of Portuguese America.

Plantations were voracious consumers of African people. Slave traders, *negreiros*, had a lower social status but were wealthier than the large plantation owners.

Rio de Janeiro became the capital of colonial Brazil only in 1763, two full centuries after its foundation. The capitalization of Rio was the recognition of its commercial preeminence. Starting in the 1730s, Rio boomed as an international city-port. By the mid-eighteenth century, it became the undisputed commercial emporium of the South Atlantic. The new status was the result of the fabulous discoveries of diamonds and gold in the last decade of the seventeenth century in what was then the Captaincy of São Vicente. When mining began to produce torrential levels of income, Portuguese authorities seeking tighter control decided to divide the São Vicente captaincy into the coastal province of São Paulo, which was left with no mineral endowments, and the landlocked province of Minas Gerais, which was separated from the province of Rio de Janeiro by the great natural escarpment of the Serra da Mantiqueira.

The discoveries of mineral wealth produced what by preindustrial standards was an economic miracle. Economic expansion induced a desperate search for passage from the highlands of Minas Gerais to the port of Rio de Janeiro. A major infrastructural achievement was the construction of the Estrada Real (Royal Road), which connected the port of Rio de Janeiro to the mineral-rich regions of Vila Rica (present-day Ouro Preto), Serro, and, at the northernmost point, Diamantina. A vast network of communications began to cover not only Rio and Minas but also São Paulo. São Paulo became an integral part of the region because of the active mule market in the town of Sorocaba, one hundred kilometers south of the provincial capital. Transportation of minerals, sugar, and imports was entirely based on mule trains. Sorocaba received burden beasts and jerked beef (to feed captives) from the Brazilian Far South, Rio Grande do Sul, and present-day Uruguay. Paulista merchants made large purchases in Sorocaba and then supplied the mines of Minas and the plantations of Rio.

Mineral wealth made Brazilian demand for African captives reach unprecedented levels. In the seventeenth century, before the mining boom, Brazil had imported half a million slaves, and at least 80 percent of them were bought by planters in the Northeast. In the eighteenth century, after the discoveries of gold and diamonds, Brazil imported 1.8 million slaves. Minas

Gerais became the most populous province in Brazil, and the majority of the *mineiro* population was African.

The arrival of the Portuguese royal court in Rio de Janeiro in 1808 made the city-port even more powerful through two simple channels: the influx of a population of at least five thousand wealthy and highly educated men (thirteen thousand Portuguese migrated in total) and the opening of the port to free trade with the rest of the world.

A third channel proved revolutionary. The Portuguese Crown began handing out nursery stocks of new varieties of coffee grown in Rio's Royal Botanical Gardens. The first seedlings of coffee had been introduced in the northern province of Pará through French Guiana. The experiment failed. The ideal agronomic environment was in the Center-South. When the royal court moved to Rio, coffee production was negligible. It had grown marginally from ten sacks in 1800 to twenty sacks in 1810 (1 sack = 130 pounds). Yet a key location with regard to altitude, weather, and quality of soil had been identified. It was the village of Rezende in the so-called Serra Acima in the southern section of the Paraíba Valley, not two hundred kilometers away from the city-port. In the 1820s, coffee became a staple in the diet of the middle classes in the United States, France, Germany, and Scandinavia (England stuck to tea). International demand and real prices soared. The twenty sacks exported in 1810 became two hundred thousand at the time of independence (1822). Coffee exports more than doubled by the time of Pedro I's abdication (1831), and a decade later, they reached the one-million mark for the first time. Coffee bushes spread from Rezende to cover the entire Paraíba Valley.

Coffee came to dominate Brazilian exports. And Brazilian exports came to dominate the world market. In the 1820s, coffee accounted for 20 percent of Brazilian foreign sales. In the 1830s, it grew to 44 percent. In 1834, coffee outstripped sugar sales for the first time, and it remained Brazil's main export for the rest of the century. Brazil produced a fifth of the world coffee output in the 1820s, a third in the 1830s, and 40 percent in the 1840s.

The rapid expansion of coffee in Rio was not only due to the combination of international prices and local factor endowments. Equally important was the extensive system of paths that had been built during the mining boom, the availability of a large pool of slave labor, and the ability of the commercial community in the port to continue importing African captives. Coffee caused slave trade to peak. Yearly totals of Africans landed in Rio grew from twenty thousand in the early 1820s to fifty thousand in the early 1830s. A factor contributing to coffee expansion was the impressive capacity of *mineiro* businessmen to transition from their old mining activities to new agricultural ventures aimed at supplying meat, dairy produce, fruits, and legumes to the population of Rio. The price of coffee was certainly a winning ticket in the commodity lottery of world capitalism. Yet Brazil's good luck at world capitalism was magnified by the availability of complementary assets—paths and slaves—inherited from colonial times, when no one could have imagined the conversion to coffee.

Until 1850, Brazilian coffee was largely *fluminense* coffee. Coffee attracted investments from the three wealthiest groups in the capital: sugar slavocrats, large-scale merchants (especially *negreiros*), and high-ranking bureaucrats. Coffee united them all into a single upper class. Partnerships and marriages connected all coffee planters within a large but close-knit network of wealth and power. The *fluminense* economic elite was perfectly aware of its "structural" political power, that is, the dependence of the government on coffee exports to collect vital revenues. Coffee barons in Brazil, like most economic oligarchies in nineteenth-century Latin America, vetoed taxes on their property and income. Yet, through exports, coffee barons produced the hard currency required for imports, and import tariffs were the fiscal basis without which governments could not function—or states could not be formed in the first place.

State Failure

At the same time the coffee economy of Rio de Janeiro was booming, the Brazilian state was collapsing. In 1835, days before his inauguration as the first elected regent of Brazil, Diogo Antônio Feijó wrote a collective message to fellow liberal politicians with ten requests that he deemed necessary for the success of his government. One request was that "in case of separation of the northern provinces, we must secure the south and use [the crisis] as an opportunity to advance with the necessary reforms."[5] From the apex of power, Feijó felt impotent to retain the provinces of the Northeast, especially Pernambuco and Bahia. Moreover, Feijó was not even certain about his ability to keep the South within Brazil's territory. Only a few weeks after the ten-point public request, he predicted in a private message that secession of the Far South, that is, Rio Grande do Sul and perhaps Santa Catarina, seemed "inevitable."[6] Almost at the same time, Antônio Francisco de Paula Holanda Cavalcanti de Albuquerque, the most prominent member of the wealthiest clan in Pernambuco, owner of a third of the sugar plantations and mills in the province, drafted a plan to transform Pernambuco and satellite provinces into a separate country. Revealing persistent centrifugal undercurrents, Holanda's project was a revival of the 1824 secessionist movement to form the Confederation of the Equator, a republic uniting Pernambuco, Caerá, and Paraíba under a confederal formula. In 1836, representative Honório Hermeto Carneiro Leão (Honório) warned in the lower house of parliament that "if the provincial legislatures keep their path, Brazil will fall to pieces [and be replaced] by multiple states."[7]

In 1839, Lord Palmerston, the British foreign secretary, received an ominous memo from a special envoy to Rio de Janeiro: "Some of my Colleagues here, and some persons for whose opinion I have much respect, think that this Empire is on the Eve of Dissolution."[8] Similarly, in 1844, after a year-long visit, the French explorer Count of Suzannet reported that "the province of Rio Grande do Sul . . . is fighting against Brazil. . . . It must be considered a separate state from the Empire." He also predicted that "San-Paolo will secede in a few years."[9]

If the breakup of Brazil seemed unavoidable both to Brazilians at the pinnacle of power and to foreign citizens whose careers depended on extracting high-quality political information, it was because appearances were not deceiving. The survival of the Brazilian state was objectively at risk. The factual basis for the opinions and predictions was the wave of provincial rebellions that swept the empire from north to south between 1831 and 1848 (see Map 7.1).

Dozens of revolts occurred in the period. Ten of them can be considered "major rebellions." Table 7.1 provides a summary description. At least three rebellions were motivated, and had the potential, to break the state. They fought for secession. At least four were motivated, and had the potential, to break the social structure. They pursued abolition. A few of them combined both secessionism and abolitionism. At least two rebellions, the Cabanagem and the Balaiada in the northern states of Pará and Maranhão, originated in feuds between rival oligarchies that morphed into an abolitionist movement

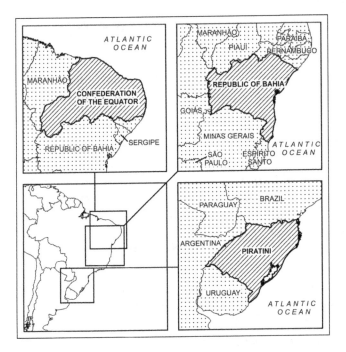

Map 7.1. Brazilian failed secessions, 1822–45

after one of the contenders, in the escalation of the conflict, chose to turn slaves into soldiers. Invariably, the oligarchic faction responsible for the military mobilization of the slave population regretted the decision. African captives became an autonomous force. The costs of a racial war dwarfed any advantage the faction had expected to obtain in its struggle against its oligarchic rival.

When Feijó was inaugurated, major revolts exploded in the Far North (Pará) and the Far South (Rio Grande do Sul), the Cabanagem and the Farroupilha. The Cabanagem, named after the typical dwelling of its social base (*cabana*, "hut") was the costliest in human lives. It shrank Pará's population from one hundred thousand to sixty thousand. The Farroupilha, named after the clothing of the rebels (ragamuffins, from *farrapo*, "rag"), was the longest. It created a separate republic, Piratini, that lasted for ten years. The purest abolitionist rebellion was the Malê revolt in Bahia. Rebels, around

Table 7.1. Major Rebellions during State Formation

Region and province	Name	Years	Secessionist	Abolitionist	Fatal casualties
North					
Pará	Cabanagem	1834–40	yes	yes	40,000
Maranhão	Balaiada	1839–40	yes	yes	5,000
Northeast					
Caerá	Pinto Madeira	1831–32	yes	no	<50
Pernambuco	Cabanada	1832–33	yes	no	<50
	Praieira	1848–49	yes	no	900
Bahia	Malê	1835	no	yes*	120
	Sabinada	1837–38	yes*	yes	1,200
Center-south					
Minas Gerais		1842	yes	no	<50
São Paulo		1842	yes	no	<50
South					
Rio Grande	Farroupilha	1835–45	yes*	no	3,400

Note: Italics indicate rebellions that were initiated before the critical year of 1837, when the Saquaremas rose to power. Asterisks (*) indicate extraordinary clarity of purpose among the leaders of the secessionist or abolitionist movement.

six hundred men, were all Yoruba Islamist slaves. They planned and executed the killings of dozens of white people and the destruction of property.

The wave of provincial rebellions was the clearest indicator of state failure in Brazil. It was also an opportunity for renewed efforts at state formation.

State failure set in motion a process of transformation at both fundamental levels of statehood: territory consolidation and violence monopolization. From 1831 to 1845, the Brazilian territory fragmented, and violence was demonopolized. In 1837, in response to failure, a new political force, the Saquaremas, emerged. Rooted in the wealth and power of the capital, it initiated a process of coalition-making and institutional change that by the end of the 1840s achieved both territory reconsolidation and violence remonopolization. The achievement was both more laborious and more consequential than independence itself.

The Roots of State Failure

Overview. To understand both the origins and the solution to the problem of state failure, it is crucial to examine Brazilian independence in comparative and historical perspective. State failure in Brazil is rooted in the fact that independence in Brazil created a new state but preserved the old regime (the monarchy) and the old government (the Braganza dynasty). No other country in Spanish America did the same. The deviation of Brazil from the Latin American pattern caused liberal agitation. In the mid-1820s, liberalism emerged as the leading challenge to the regime and the government. Liberalism achieved its goals in 1831–35. Yet liberal institutions and policies pushed the Brazilian state to the brink of collapse. Saquarema power emerged as a response to the threat of territorial dismemberment. In other words, state failure in Brazil in the mid-1830s was a direct consequence of liberal backlash against the monarch and monarchic institutions. In turn, state reconstruction in the late 1830s and early 1840s was a direct consequence of conservative reaction against liberal failure.

Independence in Installments. Brazil's independence departed sharply from the general Latin American pattern. Throughout Spanish America, independence combined four changes that occurred at roughly the same time. It affected state, regime, government, and economic policy. The change in state was the separation of the American territories from the jurisdiction of the Iberian metropolis. The change of regime consisted in the transition from absolutist monarchy to republic. The government change was the replacement of Iberian-born authorities—viceroys, general captains, and intendants—by American-born rulers, who became presidents and representatives. Finally, the change in economic policy consisted in the transition from colonial monopolies and mercantilism to market economies and free international trade. In most Spanish American countries, all four changes occurred within the span of a few years and sometimes a few months or weeks. In the territories of present-day Argentina, for instance, the month of the four-dimension change was May 1810.

   In contrast to Spanish America, in Brazil the changes associated with independence were separated by substantial time intervals, and one transformation in particular, the change of regime, did not occur at all. The official year of Brazilian independence is 1822. It is a genuine hallmark. However, 1822 in Brazil is not equivalent to 1810 in Argentina, 1819 in Colombia, or 1821 in Mexico.

Brazil achieved independence in "installments," through a string of changes occurring in 1807, 1815, 1822, and 1831. The year 1822 produced the change of state, the separation of Brazil from Portugal. The big change in economic policy, the transition from mercantilism to free trade, had already occurred a long time before, in 1808. Escaping the Napoleonic invasion of the Iberian Peninsula, in 1807 the Portuguese Crown moved from Lisbon to Brazil under the protection of the British navy. Upon arrival, the first significant measure of Prince Regent João VI was to open all Brazilian ports to commerce with the rest of the world. British protection came with a price. A treaty in 1810 ensured that English imports would pay a maximum tariff of 15 percent.

The year 1815 is key in the periodization of Brazilian independence, which has no equivalent in Spanish America. After the defeat of Napoleon and the liberation of the Iberian Peninsula (1814–15), the surviving aristocracy of Portugal demanded the return of João VI to Lisbon. The goal of Lisbon was to restore its central place within the pluricontinental Portuguese Empire. Instead of acquiescing to Lisbon's demand, João decided to elevate Brazil from the status of colony to that of co-kingdom. He thus formed the United Kingdom of Portugal and Brazil. By 1815, Brazil was still part of the Portuguese Empire, but it was no longer a colony.

Separation (independence) in 1822 was not accompanied by a change of regime or a change of government. In modern world history, the vast majority of changes of state have also included a change of regime and government. Brazil in 1822 is one of the few exceptions. In 1820, two years before independence, a liberal revolution in Portugal had compelled João VI to return to Lisbon. If he had not returned, he would have lost the throne. João's son, Pedro, became Brazil's regent. Yet Lisbon would not give up on its old imperial ambitions, especially when Brazil was rapidly becoming wealthier than Portugal. In order to restore the subordination of Brazil, the Lisbon parliament urged Pedro to join the court in Portugal. The main victim of the intended recolonization would be the elite in Rio de Janeiro, composed of high-ranking bureaucrats, slave merchants, and plantation owners, mostly Portuguese-born citizens who had migrated in 1807. They formed a strong coalition against the departure of Pedro, which they correctly viewed as a prelude to major losses in recently acquired power and wealth. Pedro, urged by the Rio coalition as well as his own ambitions to become the ruler of his own state, rejected Lisbon's demand. The natural next step was independence.

As with the flight from Lisbon in 1807, Britain was the pivotal actor in brokering Brazil's independence in 1822. British services were not free. In addition to a large compensation to Portugal (facilitated by a British loan), Brazil paid a tall bill of concessions directly to England. The concessions included a treaty that secured Britain the status of "most favored nation," which starting in 1827 extended for another fifteen years the 15 percent ceiling on tariffs for English imports. The restriction on Brazil's foreign-trade policy would seriously undermine the new country's fiscal position. It would critically delay Brazil's ability to form a state until the early 1840s. No country in Latin America was formed with such low tariffs. A minimum level of 25 percent for import duties was required.

The other major concession was Pedro I's agreement to gradually abolish the slave trade, which not only was Brazil's most profitable business but also provided the labor basis to the two other major economic sectors, sugar and coffee. The year 1830 was set as the moment of abolition. The British Empire pursued abolition for allegedly humanitarian reasons. Yet it certainly had economic reasons. The chief one was the protection of sugar production from its colonies in the West Indies (based on free labor), as revealed by the fact that England charged prohibitive tariffs on purchases of Brazilian sugar, but Brazilian cotton, also produced by slave labor, was practically free of duties. In practice, the slave trade continued until 1850, and slave labor was not completely abolished until 1888 (antislavery legislation before 1850 was toothless, largely a façade "pra inglês ver," as the Brazilian lawmakers themselves referred to it).

Given that Pedro remained in power, that the royal court was unchanged, and that top officials in Rio kept their positions, independence in 1822 caused no change in government. It did not involve a change of political regime either, since dynastic succession and royal appointments remained the dominant form of access to government power.

The Completion of Brazilian Independence. Only in 1831 did Brazilian-born citizens replace Portuguese-born rulers, which was one of the four key changes of the independence movements across Spanish America. The

change in government was the "completion" of independence for Brazil. It
was also more conflictual than the other changes in the distinctly gradual
Brazilian process. Crucially, the conflicts that caused the change of government, as well as the realignment of forces in its aftermath, defined the cleavages and alliances that set in motion the process of state formation in Brazil.

The change of government of 1831 was the abdication of Pedro I in favor
of his five-year-old son, Pedro II. The political struggle that caused the abdication was fueled by the attacks from a broad liberal coalition against the
monarch's policy record and future plans. Liberals feared that, after the death
of King João VI (1826), Pedro I would attempt to become the ruler of Portugal and recolonize Brazil from Lisbon. Liberals were certain that Pedro I valued more the power and wealth of the Braganza dynasty than the progress
of Brazil.

At the time of the struggle against Pedro I, the proposals of Brazilian
liberalism were ill defined and not always coherent. The central tenet of Brazilian liberalism was, as in most other parts of the Western world, its opposition to absolutist rule. In Brazil, liberalism combined republicanism and
federalism, that is, it pursued the reallocation of power from the executive
to the legislature, especially the elimination of the king's emergency powers, and the devolution of decision-making capacities from the imperial capital to the provinces and municipalities. Only a minority of liberals also
pursued democracy. Brazilian liberalism also included illiberal proposals,
like the exclusion of Portuguese-born citizens from power, which was usually referred to as "nativism." Finally, Brazilian liberalism included outright
antiliberal measures, such as the preservation of slavery, which was threatened by Pedro I's agreement with Great Britain.

The liberal movement was joined by supporters throughout the empire. Yet its leaders were lawmakers from Rio de Janeiro's neighboring provinces of Minas Gerais (west) and São Paulo (south) and a few journalists in
the main cities of the Center-South.

Liberal frustration with the emperor had been growing since 1824, not
two years after independence. In 1823, Pedro I had summoned a general assembly to design a constitution and modernize his monarchy into a parliamentary one. Only a few months after the inauguration of the constitutional
sessions, Pedro clashed with members of the assembly. They had opposite
interests regarding the distribution of power between the executive and the

legislative branches, as well as between the federal government and the provincial ones. Pedro, infuriated at the attempts to limit his power, closed the assembly. The abrupt decision put an end to the political honeymoon between the monarch and Brazilian-born elites, who had celebrated his 1822 decision to declare independence as a heroic action.

Brazil did produce a constitution in 1824. However, it was drafted by a Council of State whose members had been appointed by Pedro I himself. The constitution secured a long list of individual rights, an aspect that made it one of the most liberal documents in the world. Yet it also granted the emperor an extraordinary volume of institutional power. The emperor would appoint the governors of the provinces. Brazil would have to wait sixty-five years to have popularly elected provincial executives. Members of the lower house would be popularly elected, but the emperor would select the members of the Senate from a three-candidate list submitted by each province. In contrast to all other upper chambers in the Americas, the Brazilian Senate was designed to become a bastion of the emerging Luso-Brazilian nobility. Since only the emperor granted nobility titles, members of the Senate would be Pedro's most direct clients. Crucially, in addition to heading the executive branch, the emperor was endowed with "moderating power," modeled after Benjamin Constant's *pouvoir royal*.[10] The moderating power, although exercised by the same man who was the head of the national executive, was allegedly an independent fourth branch of government whose sole mission was to solve conflicts among the three other branches, in particular, to unlock stalemates between the monarch and the legislature. In practice, the moderating power was the right of the monarch to dissolve the lower house whenever the majority of representatives opposed his policy proposals. Before dissolving the lower house, the emperor was supposed to confer with the Council of State, the last relevant institutional actor in Brazil's constitutional architecture. Although the Council of State was part of the fourth branch of power and lacked legislative faculties, its members were chosen directly by the emperor, and, like the Senate, it became a redoubt of Pedro I's personal favorites, almost exclusively Portuguese-born.

Liberal with regard to individual rights, Pedro's constitution was anti-Madisonian and antinativist in the distribution of institutional power.

The emperor's concentration of power set in motion liberal opposition. It poisoned the relation between a large section of the Brazilian-born political community and the monarch. Trust was broken and would never be rebuilt. Liberal opposition originated in the lower house in 1826, the year the first legislative sessions were held (which, in stark contrast with the rest of Latin America, would never be interrupted). Political campaigning transformed congressional opposition into a social movement in less than four years.

In 1827, during the second legislative sessions, the lower house approved a bill that was a prelude to the liberal reform that would formally take place between 1831 and 1837. It created locally elected parish judges (*juizes de paz*). Local election of judges invariably resulted in control of municipal justice by local notables. The reform was a crucial tool to immunize slave traders and slavocrats against charges derived from Pedro I's abolitionist agreements with the United Kingdom. The emperor, together with the powerful caste of professional magistrates, found the liberal reform insulting.

Two factors precipitated an open clash between liberals and Pedro I. First, a long and costly war against Buenos Aires for control over the Cisplatina province (1825–28) added political ammunition to the monarch's critics. The war was concluded with the creation of Uruguay as an independent buffer country, a solution brokered by Great Britain's diplomacy. The attitude of liberal representatives and journalists against the war was highly effective in undermining both the authority of Pedro I and the prestige of the Brazilian army. The Brazilian army had suffered serious defeats by the battalions of Buenos Aires, which on paper was a clearly inferior military force. The two central liberal arguments against the war were mutually inconsistent, which of course was one of the secrets of their political effectiveness. On the one hand, liberals criticized Pedro I's geopolitical ambitions as anachronistic: Brazil needed peace for economic progress; money should not be wasted in wars but used to expand the transportation system, the great bottleneck of the export sector. Diplomacy should be used to attract foreign investors rather than to expand the territory. On the other hand, once the war was over, liberals took advantage of the loss of the Cisplatine province to humiliate Pedro I and the Brazilian army for failure against a much less resourceful rival. A fact that liberals were careful to hide from public opinion was that during the war the lower house repeatedly rejected the requests of higher levels of war expenditures submitted by the emperor. Liberal sabotage was one of the causes of Brazil's poor military performance, and Brazil's poor performance became a target of liberal criticism.

The other factor precipitating the clash between the emperor and the liberal movement was that, in the distribution of appointments, contracts, and concessions, Pedro I showed a marked preference for Portuguese-born officials and businessmen, who since 1808 had adopted the city of Rio de Janeiro as their home and were rapidly amassing power and wealth through the slave trade and coffee production. The pro-Lusitanian inclinations of Pedro were resented by liberal members of the lower house but were especially offensive to the small folk in the streets, who thought that Portuguese presence in government and commerce was blocking social mobility. Liberal politicians would not miss the political opportunity of voicing the nativist complaints of the middle classes.

By 1830, the liberal movement was an amalgam of members of the lower house, who provided political leadership, sections of the provincial elites that did not receive the Crown's favors, and an indefinite number of political outsiders, the ranks of the emerging middle class, which were thin in relative terms but had the determination and numbers to stage citywide protests. Liberalism was an umbrella for a combination of smaller political movements, which included federalism, constitutionalism, nativism, and sometimes democratic republicanism.

Pedro I abdicated on April 7, 1831, in another abrupt decision. He refused to make concessions to the liberal coalition that had demanded the appointment of Brazilian-born ministers. The liberal demand was backed up by a formal petition from the lower house, the support of low-ranking military officials, and street demonstrations in the cities of the Center-South, especially Rio de Janeiro.

Liberals in Action. The victory of the liberal movement revealed how heterogeneous the triumphant coalition was. In the aftermath of the abdication, liberals adopted three distinct political postures. The "moderates" supported monarchic rule but pursued constitutional reforms that curbed the power of the monarch; the "radicals" wanted a republic, that is, the outright abolition of the monarchy, and some of them advocated for the extension of the franchise to a much larger section of the population than the moderates were willing to accept; and the "nativists" made explicit what indirectly

all liberals were chasing, that is, positions in the civil and military administrations that hitherto had been reserved for Portuguese-born citizens.

The liberal movement disintegrated only a few short weeks after Pedro I's abdication. As often happens with broad opposition coalitions once
they succeed in toppling the government, ensuing struggles among factions
gained central stage and generated crises that were even less tractable than
the one for which the coalition was formed.

The moderate faction of the liberal coalition prevailed. It controlled
government from 1831 to 1837. Moderate domination did not result from a
gentlemen's agreement with the other liberal factions. It required force. A
key instrument for excluding the radicals was the creation of a National
Guard, which was the model military force of the emerging liberal bourgeoisie in Europe, especially France. The National Guard was a new version of
the colonial militias, which had been designed to maintain local order. The
novelty of the National Guard was that the officers were chosen by the guards-
men themselves and, given income restrictions, officers would be men of
wealth, mostly local notables, with a vested interest in protecting property
rights—which in the 1831 juncture was almost synonymous with quashing
radical agitation. By its very composition, the National Guard would also balance the power of the royal army, whose top-level officials were rightly sus-
pected of loyalty to Pedro I and Portugal. The National Guard was responsible
for demobilizing the radicals in Rio de Janeiro.

Radicals were forced out of the liberal movement, and they decided
never to return. For them, Pedro I's abdication was a genuine *journée des
Dupes*.[11] They had made a decisive contribution to the revolutionary effort
but never enjoyed the fruits of power.

Moderates created the most advanced political organization that Brazil had known thus far besides the imperial administration itself. They
founded the protoparty Sociedade Defensora da Liberdade e Independên-
cia Nacional (Society for the Defense of Liberty and National Independence).
The pillars of moderate organization were located in the capitals of São Paulo
and Minas Gerais, but smaller *sociedades* were opened and remained active
in the cities of Pernambuco and Bahia. Rio de Janeiro had its share of moderate liberals, but the most influential politicians of Rio de Janeiro were
skeptical of, if not openly hostile to, republicanism, federalism, and especially democracy.

The undisputable leaders of the moderates were the Paulista politician Feijó, the Mineiro lawyer Bernardo Pereira de Vasconcelos, and the journalist Evaristo Ferreira da Veiga e Barros (Evaristo), the founder of the newspaper *Aurora Fluminense*. On the basis of the sheer quality of its editor's arguments, the *Aurora* was able to make or break political careers and policy proposals. With Evaristo's support, Feijó became Brazil's leader between 1831 and 1837. As minister of justice and empire (1831–32) or head of government (1835–37), Feijó largely dominated the regency, the institution prescribed by the constitution to exercise the executive power in case of absence or inability of the dynastic successor. Since the regents were chosen by the lower house and had no moderating power, which would be suspended until the inauguration of Pedro II (expected in 1843, when he turned eighteen), Brazil's regime had mutated from a semiconstitutional monarchy to what in name was a "Second Reign" but in fact was a parliamentary republic.

After consolidating power, the moderates launched a series of institutional reforms. They produced a drastic transformation of the judicial system based on the creation of the jury system, which complemented the introduction of elected parish judges in 1827. Reform also included a substantial decentralization of political power, which fell short of federalism but gave provinces a much wider scope of policy action. Decentralization was embodied in the so-called Ato Adicional of 1834, the most important amendment of the 1824 constitution, which stayed in place for more than half a century. Members of the provincial executives would still be appointed by the emperor or the regents, but the amendment vastly enlarged the decision power of the provincial legislatures, which were enabled to raise all kinds of taxes except import duties, order local public works, appoint police forces, and create primary and secondary schools.

The reforms by Feijó and Vasconcelos failed to quench the radicals' thirst for change and power. Some radicals wanted full federalism. Mimicking the moderates, they created their own protoparties, the Sociedades Federais, which in general lacked the strength of the moderate model but were intimidating organizations in some provinces, like Pernambuco and Rio Grande. Other radicals pursued the creation of a republic with universal franchise. Moderates made strenuous efforts to neutralize the democratic radicals. They feared that in a democratic regime, power would slip out of their hands, either because radicals would eventually become electorally stronger or because monarchists would mount an overwhelming counterattack. Finally, the nativists, the third liberal faction, divided themselves between the moderates and the radicals, depending on whether they were able to capture political positions. Ideology was important, but office-seeking was much more powerful a motivation for nativists. Opportunism led nativists into dissolution.

Conservatives' Incipient Reaction and Moderates' Balancing Act. What would eventually become the most formidable enemy of the moderate liberals was the small but highly cohesive group of "restorationists," or *caramurus*, formally organized in the Sociedade Conservadora da Constitução Brasileira. Their leaders were Portuguese-born high-ranking bureaucrats, plantation owners, and *negreiros* of Rio de Janeiro who had been the main beneficiaries of Pedro I's reign. They wanted to turn back the clock of Brazilian history. Only hours after the abdication, they began to advocate for Pedro I's return to power.

After abdication, Pedro sailed to Lisbon to recover the Portuguese throne, which had been illegally usurped by his younger brother, Miguel, upon the death of João VI (1826). A military campaign, not a family conversation, solved the conflict within the Braganza House. Pedro's victory over Miguel and his new position in Europe had opposite effects on the liberals and the restorationists. On the one hand, it confirmed the liberals' fear that Pedro's abdication was part of a larger plan to rebuild the Portuguese empire by recolonizing Brazil. Pedro I morphed from independence hero to colonial threat. On the other, it energized the restorationists, who imagined that Pedro could use the army with which he reconquered Portugal to repress the liberals in Brazil and restore the privileges of the Portuguese-born elite in Rio.

Given the insatiability of the radicals and the determination of the restorationists, governability was the most pressing issue for the moderates. "The fatal flaw of revolutions is that they are not possible without the radicals, but then one cannot govern with them"—such was the assessment of an enlightened moderate statesman about the origins and aftermath of Pedro I's forced abdication.[12] Yet it told only half of the story. In addition to the pressure from the left by the radicals, the moderates suffered pressure from the right by the restorationists.

To rule Brazil in the mid-1830s, moderates resorted to a long-standing political method: they tried to use their diametrically opposed rivals as mutually neutralizing forces. In the moderates' plan, excluding the radicals was the condition that made possible the exclusion of the restorationists, and vice versa. Moderates persuaded many radicals that the sweeping judicial reform and the less ambitious Ato Adicional reforming provincial legislatures were big and valuable liberal conquests whose survival should not be risked by pressing for more progressive reforms, which would certainly detonate a *car-amuru* reaction. They also used the radicals when negotiating with the restorationists. To ease the passage of new legislation and to keep their grip on executive power, the moderates pointed to restorationists that without a moderate regency and some form of liberal reform, the radical wing would initiate a revolution that could put an end not only to the monarchy but also to the social order, including mainly slavery.

The success of the moderates' balancing act depended on three related conditions. Reforms had to be accepted by both radicals and restorationists; that is, the former had to be persuaded of the threat of reaction, and the latter had to be persuaded of the threat of revolution. Additionally, reforms had to be effective, which in Brazil in the nineteenth century included tangible results with regard to the overall political order and economic prosperity. Finally, the moderates had to remain united.

None of the three conditions were met.

The End of Liberal Power: Polarization, Policy Failure, and Internal Division. The moderates' bet on achieving governability though a balancing act was a resounding failure. The radicals revolted, and the restorationists reacted. For radicals, liberal reforms were not enough. For restorationists, they had gone too far. Frustration with moderate reforms triggered dozens of minor revolts. Yet, between 1831 and 1835, five rebellions had major repercussions. Four of them occurred in different provinces of the North. One exploded in the Far South.

Two rebellions of the North and the rebellion of the South were radical movements. They were fueled by "republican separatism." Acknowledging the lack of capacity to change monarchic rule in Brazil as a whole, the goal of provincial radicals was to create a separate ministate that could install a republican regime. One rebellion of the North was restorationist. Rebels hoped to incite restorationists in other provinces to follow their example, prompt the liberals to abandon power, and create the conditions for the return of Pedro I. The fifth rebellion was a pure case of slave revolt that terrified the population of Bahia. Slaves were exceptionally well organized, and they initiated a genuine "race war."

Moderate politics failed. Moderate *policies* failed as well. Both the sweeping judicial reform and the limited decentralization of power produced all kinds of effects, but not those pursued by the moderates themselves. Popularly elected justices and the jury system proved an unmitigated catastrophe. Especially susceptible to bribes by local potentates, the justices of peace and the jury members tended to favor one local faction at the expense of the other. The new judicial system became a source of political instability, defeating the purpose for which it was created, as even moderate liberal politicians acknowledged.

The Ato Adicional endowed provincial legislatures with an unprecedented level of political power. With the introduction of a degree of federalism, the moderates expected, in the long run, to bridge the gap between Brazil and the United States with regard to the quality of local governance and provincial material prosperity, as provincial legislatures would be more responsive to local demands and would compete with each other to attract private investments. Yet, before the reform could produce positive long-term effects, the short-term effects were appalling. In one province after another, the new resources available to the local legislatures became a prize to be intensely disputed between rival local oligarchies. Disputes often turned violent and morphed into full-scale rebellions.

For restorationists, as well as for some moderate liberals, liberal reforms caused what at the time were seen as the twin evils of "impunity" and "anarchy." In the city and province of Rio de Janeiro in particular, restorationists and a few moderate liberals began to fear that the failure of moderate politics and policy would prevent further expansion of the *fluminense* coffee economy, if not derail it altogether. Coffee production was rapidly becoming the leading sector of the Brazilian economy, but thus far, coffee expansion had occurred with minimal capital and infrastructural requirements. For the coffee sector to reach its full potential, the political disorder associated with moderate politics had to end. The bottlenecks of the coffee production, including outdated forms of land transportation and port facilities, required foreign capital, and foreign capital needed political order.

Finally, dissent among moderates, insinuated already in 1832, morphed into open conflict in 1835. Moderate divisions provoked the decline and fall of liberal power.[13] The divisions resulted from the political ambitions of Feijó and his collaborators, which provoked the gradual defection of key moderate leaders, whom the historian Jeffrey Needell has aptly called "the renegades."[14]

Renegades abandoned the moderates on an individual basis rather than as a group. The two pivotal renegades were Honório and Vasconcelos himself. To consolidate power, Feijó and Evaristo sponsored a change of the political regime. Formal abolition of the monarchy was a political taboo. Yet the minority of Pedro II opened a unique window of opportunity for moderates in power. The regime of the regency, as defined by the 1824 constitution, was essentially a transitory parliamentarian republic with a conservative policy bias. The element of parliamentarism derived from the fact that the executive power under the regency was a triumvirate chosen by the lower house. The conservative bias was provided by the Senate. With lifetime members chosen by the prior monarch, the Senate was designed to veto large-scale reforms.

The plan of Feijó and Evaristo to accumulate and stabilize power centered on the transformation of the regency from a parliamentarian republic into a presidential one and the elimination of the conservative bias. The presidential transformation consisted in replacing the collegial regency by a single regent, who would not be chosen by the legislature but by popular vote. The new regent would be more powerful both because he would not have to share decision-making power with coregents and because he would enjoy an independent source of legitimacy. Moderates allegedly saw the presidential republic as only a transitory regime, which would dissolve when the prince reached adulthood. Yet it would be naïve to think that Feijó and Evaristo did not anticipate that a popularly elected regent would clash against the constitutional monarch in 1843 when Pedro II turned eighteen. At that moment, the political community would almost certainly be torn between two leaders with competing claims to power, one who had been chosen by the vote of the citizenry and another who was backed by the prestige of dynastic tradition but would be seen as too inexperienced to rule. Feijó expected to transform Brazil's political regime.

Moderates achieved the full reform of the regency in 1834, and in 1835, Feijó was elected the first single regent, with the decisive support of Evaristo and his *Aurora Fluminense*. Paradoxically, when inaugurated, Feijó was already a lame duck, if not a political cadaver. The reason is that the moderate leaders had failed to produce the other planned reform, that is, the elimination of the conservative policy bias.

The big assault on the power of the Senate was attempted in 1832. It failed. The damage to the future power of the moderates caused by the survival of the Senate's power was less serious than the damage caused by the division it provoked within the moderates' ranks. Honório, a representative since 1830, rejected both the form and the purpose of Feijó's attempt at reform. The chosen route by Feijó was a coup d'état. In late July 1832, alleging lack of means to repress uprisings both from radicals and restorationists, Feijó resigned his position as minister of justice and was joined by the rest of the cabinet. Since the uprisings could be suppressed without much effort, Feijó's resignation was an obvious exaggeration. At the same time, the resignation of the other ministers could only result from a well-coordinated conspiracy. In the power vacuum, Feijó deliberately sought to amplify the sense of crisis. At the peak of his popularity, Feijó expected to be requested to return to power by general acclaim, after securing a mandate for large institutional reform. The collective resignation did force the creation of a crisis committee by members of the lower house. Moreover, the committee, under Feijó's pressure and with the tactical support of nativist representatives, decided to declare the need for constitutional reform and the transformation of the lower house into a constituent assembly.

Honório correctly guessed that the moderates' ultimate purpose was the elimination of the Senate altogether. He argued that the action of the crisis committee was unconstitutional. Honório was right. The decision-making process had bypassed the Senate. To the moderates' surprise, a majority in the lower house supported Honório's position and dismissed the proposal of the crisis committee. Honório's success in neutralizing Feijó's coup is usually seen as rooted in the logical and rhetorical quality of his parliamentary intervention, which inaugurated one of the longest and most influential political careers in nineteenth-century Brazil.[15] Yet Honório's success owed much to pure power dynamics. Eliminating the Senate was an existential threat for politicians who, despite adhering to moderate liberalism, expected to become members of the Brazilian nobility on the basis of wealth, education, and family connections. The threat was particularly acute for Coimbra-educated scions of the wealthiest *fluminense* families. Honório represented their interests. For them, a position in the lower house was a mere stepping-stone toward a seat in the Senate, an appointment on the supreme court, or a nobility title. Honório was the first "renegade" liberal. Renegades saw the regency as a truly transitory and strictly parliamentary political regime. They took for granted that, beginning in 1843, when Pedro II became emperor, they themselves would reach the level of professional seniority, intellectual maturity, and political influence required to be granted the most valuable favors that the Crown had to offer. Their future political power and their ability to protect the increasing wealth of their families crucially depended on the subsistence of the Senate as the bastion for the Brazilian nobility.

In 1835, Vasconcelos became the second prominent renegade, making the split between moderates irreversible. Vasconcelos had the same political aspirations as Feijó, that is, to capture the single-man regency. In order to block Vasconcelos's career, Feijó excluded him from a position in the cabinet and ruled against his candidacy for a seat in the Senate, either of which was only a natural reward for a founding member of moderate liberalism, the intellectual architect of the Ato Adicional, and the master legislative tactician behind its approval. Without a ministerial portfolio or a legislative seat, Vasconcelos was left without the necessary source of patronage to become the next regent. The moderates knew they were losing a major political asset. What they did not guess was that Vasconcelos would turn into an intractable enemy. After breaking away from the moderates, Vasconcelos campaigned for the reversal of the liberal reforms, which he argued had gone too far.

Vasconcelos advocated for putting an end to the "innovation race."[16] In what became the informal manifesto of renegade liberals, Vasconcelos blamed liberal politics not just for government malfunction but for state failure:

> I was a liberal. Back then, liberty was a new thing. It existed in everyone's aspirations but not in the laws. . . . Power was everything. Today, society has changed. Democratic principles have triumphed everywhere, and everywhere they put everything at risk. Before, society was at risk because of power. Now, it is at risk because of anarchy. Then and now I want to help society. That is why now I am a *regressista* [reactionary, advocate of the reversal of liberal reforms]. I am no turncoat. . . . Today I defend the country against disorganization very much like yesterday I

defended it against despotism. . . . Threats to society change: the
winds from the worst tempests are never the same. How can a
politician, blind and immovable, serve his country?[17]

The triple combination of polarization of radicals and restorationists,
moderate policy failure, and the splintering of liberal renegades made Brazil ungovernable. The defection of key moderate leaders first, followed by
the open opposition of renegade liberals later, was the death sentence of
Feijó's government.

The same process that in 1831 had achieved the completion of independence with the abdication of Pedro I morphed into state failure less than
a decade later. Moderates had received an emerging state that had already
overcome the isolated separatist movements of Pernambuco in the early
1820s. They left a state besieged by a strong, multiregional wave of provincial rebellions in the late 1830s. Liberal politics and institutional reform put
the survival of Brazil at maximum risk.

Internal division and policy failure explain the breakdown of the liberal government. What they do not explain is why, after liberal failure, Brazil experienced a *Regresso* (Restoration), as Evaristo baptized the ensuing
government coalition and its policies. The Regresso was the political force
responsible for state formation after the liberal government jeopardized the
very existence of Brazil. In 1835, Feijó himself predicted the disintegration
of the country. Foreign observers were also expecting the disappearance of
Brazil. The Regresso prevented it.

The Regresso took shape after the self-destructive measures of moderate liberals. Its emergence resulted from the combination of a structural
economic change, the steady rise of the coffee sector in Rio de Janeiro's
Paraíba Valley throughout the 1830s, and a contingent event, the unexpected
death of Pedro I in 1834, which prompted the most significant realignment
of political forces in nineteenth-century Brazil.

State Formation: Coffee Power and Saquarema Ambition

Given the coffee boom, state failure in Brazil in the 1830s seems evidence
against the theory of trade-led state formation. The opposite is the case. Two
observations are crucial to understand the impact of the coffee boom on
trade-led state formation in Brazil. First, the effects of the economy on the

polity are almost never instantaneous. In particular, the coffee boom of the 1830s in Brazil had neutral effects in the short run but decidedly positive effects in the medium run. State failure in the 1830s was followed by an extremely successful effort at state formation from Rio de Janeiro, the onset of which can be located in 1837 and its completion in 1850. The coffee boom of the 1830s in the center did not cause any of the rebellions in the peripheries. Yet revenues from coffee-centered foreign trade were vital for financing the appropriate mix of co-optation and repression through the late 1840s. A confirmation of the centrality of revenues from foreign trade is given by the fact that only in 1844 was the British restriction on maximum import tariffs lifted as the treaty of most favored nation expired. Brazilian leaders immediately raised import duties on British goods from 15 percent to a range of 25 percent to 40 percent, depending on the product. The hike in import tariffs had a negligible negative effect on the Brazilian demand for British goods, but it had a large positive impact on government revenues. They increased by 33 percent from 1843 to 1845 and by 100 percent from 1843 to 1853. The fiscal basis for trade-led state formation was only available in the mid-1840s.

Second, *politics matters*, even in the case of large-scale processes set in motion by economic transformations. State failure in the 1830s in Brazil was a case of policy failure rather than economic failure. The *fluminense* economy was contributing an increasing volume of economic resources. Yet, before 1837, neither the central elites nor the peripheral ones had the political incentives or the organizational capacity to put an end to the wave of provincial rebellions. Brazil historiography on the 1830–50 period has provided rich detail on the provincial rebellions. Yet it has failed to make the distinction between rebellions occurring before 1837 and those occurring after 1837 (in Table 7.1, pre-1837 rebellions are italicized). Rebellions before 1837 faced a national government that had few incentives to put an end to them. In 1837, largely as a reaction to state failure, a new government was formed. The new government planned and executed a reversal of the decentralization measures of the liberal regency. After 1837, rebellions, especially those of São Paulo, Minas Gerais, and Pernambuco, were a response against the recentralizing efforts of the new government. Yet, for the same reasons that the new government had decided to recentralize authority, the post-1837 rebellions found rulers in Rio de Janeiro who had a distinct interest in consolidating the territorial unity of present-day Brazil.

The actions of the elite in the city-port of Rio de Janeiro in 1837–50 were decisive for state formation in Brazil. Understanding their incentives and accomplishments is the task of this section.

A Trio of Political Entrepreneurs

Pedro I could not enjoy the fruits of the victory in Lisbon against his brother Miguel, which allowed him to regain the Portuguese Crown in early 1834. A few months later, Pedro died of tuberculosis when he was only thirty-five. Pedro's death was as consequential for Brazilian politics, as had been his decisions of 1822 (independence) and 1831 (abdication).

Pedro died at the same time that the moderate faction of the liberals was cracking.

Pedro's death made the threat of recolonization disappear. Feijó and his allies had abhorred the threat on programmatic grounds, but they had also manipulated it for political gain. One of the motivations behind the support for the moderates was fear of the intentions of the *caramurus* (restorationists). Members of the lower house who viewed Feijó as a levee against the restoration movement were left without a reason to continue supporting the moderate liberal government. The weakening of the moderates as a political force accelerated. The capacity of the liberal government to rule was also undermined. The risk of reconquest by Pedro I had helped moderates to mobilize support for a range of measures, including a bill for a perpetual ban against the first emperor's return to Brazil, which the Senate rejected by a slim majority.

The impact of Pedro's death was even stronger on the opposition than it was on the government. The death of Pedro I was a blessing in disguise for the *caramurus*. They lost their hero, but they gained unexpected coalitional power. Like-minded political forces could now partner with the *caramurus* without having the burden of being accused of conspiring against Brazil's independence.

The death of Pedro made the liberal "renegades" the epitome of the pivotal actor. With Pedro I out of the way, the *caramurus* became the renegades' natural allies. Led by Vasconcelos and Honório, the renegades recruited the support of the *caramurus* in order to form a majority in the lower house. Completing the triumvirate of the Regresso was the *fluminense* politician Joaquim José Rodrigues Torres, future Viscount of Itaboraí. Like

Vasconcelos and Honório, he was a graduate of Coimbra (mathematics). In 1835, Honório, Vasconcelos, and Rodrigues Torres created the Saquarema group. Saquarema was the coastal town, a few miles north of the city-port, where Rodrigues Torres had his main plantation. Between 1835 and 1837, the Saquaremas created the first real party in Brazilian history, the Party of Order. And the Party of Order, once in power, launched the Regresso, which put down all foci of secessionism.

Despite the Saquaremas' efforts at party formation, the trio is best seen as a collective entrepreneur rather than as a party. In contrast to the Conservative Parties of Mexico and Colombia, the goal of the Saquarema trio was domination of a multiregion territory rather than supremacy within a municipality. Its survival depended not on defeating a local rival in Rio de Janeiro, which was already bankrupt, but on obtaining the support of multiple constituencies in distant areas by delivering specially tailored packages of services to a range of local notables—the trademark of the state-making entrepreneur in nineteenth-century Latin America.

The first achievement of the Saquarema was to gain control of the lower house by 1837, which left Feijó with no option but to resign. Honório and Vasconcelos were responsible for switching former moderate representatives into a solid reactionary bloc over the sessions of 1835 and 1836. Honório brokered deals behind the scenes. Vasconcelos provided political vision through public interventions. Vasconcelos argued for the strengthening of central power as a solution to both "impunity" (caused by the liberal judicial reform) and "anarchy" (caused by the quasi-federal Ato Adicional). Honório was responsible for the Saquaremas reaching out to legislators from the Northeast, especially the provinces of Bahia and Pernambuco, whose economies were in decline but were still powerful and which carried the largest electoral weight after Minas Gerais and Rio de Janeiro. Honório persuaded them of the need for a Regresso. Shaken by violent revolts, some of which had escalated into race wars, representatives of the Northeast did not need much convincing to join the Party of Order.

The Social Basis of the Saquaremas

Rodrigues Torres, the third founder of the Saquaremas, was responsible for galvanizing the support of Brazil's most powerful economic class, the

planters and merchants of Rio de Janeiro. His mission was not complicated. Through marriage, he had become a member of the Álvares de Azevedo clan, one of the oldest and wealthiest families of Rio de Janeiro,
pioneers of sugar plantation in the lowlands (*baixada*) and large-scale slave
trade at the port. Through family connections, Rodrigues Torres contributed impressive amounts of political capital. He would recruit Paulino José
Soares de Souza (Paulino), the future Viscount of Uruguai. Rodrigues
Torres and Paulino were married to sisters, granddaughters of the Álvarez
de Azevedo patriarch. Paulino was also a Coimbra graduate (law). He became an undisputed eminence in constitutional law and designed, together
with Vasconcelos, the key measures to reverse liberal reforms.

Rodrigues Torres was the political voice of the most powerful social
network in Brazil. It was Rodrigues Torres's *fluminense* influence that persuaded moderate liberals in 1834 to appoint him the first president of the
province of Rio de Janeiro.[18] With the appointment, moderates obviously expected to strengthen their own coalition by incorporating a pillar of socioeconomic power. They did not realize they were sowing the seeds of their
own destruction. The death of Pedro I allowed Rodrigues Torres to take an
independent course of action. He became a true political entrepreneur, which
included mainly the creation of partnerships that, when Pedro I was alive,
would have been discredited as "restorationist." Rodrigues Torres persuaded
the representatives of the Rio de Janeiro provincial legislature of 1835 to join
the ranks of the Saquaremas. The *fluminense* bloc of reactionary power was
not the most numerous one, but it was comfortably the most resourceful.

As president of Rio de Janeiro, Rodrigues Torres pursued an unambiguous plan of trade-led state formation on a local scale. He focused on upgrading the transportation infrastructure of the province, which would
reduce the costs, and increase the profits, of the coffee oligarchy. Together
with Vasconcelos, he also mentored Paulino in the provincial legislature.
Paulino's rise was meteoric. Family connections helped, but his political
skills, legal expertise, and knowledge of the economy of Rio were the decisive factors. Paulino succeeded Rodrigues Torres in the presidency of Rio
de Janeiro. He only deepened trade-led state formation in the province. In
addition to the transportation infrastructure, he strengthened the police capacity of Rio de Janeiro. A larger and safer system of roads connecting the
Paraíba Valley and the port were vital for the expansion of the coffee econ-

omy. Paulino was a sophisticated political player. For the supervision of police patrolling in the valley, he trusted members of the Lacerda Werneck clan, pioneers of the spread of the coffee plantations from the Rio lowlands into the mountain ranges.

Economic partnership and family ties also connected Rodrigues Torres and Paulino to the royal court, the bastion of the Luso-Brazilian aristocracy who had migrated in 1808. They were high-ranking officials under Pedro I, owners of large plantations, and wealthy merchants. Most of them had been intransigent restorationists. They had been the chief target of radical Lusophobia. José Clemente Pereira (José Clemente) was a leader of the group. He was a member of the Teixera de Macedo clan, which had benefited from generous contracts from the Portuguese Crown to serve the coastal commerce of Africa. They were the most important slave merchants in Rio de Janeiro. After joining the Saquaremas in 1836, José Clemente campaigned for the repeal of the treaties that abolished the slave trade. In leaders like Rodrigues Torres and José Clemente, the wealthiest *fluminense* families could trust.

Hence, what distinguished the Party of Order from the moderate societies was not only superior political organization. The Saquaremas were backed by the wealth of the wealthiest city-port in South America. If a distinct Marxist claim is that political power represents the interests of the wealthy classes, then in the case of midcentury Brazil, Marxism falls short for the characterization of Saquarema power. The Saquaremas did not just "represent" the wealthy families of coffee planters and *negreiros* of Rio. The Saquaremas were *members* of those families. Some of them might have entered politics motivated by Montesquieu's aristocratic sense of honor and duty, but all of them understood that power positions were fundamental for wealth expansion and wealth protection. Every truly wealthy *fluminense* family needed a share of political power for material expansion. Political power secured contracts, favors, and, most important of all, seats in the rooms where economic policy was designed. In the division of labor within the family, some members were charged with securing a share of political power.

Yet Saquaremas were as much Marxist creatures as they were Weberian ones. For achieving wealth protection and wealth expansion, they could have followed a range of courses of action. They chose the one course of action that maximized political power, a motivation that was complementary

to, but autonomous from, the economic imperatives of their own class. As
Marxist actors, the Saquaremas protected the economy of Rio de Janeiro.
As Weberian ones, they extended domination to a larger territory. The
Saquaremas developed a distinctly political interest to project their power
beyond Rio de Janeiro and to gain influence in the other major provinces,
especially those of the Northeast, by cultivating long-term alliances with local oligarchies.

Incorporation of the Northeast:
Peripheral Demand and Central Supply

From a commercial point of view, the union between the Center-South and
the Northeast, the two large economic blocs of Brazil, made little sense for
both regions. After the coffee boom, the economic oligarchy of Rio de Janeiro did not need the Northeast to become wealthier. The formation of
Brazil was irrelevant for the coffee business. To maximize profits, what
the *fluminense* coffee oligarchy required was two eminently *local* class goods:
the enforcement of property rights and the development of infrastructure
in the area connecting the Paraíba Valley and the city-port, which included
building roads, introducing railways to replace mule trains, constructing ca-
nals and dams to prevent flooding in plantations and passages, and improvements in the port, such as new docks and warehouses. Why did the political
leaders of Rio de Janeiro spend time, money, and political capital to incorporate outlying provinces in the Northeast, especially Bahia and Pernambuco?

For Bahia and Pernambuco, economic linkages to Rio de Janeiro could
not be a motivation for union. The main consumers of the sugar and cotton
produced in the northeastern plantations were in Continental Europe and
the United States. The suppliers of textiles and hardware to northeastern
consumers were British. Given economic autonomy, why did the political
movement for secessionism in Bahia and Pernambuco not triumph?

The union between the provinces of the Center-South and those of the
Northeast can usefully be approached as a problem of supply and demand.
Given the unintended consequences of the liberal reforms, the northeastern
oligarchies "demanded" incorporation by Rio de Janeiro into Brazil, and the
central elites were willing to "supply" incorporation under very specific
conditions. The demand and the supply of incorporation had different mo-

tivations. The demand from the Northeast was rooted in the need for central state capacity to prevent and repress slave rebellion. The supply by the Center-South was purely political; it derived from coalitional considerations and the prospects of career enhancement for professional politicians in Rio de Janeiro, their allies, and their protégés.

For all the state failure caused by the liberal experiment in Brazil, it created new incentives in the hitherto secessionist provinces of the Northeast to become members of a larger country. The Cabanagem rebellion (1834), which was confined to the northern state of Pará, was the first warning sign of the potential for slave revolt in the Brazilian Northeast. Just a year later, the Malê movement caused havoc and panic in Bahia's own capital. It confirmed the worst fears aroused by the Cabanagem. Haitianism was not a "specter" any longer for the sugar barons of Bahia. Planned massacres of white people and property destruction made Haitianism a tangible reality. Fear dominated the sugar oligarchies of Pernambuco as well. The lesson was unambiguous. North of Minas Gerais, Brazil was an archipelago of Haitis, each of them ready to explode at the first political error. Slave revolts became the overriding concern of the northeastern elites in the 1830s. The danger could have been averted with the abolition of slavery, but abolition would have caused the economic ruin of the provincial oligarchs. Abolition was not the only alternative to Haitianism. Another option was central support for slave repression.

Out of fear of slave revolt, northeastern elites not only gave up the project to form a separate country. They actually created a demand for incorporation by Rio de Janeiro, which they viewed as contributing a critical level of military force. Additionally, Rio de Janeiro could provide diplomatic representation against the abolitionist pressures of Great Britain. To become separate countries, Bahia and Pernambuco would have needed British recognition. And for recognition, the obvious price demanded by the British would have been full abolition. For the Northeast, independence and slavery had become mutually incompatible goals. They chose slavery.

The outbreaks of Haitianism in the 1830s made an unmistakably positive contribution to territory consolidation in Brazil in the 1840s. They immunized the northeastern elites against secessionist aspirations. But slave revolts only contributed to the demand of incorporation by the Northeast. The missing piece is the decision of the Center-South to "supply" incorporation.

The Party of Order was the political vehicle for the incorporation of northeastern elites. Northeastern politicians with close ties to the plantation and slave owners joined the Saquaremas in the key legislative sessions of 1837. After that, they became a permanent junior partner in the Party of Order. Whenever the Party of Order captured the executive, roughly half of the ministerial portfolios were headed by a prominent Pernambucan or Bahian politician.

The chief reason for the Saquaremas of Rio de Janeiro to secure a northeastern component in its coalition is straightforward. The bastions of the liberal movement were located in the provinces of Minas Gerais and São Paulo, especially in their main cities. Given population size, Minas Gerais had the largest number of representatives in the legislature and members in the electoral college. The conservative forces of Rio de Janeiro alone could not neutralize the electoral weight of liberal-leaning Minas Gerais, let alone a unified front of Minas and São Paulo. The fact that the economies of the three provinces were highly integrated did not prevent Mineiro and Paulista politicians from disputing the power of Rio de Janeiro. Saquaremas in Rio de Janeiro needed northeastern conservatives first to balance and then to defeat liberal forces from Minas Gerais and São Paulo.

Liberalism remained strong in the provinces surrounding Rio de Janeiro well after the Party of Order had become the main political force in Brazil. The wisdom of *fluminense* reactionaries in incorporating a northeastern pillar was confirmed in 1842 when liberals revolted in São Paulo and Minas Gerais. The liberal revolts were motivated by power ambitions rather than by ideological principles. After a brief period in government in 1840, the liberals again lost power to the Party of Order. The leaders of the liberal revolts were looking for government positions and the patronage arsenal associated with them. Rebels were demobilized largely through negotiation. Only a few battles were fought. The one that marked the victory of the government occurred in the Mineiro village of Santa Luzia, which provided the liberals the informal name *luzias*. Since the 1842 defeat, the *luzias* of Minas and São Paulo accepted a secondary role in Brazilian politics. They gave up rebellion as a political method and abandoned criticism of the political order created by the Saquaremas, including chiefly the scope of the national political arena.

The institutional reversal designed and executed by the Saquaremas reveals two additional considerations in the supply of incorporation to the northeastern provinces by the Rio de Janeiro elites. The first one was the strengthening of the career of the professional judge, which, according to an informal but robust institution in nineteenth-century Brazilian politics, was often the subtitutes' bench for freshman politicians. Through a new criminal code, the Saquaremas eliminated the position of elected parish justices. The new judges would be professional lawyers appointed by the central government. The typical politician began his career as a local judge after obtaining a law degree from the University of Coimbra or, starting around 1830, in the schools opened in Olinda (Pernambuco) and São Paulo. As in Spanish America, local judges were key electoral players. Through their power to authorize eligible citizens to vote and to decide what votes were valid on election day, local judges manufactured majorities. They followed the instructions of political patrons, usually a provincial legislator, who in turn received orders from a national deputy or a minister. On the basis of merit both as a magistrate and as a political broker, the local judge expected to be promoted to a position on the court of appeals. In contrast to Spanish America, however, the next step for the Brazilian magistrate was a seat in the provincial legislature. Prominence in the provincial legislature, which depended on wise use of patronage and genuine leadership skills, propelled the magistrate into the lower house or the presidency of a minor province. Reaching the apex of their professional career, a selected minority of deputies and provincial presidents were chosen by the emperor, typically after some campaigning by a senior member of the Party of Order, to become the president of one of the five major provinces, a minister, a senator, or a member of the Council of State (the latter two were lifetime appointments). By creating a large number of new entry positions for law graduates, whose training had been directly or indirectly shaped by the Saquarema elite, the Party of Order produced a major client base, which was important both numerically and strategically, given its role in the supervision of elections. The incorporation of the Northeast into Brazil, then, translated into the ability of the Rio de Janeiro oligarchy to offer valuable jobs in Pernambuco and Bahia to their political clients. The Northeast increased the Party of Order's power to appoint and promote new generations of law-trained scions of the plantation oligarchies.

Second, in 1840, the Party of Order substantially curtailed the power of provincial assemblies through the so-called Interpretation of the 1834 amendment (Lei Interpretativa do Ato Adicional). Taking advantage of the vague wording of the 1834 reform, provincial assemblies during the liberal government had assumed powers to appoint all employees of the national administration working within the province, such as the inspectors of the customhouses, as well as to select the hierarchy of the local divisions of the National Guard. The Interpretation of 1840 restored the power of appointment to the emperor and the national cabinet. Crucially, the Interpretation aborted inchoate projects of fiscal federalism, which would have given coastal provinces like Bahia, Pernambuco, São Paulo, and Rio Grande do Sul control over the resources collected by the local branch of the customhouse. Despite the decline of the economies of Bahia and Pernambuco relative to the Center-South, the level of revenues collected at their customhouses continued to grow in absolute terms and would have been more than sufficient to fully finance the government expenditures of a midsized Spanish American country like Chile or Peru.

The Party of Order supplied incorporation to the Northeast. It provided the landowning elites of Pernambuco and Bahia with a repressive machine of last resort in case of slave rebellion. It also co-opted the political leadership of the Northeast with a share of legislative and executive power. Yet Bahia and Pernambuco paid a big price to Rio de Janeiro for their incorporation. By accepting the restoration of a fully unitarian formula of territorial governance, they gave up substantial degrees of political autonomy and a large volume of fiscal resources.

Incorporation of the South: Defeat of the Piratini Republic

Rio Grande do Sul was a prosperous rudimentary port state in 1835 when it decided to secede from the Brazilian Empire and form the República de Piratini. In contrast to the rudimentary port states of the Northeast, which were plantation economies, Rio Grande do Sul was a cattle-ranching economy, specialized in the production of jerked beef for the slave plantations of Rio de Janeiro, Bahia, and Pernambuco and of leather for export to European markets. Partly as a consequence of the type of agronomic region, a small number of rural lords controlled extensive clientelistic networks covering almost all Rio Grande do Sul. They were big landowners who supplied jobs to large contingents of rural workers and owned vast droves of horses. They could quickly turn their private economic assets into a formidable military force—a substantial cavalry—in times of war. The most prominent Riograndense lord at the time was Bento Gonçalves da Silva, to whom the empire had delegated a number of military functions, mostly related to the defense of the frontier. Yet the unitarian formula of territorial governance created a mismatch between the social power of the rural lords and the political power in the province, which was in the hands of a president appointed by the royal court in Rio de Janeiro.

Separatism and republicanism had been floating in Rio Grande's air since Brazilian independence (1822), and the successful secession of Uruguay just to the south in 1828 only reinvigorated them. In 1835, two specific grievances, one political, one economic, turned the tacit sentiment into political action: the appointment by the regency in Rio de Janeiro of a provincial president whom most local notables in Rio Grande disliked and the decline of Rio Grande's sales of jerked beef to the rest of Brazil, which was caused by fiscal and monetary policies of Rio de Janeiro (not only did Rio de Janeiro tax Rio Grande's jerked beef, but the very dynamism of its coffee sector caused currency overvaluation, which favored imports of jerked beef from Uruguay and Buenos Aires).[19]

The secession of Rio Grande cannot be understood without the ambition of Bento Gonçalves. If, after seven years of independence, Uruguay proved to be a viable state, then the sovereignty of Rio Grande, with a larger economy, was an eminently feasible project. Moreover, it would produce very tangible benefits for the Riograndense landowning class: local notables would monopolize political power by becoming presidents and ministers of Piratini; control of the customhouse in Porto Alegre would be taken from Rio, making available a new source of revenues to finance local class goods; and private business would improve thanks to an increase of exports, which in turn would be the result of the new state's autonomous ability to set a competitive exchange rate in relation to Uruguay and Buenos Aires, the rival suppliers of the slave plantations.

If one rudimentary port state in Latin America had the fundamental requisites for secession, including the ambitious and capable leadership of rural lords, it was Rio Grande do Sul. In contrast to the rudimentary port states of the Northeast, Rio Grande do Sul did not need the support of Rio de Janeiro to deal with potential explosions of slave discontent. Slave labor was substantially less vital for Rio Grande's cattle-ranching economy than it was in the rest of Brazil. Besides, the rural lords themselves had the necessary repressive capacity to obtain labor discipline. If the breakaway state failed, it was only because its rival, the power of Rio de Janeiro as reconstructed by the Saquarema entrepreneurs, was extraordinarily skilled, resourceful, and ambitious.

As expected in the lord-driven pathway of state formation, the rural lord of Rio Grande do Sul had to make an important initial investment in military capacity to form his own country. State formation through secession requires state-breaking, and state-breaking is expensive. Yet the initial investment would be more than compensated by the revenues from international trade that sovereign control of customhouses would generate. Bento Gonçalves and his associates took advantage of the generalized state weakness caused by the liberal regency. Bento correctly guessed that the imperial army would be ordered to invade Rio Grande do Sul, but he also knew that the military effort by Rio de Janeiro, which was attending to multiple fronts at the same time, would necessarily be limited. In fact, all Rio de Janeiro could do for the first few years of secession was to dispatch warships to block Rio Grande's ports so as to paralyze exports and revenues from international commerce.

After several victories in land battles, including an impressive defeat of the imperial army at the Battle of Seival, a military stalemate emerged. The interior of Rio Grande was dominated by the cavalries of the secessionist rural lords, for whom detailed knowledge of the land was a crucial advantage. On the other hand, the coast, as well as the rivers and lakes connecting the interior to the main seaports, were under the control of the Brazilian navy. The rural lords were used to horses rather than ships. Their decision to produce a navy with the help of the future Italian hero Giuseppe Garibaldi was an extraordinarily consequential event. It set in motion the process that, combined with the rise to power of the Saquaremas in Rio de Janeiro, caused its own defeat.

After five years of paralysis in naval commerce, the Riograndense lords were desperate to gain access to the sea. They had made a huge monetary and military effort in secession, but the naval blockade impeded recovery of the investment by cutting access to revenues from foreign trade. They created a small shipyard (on a piece of land belonging to Bento's sister). They built two warships. In a bold decision, instead of fighting the imperial warships stationed in the state, Piratini's leaders invaded the province of Santa Catarina just to the north, which could provide passage to the sea. In a titanic effort, they transported the ships by land to the Santa Catarina lakes with access to the Atlantic. Under Bento's sponsorship, Santa Catarina declared secession as well; it proclaimed the creation of the República Juliana and united itself in confederation with the República de Piratini.

The invasion of Santa Catarina was a pyrrhic victory, marking the zenith of the rural lords' power. The annexation of Santa Catarina created more territorial claims than what the rural lords could defend, and it was certainly more than what the monarchists in the center were willing to tolerate—the republican wave from the south was now only one state away from the empire's capital. In a desperate search for access to the sea, the rural lords of Rio Grande risked overextension, which was aggravated by the fact that in Santa Catarina they could not count on the clientelistic loyalty that made them powerful in their homeland. Even worse, overextension made the rural lords vulnerable exactly at the same time that the Saquarema entrepreneurs were preparing the Regresso, and the expiration of the British 15 percent ceiling on import tariffs made the imperial budget especially large.

In 1840, the rural lords of Rio Grande do Sul began to retreat. Rio Grande would be fully, and irreversibly, reannexed in 1845. The strategy of the Saquaremas was only partially military. They did dispatch the most prestigious general in the empire, Luís Alves de Lima e Silva, Duke of Caxias, leading an army of twelve thousand men—three times the size of the rebel army. Yet the Duke spent more time co-opting, spying, and negotiating than making war. In 1842, the Duke created a permanent division among the rebels. He promised some of them a position in the official army, which most viewed as a professional opportunity that Piratini could never provide. In 1845, the remaining rebels received an amnesty. The magnanimity revealed that the Duke was certain that co-optation and exhaustion among the enemies' ranks had worked their effects. Any attempt to revive secessionism would be a lost cause. The same increased budget that allowed funding a larger imperial army also made possible economic concessions, including the virtual elimination of taxes charged to Riograndense cattle ranchers, who were thus better able to compete with foreign providers of jerked beef.

The Saquaremas' interest in Rio Grande do Sul was political, not geopolitical. The Saquaremas did not want to incorporate Rio Grande in order to extract manpower for the imperial army. The motivation for incorporation was the appeasement of the republican sentiment, which was incompatible with Saquarema power, and the rehabilitation of the profitable customhouse of Porto Alegre. The Riograndenses lost the war and, with it, their sovereignty. Yet the rural lords received concessions that, if granted a decade earlier, would have made the war unnecessary.

Conclusions

Rio de Janeiro precociously became a leading center of trade-led state formation in 1808. In the 1830s and 1840s, coffee gave Rio de Janeiro an unprecedented fiscal capacity. Yet, according to the theory presented in Part 1, territorial expansion is *not* a priority of state-making elites pursuing the trade-led path, in sharp contrast to the pioneer western European cases. Given the relative weakness of geopolitical pressures in Latin America, what motivated Rio de Janeiro to make major political efforts to prevent Bahia, Pernambuco, and Rio Grande do Sul from leaving the Brazilian union? No study has ever asked the question. Extrapolating from the western European experience the notion that all states are naturally "territory hungry," even the most sophisticated work on Brazilian state formation has uncritically adopted the assumption that expansionist ambitions were part of Rio de Janeiro's political DNA (or, worse, that a shared sense of national identity was at work to foster unification, when in reality nationhood was a mythology created decades after state formation).

The expansionary motivation of Rio de Janeiro had two sources. First, the peripheries of Brazil, even if in relative decline, were able to generate substantial levels of revenue. They were true rudimentary port states. That is why they wanted to secede in the first place. A sophisticated political vision from Rio de Janeiro could identify economies of scale that would benefit all regions involved, deepening the path of trade-led growth both for the center and for the peripheries. The political vision primarily included a deal with the northeastern provinces by which they accepted Rio de Janeiro's rule in exchange for central support against slave rebellion. Yet such political vision required a set of actors for whom carrying it out was compatible with their professional ambition.

That is the second source of the expansionary motivation: in the mid-1830s, a realignment of forces originated a conservative political club, the privileged Saquarema circle. The Saquaremas were professional politicians—no more than ten men—who in the theoretical terms of Chapter 4 can collectively be seen as the entrepreneur of the Brazilian founding juncture. They had talents, education, and connections that no rival politician could match. They were also members of the dominant economic *fluminense* families, whose wealth derived from coffee and African captives. Superior political capital and an enormous and growing accumulation of wealth made the Saquaremas extremely powerful. Yet, for the power of the Saquaremas to count, they needed a much larger political arena than Rio de Janeiro. They could only become a dominant political group if they became indispensable to a large number of regional constituencies. Professional ambition was the motive for territorial expansion.

The Saquaremas dominated the Brazilian legislature in the late 1830s and most of the 1840s and also conquered executive power during the critical years of territory consolidation. Their intervention at the peak of political power was relatively brief. Yet the state they created was formed to last. When the opposition reached power, it found the Saquarema creation too valuable to be dismantled.[20] Remove Saquarema power, a conservative variant of the entrepreneur rooted in a major city-port, and Brazil would not exist.

EIGHT

Party-Driven State Formation in Mexico

A MASTERFUL SYNTHESIS of nineteenth-century Latin American history describes Mexico as a *failed state*: "Mexico is the prime Latin American example of Murphy's Law, to the effect that what can go wrong will go wrong. Certainly, no other Latin American country had to grapple with so broad a range of critical difficulties, whether economic and social, political or diplomatic."[1] By the mid-nineteenth century, Mexico had lost more than half the territory under its nominal control at the time of independence (1821). The territorial loss was the result of the combination of U.S. expansionism and Mexico's military weakness. From 1863 to 1867, Mexico was occupied by French troops and ruled by a European king. The loss of sovereignty was the result of Napoleon III's imperial ambitions and, again, Mexico's military weakness. Mexico's inability to defend itself was in turn the symptom of deeper fiscal causes. Mexico achieved independence with a debt of nearly eighty million pesos, a world record.[2] During the half century after independence, the average yearly fiscal deficit was seven and a half million pesos. Expenditures almost doubled revenues. Historians agree that, because of extreme fiscal unviability and territorial losses, the state in Mexico was born dead.

The consensus among historians fails to perceive that, despite major challenges, Mexico successfully avoided the level of territorial fragmentation suffered by the much smaller Central American state directly to the south, which subdivided the isthmus into five minirepublics. Between 1835 and 1867, the partition of Mexico into four successor states, which would have each been more viable than any individual splinter republic in Central America, was a more likely outcome than continued union. Yet, after 1854, Mexico prevented new territorial losses. The achievement demands that the diagnosis of the Mexican case as a failed state be corrected. More important, the revised diagnosis demands explanation.

It is well understood how and why Mexico lost territory—the conspicuous aspect of Mexico's state failure. It is a complete mystery why and how Mexico managed to preserve a territory of colossal proportions covering radically different economic and political regions—the *hidden success* of Mexico's state formation.

The explanation of Mexico's success at state formation has two components. The first one was already presented in Chapter 3: Mexico is a special but by no means deviant case of successful *trade-led* state formation. In the critical years of the mid-nineteenth century, like all other Latin American cases except Paraguay, Mexico obtained a substantial level of resources for territory consolidation that did not derive from taxation of the upper classes. To fund state formation, Mexico sold an economic *stock* (territory) instead of economic *flows* (primary commodities), which is what all other cases of trade-led state formation did. The revenues obtained from the sale of California and Arizona to the United States helped Mexico retain Yucatán. Today, California and Arizona are orders of magnitude wealthier than Yucatán. Yet, in the late 1840s, California and Arizona were virtual deserts, whereas Yucatán was one of the three most dynamic exporting regions of Mexico. Retaining Yucatán was an unambiguous success at the time.

The other component of the explanation is that Mexico was a case of *party-driven* state formation. Revenues from land sales to the United States were a necessary but not sufficient condition for territory consolidation in Mexico. After the sales, Mexico could have lost more territory. If it did not, it was because, after decades of latent and open conflict, political parties became genuinely supraregional political organizations. Parties provided the glue uniting regions that otherwise had no economic, cultural, or political connection. Parties grew in competition with one another. Rival armies and Masonic lodges in the 1820s evolved into a full-blown two-party system, pitting Liberals against Conservatives, in the late 1840s. The goal of the politicians engaged in party development was local supremacy, not state formation. Politicians joined a party in order to defeat their regional rival. The party allowed the exchange of favors among members from different regions. The unintended consequence of party development was territory consolidation, one of the two key dimensions of state formation.

The party-driven path of state formation has *positive* effects on territory consolidation but has *negative* effects on violence monopolization, the
other dimension of state formation. Precisely because in the party-driven
path a state does not exist before parties are formed, parties are hybrid political organizations, which combine electoral capabilities and military assets. Electoral competition regularly morphs into violent conflict. The
two-party system in a stateless context is actually a *duopoly of violence*. Civil
war, open or latent, is a permanent feature of the political arena in the party-
driven path of state formation.

In Mexico, a major temporal gap separated territory consolidation
(mid-1850s) from violence monopolization (late 1870s). The gap is the distinctive effect of the party-driven path of state formation. A prolonged civil
war between Liberals and Conservatives (1854–67) resulted in a decisive victory by the Liberal Party. The Liberal triumph (1867) paved the way to violence monopolization.

What follows is the party-driven component of the explanation of state
formation in Mexico. The first section describes the outcome to be explained.
It highlights Mexico's hidden success. The second section reviews Mexico's
colonial background, which is the key to understanding the emergence of
the Conservative/Liberal cleavage in the late 1840s. The third section traces
the emergence of the two-party system and shows how party formation had
the unintended effect of state formation qua territory consolidation.[3]

Outcome: Hidden Success

The consensus vision among historians is that before 1867 Mexico was a
failed state. In a brilliant synthesis of the latest advances in historical research, Brian Hamnet describes the century from 1767 to 1867 as a transition from a prosperous society to a weak and truncated state. Similarly, for
David Bushnell and Neill Macaulay, the first half century of Mexico's independent life was marked by unmitigated economic and political "decline."[4]
Moreover, according to Josefina Zoraida Vázquez, the most important
question about Mexico before the late 1860s is "how and why the wealthy
and prestigious New Spain, in a matter of a few decades, became an unstable, bankrupt nation, incapable of governing itself and preventing U.S.
invasion?"[5]

The consensus vision is not necessarily wrong. Yet the characterization of Mexico as an economic and political failure is based on generalizations that fail to separate distinct dimensions of economic and political performance. It is certainly the case that on several dimensions Mexico "declined" compared to the Viceroyalty of New Spain. However, it is also true that on the specific dimensions of party formation and territory consolidation, Mexico was a success relative both to the historical record of other Latin American cases and to reasonable counterfactual trajectories that Mexico could have followed.

After identifying the dimensions of decline and reviewing the factual basis for it, this section offers a precise characterization of Mexico's success at state formation. A better understanding of state formation in Mexico requires the theoretical discipline of using the technical definition of the state in order to separate dimensions of failure and dimensions of success, as well as choosing an adequate set of historical and counterfactual comparisons. Analytical rigor produces a new vision of the Mexican state-formation process, which allows the highlighting of key achievements in a context that can otherwise be seen as one of generalized decline.

Generalized Decline

The consensus vision of Mexican generalized failure by the mid-nineteenth century has strong empirical support, which makes Mexico's success at territory consolidation all the more remarkable. Among all Latin American countries, Mexico certainly provides the starkest overall contrast between the last decades of colonial rule and the first five decades of independent life. Three trends jointly characterize the decline.

First, the production of silver, Mexico's main export, decreased from twenty-six million pesos the year before the first insurrections against Spanish rule (1810) to six million pesos the year after independence (1822). After independence, every major mining center in Spanish America suffered a great delay in recapturing colonial levels of mineral output. But none experienced more dislocation than Mexico. Mines had suffered from flooding and subsidence during the wars of independence, and large sections of a relatively advanced system of routes had fallen into disrepair. Expecting a fast recovery, Mexican economic elites and especially foreign companies made large investments in refitting the traditional Mexican mines. Economic hopes were crushed. Turning mines profitable again and restoring the transportation system demanded much more time and capital than originally expected. Because of economic decline, Mexico entered into a semipermanent state of fiscal "penury."[6]

Second, in colonial times, political stability was the norm, and it was sustained with only a minimal military force. By contrast, between 1821 and 1867, only one government transferred power to the following according to constitutional methods. All other rulers were replaced through coercion. Mexico's army was gigantic by Latin American standards. At the time of independence, it was fifty thousand men strong, and the military payroll consumed half the Mexican budget. Yet the army was not a cohesive force. After independence, the army was divided into seventeen semi-independent sections (*comandancias*). Several commanders turned the men and weapons at their disposal into private armies, which helped them establish patrimonial rule over large territorial pockets. Because of the lack of coordinated action by the generals, Mexico's army was extremely ineffective, which in turn explains the third and last trend.

Finally, Mexico lost more than half of its territory on a permanent basis, and for a period, it lost sovereignty altogether (see Map 8.1). In 1823, the rebellion of the caudillo Antonio López de Santa Anna against Agustín de Iturbide, Mexico's first ruler, resulted in the secession of Central America. Twelve years later, Texas claimed independence. In 1848, military victory allowed the United States to annex Texas, Arizona, New Mexico, and California. In the early 1860s, Mexico's army could not prevent an invasion from Napoleon III.

Given geopolitical pressures, internal political turmoil, and economic and fiscal penury, what is remarkable is that Mexico's territorial losses were not bigger.

Success: Relevant Comparisons

Against the colonial benchmark, independent Mexico looks like a failed state. Yet colonial Mexico does *not* provide the most instructive contrast. More informative is a comparison with a counterfactual Mexico divided into several separate countries, a fragmentation that did occur in the much smaller

Map 8.1. Mexico in 1822

territory of neighboring Central America. Present-day Mexico could have divided into four sovereign units. The corridor connecting México City to the port of Veracruz through Puebla would have been the core of one country. Three republics could have seceded from the core, each one larger and economically more powerful than Central America's successor states. The Yucatán Peninsula, with its own port and a vibrant plantation economy, could have formed a separate country. Likewise, Jalisco and Zacatecas in the West could have produced a two-state confederation with a vast Pacific coastline. Finally, profiting from commerce with neighboring United States, the northeastern states of Sonora, Chihuahua, Coahuila, Tamaulipas, and Nuevo León could have created a new country, either jointly or individually (see Map 8.2).

According to the economic theory of territorial combinations presented in Chapter 4, the México City–Veracruz core, the Yucatán Peninsula, Jalisco-Zacatecas, and the cluster of northern states were at least

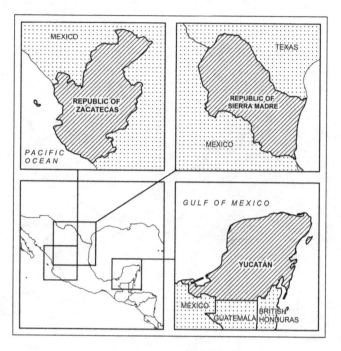

Map 8.2. Mexican failed secessions, 1824-38

rudimentary port states. Each of them had the economic incentive and the fiscal capacity for "small-scale" state formation, that is, the formation of an independent country by seceding from, or rejecting the incorporation of, neighboring regions.

The success at territory consolidation in Mexico is remarkable because the counterfactual fragmentation into four independent states has a solid factual basis. First, the example of Central America shows that when regional economies (a) have commercial linkages to international markets that are stronger than linkages among each other and (b) are endowed with a port that can collect revenues from international trade via import tariffs, their leaders develop a strong incentive to form independent states. In Yucatán, the Zacatecas-Jalisco axis, and the northeastern states of present-day Mexico, international linkages and the ability to collect revenues from foreign trade were even stronger than in any of the successor states of Central America.

Second, Mexican fragmentation was for long junctures before the mid-1850s a more likely outcome than continued union. In 1823, the same year that Central America seceded from Mexico, Jalisco became a "free and sovereign state." Given the close commercial relations between Zacatecas and Guadalajara, Jalisco's capital, Zacatecas seceded too. The confederal constitution of 1824 made reincorporation appealing to Jalisco and Zacatecas. The introduction of a unitarian formula in 1836 led Zacatecas to secede. Yucatán and the cluster of northeastern states followed the example. The three regions were the only ones to experience mild prosperity in the context of generalized stagnation. Yucatán exported sisal to the United States; Zacatecas made new discoveries of silver veins; and the northeastern states' cattle-ranching economy supplied a sustained demand from the U.S. South.

Yucatán had every condition to form a ministate. It would have been a more viable country than Guatemala, the strongest successor state after the fragmentation of Central America. Separated from Mexico's center by impenetrable jungles, Yucatán was connected to Veracruz only through navigation across the Gulf of Mexico. The time of travel to Veracruz was similar to the time of travel to New Orleans, which was Yucatán's main market for the emerging sisal sector. The fiber produced from the henequen cactus was the key input for rope and twine. In the 1830s and 1840s, sisal created substantial fortunes among the Yucatecan landed elites. By skipping traffic with Veracruz, Yucatán could have its own customhouse in Sisal, the state's main seaport. Sisal collected Yucatán's own revenues. For Yucatán, union with Mexico meant a net economic and political loss. It is a twin case of Piratini (Rio Grande do Sul) in relation to Brazil. No other region in Spanish America worked so intensely to remain an independent republic as Yucatán did in the early 1840s. In fact, before annexation to Mexico in 1847, Yucatán tried to become an English protectorate, a Spanish informal colony, and a U.S. state. Yet Yucatán eventually became Mexican.

In the late 1840s, Mexico's borders looked like they do today, but they were not consolidated. Although it did not occur, more territorial change was possible. The northeastern states of Coahuila, Tamaulipas, and Nuevo León threatened secession every time a unitarian formula of territorial governance replaced a confederal or federal formula. The República de Río Grande, which united all three states, was a short-lived state created in January 1840. It expressed strong secessionist undercurrents, which erupted again in 1850 with the creation of the República de la Sierra Madre. The secessionist republic was sponsored by Santiago Vidaurri, a political and military leader similar to other caudillos in Spanish America who successfully opposed large-scale state-formation projects and carved out a smaller independent country that was coterminous with his network of patronage relations, like Páez in Venezuela (a successor state of Gran Colombia) and Carrera in Guatemala (splinter of the Central American Federation).

During the Reform War (1858–61), Liberals and Conservatives fought a major civil war that would decide the survival of precolonial and colonial institutions, including collective property rights of indigenous communities, the wealth and status of the Catholic Church, mercantilist privileges of the aristocracy in México City, and the immunities of the army (*fueros*). The war divided Mexico not only along ideological lines but also along territorial ones. Two parallel governments, one centered in México City, the other in Veracruz, coexisted throughout most of the conflict. A persistent stalemate could have led to the division of the country into two halves. Finally, when in 1862 Mexico became a semicolony of the French Empire, no one imagined that five years later, due to the rise of Germany, Napoleon III would decide to recall the troops in Latin America in order to defend his position in western Europe and thus to restore Mexico's sovereignty by default. Continued French domination, the most reasonable outcome to expect in the mid-1860s, would have probably provoked secessions of splinter states that could not tolerate foreign invasion or monarchic rule.

In sum, it is still an enigma how and why Mexico managed to prevent the secession of Yucatán, Jalisco/Zacatecas, and the northern states, the neglected success of Mexican state formation. Despite unique challenges and substantial territorial losses, Mexico's center managed to form a territorial colossus that incorporated multiple peripheries, at least three of which were rudimentary port states. In Latin America, only Mexico combines so many different political and economic regions. Remarkably, the combination was produced with a fraction of the fiscal resources available to the elites of Rio de Janeiro or Buenos Aires, the capitals of the other two colossuses. Present-day Mexico is much smaller than the Viceroyalty of New Spain. However, it is much larger than the territory that should have resulted from the quadruple combination of U.S. expansionism, fiscal penury at the center, autonomous economic growth in a few peripheries (Yucatán, Zacatecas, and the northeastern states), and generalized politico-military fragmentation after independence.

One component of the explanation of Mexico's success is rooted in the availability of financial resources derived from the sale of large tracts of land in the 1840s. Yet this component of the explanation only accounts for the capacity to reannex secessionist regions, not for the willingness to do so. It also does not explain why territory consolidation in Mexico predated violence monopolization by several decades. To address both issues, it is crucial to see Mexico as a *party-driven* variant of the trade-led state-formation process. Party formation in Mexico is a direct legacy of colonial society.

The Colonial Background to Party Formation

Mexico is the heartland of what in colonial times was the Viceroyalty of New Spain. Out of the four Spanish viceroyalties in Latin America, New Spain was comfortably the wealthiest. Mexico's central plateau was endowed with extraordinary mineral wealth, especially silver. New Spain was the largest Iberian colony. It was also the most developed in every economic, social, and institutional aspect. The level of development of New Spain explains why political divisions in independent Mexico quickly evolved into the purest form of Conservative-versus-Liberal cleavage. Conservatives and Liberals fought over the persistence of colonial forms of corporate privilege.

From an economic perspective, New Spain's silver mines were more productive than those of Peru and Upper Peru (present-day Bolivia), the other major mining centers in colonial Spanish America. Annual royal revenues from Mexico grew from two million pesos to twenty-five million over the course of the eighteenth century. Silver mines were only a fraction of Mexico's total economic activity, about two-thirds of which was agricultural. Agriculture in Mexico was more diversified than in any other Iberian colony. Large estates, or *haciendas*, owned by either the white elite or the church, produced a range of cereals, including wheat and corn, as well as beef, mutton, hides, and wool. In indigenous villages, property was divided into private plots and communal pasturelands, or *ejidos*. Villages specialized in small-scale farming production, including fruits, poultry, eggs, peppers, and cochineal (a dye derived from cactus bugs that for long periods was New Spain's second-leading export product). Three-quarters of the Mexican indigenous population, roughly 60 percent of the total, were agricultural workers. Most indigenous peasants lived in poverty, slightly above subsistence level.

From a social perspective, the network of cities in New Spain was three times as large and four times more populated than that of New Granada, the other viceroyalty with a large number of cities (present-day Colombia, Venezuela, Ecuador, and Panama).[7] In no other section of the Americas was the Catholic Church more powerful with regard to the number of followers and economic wealth. By the end of the eighteenth century, the Catholic Church was the single largest landowner in New Spain. Its rural property was worth around two hundred thousand million pesos. Finally, economic groups in New Spain had a long tradition of being organized in guilds, *consulados*, which were granted special commercial privileges by the Crown in Madrid or the viceroy in México City (only Lima had comparably powerful *consulados*). Profiting from mercantilist policies, members of the *consulados* obtained monopolistic rights to produce and sell tobacco, cotton, salt, and pulque (an alcoholic beverage derived from the maguey plant), as well as exclusive rights to lend money and distribute imports from the big Cádiz merchant houses. The wealth of the upper class derived from political access to colonial authorities. Its members were a *rentier aristocracy* concentrated in México City and the port of Veracruz.

The level of economic, social, and institutional development in New Spain was a proximate cause of party formation and, through it, a distant cause of territory consolidation.

Party-Driven State Formation

Mexico pioneered the party-driven variant of trade-led state formation. State formation was an unintended but direct effect of party formation. The Conservative-versus-Liberal cleavage that crystallized around the late 1840s was in turn a direct outcome of the maturity reached by colonial institutions and society before the wars of independence. Colonial institutions such as the church and colonial classes such as the rentier aristocracy had acquired so prominent a place by the time of independence that a struggle between advocates and defenders of colonial privilege was bound to emerge in the context of political mobilization created by the collapse of the Spanish Empire.

Precisely because political and social stratification in colonial times had developed more fully in Mexico than anywhere else in Spanish America, postindependence political struggle rapidly evolved into a partisan fight between Conservatives and Liberals over the preservation of colonial legacies. The multiplicity of urban centers encouraged the formation of partisan networks across regions, especially among Liberal politicians, who depended on mutual help for political survival.

In turn, party-driven state formation in Mexico explains the substantial temporal gap between territory consolidation (mid-1850s) and violence monopolization (late 1870s). It separates Mexico, together with Colombia and Uruguay, from the cases of port-driven state formation in Argentina and Brazil and the cases of lord-driven state formation in Peru and Venezuela.

Wrong Interpretations

The thesis that parties contributed to state formation in Mexico is a radical departure from conventional accounts by historians. A strong tradition in Latin American history claims that the rudiments of the Mexican state before 1855 were the outcome of a *lord-driven* process. The tradition is rooted in the vision crafted by the brilliant statesman and historian Lucas Alamán: "The history of Mexico in this period [1822–55] might accurately be called the History of Santa Anna's revolutions. . . . His name plays the main role in all the political events of the country, and its destiny has become intertwined with his."[8] The irony of this influential passage is that Alamán himself was a major contributor to *party-driven* state formation in Mexico. Alamán was the formal founder of the Conservative Party in 1848, which, in competition with the Liberal Party, had the unintended effect of making a much more significant contribution to territory consolidation in Mexico than did any individual warlord, including General Antonio López de Santa Anna. Santa Anna's contributions were largely *negative*. Santa Anna provided disastrous military leadership in the Mexican-American War, interfered with a more rapid formation of political parties, and wasted fiscal resources like few leaders in nineteenth-century Latin America.

If Santa Anna was not an agent of state formation, even less so was the army to which he belonged. Mexico's army was unique in Latin America. It was the only one to result from the merger of the royalist troops and the

insurgent guerrillas. It was so large that its payroll was the single most important cause of the state's fiscal indigence; it was so fragmented into uncoordinated chieftains that it aggravated civil conflict; and it was so ineffective that it
could not prevent foreign occupation and large territorial losses.

Parties have traditionally been seen as agents of state failure, even by
party leaders themselves. It is certainly true that they caused civil war, with
minor episodes in 1835 and 1840 and major ones in 1857–60 and 1867. Their
contribution was negative to violence monopolization. Yet they made a major, albeit slow-moving and largely invisible, contribution to territory consolidation. Precisely because party formation was a slow-moving process, the
very protagonists failed to see the unintended consequences for territory consolidation. "The owl of Minerva spreads its wings only with the falling of
the dusk."

Basic Chronology

The two-party system of Mexico in the mid-nineteenth century had its roots
in the Independence period. The formation of Conservatives and Liberals
as rival parties occurred over the course of three major junctures of party
formation:

1. *The transition from rival armies to competing lodges (1810–24).*
   This juncture in party formation covers the period of the independence wars (1810–20), the achievement of independence
   and the First Empire (1821–23), and the foundation of the First
   Republic under a quasi-confederal formula of territorial governance (1824).
2. *Partisan warfare (1824–54).* This juncture inaugurated the period of Failure, which Mexico shared with all other Latin
   American countries except Chile and Paraguay. It covers what
   in Mexican historiography is usually known as the First Federal Republic (1824–34), the Centralized State (1834–45), and
   the Second Federal Republic until Santa Anna's dictatorship
   (1846–54).
3. *Liberal triumph (1855–70).* This juncture covers the so-called
   Reforma, a large-scale Liberal reform program that was initi-

ated in 1855 and culminated in 1876, and the subperiod known
as República Restaurada (1867–76). The Liberal reform was
interrupted by both a major civil war (1857–60) and a foreign
invasion (1862–67). During both interruptions, a Conservative
bid to regain power backfired on the party and eventually
caused its irreversible bankruptcy.

Each period of party formation will be analyzed in turn.

From Rival Armies to Competing
Masonic Lodges: 1810–24

Between 1810 and 1824, two protoparties were formed. In 1810, the original
axis of conflict was Mexican independence versus Spanish colonialism. Rival political groups were essentially war machines. After ten years of armed
conflict, both groups temporarily embraced independence. In 1823, the
struggle resumed. The fight was over the form of government: centralized
monarchy versus federal republic. Under the new line of conflict, rival political groups organized as competing Masonic lodges. The transition from
armies to lodges did not cause the extinction of the use of violence to gain
control of government. Yet the transition did expand the repertoire of methods of political competition, including mainly party formation.

Independence and Empire (1810–23). From 1810 to 1823, political parties
were nonexistent in Mexico. The key political actors were rival armies: insurgents versus royalists. At the time of independence, the most prominent
leader of the insurgent movement was Vicente Guerrero. The commander
of the royalist army was Agustín de Iturbide, son of a Basque merchant of
Michoacán. The rival groups were military organizations, but they pursued political goals. Since 1810, the goals had been mutually incompatible: independence versus colonialism. In 1820, an exogenous event, the
liberal revolt in Spain, made the rival armies temporarily converge on the
goal of independence.

Under Iturbide's leadership, the bulk of the royalist army in Mexico
switched sides in 1820. Suddenly, royalists and insurgents agreed on the top
political priority. They both embraced independence, but they did so for

opposite reasons. Iturbide, like the other royalist officers, was a monarchist. He was horrified by the liberal victory in Spain and feared that liberalism would spread throughout Mexico. Insurgents, for their part, unanimously favored republican rule. Their preferences regarding other institutional and policy issues, like the formula of territorial governance and the status of the church, were largely ill defined and varied across lower-level leaders. A small group within the insurgents, which would grow stronger over time, embraced what in retrospect can be seen as a liberal plan of action. The plan pursued a radical attack on colonial institutions and social structures and advocated the introduction of laissez-faire economics, federalism, democratic reform, the abolition of military privileges, the disentailment of indigenous communal land, and the confiscation of church property.

In 1820, the insurgents' chances of winning the war were negligible. The insurgent army had for a long time deteriorated into guerrilla bands. Guerrilla fighters were especially recalcitrant in the *tierra caliente* (hot country), the present-day state of Guerrero. The central plateau, including México City, and the key port of Veracruz, as well as the communications between capital and port, were under firm royalist control.

Iturbide's volte-face gave his rivals an opportunity for a tactical alliance. Insurgents obtained independence, their historical priority, but sacrificed the creation of a republic, their second objective. The minimalist compromise between royalists and insurgents was expressed in the Plan de Iguala, and the army claimed for itself the role of guaranteeing its four main clauses: independence from Spain, monarchic rule, preservation of the Catholic religion, and reconciliation between Spaniards and Mexicans.

The contradictory alliance sustaining Iturbide made his tenure as emperor of Mexico inevitably brief (early 1821 to mid-1822). Iturbide's fall revealed that Mexico was ungovernable. In 1823, Mexico joined most other Latin American countries in the Failure period. Failure in Mexico became especially virulent. In no other Latin American country did both armies fighting over independence survive, let alone merge. The consolidated army had deleterious effects on state formation. Its cost made fiscal crisis a chronic feature of the Mexican state.

After independence had been achieved, political differences between monarchists and republicans were front and center. Monarchists had a much more precise institutional agenda, which included a strong, dynastic executive power under minimal control of a legislature, a close alliance with the

Catholic Church, a unitarian formula of territorial governance, and limited civil and political rights. Republicans only agreed on the rejection of monarchic rule. The majority but not all of them favored federalism, freedom of the press, and universal suffrage. Initially, only a minority of republicans opposed the power of the Catholic Church.

Republican forces grouped together the surviving generals of the insurgent army, including mainly Guerrero and Guadalupe Victoria, some new protoprofessional politicians, like Valentín Gómez Farías, an ardent antichurch liberal, and General Santa Anna, a former staunch Iturbidista who switched sides when he perceived that Iturbide's support had begun to crumble. A constant in Santa Anna's political career was his talent to switch sides in anticipation of changes in public opinion. Santa Anna was the ultimate political chameleon.

A divided army and the cleavage between monarchists and republicans were the catalysts of Failure, which lasted until the mid-1850s. The monarchic-republican cleavage was the basis of prepartisan political organizations, and the struggle between the parties that evolved from that cleavage created a state of semipermanent civil war until 1867.

However, in sharp contrast to the divided army, the conflict between protoparties fueled *party formation*. Partisan conflict, when turned violent, blocked state formation qua violence monopolization. Yet, as an engine of party formation, partisan conflict fostered state formation qua territory consolidation. The latter was an unintended, invisible, but powerful process.

Masonic Lodges and Confederal Constitution (1823-24). The fall of Iturbide initiated a new constitutional process in 1823.[9] It also pushed political actors to organize themselves. The vehicle of political organization was not the political party. It was the Masonic lodge. The Scottish Rite lodge gathered most members of the former colonial elite of México City who had strong vested interests in the preservation of mercantilist policies and economic monopolies.[10] The *escoceses*, as members were known, also favored monarchic rule, limited political participation, and a unitarian formula of territorial governance, which were the institutional means to protect aristocratic social and economic privilege. The plan of the *escoceses* was to craft a coalition between the army, the church, and the rentier aristocracy of the México City–Puebla–Veracruz corridor. The coalition would provide the social and organizational support for a government under *escocés* hegemony. The quest

for power pushed *escoceses* into multiple tactical alliances and policy compromises. Yet the pillars of their coalition—army, church, and rentier
aristocracy—remained immutable.

In response to the formation of the Scottish Rite lodge, several former
insurgents, emerging politicians in the capitals of the central states, and oligarchies of peripheral states founded the York Rite lodge. They shared only
two well-defined institutional goals: republicanism and federalism. The social basis of the *yorkinos* was not as clear as that of the *escoceses*. To the re-
gret of Marxist analysts, *yorkinos* lacked a social basis, and they were a purely
political movement. Some *yorkinos* promoted the incorporation of peasant
communities. Yet peasant communities were not part of the social basis, and
those *yorkinos* who wanted to include them largely viewed peasant communities not as equal political partners but as providing a following that would
strengthen an agenda of reforms that would directly attack the privileges of
the three pillars of the proto-Conservative coalition.

The secret nature of the lodges meant that private conspiracies rather
than public debates and electoral campaigns were the main locus of decision-
making in the 1820s and early 1830s. The lodges began to morph into protoparties in the late 1830s when members discovered the political benefits
of producing public interventions, through the press, manifestos, or speeches,
and of adopting partisan labels that signaled the constellation of interests and
fellow politicians to which they belonged.

A large number of politicians before midcentury were neither *escoceses*
nor *yorkinos*. They were moderates, defined by one similarity and multiple
differences with the *liberales puros* of the York Rite (purist liberals). Like
the *yorkinos*, moderates opposed colonial privilege. In contrast to the purists, the moderates' support for federalism, laissez-faire, and democracy was
conditional on the changing circumstances of the country, including the fiscal standing of the central government, the threats of foreign invasion, and
the level of education of the general public. Also, in contrast to the *puros*,
moderate politicians were skeptical about popular mobilization. The ideological flexibility of the moderates, rooted in a subtle understanding of evolving practical challenges rather than in philosophical inconsistency, made
future conservatives and purist liberals compete for their support.

Yorkinos and moderates were responsible for drafting the 1824 constitution, which, in comparison to the U.S. document, was more confederal and

less liberal.[11] The influence of the moderates, combined with fear of retaliation by the coalition behind the *escoceses*, left intact the system of corporate privilege, including ecclesiastic and military immunities.

Partisan Warfare: 1824–54

The 1824 constitution quickly became a dead letter. A constitutional breakdown occurred in 1828, when a moderate candidate won the presidential election and the York Rite *puros* staged a coup to install Guerrero in the presidency.

Historians usually blame the constitution's own flaws of institutional design for the breakdown. Yet such a conclusion does not survive comparative historical analysis. The cause of the constitutional breakdown in 1828 was Mexico's structural ungovernability. The 1828 episode was not an isolated event in Mexico's history, and Mexico's ungovernability was not unique in the region. Constitutional breakdowns recurred in 1829, 1832, and 1835 under the same constitution and in 1841, 1843, and 1845 under a different constitution, which introduced a unitarian formula of territorial governance.

Mexican ungovernability was the effect of the appalling economic conditions affecting all Latin American protostates after independence, which translated into desperate fiscal crises. Like Buenos Aires, Gran Colombia, and Peru, Mexico defaulted on its foreign debt in 1827. Mexico's ungovernability was aggravated by the political polarization between the *yorkinos* and the rentier aristocracy of México City. Polarization was not unique to Mexico either. It dominated partisan politics in Bogotá and Buenos Aires for long periods.

Fiscal penury and political polarization were not unique to Mexico, but in Mexico they were extreme. They were both symptoms of even deeper causes. The performance of the export sector relative to colonial standards was poorer in Mexico than anywhere else because of the severe damage to the mining industry and the transportation system during the wars of independence. Anemic exports translated into a weak flow of imports, which caused a drastic reduction of government revenues. At the same time, an inflated army made government expenditures soar. Large fiscal deficits were the chronic result. Between 1821 and 1867, expenditures averaged seventeen and a half million pesos; revenues averaged only ten million.[12]

Poor economic performance was compounded in Mexico by the legacy of a highly developed colonial society, which included an unparalleled level of inequality between the rentier aristocracy and the large population of rural workers. Hence, in Mexico, the stakes of the struggle over the abolition of colonial privilege were especially high. Extreme political polarization was a natural reflection of them.

A precursor to civil war, political polarization was nevertheless a big step forward in party formation. Party formation included the mobilization of diverse regional interests, which in turn made a major, albeit unintended, contribution to territory consolidation. Political polarization and party formation grew out of successive failures by alternating protoparties to provide a solution to Mexico's fiscal, economic, and geopolitical challenges during their tenure in power.

The Conservative-Liberal Pendulum (1828–35). President Guerrero found no solution to Mexico's fiscal weakness and political polarization. Not even the defeat of a Spanish attempt to reconquer Mexico prevented Guerrero's fall. The Catholic Church played a key role in undermining Guerrero's authority. With an empty treasury, Guerrero obtained some funds by selling church property. Guerrero was also a friend of the U.S. ambassador Joel Roberts Poinsett, who had played a pivotal role in the formation of the York Rite lodge. To prevent further property confiscation, the church mounted a campaign accusing Guerrero's government of falling under Protestant influence—a trivial charge from a contemporary perspective, it was a destabilizing blow in early nineteenth-century Mexico.

The defeat of the Spanish invasion was capitalized on by Santa Anna rather than by Guerrero. Spanish troops landed in Tampico in July 1829. Santa Anna led the defense, and victory made him an instant national hero. It was Santa Anna's primitive accumulation of political capital. He had already built an extensive network of patronage in his native state of Veracruz, which secured him influence over the port's customhouse, a vital source of public revenues. Additionally, victory over the Spaniards gained him unconditional loyalty from a large contingent of soldiers. Santa Anna became an indispensable pillar of Guerrero's government.

Once the external threat was overcome, the campaign against Guerrero resumed. Attacks from the church and its civilian allies forced Guerrero to remove his liberal ministers and forced Poinsett to leave the country.

Santa Anna sensed that the change in public opinion was irreversible and withdrew his support for Guerrero.

In November 1829, another coup replaced the president. The new rulers were the general Anastasio Bustamante as president and the mining engineer Lucas Alamán as minister of foreign and internal affairs. Bustamante contributed the military power. Alamán was the policy maker. Alamán was a conservative *avant la lettre*. Alamán's institutional and policy preferences were the exact opposite to those of the *yorkinos* who had supported Guerrero. Alamán made every effort to secure and upgrade the system of corporate privilege inherited from the colony. The most prominent example was the creation of the state-owned Banco de Avío, a precocious developmentalist experiment aimed at subsidizing the textile industry of Puebla, which was controlled by a handful of magnates of the colonial rentier aristocracy. Puebla's textile output was supposed to substitute for English imports. To deal with the fiscal crisis, Alamán sold the deficit-ridden public monopoly of tobacco to a wealthy group in México City. The government also eliminated a large number of public jobs, which included a reduction in the size of the army, a measure that only a general with impeccable military credentials like Bustamante could implement.

Risking further political polarization, the new government shut down *puro* newspapers, deposed federalist governors, and purged the legislatures. Bustamante's government also created a liberal martyr. In 1830, former president Guerrero revolted in the South after gathering a small force of guerrilla fighters. The army remained loyal to Bustamante and rapidly repressed the revolt. Guerrero was captured in January 1831 and executed in February by order of the central government. The short-term gain for the conservatives was plain. Yet the martyr was a major source of long-term political capital for the liberal cause.

In less than two years, Mexico's economic weakness and political polarization also proved lethal to the Bustamante-Alamán government. Yet the Bustamante-Alamán government made a major contribution to party formation. It created a conservative partisan network. Although the network did not aggregate interests across all regions in Mexico, it extended throughout the central east-west corridor from Jalisco (Bustamante's state) to Veracruz. It included Guanajuato (Alamán's state), México City, and Puebla, the state to receive the largest number of political favors from Alamán. Inadvertently, Bustamante and Alamán also contributed to the formation of the Liberal

Party. As Bushnell and Macaulay succinctly put it, "Under the oppression of Bustamante's proclerical dictatorship, [*puros*] had strengthened their commitment to liberalism."[13] Failure of government performance was the visible outcome, but it was combined with unambiguous success at party formation, a development missed by the very protagonists.

In 1832, *puro* conspirators were joined by a disgruntled group of army officials, who still resented Bustamante's downsizing, to topple the government. The leader of the coup was none other than Santa Anna, who had also been a key figure in the 1828 coup favoring Guerrero. This time, Santa Anna not only broke the old government but also made the new one. He became the new president. If Santa Anna's main talent was his ability to anticipate changes in public opinion, a complementary virtue was his ability to acknowledge that Mexico's structural problems could not be solved within the time horizon of any individual government. In three out of his five presidencies, Santa Anna delegated power to his vice president and moved to his Manga de Clavo hacienda in Veracruz, a rural property that grew to cover half a million acres. Political pragmatism rather than sloth was the motive behind Santa Anna's delegations. In Manga de Clavo, Santa Anna avoided responsibility for his delegates' failures. He would move to the capital only to take credit for his delegates' successes or to clean up their mistakes.

During Santa Anna's first presidential term, the vice president was Valentín Gómez Farías, a radical liberal. His institutional and policy preferences were the polar opposite of Alamán's. His closest collaborators were José María Luis Mora, the dean of Mexican liberal thought, and Lorenzo de Zavala, whose federalist convictions made him prefer Mexican disintegration over union under a unitarian formula. The new government favored the purest form of federalism and was convinced that economic laissez-faire and a frontal attack against church power would solve Mexico's economic problems. Confiscating church property could certainly restore the government's fiscal health. The disparity of wealth between church and government in Mexico had no parallel in the world.

Gómez Farías attempted the first large-scale liberal reform in Mexico. Yet, before it could produce any positive results, the reform was aborted by its own patron, Santa Anna. The liberal reform faced the classical problem of many large-scale policy changes: its short-term losers made their grievances felt much earlier than the general population could enjoy the long-term benefits. Textile magnates in Puebla and monopolistic tobacco producers in Veracruz were furious at free-trade policies. Mexican consumers preferred British textiles and Cuban cigars. Imports were better and cheaper. Gómez Farías abolished the mercantilist protection of the rentier aristocracy and forced it to lose substantial captive markets. The church naturally opposed Gómez Farías, who initiated his attack by secularizing education. The army suffered another downsizing and was threatened to be replaced by provincial-level civilian militias. Gómez Farías deepened the spiral of political polarization by sponsoring a law, the Ley del Caso, that allowed the government to exile political rivals. Fifty politicians were exiled, mostly conservatives, including former president Bustamante.

Santa Anna quickly perceived that grievances against Gómez Farías would pile up indefinitely. Before he was held responsible for Gómez Farías's failures, Santa Anna moved to the capital, resumed presidential power, expelled the liberals, and suspended the confederal constitution. Embracing the dominant trend in public opinion, Santa Anna switched political sides and surrounded himself with conservatives.

Gómez Farías's government made a negative contribution to the violence-monopolization component of state formation. Like the Bustamante-Alamán government, the Gómez Farías government made a U-turn in relation to its predecessor's policies. Radical policy changes compressed within short periods, especially when they produced no solution to Mexico's structural problems, fueled political polarization. In turn, political polarization was the precursor to violent partisan conflict.

Yet, exactly like the Bustamante-Alamán government, Gómez Farías made a major contribution to party formation. Gómez Farías defined a clear set of policies that could gather the support of a large number of fellow politicians and a substantial portion of the public. Short-term losers caused the government breakdown, but those who expected to become winners of Gómez Farías's policies, including potential buyers of the church's rural property, would form a distinct political constituency. Also, as manifested in the divergent geographical roots of Gómez Farías (Guadalajara), Mora (Guanajuato), and Zavala (Yucatán), the liberals were aggregating interests across multiple regions. Liberals were definitely more successful in multiregion coalition-making than conservatives were because they advocated federalism, the choice of formula for territorial governance of most peripheral politicians.

Federalists versus Centralists (1836–44). Reflecting widespread disillusionment with radical liberalism, Santa Anna created a new government dominated by advocates of the reversal of liberal reforms. His collaborators defended the introduction of a unitarian formula of territorial governance. They founded the Centralista political movement, which, despite acknowledging the advantages of the federal formula on general grounds, considered it unsuitable to provide a solution to the specific challenges facing Mexico since independence. For the Centralistas, provincial militias were harmful to the economy because they diverted men away from productive work. By fragmenting the means of violence, they also contained the seeds of civil wars.

In early 1835, provincial militias were abolished. Secessionist reactions followed immediately in Texas, Zacatecas, and Yucatán. All three regions feared confiscatory taxation. The risk of Mexican territorial dismemberment reached an unprecedented high. Santa Anna himself led the military expedition to repress secessionists in Zacatecas and Texas. He succeeded in Zacatecas. He failed in Texas, where he was captured. Defeat in Texas pulverized Santa Anna's political capital. In 1836, the legislature drafted a new constitution, the Siete Leyes, which introduced a unitarian formula of territorial governance, so that state governors would be appointed by the president. The new fundamental laws also created a fourth branch of government, the "Supreme Moderating Branch," which would check that the other three branches did not infringe on each other's jurisdiction.[14]

Drastic constitutional reform caused polarization to reach new levels. Former *yorkinos*, together with former liberal governors of peripheral states who had been displaced from provincial power, began to call themselves Federalistas to signal opposition to the new Centralista constitution. Centralists and federalists were at best oligarchic parties in formation. Neither of them had a policy platform or internal rules to stage candidates. Yet, as if being in the opposition incentivized organizational development, federalists were a clear evolution in relation to *yorkinos*. The territorial network of federalists became larger as centralism galvanized a common front among formerly self-sufficient oligarchies in San Luis de Potosí and Tamaulipas in the North, Oaxaca and Chiapas in the South, and the states of central Mexico.

In 1837, the same year Santa Anna returned from his Texas prison, Bustamante was elected president for a second time. Bustamante decided to give moderates a chance to run the government. The hope was that moderate policies would put an end to political polarization and thereby achieve governability. The secession of Yucatán and Texas, coupled with federalist revolts in the Northeast, pushed Bustamante and his moderate partners to submit a request to the newly created Moderating Branch for the restoration of the federal formula. Controlled by unconditional centralists, the Moderating Branch turned down the request. The veto of the Moderating Branch, a quick decision by an ephemeral institution, was extremely consequential. It ruled out what in retrospect can be seen as a developmental path in which internal political conflict and opportunities for external threats were drastically reduced. In 1837, a federal formula would have appeased separatist regions and thereby given no excuse for foreign invasion.

Two events brought Santa Anna back into political life. First, Bustamante left the capital to fight the federalists in the Northeast. Second, the French government authorized the invasion of Veracruz in order to obtain reparations for economic damage suffered by French nationals. Topping the list of damages was a pastry shop owned by Monsieur Remontel, which gave the conflict the name, Guerra de los Pasteles (Pastry war). Most damage had occurred during lootings in the context of political turmoil in México City during the last months of Gómez Farías's tenure. Santa Anna's intervention did not save Mexico from paying an exorbitant indemnity of six hundred thousand pesos (the most expensive pastries in history). Santa Anna lost his leg in the fight and instantly became a model of superhuman patriotic sacrifice. He regained some of his former political prestige. In the absence of Bustamante, Santa Anna was appointed interim president. This was his second presidency.

Fiscal penury, and an abundant dose of corruption, led Santa Anna to borrow money from expert financial speculators, or *agiotistas*, who obtained interest rates of 300 percent. In less than five months, Santa Anna lost the confidence of the legislature and the Moderating Branch. Bustamante resumed presidential office. The central government was bankrupt, and bankruptcy prompted desperate measures. Weak revenues became anemic because of corruption at the Veracruz customhouse, most likely instigated by Santa Anna. Bustamante raised import tariffs, but the measure backfired because it reduced legal imports and stimulated contraband. The public monopoly of tobacco was restored, but the government lacked the capacity to prevent illegal production and commerce. The working costs of the monopoly, which included salaries and payments to legal producers, were far higher than its revenues. The Banco de Avío became insolvent. Key institutions of mercantilism were bankrupt.

In 1840, a string of political crises gave Bustamante's government a lethal blow. Former president Gómez Farías revolted against the government. He gathered a following of federalists in México City. A mini civil war followed. The ranks of the moderates suffered an exodus from both ends of the spectrum. Some moderates radicalized. Others became openly conservative. One of them spoke on behalf of several former *escoceses*. In a letter to the president that was highly publicized, he argued that Mexico needed to import a European king. For conservatives, not even the centralized republic was strong enough to prevent fragmentation. Republicans made a scandal of it. Secretly, Alamán and other conservatives started to conspire to create a monarchy. Unintentionally, the polarization of 1840 and the monarchic manifesto deepened the process of party differentiation. As if Bustamante did not have enough problems, Great Britain, a traditional ally of conservative governments, acknowledged the independence of Texas. Republicans *and* conservatives now made a scandal of it.

As the fiscal weakness of the government deepened, causing presidential paralysis, the string of political crises prompted both conservatives and moderates to abandon Bustamante. For conservatives, Bustamante's defense of the federal formula was treason. For moderate federalists, Bustamante's military action against provincial revolts made him unreliable. A new military coup was imminent. The first experiment at political moderation was a resounding failure.

In August 1841, General Mariano Paredes, a conservative from Guadalajara, revolted against Bustamante. For Paredes, the solution to Mexico's problems was more centralism, possibly a dictatorship in preparation for monarchic rule. Santa Anna and his loyal military following, together with the rest of the army, supported the coup. Santa Anna was Paredes's military and political senior. He became provisional president in October and called for elections for a new constituent congress.

Since 1835, Santa Anna favored conservative policies, but he was the only politician to avoid fixed partisan affiliations. Moreover, in his new presidency, Santa Anna appointed a liberal finance minister. The decision was the key component of a new technique of revenue extraction that Santa Anna would only perfect over time. He blackmailed the church to lend money. He made the reasonable argument that, if he did not rule the country, the liberals would, and a liberal government would pursue confiscation of church property, a much worse outcome. A liberal finance minister was, at the same time, a display of Santa Anna's power to contain liberalism and a threat of rapid punishment if the church did not accede to his financial requests.[15]

Legislative elections, apparently free, produced a majority of federalist representatives. The army closed the congress because the drafts for a new constitution were too liberal and threatened the army's immunities. In 1843, a special committee of conservative landowners, clerics, lawyers, and army officers produced a new constitution that was tailor-made for a dictatorship. The only consensus candidate to assume dictatorial powers was Santa Anna. The 1843 constitution enhanced presidential powers vis-à-vis the legislature and eliminated the Moderating Branch. However, Santa Anna's mismanagement of government revenues—wasteful use of funds collected for a campaign to recover Texas, coupled with excessive fiscal extortions of his conservative allies—provoked a new coup by Paredes, which the new congress and the rest of the army supported. In 1844, Santa Anna was exiled for life, and General José Joaquín Herrera, a moderate, assumed the presidency.

On the Brink of Collapse: Internal Conflict and External War (1844–48). President Herrera's inauguration roughly coincided with the prelude to the most serious crisis ever faced by a Mexican government. The United States began preparations for invasion, whereas Mexico was militarily and financially incapable of any resistance. Aware of the country's weakness, Herrera tried to negotiate a diplomatic solution that perforce acknowledged that Texas belonged to the United States. A negotiated settlement was the only way out for Mexico, but partisan polarization made Herrera's proposed solution unviable. Paredes mounted a third coup, accusing Herrera of treason. The army supported Paredes, who finally became president. Paredes and Alamán revived the idea of establishing a monarchy with a European king who could contribute enough military power to counter U.S. expansionism.

Before Alamán could find a suitable monarch, in mid-1846 the United States already occupied large areas of northern Mexico. Unable to defend the country, Paredes's presidential power evaporated. Santa Anna, exiled in

Cuba, and Gómez Farías, exiled in New Orleans, revived their old partnership as if Santa Anna's firing of Gómez Farías in 1835 had never occurred. Santa Anna obviously did not think much of the memory of the Mexican public. The new partnership was meant to be the beginning of an emergency coalition for national salvation.

Mexico had tried almost everything: pure liberal and federal governments, pure conservative and centralist governments, and moderate governments. Political polarization devoured every government's capacity to rule. A broad-based coalitional government in the context of a national crisis could work. The new edition of the partnership between Santa Anna and Gómez Farías represented a reconciliation between the military strongman who had gained the trust of an array of conservative interests and the civilian politician with exemplary liberal convictions. Gómez Farías led a self-proclaimed federalist revolt, which restored the constitution of 1824 (Plan de la Ciudadela). Both the political society and the general public extended a line of credit to the new coalition. Santa Anna became president for the fourth time. To lead the army against the United States, he moved to the North and delegated power to his vice president, Gómez Farías. Gómez Farías's exclusive mission was to find the financial resources to wage the war. He confiscated church property valued at ten million pesos. Facing church protest and conservative reaction, Santa Anna repeated old methods, only perfected. As in 1835, in March 1847, he returned to México City, annulled Gómez Farías's measures, and abolished the vice presidency. In the process, he blackmailed the church to lend one and a half million pesos.

No fiscal and military resources were enough to prevent a total victory by the United States. U.S. troops occupied Mexico's capital on September 15, 1847. Santa Anna resigned the following day.

In 1847, Mexico had become a completely different political entity than what it was only twenty years earlier. It was a new, much smaller, state. It could shrink further. Yet two parties had been created. They were the only political organizations that had become stronger since independence, when they were only small and secret associations.

Political polarization had been unstoppable since 1810. After independence, it had been the proximate cause of every government breakdown. It was also the cradle of successful partisan organization. Intensified partisan conflict after the Mexican-American War would make things worse before they got better. Partisan conflict further destroyed the Mexican state along the violence-monopolization dimension, but it eventually helped to strengthen the territory-consolidation dimension.

Partisan Conflict in Pure Form: The Superior Stage of Party Formation (1848–54). General Herrera, the former moderate president, assembled the dispersed battalions of Mexico's army and sponsored the formation of a new government in nonoccupied territory. The United States' overwhelming victory in 1847 revealed the wisdom of Herrera's attempt to negotiate a diplomatic settlement two years earlier. Now Mexico had no option but to accept whatever terms the United States wished to propose, which would doubtless be much worse than those that could have been obtained by Herrera in 1845 but had been rejected by both federalists and centralists.

The end of the Mexican-American War was followed by the first successful step in trade-led state formation in Mexico. It was based on three pillars: the U.S. indemnity, fifteen million pesos; the recovery of mining activity, which reached the export levels of preindependence times; and the discrediting of the army as a consequence of its disastrous performance during the U.S. invasion.

The U.S. indemnity contributed to state formation qua territory consolidation. It financed the reannexation of Yucatán. The Yucatecan elite abandoned its separatist project in exchange for central help in the repression of the peasant rebellion. The export bonanza gave the political and economic elites a preview of the virtuous circle of trade-led state formation. An export boom made possible a larger flow of imports, which in turn increased government revenues. Fiscal surpluses allowed politicians to entrench their power by providing key class goods, including social peace and property rights. A better supply of class goods increased the profits of the economic elites by enhancing export capabilities. Finally, the elimination of the old army from the political scene removed interferences to further party formation. The end of military coups created the possibility that civilian politicians could complete their terms in office, which in turn would allow partisan policy programs to produce the intended results and to be judged by the public beyond the short-term sacrifices they usually required.

In 1851, Herrera became the first Mexican president to complete his term and hand office to his legal successor. The new president was General

Mariano Arista, a moderate. Yet it was too late for moderation. Exactly two years after assuming the presidency, Arista was forced to resign.

The fall of Arista, when most conditions favored effective government for the first time in Mexico's history, provides a unique opportunity for causal inference. The end of army intervention in politics was obviously a necessary but not a sufficient condition for government stability. The comparison between the first government of Herrera (1845) and that of Arista is most instructive. They both fell after trying to walk a middle course that avoided criticism from both conservatives and radicals. In contrast to Herrera's first government, Arista's government received tailwinds from the international economy and the dissipation of geopolitical threats. Moreover, after 1847, the army had lost its king-making power. Given the comparative absence of geopolitical, fiscal, and praetorian challenges during Arista's presidency, parties were left as the main, if not the only, cause of government failure. Partisan polarization had become the master force in Mexican politics. It destroyed governments in the short run, but it contributed to state formation qua territory consolidation in the long run.

A breakdown caused by parties can in turn be interpreted as an ideological phenomenon or as a purely political one. According to the ideological interpretation, Arista's moderate course of action was too radical for conservatives and too conservative for radicals. Arista's fall would be a reflection of the level of ideological polarization that dominated Mexican politics, which had acquired a life of its own. Polarization persisted despite the fact that traditionally divisive geopolitical and fiscal problems had subsided.

On the other hand, a purely political interpretation builds on the fact that, after decades of conflict, radicals and conservatives had finally become full-blown political parties, whereas moderates lacked party organization. Alamán formally founded the Conservative Party in 1848. The radicals were fully structured as a party, which became known as the Liberal Party, in the mid-1840s. Partisan voracity for power led both Liberals and Conservatives to destabilize Arista, who had no base of organized support.

Both the ideological and the political interpretation account for Arista's fall as the result of the joint, albeit uncoordinated, attack by two rival parties. It is hard to adjudicate which interpretation is right because both Conservatives and Liberals depicted themselves as parties of ideas and campaigned against Arista on policy grounds. The political interpretation is stronger because it also accounts for subsequent political conflicts, in which the office-seeking motivation clearly trumped policy preferences.

The fall of Arista reveals two opposite aspects of party formation in mid-nineteenth-century Mexico. Both the Conservative Party and the Liberal Party were strong enough to undermine presidential power. They orchestrated electoral campaigns through the press, held public meetings, and propagated negative propaganda, and their most influential members met regularly to plan conspiracies. Yet neither party had a strong candidate to replace Arista. Partisan conflict in Mexico made possible the apparently impossible. Santa Anna, who had to move to Colombia after his embarrassing performance in the war against the Untied States, became the candidate of *both* parties. Alamán, in a letter to Santa Anna, showed the true colors of the Conservative program. Mexico needed to rebuild the army, let the church provide spiritual union to a country that lacked one, promote a mercantilist form of economic development, and find a proper monarch, that is, a Bourbon or Hapsburg prince, who Alamán was convinced would unanimously enjoy unquestioned legitimacy. Miguel Lerdo de Tejada, member of a new generation of Mexican Liberals, also tried to have Santa Anna's ear. He likewise wrote a detailed program of Liberal reform. It included a number of infrastructural developments, from telegraphs to railways, that would boost export-led growth through free trade. It also defended the disentailment of the church's rural property, which would put an enormous amount of assets to productive work. Lerdo's program was antithetical to that of Alamán.

Santa Anna was confident in his ability to manipulate collaborators and to please rival partisan groups. In April 1853, he assumed the presidency of Mexico for the fifth time (it would be the last). Santa Anna suspended the constitution and became a full-blown dictator. Alamán was appointed minister of internal and foreign affairs, a position from which he could search for his prince. Lerdo became undersecretary of development to carry out infrastructure projects. Finally, to blackmail the church, Santa Anna appointed the Liberal Antonio de Haro y Tamariz as minister of finance. Initially, both parties supported Santa Anna, each assuming it would eventually prevail over the other. Mexican parties were blinded by ambition: nothing in Santa Anna's record gave reason to expect that his fifth presidency would be anything but an unmitigated disaster.

Government expenditures ballooned, in part because of a precursor attempt to create a personality cult. Santa Anna gave himself the regal-sounding title of "Most Serene Highness." A deficit of nearly twenty million pesos was supposed to be covered with bonds guaranteed by church property. Blackmailing the church did not work this time around. Conservative protest forced Haro to resign. For the last time, Santa Anna resorted to a uniquely Mexican source of revenue: the sale of sovereign rights to land that was de facto occupied by the United States. Just before Santa Anna's assumption of the presidency, the United States had seized present-day southern Arizona, which in Mexico was known as La Mesilla. Santa Anna had no power to repel the invasion but was eager to get cash out of it. Through the "Gadsden Purchase," Mexico obtained ten million pesos. The death of Alamán in June evaporated the Conservatives' hope to control Santa Anna. Santa Anna's increasingly autocratic methods, which included censorship of the press and exile of progressive politicians, alienated Liberals.

Both parties withdrew their support for Santa Anna. At the same time, they began preparing to clash against each other. Santa Anna's pomp could not hide the fact that, by the end of his first year in office, his career was finally over. For either ideological or purely office-seeking reasons, the old rivalry between conservatives and radicals was ready for a new round of conflict. This time, conflict would be different. Protoparties had become real parties. The army and Santa Anna would not be there to interfere with civilian politicians. Finally, the world economy was more than ready to reward the winner of the civil war with the necessary fiscal resources for successful trade-led state formation.

In February 1854, what seemed to be just another military coup, with the limited goal of replacing an old general with a new one, was actually the first step in what would become the Reforma, a large-scale program of Liberal change, which had unintended but massive repercussions for party formation and state formation. In March, the military movement mutated into a revolution. The revolution offered a program, the Plan de Ayutla, and capable leadership took it over, including Ignacio Comonfort, a wealthy merchant of Puebla, and Juan Álvarez, Guerrero's successor as the caudillo of the *tierra caliente*. In 1855, the Liberal revolution forced Santa Anna to resign and sail into exile. He was "soon a forgotten man."[16]

Liberal Triumph: 1854–76

By the mid-nineteenth century, Mexico had created the pillars of party-driven state formation. As in Colombia and Uruguay, it was political parties, rather than a dominant economic class or a shared sense of nationhood, that created durable networks of supraregional loyalty. Alliances were formed through partisan rivalry, which manifested itself in protracted, often violent, political conflict. Permanent civil war meant state failure, the lack of violence monopolization. Yet civil war between partisan networks cutting across regional lines was a key driver of territory consolidation, the other component of state formation. The unintended unifying effects of partisan conflict were more remarkable in Mexico than in Colombia, whose regional economies enjoyed much larger complementarities, let alone Uruguay, which is essentially a single-region country.

Onset of Liberal Reform (1855–57). At the head of an army of native Mexicans, Álvarez gained control of México City in November 1855. He was chosen president by an assembly composed of second-level leaders of the revolt and Liberal politicians who returned from exile or were released from prison. Álvarez was a regional caudillo, not a national leader. Rather than be the head of national politics, he preferred to consolidate power in the newly created state of Guerrero (the former Pacific coastal zone of the state of México). After only two months in power, Álvarez appointed the moderate Comonfort as interim president and returned to Guerrero. Comonfort was only the figurehead of a group of policy makers who did not believe in moderation.

Three returned exiles took the reins of the new government: Melchor Ocampo from Michoacán, Miguel Lerdo de Tejada from Veracruz, and Benito Juárez from Oaxaca. The three men met in their New Orleans exile. They were all radical Liberals. The first important action of the new government, the Ley Juárez, was the abolition of the ecclesiastical and military *fueros*, the corporate judicial immunities inherited from colonial times. The second action, the Ley Lerdo, was the abolition of corporate ownership of rural and urban real estate. Individuals who occupied church land or *ejidos* would become the new owners. Rental payments were to be converted into mortgage payments. Unoccupied land would be declared vacant and sold at auction. The church was the main target in the execution of the law. In half a year, the Liberal government had created individual ownership of real estate valued at twenty-three million pesos. Eighty-five percent of the reassigned property had belonged to the church.

The church did not remain passive. Initially, it tried to limit the effects of the Ley Lerdo by negotiation. Instead of concessions, the government responded with new attacks. It prohibited priests from charging fees for administering sacraments. Sacraments had an enormous demand from the indigenous population, which was mostly poor and was forced to spend a large portion of their income on baptisms, marriages, and funerals. The church switched from negotiation to confrontation. The cash flowing into the church's coffers as a result of the disentailment of its rural property was in turn transferred into a war chest to finance the overthrow of the Liberal government.[17]

In 1857, a new constitution, drafted by radical Liberals, incorporated the Lerdo and Juárez laws. The privatization of church property and the abolition of *fueros* acquired constitutional status. The silence of the new constitution regarding religion was implicitly the adoption of religious toleration. No prior Mexican government had dared go that far.

Conservative Backlash and Civil War (1858–61). As if following basic laws of Newtonian physics, the strength of the Conservative reaction was proportional to the depth of the Liberal reform. In December 1857, Conservative army officers, with the financial and ideological support of the Mexican Catholic Church and the Holy See, staged a coup. The army closed the congress. Comonfort departed to exile in the United States. Yet, after a three-year conflict, the Conservative reaction failed. The army was a much weaker political actor than in the past. The Liberal Party, in turn, was much stronger.

In contrast with responses to all prior coups, the Liberal resistance was effective this time around. Juárez, who as chief justice was the legal successor to Comonfort, moved the government to Veracruz, while Conservative military officers held the capital. Parallel governments formed two armies.[18] The duopoly of violence prompted the Guerra de la Reforma, the largest civil war in the century spanning from independence to the Mexican Revolution (1910).

Half of the Mexican states were under Liberal control; the other half were ruled by Conservative governors. Liberals controlled the states with the most active ports, including Veracruz on the Caribbean and Acapulco on the Pacific, and the three northeastern states bordering the United States. The five states, especially Veracruz, were vital sources of revenue, which derived almost entirely from import tariffs. Liberals also ruled the prosperous state of Zacatecas. Mexico's densely populated heartland, including México City and the states of México and Puebla, was governed by Conservative generals. To the south, bordering the heartland, Oaxaca was also Conservative. Urban and rural masses in the heartland were largely Conservative. The urban poor were deeply Catholic. The rural poor were deeply Catholic *and* devoted to the communal lifestyle threatened by Liberal reform.

Remarkably, military control of distinct territories did not result in the partition of Mexico into a Liberal country and a Conservative one. Examples of secession following partisan conflict surrounded Mexico. Exactly two decades earlier, Conservative Guatemala had seceded from the Liberal-dominated Central American Federation. And before the Mexican conflict was over, the United States was already divided into two territorial units fighting over major institutional reform.

The main reason for continued union in Mexico was not the existence of superior bonds of national identity shared by Mexicans of both territories. Rather than cultural harmony, what united the Liberal and Conservative halves was, quite paradoxically, partisan conflict. Some forms of political conflict have unifying effects. Over the course of the prolonged confrontation between the Mexican parties, both parties, especially the Liberals, managed to create an extensive network of professional or semiprofessional politicians that had penetrated the rival's bastions. Interparty conflict deepened and extended intraparty loyalty.

In Mexico's heartland, a Conservative bastion, Liberals had created key political and economic constituencies. Liberal politicians in the capital expected a mix of professional and ideological rewards from a possible Liberal triumph. Crucially, new economic groups in the heartland also expected to profit. The old rentier aristocracies of Mexico and Puebla were staunchly Conservative. Yet the pioneering experiments at free trade and privatization of the early 1830s had prompted the emergence of a new kind of landowner in the central plateau, with a distinct material interest in the triumph of the

Liberal Party. For the new landowner, Liberal reform would create the opportunity to acquire additional rural property as a consequence of further progress in the disentailment of church and *ejido* land. In the sections of the territory under Liberal control, Juárez proceeded to nationalize church property without compensation. He auctioned it to increase the Liberals' war chest. The example terrified the church in the Conservative states of Mexico, but it also caused delight among the most recently formed groups of the upper class.

The fact that the Liberal Party had both political and social support in the Conservative heartland was a chief cause of Liberal victory in 1861. Another key cause was Liberal control of the states with the most profitable customhouses. Since a large fraction of Mexico's imports were consumed in the heartland, the population of the states under Conservative rule helped finance, through import tariffs, the Liberal government and its army. The fiscal field of the war was biased against the Conservatives. The weakness of the official army, the main grievance of which was the abolition of the *fueros*, was the final cause of the Liberal victory. When the conflict broke out in 1857, the Liberals had no army. Although they knew the risks of military backlash by the Conservatives, they did not prepare for war. The Liberals improvised an army, turning lawyers, journalists, and local notables into generals. It was enough to win.

The Liberal victory was decisive, an indication of the irreparable damage suffered by the official army in 1848. Yet it was transitory. Precisely because the Conservatives had exhausted their financial and military forces in Mexico, they searched for a foreign ally. They found one in Napoleon III.

The Conservatives' Last Resort: Foreign Alliance (1862–67). The civil war left Mexico with a massive debt. The Conservatives had borrowed large sums from European bankers. The Juárez government was forced to default on its foreign loans. Britain, Spain, and France showed no mercy. They agreed to occupy Veracruz and collect capital and interest by appropriating customs revenues. At the same time, Conservative exiles in Europe convinced Napoleon III that France should take several steps further and transform the financial dispute into an imperial crusade. Napoleon III sent thirty thousand soldiers to occupy Mexico and puppet Archduke Maximilian of Austria to rule it. For Conservatives, it was a dream come true. The restoration of a Hapsburg monarchy would bring back what they viewed as the golden age of colonial rule, reviving the splendor attained by New Spain before the eighteenth-century Bourbon reforms (Conservatives found the Bourbons too progressive compared to the Hapsburgs).

The willingness of Conservatives to engage in international alliances that compromised Mexico's sovereignty in exchange for partisan gains caught the Liberal government off guard. But the Conservatives were in for a bigger surprise. Maximilian I, the new Mexican emperor, embraced a decidedly liberal policy agenda.

The French military force was overwhelming. There was nothing the Liberals could do to defeat it. Maximilian's policies were a continuation of the Liberal reform, except for the regime type. The fact that Juárez organized a Liberal resistance despite the lack of military capabilities and the absence of policy incentives indicates how developed the Mexican Liberal Party was. It had become, above anything else, a formidable office-seeking machine. Crucially, it had multiple territorial extensions. Juárez moved the government to unoccupied enclaves on the border with the United States.

Liberal resistance endured four long years—enough to receive a stroke of luck. Late state-formation efforts in Prussia had indirect but decisive repercussions on the formation of the Mexican state. The process of German unification was an unmistakable threat to Napoleon III. In early 1866, Napoleon decided to concentrate troops in Europe. In May, the French occupation army began to withdraw from Mexico—and to abandon Maximilian. The naked emperor decided to request backup from the remaining Conservative generals. The desperate measure was the death sentence for both Maximilian and the Conservative Party. Militarily anemic and politically discredited, the alliance between the emperor and the Conservatives was easily defeated by the Liberals, who were able to recapture most of the country, including the capital, by February 1867. June 19 was an eventful day: Maximilian and the two most prominent Conservative generals were executed. The Conservative Party died with them. Édouard Manet produced five paintings to tell and retell the story of the execution.

Territory Consolidation (1867–Present). Liberal victory inaugurated what in Mexican historiography is known as the República Restaurada. The expression refers to a change of regime, from monarchy back to republic. Yet the change of regime was a minor political transformation compared to the change in the status of the Mexican state. The Liberal triumph was the

culmination of territory consolidation in Mexico. Through party formation, Liberal politicians had created a large multiregional organization.
Partisan linkages were the strongest cement across Mexican provinces. The
struggle of the Liberal Party to survive had the unintended effect of contributing to the undivided territorial survival of present-day Mexico. A
strong party consolidated a large territory.

The party-driven path to state formation was embedded within the
general trade-led pattern. Already under Maximilian's imperial rule, "imported" pacification secured by a foreign army and a new round of liberal
economic reforms combined to encourage a boom in foreign investments,
which included a big push in the construction of the railway connecting
México City and the port of Veracruz. The definitive triumph of the Liberal Party in 1867 extended the positive international outlook for Mexico.
For six crucial years, right before the 1873 world economic crisis, Mexico
entered the virtuous circle in which pacification enhanced the prospects for
economic modernization via foreign investments and commodity exports,
and economic modernization in turn deepened pacification through higher
volumes of revenue derived from foreign trade.

The territory-consolidation chapter of Mexican state formation was
closed by the victory of the Liberal Party. The victory could also open the
chapter of violence monopolization. It did. But it did not close it. In effect,
after 1867, military challenges to Liberal supremacy were extinguished.
What the Liberal victory could not prevent was violence from *within* the
party. The Liberal victories in 1861 and 1867 were based on improvised
military mobilization. Power was delegated to local notables, a process that
is the perfect incubator of caudillo rule, as discussed in Chapter 2. Liberal
caudillos remained quiet, except for the popular General Porfirio Díaz
from Oaxaca. Porfirio challenged Juárez's supremacy in late 1867. He was
defeated. Ten years later, Porfirio tried again. He had become the strongest
strongman in the land. Sebastián Lerdo, the younger brother of Miguel,
had succeeded Juárez in 1872. When he sought reelection in 1876, Porfirio
campaigned under the slogan of "no reelection." Porfirio became president. Investment and trade opportunities from the United States allowed
Porfirio to pursue a recharged version of trade-led state formation, which
took pacification and economic modernization to unprecedented levels. In
1884, Porfirio forgot his past complaints against reelection. He saw it fit to
rule Mexico in perpetuity. He had achieved pacification.

NINE

Party-Driven State Formation in Comparative Perspective

Colombia and Uruguay

COLOMBIA AND URUGUAY are the two final cases of party-driven state formation in Latin America. As in Mexico, competing partisan forces in Colombia and Uruguay were the crucible for supraregional loyalties connecting political elites from distant localities when other linkages were nonexistent. Two parties dominated the emerging political arena in Colombia and Uruguay. Whereas in Colombia, as in Mexico, party loyalties got structured around a Conservative-versus-Liberal cleavage, in Uruguay the struggle was essentially between nearly identical liberal parties, Colorados versus Blancos.

The analysis of territory consolidation in Colombia and Uruguay confirms the insight that was crucial to understand the process of state formation in Mexico: the very activity of coalition-making over the course of partisan competition for power—and *not* a master plan of institutional reform or a shared sense of nationhood—is a key driver in the creation of countries (the only true alternatives being a political entrepreneur or a rural lord dominating a rudimentary port state).

Programmatic differences between parties were substantial in Mexico, moderate in Colombia, and negligible in Uruguay. Partisan ideologies were sufficiently different across Mexico, Colombia, and Uruguay so as to leave the competitive logic of party formation—the only antecedent condition shared by all three cases—as the sole political motivation for territory consolidation. Naked political competition trumped partisan ideology in the creation of Colombia and Uruguay, as it did in Mexico.

In Colombia, the colonial past decisively shaped partisan divisions, the same way it did in Mexico. A colonial legacy of multiple urban centers, each with its own partisan divisions, provided the basis for the creation of multi-region political networks based on the exchange of mutual help among Colombian local notables operating from different cities but sharing a larger political agenda. As in Mexico, the Colombian division between Liberals and Conservatives was fueled by opposite responses to the ability of the Catholic Church to survive the wars of independence with abundant reserves of cultural and economic power.

Yet an important programmatic difference separated the Colombian Conservatives from their Mexican counterparts. The Colombian Conservatives were substantially less "conservative" in relation to the colonial past than the Mexican ones were. Crucially, in contrast to Mexican Conservatives, who both were pro-monarchy and favored state-sponsored development, Colombian Conservatives were devoted republicans, and they largely advocated free markets. Also, whereas Mexican Conservatives were unconditional supporters of a unitarian formula of territorial governance, Colombian Conservatives were flexible and opportunistic. They switched preferences between federalism and unitarianism as political circumstances changed. When public opinion reached a consensus for one particular formula, they moved in unison with their Liberal rivals.

If in Mexico the struggle between Liberals and Conservatives was about *whether* to abolish colonial institutions, in Colombia it was about *how fast* to do it. In the context of Mexican politics, Colombian Conservatives would have been considered "moderate" Liberals who differed from pure Liberals in claiming that the transformation of colonial institutions needed to be gradual. The transformations included the elimination of corporate privilege, like the judicial immunities of the military and the clergy, the privatization of church assets, and the secularization of education.

In Uruguay, the ideological distance between Colorados and Blancos was negligible. Lacking mineral wealth and abundant indigenous labor, the River Plate basin in colonial times was of marginal interest to the Spanish Crown. And the territory of present-day Uruguay occupied a peripheral position within an already peripheral domain. In what was only known as the "eastern bank" (Banda Oriental) of the River Plate, the Spanish Crown only built military outposts to deter Portuguese invasions. Independent Uruguay was uniquely exempted from the whole array of colonial corporations, including a powerful church, a military aristocracy, commercial guilds, or protected indigenous communities. The contrast with Colombia and especially Mexico could not be sharper. Uruguay simply lacked a colonial legacy about which rival political forces could fight. Both Uruguayan parties were unambiguously liberal in embracing economic freedoms, civil liberties, and representative government. Both parties ritually honored José Gervasio Artigas's independence program, and they both surgically purged from it his socialist ideas. Large landowners provided leadership to both parties, so Artigas's old proposal of land reform never became a party platform.

In sum, as a function of the weight of the colonial legacy, which was the heaviest in Mexico and the lightest in Uruguay, the three cases of party-driven state formation structured three distinct party systems. Variations in interparty ideological distance across the three cases were formidable, ranging from utter incompatibility in Mexico to virtual equivalence in Uruguay. Yet the three systems of parties had identical effects on state formation. The contents of party platforms mattered much less than the dynamics of party competition did. By creating supraregional organizations, the struggle between parties had a decidedly positive effect for territory consolidation, the first component of state formation. It also had a negative short-run impact, compensated by a positive long-run legacy, on violence monopolization, the second component.

This chapter is divided into three sections. The first and second sections analyze how party formation contributed to state formation qua territory consolidation in Colombia and Uruguay, respectively. Both in Colombia and in Uruguay, the path leading to territorial consolidation was one among a set of three possible developmental trajectories. One of the alternative possible trajectories was the formation of a larger state, in relation to which Colombia and Uruguay would have become a subnational unit, and the other was the fragmentation into smaller territorial units. The logic of party formation preceded territory consolidation and closed down the two alternative paths in both cases. The third section documents the contribution of parties, once fully formed, to state formation qua pacification, an outcome that fell short of violence monopolization but was instrumental for trade-led development.

Territory Consolidation in Colombia:
Party Formation as the Driver of Union
Liberals versus Conservatives
in Colombia

Present-day Colombia roughly corresponds to the territory known as Nueva Granada from independence in 1819 to 1863. "Colombia" was the name created by Bolívar in the late 1810s to designate the union of the territories belonging to the former Viceroyalty of New Granada, which included, in addition to Nueva Granada, Venezuela to the east and Ecuador to the south (Map 9.1). Bolívar's Colombia collapsed shortly after the Liberator's death in December 1830. To avoid confusion between Bolívar's Colombia and modern Colombia, introductory history books refer to the former as "Gran Colombia." Purist historians find "Gran Colombia" an awkward label, which eliminates altogether "Nueva Granada" from the historical record.[1]

Purists are right for a fundamental reason in political analysis. Assuming that present-day Colombia existed in 1830 is equivalent to reading history backward, which buries the fact that many leaders of Nueva Granada in the 1830s avoided appropriating the name "Colombia" for the eminently political reason that they considered that reunification with Venezuela and Ecuador was still possible. They reserved the name "Colombia" for such a potential outcome. Only in 1863 did leaders of Nueva Granada adopt for the first time a version of the name, the Estados Unidos de Colombia (United States of Colombia).

Colombia as Outcome:
Three Possible Futures in 1830

In the early 1830s, Nueva Granada faced three future scenarios: reunification with Venezuela and Ecuador, further fragmentation into minirepublics, and consolidation of the territory of present-day Colombia.

Reunification was the first path to be abandoned. In the early 1830s, Páez consolidated caudillo rule in Venezuela. He achieved hegemony by combining military command over the rural population of the interior, the Llanos, and support from the economic elites of the coast, to which he de-

Map 9.1. Gran Colombia, 1819–31

livered the class goods required to export cacao and coffee. Within a larger political unit, which merged Nueva Granada and Venezuela, Páez would not be nearly as powerful as he had become in the small successor state. In a larger territorial unit, Páez would have had to negotiate policies and compete for government positions with politicians coming from all directions, including Bogotá, Cartagena, Medellín, and Popayán, cities with well-established ruling classes. Páez was one among several agents responsible for the breakup of (Gran) Colombia. Yet, once he entrenched his power in Venezuela, Páez became the single most formidable obstacle against re-unification. If Páez first contributed to the collapse of Bolívar's project of large-scale state formation, he then made sure that the separation of Venezuela became irreversible.

For decades after the collapse of Colombia, then, Nueva Granada's options turned binary: territorial consolidation or further fragmentation. In the 1830s, several forces pushed Nueva Granada to mirror the trajectory followed by Central America. Central America had first seceded as a whole from Mexico (1823), and two decades later, it partitioned into five minirepublics. The breakdown of (Gran) Colombia in 1830 could have been followed by the partition of (smaller) Nueva Granada into the equivalent of four Ecuadors and two Panamas.

From a geographic point of view, Nueva Granada is an enormous challenge for state formation. It is the only country in which the gigantic Andean mountains divide themselves into three separate chains, or *cordilleras*. Two rivers, the Cauca and the Magdalena, run between the western and central chains and between the central and eastern chains, respectively. The most important population centers of Nueva Granada were interior cities, except for Cartagena. In no other country of the Americas was it so expensive to build passage between the main cities and the main waterways. Most passages required mule trails and human porters, long days of travel, and high risks, including rains, flooding, landslides, and tropical diseases. Once the river was reached, navigation was no panacea. Before the introduction of steamboats in the 1850s, it could take up to six weeks of travel in pole boats to connect the Upper Magdalena and the Caribbean, the door to the outside world. Economic relations between the cities were minimal, communications infrequent.

From 1830 to 1880, Nueva Granada was a failed state. Its territory was repeatedly broken down into three to six distinct political units, depending on the year the count is taken. Some ministates wanted secession. Some wanted a combination with a reduced number of other splinters of Nueva Granada. And some wanted to join neighboring countries.

In the early 1830s, at the same time that some Granadan leaders were still dreaming about reconstructing Bolívar's large country by merging with Venezuela and Ecuador, an array of local powerholders were taking concrete actions to create ministates in which they could reign supreme. Nueva Granada was de facto split into six ministates: (1) the eastern Andean range, a vast area centered around Bogotá, the aspiring capital, which included the valley of the Upper Magdalena River, the most important waterway connecting the interior to the Atlantic; (2) the isthmus of Panama; (3) the Caribbean coast, a corridor running from the border with Panama to the mouth of the

Magdalena River, whose capital, Cartagena, had been a major city-port in colonial times; (4) Cauca, which included the highlands bordering Ecuador, the valley of the Cauca River, the second most important internal waterway, and a long strip of Pacific coast reaching Central America; (5) the plains of Casanare northeast of Bogotá, an area that belonged to the same topographical area as the Venezuelan Llanos; and (6) Antioquia, the core of the western Andean range, which, thanks to abundant gold deposits and a uniquely entrepreneurial elite, was the wealthiest region in northern South America.

Secessionist attempts by Nueva Granada's ministates were brief but recurrent, revealing strong centrifugal undercurrents. Casanare requested incorporation into Venezuela. Antonio Páez, Venezuela's president, had recently played a pivotal role in causing the dissolution of (Gran) Colombia, which gained him the animosity of several lieutenants of Bolívar who wanted to keep alive the Liberator's big political project. Páez prudently turned down Casanare's offer to avoid opening another battlefront. Cartagena and Antioquia had already initiated a local process of party formation that would gradually turn them into conservative bastions. They were both skeptical of the pace of reform of liberal leaders in Bogotá, including drastic cuts to the church's economic resources and its authority over schools. Yet, in contrast to conservative bastions in Central America, Antioquia was a landlocked region, and its secession from liberal Nueva Granada would have required partnership with another conservative region endowed with a seaport.

Cauca was a special political entity. It was Cauca that could have provided Antioquia with access to the sea and formed with it a separate country. In fact, a fourth successor state of Bolívar's Colombia, uniting Antioquia, Cauca, and Cartagena, was a plan shared for years by local notables in all three regions.[2] Cauca possessed an old colonial aristocracy, which had become wealthy from exploiting the first substantial gold mines in the viceroyalty. Mining in Cauca was virtually exhausted by the time of independence, but the local aristocracy, which had built the cities of Popayán and Pasto, minireplicas of nearby Quito, still commanded large amounts of political capital.

If the Popayán aristocracy did not put more effort into the plan of creating a fourth successor state, it was not because it shared with Bogotanos and Antioqueños a sense of Granadan nationhood, which did not exist even in inchoate form. On the contrary, the reason was that some of the members of the Popayán aristocracy envisioned joining Ecuador. The highlands of Ecuador, which hosted the city of Quito, and the southernmost area of Cauca were a single geographic and cultural entity. Catholicism had grown deep roots among both the white aristocracy and the large Quechua population. Crucially, the churches of Popayán and Pasto belonged to the diocese run by the archbishop of Quito. A common aristocratic background and a shared ecclesiastical jurisdiction with Quito were a more meaningful linkage than political ties with Bogotá.

The retention of the Cauca region within Nueva Granada was the key to preventing full disintegration. Most other regions considering secession, especially Antioquia, needed Cauca to break away from Bogotá. Paradoxically, it was partisan divisions within Cauca that prevented separation from Nueva Granada. Divisions pushed rival political groups of Cauca—led by the mortal enemies José María Obando and Tomás Cipriano de Mosquera—to insert themselves within broader partisan networks linking together Bogotá, Antioquia, and the Caribbean.

Civil wars pushed Nueva Granada to the brink of disintegration in the late 1830s and again in the early 1860s. Wars turned Granadan regions into semisovereign states. In the late 1830s, a rebellion in Pasto in defense of the Catholic Church escalated into a multilateral civil war in which almost every region fought for independence. All the secessionist regions, except for Antioquia, became dominated by *state-breaking* warlords, or "Supreme Captains," the title they gave themselves. The warlords inspired the name of the protracted conflict, the Guerra de los Supremos. The legacy of the war was so long lasting that two decades later, President Mariano Ospina, the founder of the Conservative Party, took desperate measures to keep together the territory of Nueva Granada. First, he revived negotiations with the United Kingdom to transform the country into a British protectorate. After the United Kingdom turned down the offer, Ospina requested annexation to the United States. Ospina's attempted solutions seem exaggerated but were only proportional to problems that, given his position and talent, he sensed better than anyone else. Among many other problems, a central challenge was that the Liberal Party was entering a phase in which its new leaders were willing to experiment with radical institutional reform. Ospina predicted that radical reform would be a source of political chaos. He was right.

In the early 1860s radical Liberals successfully campaigned for a version of political decentralization that was much closer to the confederal formula than to the federal one (as defined in Chapter 4). The 1863 constitution, which finally appropriated the name "Colombia" for Nueva Granada, introduced the most extreme version of confederal association ever implemented in the Americas. It allowed the nine constituent states to build their own armies. The authority of the federal government to intervene in subnational affairs was so drastically curtailed that states could go to war with each other and the president had to remain idle. In the 1870s, the military capabilities of at least three states, Antioquia, Cauca, and Cundinamarca, were individually superior to those of the national army. Nueva Granada had become an international system of states in all but name.

The governments of the Regeneration period (1880–99) were the backlash against radical decentralization. Even Liberals admitted the need for institutional reversal. As if following the laws of Newtonian physics, the Regeneration drafted a new constitution in 1886 that reintroduced unitarianism, the opposite formula of territorial governance. Provincial armies were abolished. The road to secession was finally closed down. Regions were deprived of the physical means to pursue it.

Only the most naïve version of formal institutionalism would argue that Colombia did not fragment further because of constitutional reform. Increasingly strong partisan networks account for the ability of the country to overcome major secessionist challenges. As the rivalry between Conservatives and Liberals intensified, cross-regional linkages among local elites belonging to the same party grew stronger. Partisan linkages rather than constitutional texts kept Colombia together.

Colombia's most important civil war, the Thousand Days' War (1899–1902), was an indisputable sign of state failure qua violence monopolization. Yet, by that time, the Colombian state was a success with regard to territory consolidation precisely because Colombia's parties—the contenders of the war—had both become supraregional alliances cutting across the borders of economic or political subunits. Unintentionally, party formation overcame the challenges of geography. It gave political integration to a territory that completely lacked a natural one.

Explanation:
Partisan Division, Territorial Union

In Colombia, the process of party formation was completed *before* the process of state formation. In turn, the formation of the two dominant political parties was preceded by a power struggle between prominent independence leaders who were largely indistinguishable with regard to their policy platforms, let alone their political ideology. Over the course of the struggle, leaders in Colombia made a number of tactical alliances with specific social groups, like the Catholic Church in Cauca or the artisans of Bogotá. Some but not all the tactical alliances became long-term partnerships.

In the transformation of tactical alliances into permanent coalitions, political leaders selected groups depending on electoral dividends. It is in such transformation where the pristine emergence of political parties can be discerned. The process of party formation in Colombia involved two transitions: from personal rivalries to partisan struggles and from groups structured around private linkages—loyalty to circles of friendship—to electoral machines representing the interests of anonymous constituencies, which had become permanent partners in preceding rounds of group selection.

The rudiments of party formation can be found in the personal rivalry between Simón Bolívar and Francisco de Paula Santander during the (Gran) Colombia period (1819–30), that is, three full decades before the two Granadan parties acquired permanent organization, formal names, and policy platforms. Even in the successor state of Nueva Granada, disputes between Mosquera and Obando in the mid-1830s and early 1840s, which were crucial in creating proto-Conservative and crypto-Liberal organizations, were still based on personal animosities and loyalties rather than economic or social interests.[3]

The key period of party formation was remarkably short, from 1826, when Nueva Granada was still part of (Gran) Colombia, to the late 1840s, when Ospina, in partnership with young José Eusebio Caro, gave the Conservative Party its permanent name and, more important, a comprehensive policy platform. Before 1850, four events helped to sort political leaders and active citizens into two distinct political communities: (1) the breakdown of (Gran) Colombia in 1830, which had the dual effect of separation from a large territory and of linking together the regions of a smaller one; (2) the first competitive presidential election in Nueva Granada in 1836; (3) the War of the Supreme Captains in the late 1830s; and (4) the emergence of a young generation of university-educated liberal activists in the mid-1840s. Each of these steps in party formation will be analyzed in turn.[4]

The Collapse of (Gran) Colombia: The Negative Partisan Impact. Early partisan divisions caused the breakdown of Bolívar's Colombia, which in turn had a decisive impact on party cleavages in the successor state of Nueva Granada. The collapse of Colombia is customarily attributed to the secession of Venezuela, which started struggling for separation in 1826 under the leadership of Páez. Yet the collapse of Colombia was overdetermined. Much less visible but probably more powerful was the ambition of Santander and his circle of civilian associates to get rid of Bolívar and his military lieutenants.

In 1828, after colossal military achievements in Lower Peru and Upper Peru (aptly renamed Bolivia), Bolívar returned to Colombia to deal with secession threats. Bolívar was perfectly aware that, once the Spanish threat of reconquest had extinguished, the reasons for the union of (Gran) Colombia would virtually vanish. He made a desperate attempt to prevent disintegration by assuming dictatorial powers. He expected that his prestige would silence dissidence. The expectations were reasonable, but the solution backfired. It proved incompatible with the distribution of power that had consolidated through the 1820s. To lead the campaign in Peru, Bolívar had sponsored the rise of three vice presidents in (Gran) Colombia, who would separately run Venezuela, Nueva Granada, and Ecuador. Two of his Venezuelan lieutenants, Juan José Flores, ruler of the Ecuadorean section, and Páez, ruler of the Venezuelan section, owed their military careers to Bolívar and would not question his dictatorship of 1828.

In Nueva Granada, things were different. Santander, the ruler, abhorred dictatorship. Santander was a true liberal *avant la lettre*. Santander's collaborators were probably less principled, but Bolívar's autocratic methods in the late 1820s were a death sentence to their political careers. The majority of military generals in Colombia were Venezuelan, and Bolívar's dictatorship relied heavily on them. Bolívar closed the congress, so politicians of Nueva Granada were suddenly deprived of all sources of institutional power. At the time of the collapse of Colombia, Venezuelan generals left Nueva Granada (although not Ecuador). Yet Nueva Granada had about a dozen native generals, each endowed with a substantial following. Most of them remained loyal to Bolívar even in his dictatorial phase. In a remarkable turn of events, which would set Nueva Granada apart from most South American countries, the military power of Bolívar's lieutenants was defeated by the prestige of the constitutional opinion shared by the vast majority of politicians in Bogotá, Antioquia, and Cauca, led by Santander.

It was the partisan struggle between the supporters of a Bolivarian dictatorship in (Gran) Colombia and the advocates of the rule of law in Bogotá, who had a distinct interest in the preservation of politics as a professional career, that decisively contributed to the rise of separation schemes in Nueva Granada. If Páez and Flores wanted secession, it was not because they were leaders of a different party. They had no parties. They wanted separation because they were caudillos who could secure political supremacy within a smaller area. Only in Nueva Granada did a protoparty, liberal in the sense that it rejected dictatorship, gather the support of almost the entire political community. For them, the territory of the state had to shrink because the regime of the larger state was a dictatorship. The liberal protoparty caused state failure on a pan-Colombian scale. However, it also forged state formation in the smaller territory resulting from the departure of Venezuela and Ecuador.

The Rise of Nueva Granada: The Positive Partisan Effects. The generalized disappointment with Bolívar's dictatorial methods could presumably provide a common platform of constitutional, explicitly antiabsolutist values to the whole spectrum of political notables ruling Nueva Granada's main cities. It did, but not for long. It was not shared values that united Nueva Granada in the long run. On the contrary, it was partisan conflict.

The shared anti-Bolivarian animosity and the fresh memories of the dictatorship explain why Santander, the first president of Nueva Granada (1832–37), was a consensus candidate for the first presidency. The consensus was ephemeral. Two unrelated men, from radically different places and professions, were the source of discord. One of them was Bolívar. The other was Jeremy Bentham, the utilitarian English philosopher.

In the mid-1830s, after the foundational rejection of Bolívar's dictatorship, all Granadan politicians agreed that the army should be reduced to avoid the risks of praetorian assaults on political power. Governments of all stripes steadily reduced the number of soldiers. Gran Colombia's army was twelve thousand men strong. The first government of Nueva Granada (1832–37) reduced it to three thousand, and by the mid-nineteenth century, it was less than one thousand men strong and had no navy (one thousand men was a ludicrous figure by Westphalian, war-led standards of state formation).

A small wedge cracked the general Santanderean consensus: Nueva Granada politicians disagreed about the best approach to demobilize the military officers who had been loyal to Bolívar's dictatorship. Some wanted rapid and complete removal from public office. Others advocated a conciliatory, gradual approach.

During Santander's presidency, Bentham was the second source of conflict. Santander sponsored the inclusion of Bentham's texts in the core curriculum of the law schools. For devout Catholics, utilitarianism was a subversion of traditional moral values. The church responded by threatening students who used Bentham's books with excommunication. That Bentham's ideas could spark major public antagonism is quite unimaginable by twenty-first-century standards. Yet, even by nineteenth-century standards, conflict over Bentham grew out of proportion. What politicized Bentham were other measures by Santander and the opportunity seen by members of the incipient opposition to fish for electoral dividends in the many rivers of a highly pious society. In addition to sponsoring utilitarian education, Santander closed monasteries with small numbers of friars. For Santander, the church caused a waste of assets that a poor economy could not afford to lose. The career of priesthood distracted young men from productive work, and mortmain property took up land that could be used for cultivation. Most Granadan politicians agreed with the need to curb the economic and ideological power of the church. They disagreed about the speed of transformation.

The Election of 1836 and the Márquez Presidency. Neither Bentham's texts nor Bolívar's legacy would have created a permanent political division had they not been seen as powerful electoral magnets in the presidential campaign of 1836 to decide Santander's successor. Remarkably, the government's candidate, Obando, lost the election. Given the phenomenal "incumbent advantage" that marked Latin American politics throughout the nineteenth century and given that Santander, the main living hero of independence, was still enormously prestigious, the government's defeat revealed a major novelty in the emerging political arena. What a few years earlier was only a tenuous, amorphous current of opinion against Santander's reforms had acquired in 1836 a formidable ability to coordinate efforts for voter mobilization across regions. The effort was the first rudiment of a political party.

The winner of the 1836 election was José Ignacio Márquez, one of the many politicians who had opposed Bolívar's dictatorship in 1828 and supported Santander's ascension to power in 1832. Márquez was voted in by citizens who wanted a more conciliatory approach both to the Catholic Church and to the Bolivarian military. They wanted change, but it had to be more gradual than the transformation led by Santander. Márquez also received the support from pro-Santander politicians who were skeptical about Obando's candidacy. This was the case of members of the upper classes in Cartagena, Medellín, Popayán, and especially Bogotá. In contrast to Márquez, who was a civilian, Obando was a military veteran, a caudillo with a strong following among the rural poor of Cauca. Although Obando fought against Bolívar's dictatorship, the public still distrusted warlords of all kinds.

Márquez wanted his presidency to heal the wounds between devout Catholics and supporters of Bolívar on the one hand and the radical liberals pushing for fast reform, *liberales exaltados*, on the other. Under Márquez's presidency, Santander became the opposition's leader. His newspaper, *La Bandera Nacional*, became a frightening political weapon. Although Santander had been aware of the need for reconciliation during his own term, as the leader of the opposition, he decided to scrutinize every appointment made by Márquez with a magnifying glass, searching for potential contamination by religious archaism (i.e., Catholicism) or hidden dictatorial ambitions (i.e., Bolivarianism). From the opposition, Santander found that his future political career was best served by mobilizing a well-defined portion of the general public, which was marked by an aversion to colonial institutions that interfered with free markets (from slave labor to public monopolies) and to Bolivarian methods or rule (government by decree and military intervention).

Santander's partisan opposition was an obvious headache for Márquez, and it deliberately undermined his capacity to rule. Yet, unintentionally, it made a major contribution to state formation qua territory consolidation. Santander's critical arguments were issue specific rather than region specific. His plan was to mobilize support for an agenda of institutional reforms irrespective of locality, thereby linking together distant communities of leaders, activists, and citizens.

Showing a remarkable capacity for collective action, many devout Catholics decided to create a network of Catholic societies in all major cities, like Bogotá, Cartagena, and Popayán. The societies were a club rather than a party, but they embraced a political mission. Their members had been quick to realize that, depending on who was at the pinnacle of power, politics in independent Nueva Granada could cause irreparable damage to the church. The societies were meant as a barrier to change. Márquez shared the liberal diagnosis that the church was a burden for Nueva Granada's economy and government. He had no part in the creation of the societies. Yet the game of politics, and the opposition schemes within it, had already become unstoppable in Bogotá. As a consequence, the rumors linking the Catholic societies to Márquez's government, although entirely false, were taken as an obvious truth by the public.

The opposition eventually cornered Márquez's government into doing what Márquez had never intended to and what the opposition had always feared. The moderate liberals supporting Márquez began to rely on Bolívar's former lieutenants, in part out of fear of radical rebellion and in part because of the defection of other military officers. A key partner of Márquez was Mosquera, a staunch Bolivarian general from Popayán who had been defeated in battle by Obando a few years earlier when loyalist Bolivarians decided to take arms to defend the dictatorship.

The alliance between moderate liberals and former Bolivarians was the kernel of the Conservative Party. Another personal struggle, between Mosquera and Obando, pushed party formation a step further. Mosquera and Obando hated each other. They fought for control over the army. Obando wanted to purge the army of Bolivarian officials, whereas Mosquera pursued the subordination of the army to Bolivarian generals. Once Mosquera was appointed by Márquez to the war portfolio, he sought to eliminate Obando.

The War of the Supreme Captains, 1839–42. A standard political gambit was the prelude to the military clash. In 1839, Obando was officially accused of the assassination of Marshal Antonio José de Sucre (June 1830).

Sucre's loyalty to Bolívar was unconditional. A man of exceptional military and administrative talents, second in independence achievements only to San Martín and Bolívar, Sucre would have been the natural successor of Bolívar as president of (Gran) Colombia. The accusation against Obando lacked any kind of factual evidence. Yet it was a reasonable one. Flores, the military ruler of Ecuador, conspired to have Sucre killed because the continuation of Bolívar's plan by his loyal marshal was incompatible with Ecuador's secession. Santander himself had tried to have Bolívar killed in 1828. And Obando was a close associate of both Flores and Santander. Obando and Flores entertained the scheme of forming a "Great Ecuador" by annexing Cauca, Obando's base. Santander in turn had chosen Obando in 1836 to succeed him as president of Nueva Granada. If Obando was not responsible for Sucre's assassination, it was not for lack of motivation or accomplices.

Mosquera launched an official pursuit of Obando. In desperation, Obando revolted in early 1840, leading a vast clientele of rural workers from Cauca. Obando's rebellion was imitated by a number of smaller caudillos throughout the territory of Nueva Granada, inaugurating the War of the Supreme Captains. To face the challenge of Obando and the other liberal rebels, Márquez's government was forced into a closer alliance with the Bolivarian generals.

The government won, but the war, which lasted almost three years, was an unmitigated economic disaster. Yet, from a political perspective, at the same time that the war placed Nueva Granada on the brink of disintegration in the short run, it had crucial stabilizing effects in the long run. The most prominent short-run effect was the enhanced risk of fragmentation of the recently created territory of Nueva Granada into a number of fiefdoms ruled by rural warlords. The cross-regional linkages at the level of partisan public opinion built by Santander and his circle were trumped by the ambition of local warlords to carve out their own minicountries. Moreover, the government itself, lacking sufficient military capabilities, became a sponsor of partial territorial dismemberment. In order to secure enough soldiers and arsenal to defeat Obando, Márquez promised the Ecuadoran president that Nueva Granada was willing to give away the city of Pasto in exchange for military support.

Yet the War of the Supreme Captains had two positive political effects on party formation that in the long run would prove crucial for territory consolidation. First, the alliance between the Márquez government and the Bolivarian generals—which was initially a war machine—turned into a protoparty that became known as the Ministeriales. They were only one step away from the creation of the Conservative Party. They only needed a new challenge from their rivals and new leadership to provide partisan structure (i.e., organization and platform).

The most important development during the War of the Supreme Captains was the very dispute between Mosquera and Obando. The dispute was a mix of personal vendetta and political conflict. The dynamics of the dispute closed down the two alternative paths for the pivotal Cauca region, which were annexation to Ecuador or creation of an independent state (together with Antioquia). The reason is that both Obando and Mosquera were natives of Cauca, where each of them had a formidable following. During the war, both Caucano generals learned that extinguishing the power of the rival was nearly impossible and that, to prevent defeat, they required fiscal, military, and political support from Bogotá. As much as they fought each other, Obando and Mosquera made major political efforts to secure allies outside Cauca, from the Caribbean and especially the eastern *cordillera*. The competitive search for outside allies resulted in the unintended political attachment of the region to the emerging political arena of Nueva Granada.

In sum, the War of the Supreme Captains almost disintegrated New Granada. Yet the aftermath of the conflict was the unintended but definitive incorporation of Cauca into the political networks centered in Bogotá. Too busy fighting each other, protagonists did not notice the development. Too immersed in the details of the war, historians have not perceived it. With the party-driven incorporation of Cauca into Nueva Granada, the chances of secession by other outlying regions fell dramatically. It was a hidden but foundational event in Nueva Granada's party formation and, indirectly, in territory consolidation.

Completion of Party Formation. The victorious alliance between Márquez and the Bolivarian military prompted the elevation to power of two generals with the most distinguished performance during the war, Pedro Alcántara Herrán and Mosquera himself, both of whom became presidents, in 1841–45 and 1845–49, respectively. The power of Herrán and Mosquera essentially fulfilled the ominous prophecy that radical liberals had helped to cultivate.

In the late 1840s, under the leadership of Ospina, a prominent lawyer and journalist, the "ministerial" alliance developed into a full-blown partisan organization, the Conservative Party. In contrast to the moderate and ministerial predecessors, Conservatives built an open alliance with the Catholic Church. Although Conservative voters and the pious population certainly believed in the ideological affinity between Conservatism and Catholicism, both the leaders of the party and the leaders of the church viewed the partnership in instrumental terms. The church proselytized in favor of a social order compatible with Conservative power. In exchange, Conservative leaders secured political protection of the church, especially vis-à-vis radical reform, which threatened the confiscation of ecclesiastical property, the full secularization of education, and the adoption of religious tolerance.

The leaders of the Conservative Party did not differ with regard to social class from the founders of what a few years later would become the Liberal Party. They were all members of the educated elite, typically holding a law degree. As the historian Frank Safford has shown, the notion that Conservatives were landowners whereas Liberals were merchants is wrong, among other reasons because most members of the upper class were landowners and merchants at the same time.[5] The attribute that most consistently differentiated the elite of the Conservative Party from other political leaders was a history of family control over the administrations of New Granada's main cities in colonial times. Nineteenth-century Conservatives were generally descendants of prominent civil servants in eighteenth-century Bogotá, Cartagena, and Popayán. The alliance with the Catholic Church and the Bolivarian military, then, created a constellation of interests that resembled that of the Mexican Conservative Party, and it was also marked by the defense of corporate privileges, including judicial immunities, government contracts, and control over the selection and education of new recruits into the civil, military, and ecclesiastical hierarchy.

Party formation was completed shortly after the Conservatives lost the presidential election of 1848. The winner was the Liberal José Hilario López. His victory was the result of divisions within the Conservative Party, which presented multiple presidential candidates. The rise of López marked the beginning of a three-decade period in which the Liberal Party ruled almost uninterruptedly. The period of Liberal dominance was characterized by the rise to power of a new generation of university graduates willing to experiment with large-scale political reform, with an emphasis on the elimination of colonial institutions, especially slavery; government monopolies, like the salt and tobacco *estancos*; and church privileges. The intellectual leader of the new generation of Liberals was Manuel Murillo Toro, who became president twice.

The Liberal reform of Colombia was similar to the Liberal reform of Mexico. If it was not more radical, it was only because the power of the Mexican Catholic Church dwarfed the power of the Colombian one. In Mexico, the church was the largest landowner, so the confiscation of church property was equivalent to land reform, even if the reform did not create a large class of small landowners. In Colombia, most church property was urban.

From the perspective of party-driven state formation, the key Liberal reform was the introduction of universal suffrage in 1853. It was an attempt at democratization, and democratization in turn reflected the interests of a coalition that was too heterogeneous to last. It was supported by the young Liberal intellectuals and the artisans of the city of Bogotá, an economic class that, in its political awareness and organization, had no parallel in Latin America at the time.

The Bogotá artisans were crucial in the rise of the Liberals to power in 1849. Yet, for them, the Liberal reform was a textbook case of a *journée des Dupes*.[6] The young Liberal intellectuals became the main political beneficiaries of the government change and gradually marginalized the Bogotá artisans from power, adopting policies that clearly damaged their interests. The artisans had originally organized as an interest group. Their chief demand was protection from European imports, especially clothing and simple hardware. Their only other demand was democracy, but they wanted democracy as a means to protect their economic interest. The new Liberal generation made a tactical alliance with them, which dramatically failed to become permanent. Liberals were more ardent defenders of free trade than Conservatives were. In 1853, in response to laissez-faire policies, the artisans organized to take the streets, protest, destroy property, and intimidate members of congress with firearms. The reaction of the young Liberal leaders revealed their upper-class background. They joined the Conservative elite, civilian and military, to repress the protest. Repression was so effective that the artisans never mobilized again.

The betrayal of the artisans by their Liberal allies also revealed the deeper structural constraints on state formation analyzed in Part 1. When state formation took the party-driven path, parties formed and evolved within the clear limits established by the requirements of the trade-centered process, which heavily depended on free international commerce.

The relatively brief intervention of the artisans in nineteenth-century politics had two lasting effects. First, it helped define the boundaries of the social interests represented by the Liberal Party and of the economic policies adopted by Liberal governments. Disruptions to trade-led state formation generated outside the upper classes would not be tolerated. Second, the artisans of Bogotá created the rudiments of mass political organizations, which had impressive diffusion effects. In the early 1840s, the artisans had created the Society of Artisans, which at the time was a mixture of mutual-aid society and pressure group. In the context of the competition between Conservatives and proto-Liberals in the late 1840s, the artisans refunctionalized their society to provide political support to Liberal candidates. The society was accordingly renamed the Democratic Society, which in addition to demanding universal suffrage worked to increase the literacy of its members so that they could gain the right to vote before suffrage restrictions were lifted. The Democratic Society of Bogotá served as an organizational model for the pro-Liberal popular classes in other cities. Democratic societies mushroomed throughout Nueva Granada. Imitation did not stop there. After the Liberal success of 1849, pro-Conservative popular classes organized their own societies, ostensibly for the defense of the Catholic religion and the traditional church. Conservative popular societies were not pure plagiarism. They were also a reaction to Liberal policy, which gradually expanded secular education, closed small monasteries, and introduced the principle of religious toleration. For Liberals, religious toleration was a crucial step toward attracting high-human-capital immigrants from Germany and Scandinavia. For Conservatives, it was blasphemy.

No political process is complete without an element of irony. The creation of popular societies and the adoption of universal suffrage, both Liberal initiatives, ended up tipping the electoral balance in favor of the Conservatives. Throughout the second half of the nineteenth century, the

Conservatives were more popular than the Liberals were. If Liberals remained in power from 1849 to 1876, it was because, entrenched in the government, they applied surgical doses of fraud and force in critical political times.

In sum, by the mid-nineteenth century, the political arena of Nueva Granada was fully occupied by, and organized into, two rival political forces. Liberal and Conservative leaders shared economic interests. They wanted Colombia to become a leading exporter of tropical goods, in addition to gold. Although they distinguished themselves on cultural issues, the rivalry was essentially rooted in the competition for government positions. Party leaders created gentlemen's clubs and newspapers. The popular sector of each party had its Democratic or Catholic Societies. Clubs, newspapers, societies, and campaigns linked together political communities from distant localities. Party formation preceded and caused territory consolidation in Nueva Granada.

Territory Consolidation in Uruguay: Party Formation as the Driver of Union
Liberals versus Liberals in Uruguay

The political struggle between Colorados and Blancos in Uruguay had no basis in class divisions. In contrast to Mexico and Colombia, partisan cleavages cannot be traced to the colonial legacy. Uruguay lacked colonial corporations that could pit defenders of Bourbon traditions against advocates of radical reform. At the origins of the Uruguayan partisan cleavage lay the personal rivalry between two caudillos, Manuel Oribe (Blanco) and Fructuoso Rivera (Colorado), both of whom had been lieutenants of Gervasio Artigas, Uruguay's independence hero. Yet, as in Mexico and Colombia, party formation in Uruguay predated and caused state formation.

Uruguay as Outcome: Three Possible Futures in 1835. Artigas had been a special independence hero. In 1811, he joined Buenos Aires in the fight against Spain. Three years later, in sharp disagreement with Buenos Aires's centralizing policies and upper-class bias, Artigas struggled to create a new state. Against centralization, Artigas's new state was a confederation of present-day Uruguay and the provinces of Entre Ríos, Santa Fe, and part of

Córdoba in present-day Argentina, the Liga de los Pueblos Libres (Map 5.3). Against upper-class power, the new state promoted the creation of a large class of small farmers through land reform.

In a clear indication that political ambition was a stronger force than any inchoate Rioplatense national sentiment was, the leaders in Buenos Aires decided to deal with the territorial and social threat created by Artigas by allowing the Brazilian Empire to invade Uruguay in the late 1810s. Artigas and his followers could fight Spain and Buenos Aires, but the addition of a third enemy proved lethal. Brazil annexed Uruguay and renamed it the Cisplatina Province. Artigas was banished to Paraguay and never returned.

Uruguay is the only South American country that gained independence from another South American country. In 1825, the independence campaign of Uruguay was initiated by the "Thirty-Three Men from the East," a crusade by a minuscule group of exiles in Buenos Aires. With only nominal support from Buenos Aires, the crusaders sailed to Uruguay to challenge Brazilian rule. They were led by Oribe and Juan Antonio Lavalleja, another former lieutenant of Artigas. Rivera had remained in the Cisplatina under Brazilian rule, but he quickly joined the independence movement. Initial military success, and the willingness of Oribe and Lavalleja to lead Uruguay into a union with Buenos Aires, prompted the government of Buenos Aires to enter the fight.

Buenos Aires and Brazil soon reached a military stalemate. The land was dominated by Buenos Aires, but the rivers were controlled by Brazil. The end of the stalemate was brokered by Great Britain, which sponsored the creation of Uruguay as an independent state in 1828. The negotiation of Uruguay's independence is known as the "Ponsonby Mission" after the prestigious English diplomat. British commercial interests benefited from the creation of Uruguay in multiple ways. A neutral buffer zone between Buenos Aires and Brazil would prevent conflict between England's two main commercial partners in the South Atlantic and thereby contribute to the reliability of trade flows. Also, a small republic like Uruguay, much more vulnerable to foreign pressure, would ensure that the port of Montevideo became another node within Great Britain's vast economic empire.[7]

British protection and stalemate between Uruguay's more powerful neighbors largely explain the early emergence of Uruguay as an independent state. Yet, starting in the mid-1830s, when both the Ponsonby mission and the agreement between Buenos Aires and Rio de Janeiro became a distant memory, the developmental paths of Uruguay were reopened. In addition to the preservation of Uruguay in its 1828 territorial form, two types of scheme were considered. One involved further fragmentation by the separation of the city-port of Montevideo from its rural hinterland. A key component of the scheme was the creation of an entrepôt under the protection of some international power that would defend it against incursions from warlords in the rural hinterland and that would also become an arbiter to secure property rights and solve conflicts between factions within Montevideo. The menu of arbiters included France, an Italian prince, a joint Argentine-Brazilian commission, and of course Great Britain.[8]

The other scheme, by contrast, contemplated territorial expansion, the creation of "Great Uruguay," which was a revival of Artigas's Liga de los Pueblos Libres, except that it included the mighty Rio Grande do Sul, which since 1835 had become an independent republic that rejected the monarchic regime of Brazil and needed external allies to secure its international survival. The main sponsor of the Great Uruguay project was Rivera. In 1842, it almost became a reality.

The rise of present-day Uruguay and the elimination of alternative paths since 1828 are intimately linked to the process of party formation.

Civil War and Party Formation: 1839–43. Only a decade after independence, the first civil war exploded in Uruguay. It lasted fifteen years, hence its name, Guerra Grande (Big War). The struggle was the crucible of Uruguay's two parties. Rivera, the first president of independent Uruguay, was succeeded by Oribe. Through an informal power-sharing agreement, during Oribe's presidential term, Rivera became the military commander of the rural areas beyond the city of Montevideo. Fearing a coup, Oribe removed Rivera from his position in 1836, which of course only precipitated the insurrection. The personal rivalry soon escalated into a conflict between nearly identical rural armies, which distinguished themselves by the color of a piece of clothing. Oribe ordered his soldiers to wear a white headband (hence, Blancos) and Rivera commanded his followers to turn their wool ponchos inside out. Ponchos came in multiple colors, including white, beige, and light blue, but their linings were uniformly red (hence, Colorados).

Both Oribe and Rivera were state-breaking caudillos, as defined in Chapter 4. Their warlord qualities were enhanced, if not created, by the economic context.[9] Uruguay was a primitive pastoral economy. Land titles existed, but rural estates were not enclosed. The use of barbed wire to fence pastures was introduced only in the 1870s. The main activity was cattle breeding, but livestock was of dismal quality. It produced three staples: hides, tallow, and jerked beef, which was sold to slave plantations in Brazil and Cuba. Precisely because violence was not monopolized, incentives to upgrade fencing and livestock were minimal. For a number of Uruguayan cowboys, cattle rustling was as profitable as cattle breeding. Rural banditry was riskier than ranching, but the barriers to entry were much lower. In the Uruguayan countryside, since Artigas's times, a special class of small cattle breeders consolidated. They owned no land, only a few head of livestock. They were not bandits, but they illegally used the pastures of large landowners, often absentee lords, to feed their cattle.

In the context of a primitive pastoral economy and a stateless society—populated by backward landowners, countless bandits, and a large class of small cattle breeders—the caudillo became an indispensable source of protection. Caudillos offered protection to large landowners who needed to evict intruders, to bandits who had a feud with a rival ring of rustlers, and especially to the small folk, who were defenseless against everyone else. Midcentury Uruguay was an anarchical, violent society.[10] Rivera and Oribe led large-scale protection rackets. They were the rudiment of political parties.

The Big War was made bigger by the participation of foreign powers, including Buenos Aires, Brazil, provinces in present-day Argentina that rivaled Buenos Aires, France, England, and a legion of volunteers led by the future Italian unification hero Giuseppe Garibaldi.

Buenos Aires supported the Blancos, and Brazil the Colorados. Buenos Aires was ruled by the dictator Juan Manuel de Rosas, a large landowner. Rosas represented Buenos Aires's interest in consolidating its leadership as the main port of the River Plate and the center of the meat-salting industry. Rosas wanted to force the cattle breeders of Uruguay to become captive suppliers of Buenos Aires's *saladeros*, the meat-salting plants. Rosas provided enormous amounts of financial and military aid to Oribe. He expected in return the hegemony of Buenos Aires over the navigation of the entire system of rivers in the River Plate basin. The port of Buenos Aires was already an abundant source of revenue. The subordination of Montevideo would make it a colossal one.

In supporting the Colorados, Brazil wanted Rivera to produce a satellite government that would protect the Brazilian citizens who had bought land in Uruguay while it was a province of the empire, as well as to push southward the border between Uruguay and Brazil, which was an open, ill-defined frontier. Additionally, for Brazil to access its own interior in the Matto Grosso, it required free navigation of the River Plate and its tributaries (overland passage from Rio de Janeiro was impossible). From Brazil's perspective, if Rosas controlled both sides of the River Plate, access to Matto Grosso would be subject to his discretion, if not his extortion.

The French, the English, and Garibaldi also sided with the Colorados. The French and the English wanted free trade, and free trade required free navigation. Garibaldi wanted adventure.

The Long Siege and Disintegration Risks: 1843–51. After almost four years of combat, Colorados and Blancos reached a military stalemate, which created a remarkable territorial configuration for a country the size of Uruguay. The Colorados dominated the city-port of Montevideo. The Blancos dominated the rural interior. The Blancos made several attempts to defeat the Colorados entrenched in Montevideo, but they all failed. Montevideo had become a fortress, the Troy of the River Plate, according to Alexandre Dumas. The power of the French navy became vital in providing supplies to the Montevideo population.

The Big War morphed into a long siege (Sitio Grande), during which Colorados in Montevideo were strong enough to resist invasion but not strong enough to exert control beyond the city walls. The smallest South American country had become two separate territorial units. The government of Montevideo, called "La Defensa," was de facto a French protectorate, and the government of the interior, "El Cerrito," depended on Buenos Aires's support. State failure in Uruguay during the 1840s was not due to the rise of a duopoly of violence. The precise manifestation of failure was the emergence of two microstates, each of which had the monopoly of violence within its own boundaries and its own foreign protector.

Starting in 1843, the war between rival parties in present-day Uruguay could not be classified as either civil or international before it was over.

Partisan divisions roughly coincided with territorial boundaries. In contrast to civil wars in which partisan cleavages cut across geographical boundaries and rival armies are intermingled within the same territory, the war of Uruguay could in principle be solved by simply partitioning the Colorado area from the Blanco area, with the expectation that the remaining partisan minorities in each area would migrate to the other area, as in fact had begun to occur. Had partition occurred, the war would have been an international one. Montevideo would have become a microstate similar to the city-ports of the Hansa League or Panama.

Yet not only did Uruguay stay united, overcoming the schism between city and countryside, but it also remained independent. Independence ruled out two outcomes: absorption by a larger neighbor, which would have been a natural development given the geopolitical weakness derived from prolonged internal turmoil; and the formation of a confederation with other subunits within the vast River Plate basin, which could have profited from the fact that Montevideo was the best natural port in the entire River Plate basin.

It would only be a slight stylization of the factual record to claim that union was achieved by merit of Uruguay's internal actors, whereas independence was a gift from external forces (a repetition of the 1828 process). An evolving balance of international power had a crucial impact on Uruguay's independence after the Big War. Internal union, however, was an unintended outcome, as in all other cases of party-driven state formation. It was a by-product of party formation, resulting from the combination of new political dynamics in Montevideo, the Uruguayan center, and old partisan divisions in the hinterland, the periphery. The next two sections explain, in turn, independence and union.

Uruguay's Independence in the 1850s: International Luck. Uruguay remained an independent state because of events outside Uruguay. A simple explanation of the fact that Uruguay was not annexed by a more powerful country is that so many foreign rulers were interested in it that they neutralized each other. The same way that France did not invade Uruguay in order not to risk a war with the United Kingdom, Buenos Aires did not want to risk a war with Brazil, and vice versa. Yet the explanation based on mutual international vetoes, valid for the 1830s and 1840s, hides key changes in the early 1850s, which add fundamental historical detail and illustrate the impact of the Commercial Revolution discussed in Part 1.

Uruguay's Big War was over only when the balance of international power changed. In 1851, the ministate of Entre Ríos in present-day Argentina decided to challenge the hegemony of Rosas in Buenos Aires. Rosas had strangled Entre Ríos's fiscal position by impeding free navigation along the two rivers, the Paraná and the Uruguay, connecting the ministate to the Atlantic. Exerting "navigation despotism," Rosas forced all ships with cargo for the ministates in the Upper Littoral and the Interior of present-day Argentina to stop at the port of Buenos Aires and pay import duties. Naturally, Rosas did not share the revenue collected. It was all spent within the boundaries of Buenos Aires. Urquiza and Entre Ríos had been loyal to Buenos Aires throughout the 1840s. Like the other ministates, Entre Ríos was too weak to question Rosas's policies. Yet, despite Rosas's hegemony, Entre Ríos managed to grow its economy in the 1840s. Its cattle-ranching activities began to catch up with those of Buenos Aires.

Incipient economic development gave Entre Ríos incentives and resources to challenge Buenos Aires's trade and navigation policies. Through remarkably speedy diplomatic negotiations, Entre Ríos made an alliance with the Colorados of Montevideo and with Brazil, both interested in the destruction of Rosas's power. Urquiza offered his partners the free navigation of the rivers of the River Plate system. Urquiza's promise was utterly credible, for he himself would be the main beneficiary of free navigation. In exchange for Brazil's and Montevideo's support, Urquiza committed to force Oribe's Blancos to lift the siege. Oribe's only foreign support had come from Rosas. The combination of the power of Urquiza's horsemen, the Colorados entrenched in Montevideo, and the Brazilian army defeated Rosas in 1852. Rosas's fall left little option to the Blancos other than military demobilization, which finally put an end to the Uruguayan Big War.

If Uruguay was not annexed by any country before 1850 because of the mutual veto of powerful international players, after 1850 it was not annexed because it lost its geoeconomic value. The reason was the end of Rosas's monopoly. Buenos Aires's trade restrictions fell together with the dictator. Free navigation of the entire River Plate basin finally became a reality, which made direct control of Uruguay a much less attractive option. Entre Ríos producers did not need Montevideo's harbor to export hides and jerked beef; the

French and the English merchants could trade freely with the other ministates of present-day Argentina and Paraguay without paying extra fees to Buenos Aires; and Brazil could reach the Matto Grosso through newly internationalized rivers. Uruguay was a completely dispensable geopolitical prize in a context where trade expansion rather than territorial expansion had become the dominant goal.

Great Uruguay: The Path Not Taken. If the path of annexation was closed down for Uruguay, so was the path of territorial expansion. Uruguay is the smallest state of South America because the project of expansion into Great Uruguay was aborted. Efforts made by Uruguayan leaders to form a union with nearby ministates of similar strength failed. The decade of the 1840s, which Uruguay spent entirely at war, was the right juncture for the formation of a confederation linking together Uruguay, Rio Grande do Sul in present-day Brazil, and the ministates of the Upper Littoral in present-day Argentina. Since 1835, Rio Grande do Sul had become an independent republic, Piratini, and it needed outside allies to resist reannexation attempts from Brazil. Rivera, the Colorado leader, spent several seasons in Piratini, exchanging promises of mutual military support with its leaders. Additionally, under Rosas's dictatorship, Montevideo offered the Upper Paraná ministates in present-day Argentina the perfect maritime outlet.

Great Uruguay made a lot of sense, in geographic, economic, and even geopolitical terms. Geographically, Great Uruguay was the landmass corresponding to the large area of the River Plate basin, with the exception of Buenos Aires. Economically, with the partial exception of Corrientes, all subunits in Great Uruguay were pastoral economies based on extensive cattle ranching, a prosperous meat-salting industry, and exports of jerked beef to Rio de Janeiro and Havana and of hides to western Europe. Geopolitically, the formation of Great Uruguay would have created a state that had nothing to fear from Buenos Aires or Rio de Janeiro.

In 1842, the rulers of Santa Fe, Corrientes, and Piratini met with Rivera in Entre Ríos and agreed on the formation of Great Uruguay, an expanded version of Artigas's old Liga de los Pueblos Libres.[11] Two obstacles proved fatal. First, Entre Ríos was still a client state of Rosas, and its leaders feared that the challenge to Rosas was premature. Without Entre Ríos, less prosperous and less powerful ministates like Santa Fe and Corrientes could not challenge Rosas either. Second, Rivera gradually lost the trust of the leaders of Piratini. They were uncertain as to whether Rivera genuinely wanted union or whether he was just manipulating Piratini to obtain munitions and manpower against his enemy Oribe. Both obstacles illustrate a larger theoretical point. Caudillos, like the ones who dominated Entre Ríos, Santa Fe, and Rio Grande do Sul, as well as Rivera himself, are poor leaders of large-scale projects of state formation. They prefer to form a state whose territory is coterminous with the spatial extension of their network of clients. Small-scale state formation secures for caudillos the pinnacle of the clientelistic hierarchy. The merger of separate caudillo networks, although not impossible, creates great uncertainty for individual caudillos about their future share of power within the larger territory. Promises of power sharing by caudillos carry little credibility. The moment a caudillo gains a clear economic or military advantage, due for instance to a better cattle-ranching season, he has an incentive to renege on prior agreements and make a bid to dominate the other caudillos.

Explanation: Territory Consolidation through Party Formation, 1850–75

For more than eight years, the city-port of Montevideo was Colorado, and the rural hinterland was Blanco, each dominated by a rival caudillo (1843–51). At various junctures, conditions seemed ripe for permanent separation and the consolidation of two microstates.

What stopped Uruguay from partition was the fact that, by the end of the 1840s, the city of Montevideo experienced the birth of competitive oligarchic politics. The new political activity in Montevideo was led by university-trained politicians, the so-called *doctores* (jurists), who were appalled by the human and economic destruction caused by the war.[12] They launched a prolific debate about the impact of rural warlords and partisan politics on the prospects of Uruguay's development. Initially, most members of the Montevideo political oligarchy put aside minor ideological differences and agreed on the need to establish a durable peace, which for them required overcoming the old division between Colorados and Blancos, breaking down existing caudillo political networks, and creating purely electoral political parties (i.e., purged of military-insurrectionary components). Yet it was not the declared goals of the *doctores* that prevented Uruguay's fragmentation. Rather, it was the unintended consequences of their actions.

The mission of replacing the old partisan loyalties with new ones was a resounding failure. Moreover, for the remainder of the century, rural caudillos continued to play a decisive role. Yet, in the long run, the urban political oligarchies, through unexpected combinations, transformed Blancos and Colorados from rival armies into fully fledged political parties. The renovated traditional parties were marked by an acute understanding of the need to solve political differences via peaceful means, including electoral competition, policy bargaining, and power sharing. The *doctores* failed at creating new parties but unintentionally succeeded at transforming the old ones. Such transformation contributed both to territory consolidation and, as we will see in the last section, to pacification.

The key to territory consolidation was the combination of two contrasting legacies of the Big War: the fragility of the consensus among the new political oligarchy in the city and the persistence of the old partisan divisions in the countryside. Over time, the new political oligarchy split about issues of strategy in relation to the resilient nature of rural power, and, in a classical problem of collective action, even the most ardent opponents of caudillos and old parties capitulated to the need to make deals with them. The initial drive of the city to reform politics in the countryside, after several failed attempts, mutated into opportunistic alliances through which the *doctores*, in competition with each other, opted to join the old parties of rural origin. The former bands of pastoral warlords and clients were each to incorporate a distinct subgroup of urban jurists.

Uruguayan traditional parties were born from the unexpected combination of rural caudillos and urban *doctores*. City and countryside became linked, and Uruguay's territory unintentionally consolidated, by the race of rival urban politicians to obtain the support of the caudillos and their traditional followers. The emerging two-party system proved stronger than any other social or political organization in Uruguay. The parties certainly predated by decades the existence of a national identity. Colorados and Blancos came to dominate Uruguayan politics, and thereby to consolidate the Uruguayan territory, through two critical challenges: the so-called fusionism of the 1850s and the sequence of constitutionalism and militarism from 1872 to 1890. Both challenges put at risk the very survival of the parties.

In overcoming the challenges, the parties become so strong that they dominated Uruguayan politics through the following century.

Fusionism (1850–64). The endurance of the partisan divisions and caudillo
power in the countryside was tested twice in the decade after the Big War.
In 1851, under the auspices of Urquiza and the Brazilian army, the vast majority of university-trained politicians in Montevideo agreed on the need for
"political fusion," a plan for a grand coalition of national salvation that would
pursue the shared goal of postwar economic reconstruction and postpone
debate about less urgent matters. Fusion failed.

The struggle between Blancos and Colorados had been too intense and
prolonged to allow for the dissolution of partisan loyalties. Rival parties
blamed each other for massacres. Under such conditions, partisan identifi-
cations are extremely durable, and subsequent fusion becomes a chimera.
In 1855, while the fusionist government in Montevideo was designing plans
to marginalize rural warlords from public office, Venancio Flores, an emerging Colorado caudillo, received the support of an opportunistic wing of jurists in Montevideo to topple the government. Urban politicians from both
parties reacted by joining forces and creating a third party, the Liberal Union,
which invoked the superiority of the rule of law over the rule of men. It was
a new failure. Flores agreed with the rival caudillo Oribe to support a presidential candidate who would defeat the Liberal Union.

The agreement between rival caudillos in 1855 revealed three novelties
in Uruguayan politics. First, when their survival was at risk, rival caudillos
were better at collective action than urban politicians were. Second, rival caudillos, out of personal ambition or a superior understanding of political
reality, did not even consider fusion, which helped preserve the traditional
divide between Blancos and Colorados. They could negotiate truces, but
merger was a political taboo. Finally, caudillos discovered that agreements
were possible and often useful. The Flores-Oribe agreement, fragile as it was,
contributed to a rapid revitalization of Uruguay's economy, which the war
had pushed back to nearly subsistence levels.

In 1860, a new president, Bernardo Berro, made another attempt at fusion. Berro's strategy was more sophisticated than the plan of prior fusionists. He expected transformation of partisan politics to be a gradual process,
not a change that could occur overnight by presidential decree. Berro did

not renege on his Blanco sympathies and dispensed with the idea of creating a third party. He aimed at collaboration between Blancos and Colorados and appointed several Colorados to prominent decision-making positions. Yet Berro, pursuing a patriotic goal, made a critical political mistake. As part of the plan of economic reconstruction, Berro took the brave decision of revoking trade and tax concessions that Montevideo had granted to Brazil a decade earlier in exchange for military help against Oribe. Berro became a lamb among wolves. Brazil began to search for a presidential candidate who was willing to extend the concessions threatened by Berro, and Flores had no scruples about receiving foreign help against a Blanco government. In 1863, Flores began a military campaign against Berro. A few months later, Flores was again president of Uruguay.

Flores's restoration of Colorado power only deepened partisan divisions. As fusionists feared, the hegemony of one party would cause the insurrection of the opposition. In 1870, a new Blanco warlord, Timoteo Aparicio, launched the Revolution of the Lances, named after the *tacuaras*, a rudimentary lance made by tying a knife to the end of a bamboo pole. The ensuing civil war lasted two years. The Colorados prevailed, but Blanco power was far from extinguished. To prevent new rebellions, the Colorados committed to sharing power with the opposition by appointing Blanco politicians to rule four out of the thirteen departments of the interior.

The Sequence of Constitutionalism and Militarism (1872–90). By the end of the Revolution of the Lances, the urban political elites of Montevideo, frustrated by the recurrence of conflicts, made a different attempt to transform old partisan loyalties. They called themselves *principistas*, or constitutionalists, an allegedly improved revival of the fusionists of the 1850s. In contrast to the fusionists, the constitutionalists did not aim to eliminate Blancos and Colorados. They aimed to provide them with "principles," which was a distinct policy platform with a common core that acknowledged the value of the rule of law and parliamentary representation.

After three years of holding an overwhelming influence on national politics (1872–75), the constitutionalists were ejected from power through a military coup. The coup was not motivated by the resentment of old partisan organizations but by frustration from the new economic sectors that had grown wealthier after the peace brokered by Oribe and Flores in the mid-

1850s. The leader of the coup was not a rural caudillo but a professional soldier, Colonel Lorenzo Latorre. Peace had created incentives for the rural sector to initiate an incipient modernization, which heavily relied on the substitution of cattle ranching by sheep farming and the upgrading of wool quality through the introduction of new breeds. A chief complaint against the constitutionalists among the emerging commercial and rural bourgeoisie was that they focused on institutional reforms that added no value to the export sector at the expense of providing the policies required to deepen economic modernization. The emerging bourgeoise essentially demanded the supply of class goods characteristic of trade-led state formation, as defined in Chapter 1. The government of Latorre delivered exactly that: consolidation of land titles, modernization of the rural police to prevent banditry, laws against vagrancy to create a disciplined workforce, and incentives to the use of barbed wire to enclose private pastures.

Paradoxically, constitutionalism followed by militarism pushed party formation in Uruguay into the next stage. The new leaders of the parties, especially the Colorados, seemed to have learned the fundamental lessons from prior defeats at the hands of antipartisan jurists, rival caudillos, and professional soldiers. In 1890, a new Colorado government, led by Julio Herrera y Obes, consolidated a partisan machine that would rule Uruguay for decades to come. The renovated Colorado party was a combination of multiple components, including actors, resources, and policies, that had proven the most politically effective since 1830. The rural core, based on clientelistic networks, was complemented by a wing of experienced urban politicians capable of supplying class goods to modern landowners and urban merchants and of mobilizing public opinion behind the virtues of civilian rule (against the evils of military intervention). In order to survive, the Blancos had no choice but to imitate the Colorados' coalitional components and policy proposals.

Although the two parties became nearly identical machines based on a coalition of a large rural constituency and a section of the urban political oligarchy of Montevideo, the rural component had political primacy. The birth of oligarchic politics in Montevideo in the 1840s, the center, fostered the multiplication of political motivations, projects, and interests. In the city, political options were far from binary. Some leaders embraced the elimination of old parties; some pursued the creation of a new, entirely urban political party; and some hoped to provide modernizing leadership to the old parties. They also disagreed regarding the relative weight among the institutions of republicanism (division of powers), liberalism (individual rights), and democracy (universal suffrage).[13]

Yet it was the preexisting, strictly dichotomous division of the countryside, between Blancos and Colorados, that placed persistent constraints on the political action by the new generation of urban politicians. The old rival organizations of the rural areas drastically reduced the number of options available to politicians in the city.[14] The center provided new leadership, but the political cleavages had been set in stone by the periphery. Peripheral cleavages forced urban politicians who aspired to make a professional career to build linkages with constituencies they initially despised and wanted to marginalize. Such partisan linkages, channeled through the structures created by the rural children of Artigas, provided union to a country that had no other basis to stay together.

Pacification without Violence Monopolization: Colombia and Uruguay Diverge from Mexico

Colombia and Uruguay illustrate an intermediate outcome of party-driven state formation that was absent in the Mexican case. When parties are the most powerful organization in an emerging state, pacification can occur *before* violence monopolization. Violence monopolization is the most solid path to pacification, but it is not the only one. Another path is an agreement between the two rival parties to share political power. Armed conflict between political parties typically occurs because one of them believes it is underrepresented in government. The solution to insurrections is to adjust upward the share of power corresponding to the underrepresented party, which is essentially an issue in institutional engineering and can be achieved by granting the minority party junior positions in the executive cabinet, a larger number of seats in the legislature (which requires a reform of the electoral laws), or full control of subnational units (federalism or some substitute form of territorial power sharing).

The trajectories of party-driven state formation in Colombia and Uruguay have two commonalities. First, both countries experienced a long period, of about seventy years, of open or latent civil war provoked by partisan struggle. Party formation takes decades to produce its fruits, and, absent a monopoly of violence, protoparties resort to all kinds of method to achieve supremacy, including certainly violent insurrection. In both cases, partisan wars destroyed productive assets and scared future investors, which resulted in decades of economic backwardness. Second, in both countries pacification was achieved through the adoption of a very specific formula of power sharing between parties, the so-called incomplete vote, after a major clash in the late 1890s and early 1900s. The incomplete vote is a hybrid form of electoral regime, an intermediate solution between majoritarian rule and proportional representation, which in both countries secured the minority party a third of the seats in the legislatures. The formula was the central clause in the peace treaties of the last round of conflict between the parties. The peace treaties, the Tratado de Neerlandia and the Tratado de Wisconsin (1902) in Colombia and the Pacto de la Cruz (1897) and the Tratado de Aceguá (1904) in Uruguay, are rather exotic legal documents in the standard historiography of Latin American. Yet, from a Hobbesian perspective centered on state formation, they are more fundamental than the constitutions themselves. They caused the transition from civil war to political order.

Partisan Warfare and Economic Backwardness

The War of the Supreme Captains and the Big War had a foundational effect on the two-party system that came to dominate Colombia and Uruguay. The War of the Supreme Captains was the cradle of the "ministerial party," which in turn morphed into the Colombian Conservative Party less than a decade later and motivated diverse elements in the opposition to organize the Liberal Party. The effects of the Big War in Uruguay were even more direct than in Colombia, for the former rival armies, Blancos and Colorados, became opposing political parties without any substantial mutation in their leadership and constituencies.

None of the foundational wars were decisive. Not only did both contenders survive the wars, but in both countries the two emerging parties retained a critical amount of military capabilities, including arsenals, military leadership, ready troops, and logistical know-how. The end of the foundational wars could have led the demobilized political forces to stop fighting and start competing by peaceful means. Given the security dilemma created by the duopoly of violence derived from the military parity between the parties, the peace agreements at the end of the wars were soon dead letters. They were temporary truces. Colombia experienced another seven major civil wars through 1902, and Uruguay, another five through 1904. In all twelve cases of conflict, civil wars were prompted by "party revolutions," that is, rebellions by the opposition.

From an economic perspective, the foundational civil wars were incredibly destructive.

Colombia. The War of the Supreme Captains cut flows of international trade in half. Dozens of landowners went bankrupt because both armies were voracious consumers of cattle. The opportunity costs were likewise enormous. Incipient progress in the growth of tropical exports, especially cacao, was aborted. The first efforts at steam navigation of the Magdalena River, which a decade later would prove a key artery in Colombia's communications, were abandoned. Tellingly, the war wrecked the only steamboat that had begun to make regular trips. Only one conflict, the Thousand Days' War (1899–1902), was more destructive than the foundational war. Thousands of young men died. As a consequence of the war, Colombia lost the isthmus of Panama, which took advantage of weakness in Bogotá and support from Washington, DC, to gain independence in 1904.

The direct damage caused by the worst wars was dwarfed by the economic opportunities lost to the fear among investors that conflict, open or latent, had become a natural state of affairs. The relevant comparison is provided by the area of the Paraíba Valley in south-central Brazil. Paraíba began to export coffee in the 1830s, and by the 1840s, the economy of Rio de Janeiro was booming. In Colombia, the land suitable for coffee cultivation was more dispersed than in Brazil. Yet almost all Colombian regions produced coffee of higher quality. Open or latent civil war retarded the initiation of large-scale coffee exports by no less than four decades. Only in the last decade of the nineteenth century did coffee begin to dominate Colombian exports.

Uruguay. The Big War was the most destructive in the country's history. It caused a demographic and economic catastrophe. Cattle fell from over six million head in 1843 to two million in 1852. The rural economy of Uruguay returned to subsistence levels. A higher but less visible economic cost of the Big War in Uruguay was the lost opportunities to modernize the export sector. Buenos Aires provides a reasonable counterfactual. Starting from a nearly identical baseline, marked by a pastoral economy centered on extensive ranching of wild cattle, during the 1840s Buenos Aires began to export lambs' wool to Continental Europe. The wool industry had strong productive linkages to the other sectors and thereby caused the takeoff of Buenos Aires's economy. Before the Big War, a few pioneers in Uruguay had begun to experiment with sheep farming. Yet the war stopped progress in its tracks. As a consequence, Uruguay missed critical years of sustained international demand. Its sheep-farming sector lagged that of Buenos Aires by about two decades. The lag, which prevented Uruguay from becoming an export economy in the nineteenth century, was almost entirely attributable to civil conflict.

Pacification through Electoral Reform

Civil wars created political parties in Colombia and Uruguay, and *then* political parties engaged in chronic civil war. Additionally, civil wars caused economic backwardness. Pacification became a strong demand by economic elites who saw business opportunities evaporate year after year.

Only political parties, the very source of the problem, could provide a solution. Enduring peace proved difficult to achieve. Pacification required that political parties overcome a large collective-action problem, for the expected partisan gain from insurrection was usually higher than the share of economic prosperity derived from collective peace. Another obstacle to pacification was the government's lack of credibility. To appease the opposition, governments could promise to share positions of power. Yet governments repeatedly reneged on their promises as soon as the opposition party demobilized and the revolutionary threat subsided. In the last four decades of the nineteenth century, Colombian and Uruguayan parties made various attempts at pacification, all relying on different forms of power sharing. Most of them provided transitory relief. Only at the very end of the century did parties discover techniques to make promises of power sharing credible and peace sustainable.

Colombia. In the mid-1890s, the ruling Conservative Party of Colombia split into a moderate faction and a hardliner one. Both factions expected a Liberal rebellion motivated by exclusion from power. Conservatives had monopolized government positions, at all levels and in all branches, for an entire decade. What differentiated the moderates from the hardliners was the willingness to avoid a new civil war by sharing power with the Liberals. Hardliners controlled the presidency and were the strongest bloc in congress. In 1898, the moderates drafted a reform to introduce minority representation through the incomplete vote formula, which would allocate two-thirds of the seats at stake in each jurisdiction to the majority party and the remaining third to the runner-up, thus securing Liberal representation. A moderate Conservative, acknowledged as Colombia's top expert in electoral engineering, claimed that the preservation of majoritarian rule was equivalent "to declaring that only the party in power has the right to vote, consolidating a tyranny by scientific means."[15]

When moderates proposed the formula of the incomplete vote, Rafael Uribe Uribe, the only representative of the opposition in congress, led its defense. He claimed that "Colombia's biggest problem is that of peace. This problem can only be solved in one way: by giving justice to the Liberal Party."[16] Justice for the Liberal Party had a very precise meaning: the breakup of the Conservative monopoly over government positions. Uribe reviewed Colombia's recent political history in order to make a prediction. "In thirteen years, only two Liberal representatives went to Congress. . . . We have never had a seat in the Senate. . . . We have had nobody in the ministries, in the governorships, in the judicial branch or the electoral boards to protect and defend us." Uribe's prediction was a threat of war:

> I am not coming here as the Roman consul before the Senate of Carthage, bringing in his uniform the options "war or peace" for you to choose. I am just predicting the unavoidable. I am just warning that this, which today is a peaceful petition in favor of our rights, if you deny it, tomorrow will become a demand backed by the arms. . . . Give us the freedom to make public and defend our rights with the vote, the quill, and the lips; otherwise, nobody in the world will have enough power to silence the barrels of our rifles.[17]

Faced with the option of concession or war, hardline Conservatives chose war. No politician in 1898 foresaw the devastating magnitude that the war would have. The "little skirmish of three months" that some in the government had predicted ended up becoming the Thousand Days' War (October 1898–November 1902), the most destructive civil war in nineteenth-century Latin America. After the Conservative victory in the Battle of Palonegro (May 1900), the Liberals' chances of capturing the government evaporated. Yet Liberals kept fighting, with the expectation of extracting political reform.

Probably both Conservative and Liberal politicians would have changed their decisions on the eve of war if they had known that, by the end of 1903, thousands of young men would die, the territory of Panama would be lost, and the Colombian economy would suffer four years of paralysis in some regions and massive destruction in others. Preventing future wars became a top priority for political leaders of almost every affiliation. For the first time since the creation of parties, a broad bipartisan agreement was created in the second half of 1902, and it consolidated after the loss of Panama in 1904. The consensus was built around a shared diagnosis of past ills and future remedies. Several hardline elements in the Conservative Party converged on the vision of the moderates, who insisted that the blame for political chaos had to be put on the *vieja iniquidad* (old injustice), a celebrated formula to describe the persistent political exclusion of the opposition.[18]

Two treaties, signed by different Liberal generals, put an end to the war. In both treaties, the government committed to sharing power with the Liberals (Tratado de Neerlandia, clause 14, and Tratado de Wisconsin, clause 7-B). In the 1904 elections, with the support of moderate Conservatives and Liberals, General Rafael Reyes was chosen president under the slogan "Peace and Concord." Soon after he took office, a stalemate with congress, formed under the previous presidential term, led Reyes to dissolve it. The step helped Reyes to marginalize remaining hardline Conservatives. Instead of calling another congress, the new president decided to reform the constitution and call a constitutional assembly, which was inaugurated in March 1905.

The new president and the assembly promptly applied the remedy prescribed in the postwar shared diagnosis. In April, the executive power proposed a constitutional amendment introducing "minority representation."

The legislative process was as fast as formal procedures allowed (four days), and the amendment received unanimous support. The bipartisan commission that studied the proposal claimed, "This reform is the peace for the future; it is the first time that national unity is formally proclaimed . . . for no Constitution since 1811 had had the courage to acknowledge the right of minorities to be represented; that was the cause of the countless civil wars that have ruined the country."[19]

A few weeks later, a new electoral code was approved, in which the incomplete vote was the specific formula chosen to fulfill the amendment's goal. Article 33 stated that two-thirds of the seats in both houses of congress, as well as in regional legislatures and electoral boards, would correspond to the electoral majority, and the remaining one-third would correspond to the minority.

The legacy of electoral reform in Colombia was a durable peace. The causal linkage between power sharing and pacification is reflected in the testimony of the finest analysts of the time, including Julio H. Palacio and Pedro Navarro. According to Palacio, the blockage of the reform proposal by hardline Conservatives in 1898 "was the *causa principalísma* [most principal cause] of the devastating war." And vice versa: "for me, the true father of peace in Colombia . . . is General Reyes, who facilitated minority representation. Without [him], the peace treaties of Neerlandia and Wisconsin would have been dead letters for a long time, and another war would have disintegrated the country."[20] Navarro, in turn, confidently asserted that the incomplete vote was "the best law of Reyes's dictatorship: Colombia owes to it the internal peace that it has enjoyed for the last 33 years [writing in 1935], the basis of its progress and material well-being."[21]

Uruguay. Although the incomplete vote is an exotic species of electoral rule, it found fertile soil in Uruguay, where it replaced majoritarian rule in 1898. In Uruguay, reform was introduced by a government that feared revolution by the opposition more than it feared electoral defeat. Like the Conservatives in Colombia, in late nineteenth-century Uruguay, the Colorado party was confident that it had the support of the majority of the population. Yet the Colorado government sponsored an electoral reform that produced a substantial cut of its share of seats in congress. The only possible strategic motivation for reform, then, was appeasement. Like the Colombian Liberals, the Blancos in Uruguay proved that they were willing to go to war to challenge the Colorados' monopoly of government positions.

The institutionalization of minority representation in Uruguay was a direct consequence of the uprising led by the Blanco warlord Aparicio Saravia. The intimate connection between pacification and electoral reform is revealed by the fact that the introduction of the incomplete vote was the main clause in the Pacto de la Cruz (September 1897), the peace agreement that put a formal end to Saravia's rebellion. The rebels also extracted the concession of increasing the number of departments controlled by Blanco bosses from three to six.

In 1903, the Colorado government appointed Blanco leaders to only five departments, that is, one less than the number agreed in 1898. Saravia revolted again in 1904. The new rebellion was Uruguay's last civil war. Saravia mobilized thousands of rural workers, but only a few Blanco caudillos and an even smaller number of urban leaders adhered to his movement. Saravia was defeated, and pacification was accomplished. The 1904 uprising provided critical lessons to both parties. From the initiation of the rebellion, the Colorados learned that even small violations of the power-sharing agreements could instigate armed opposition. From the end of the rebellion, the Blancos learned that the share of power obtained in 1898 was large enough to please most of its leaders and dissuade them from taking military risks.

In 1905, sensing that Uruguay was entering a new era of peaceful co-existence between the two parties, José Espalter, a prominent Colorado legislator, drew natural counterfactual conclusions:

> Those who live in the country know that we could have avoided the Blanco revolution of 1897, and perhaps all other rebellions as well, if we had introduced an electoral system that allowed Blancos to have a minority in Congress. Someone heard one of our great statesmen saying: "give Blancos twelve legislators, and we will prevent war." War was not prevented because the opposition was not granted even one representative. The basis of peace was the law of incomplete vote, which allowed the minority to get a third of the representation. The law of the third is in fact the peace![22]

Conclusions:
Comparative Party-Driven State Formation

In Mexico, partisan division, and the dynamics of party competition, unintentionally unified the largest territory. Yet Mexico is not the only case of party-driven state formation. Colombia and Uruguay provide additional evidence of the impact of party formation on territory consolidation and violence monopolization. As in Mexico, competing partisan forces in Colombia and Uruguay forged supraregional networks connecting distant political elites when other linkages uniting the regions of an emerging state were virtually nonexistent. In all three cases, two parties dominated the political arena, Conservatives versus Liberals in Colombia and Mexico, and Colorados versus Blancos in Uruguay.

In all three cases, the transition from protoparties to full-blown political parties comprised not only the creation of electoral machineries for voter mobilization but also the development of rival armies for partisan warfare, including an arsenal of weapons, a cohort of warlords ready to lead large contingents into the battlefield, and constant preparations for insurrection when in opposition.

The amphibious nature of political parties, in part electoral machines and in part partisan armies, is the key to understanding the separation between territory consolidation and violence monopolization in Mexico, Colombia, and Uruguay. In all three cases, the borders of the territory consolidated decades before violence was monopolized. The temporal gap separating the two fundamental dimensions of state formation provides the conditions for the existence of countries in which territorial borders are demarcated but violence is atomized, oligopolized, or duopolized. Since all three countries were dominated by two parties, each with its own military capabilities, Mexico, Colombia, and Uruguay were marked by a persistent duopoly of violence, which, in line with the fundamental security dilemma, caused open or latent civil war. Civil wars have many repercussions. One of them, critical in all three cases, was to retard the very process of trade-led state formation, as pacification was the chief precondition for the expansion of the export sector.

In all three cases, paraphrasing Tilly, parties made war, and war made parties. Each round of conflict increased the internal cohesion of the contenders, intensified old animosities, and mobilized new loyalties, especially among hitherto neutral citizens who suffered the loss of family and friends, as well as confiscation of property in the course of pillaging raids by one of the parties.

In all three cases, party formation unintentionally contributed to territory consolidation by creating multiregion coalitions. In all three cases, party formation was inimical to violence monopolization in the short and medium run. Yet, once fully formed, parties were crucial agents in the transition from violent contestation of power to peaceful, purely electoral, political competition. When led by parties, civil wars, even if prolonged, do not last forever. War ends when one of the parties defeats the other one (Mexico) or when, worn out by conflict, both parties agree to sustain a durable truce and jointly decide to pursue political conflict by other means (Colombia and Uruguay).

Lord-Driven State Formation

Central America, Venezuela, and Peru

WARLORDS WERE CENTRAL POLITICAL agents in the critical period of state formation in Latin America. Five Latin American states were formed by caudillos: Venezuela, Peru, Guatemala, Ecuador, and Paraguay. Naturally, not all warlords formed states. The five caudillos who succeeded at state formation are a special selection among dozens of warlords who emerged in the region before 1850. They rose first as a consequence of improvised methods of military mobilization against Iberian rule, by which a revolutionary center delegated defense responsibilities to a local notable— like Artigas in present-day Uruguay or Obando in present-day Colombia. Later, lords gained prominence in the diffusion of private armies as a consequence of the failure to form states by the first generation of postindependence rulers—like Facundo Quiroga in the Andean ministates of present-day Argentina and Rafael Carrera in the Central American Federation.

State-making lords are the closest type of state-formation agent to the western European warrior. Latin American lords and western European warriors share the initial source of power that allowed them to launch their political careers, that is, military capabilities, including primarily clients who worked the fields in times of peace and were ready for combat in times of war.

Yet the five Latin American lords who succeeded at state formation were different from the western European warriors in two fundamental ways. First, in an apparent paradox, a common denominator of all five lords was their dual success both at state-*breaking* and at state-*making*. They formed *small* states after breaking *large* ones. Gaspar de Francia formed Paraguay in the early 1810s as a successor state of the United Provinces of the River

Plate, which collapsed in 1820; Venezuela under Páez and Ecuador under Flores caused in 1830 the breakdown of the (Gran) Colombian state founded by Bolívar; in 1839 Peru broke away from the Peru-Bolivian Confederation, an attempt by General Santa Cruz, a former Bolívar lieutenant, to unite Lower and Upper Peru; finally, Rafael Carrera led Guatemala to independence and gave the death blow to the Central American Federation in 1838.

The link between rural lord and small size is straightforward. The size of the splinter state was compatible with the extension of the clientelistic network at the basis of caudillo power. For all five caudillos, larger states would have created risks to their political career by incorporating regions with new aspirants to central power. The contrast with the western European warrior could hardly be sharper. The western European warrior wanted to incorporate as much territory as possible. The limits to territorial expansion were given by the risks of overextension, that is, of absorbing more regions than the warrior was capable of defending. The Latin American caudillo built a coalitional basis for internal supremacy, not a military bastion for international survival. The Latin American lord demarcated the territory in which he could reign supreme, irrespective of the outside geopolitical threats, which were largely negligible, as noted in Part 1. The difference in scale of lord-driven state formation between Latin America and Europe revealed the fact that, in contrast to the anarchic international society surrounding western European state formation, states in Latin America were formed under a clear international hierarchy, topped by Great Britain, France, and, in the case of Mesoamerica, the United States.

The second difference with the European warrior is that, once in power, the Latin American lord rather quickly mutated into a "merchant," a market-maker who prioritized the expansion of commercial opportunities over the expansion of territorial possessions. Like political entrepreneurs and party leaders, rural lords became experts in supplying the two key class goods, pacification and infrastructure, required to set in motion the export sector of the economy. The only exception to the pattern is Paraguay, which had no commodity to offer to international markets. Not surprisingly, Paraguay is the only case of war-led state formation (a venture that half a century later proved dramatically suicidal).

Beyond the five state-making caudillos, the vast majority of rural lords followed one of three distinct trajectories: they were co-opted by political entrepreneurs (e.g., Urquiza by Mitre in Argentina); they were absorbed into the networks of emerging political parties (e.g., Obando by the Colombian Liberal Party or Álvarez by the Mexican one); or the region they dominated was annexed by a larger territory (like Rosas's Buenos Aires into Argentina or Bento's Piratini into Brazil). Hence, with the exception of the founding five, which were (large-scale) state-breakers and (small-scale) state-makers, the vast majority of rural lords became *state-taking* rural lords.

This chapter is organized in three sections and analyzes lord-driven state-breaking and state-making in three cases: the collapse of the Central American Federation (1822–38), followed by the rise of Guatemala as its main successor state; the formation of Venezuela in the aftermath of the dissolution of (Gran) Colombia (late 1820s); and the breakdown of the Peru-Bolivian Confederation and the emergence of Peru (early 1840s). Each case illustrates a key aspect of the process in pure form.

The collapse of the Central American Federation is a case in which a lord-driven process of small-scale state formation trumped the large-scale process of party-driven state formation. As in Mexico and Colombia, the colonial legacy structured in Central America a party system based on the Conservative-versus-Liberal cleavage. Yet dissatisfaction with liberal reform gave a rural warlord, Rafael Carrera, the opportunity to form a "popular conservative" coalition, which could maximize power over the truncated territory of present-day Guatemala. Union with El Salvador or Nicaragua complicated Carrera's professional career. The rise of Venezuela under the leadership of José Antonio Páez illustrates the rapid assimilation by a triumphant caudillo of dominant economic interests, which in the case of Venezuela centered on the promotion of coffee and cacao exports from the coast. Finally, the rise of Peru under the leadership of Ramón Castilla occurred in the aftermath of the caudillo's collaboration with the destruction of the Peru-Bolivian Confederation. Peruvian state formation was based on the export of a fertilizer, guano, that, in contrast to all other export commodities in Latin America, required almost no physical infrastructure. Guano also provided the ruler who happened to be in power during the price boom an instant winning lottery ticket manifested in torrential flows of monetary resources to consolidate his small-scale territorial project.

The Breakdown of the Central American Federation and Carreras's Guatemala

Overview

Central America gained independence from Spain in 1822 as a jurisdiction of Mexico. A year later, Central America seceded from Mexico. It remained a single state for almost two decades (Map 10.1). Its founders called it the Repúblicas Unidas del Centro de América (United Republics of the Center of America), from which the modern toponym derives.

Central America is important not for its geographical scope—the size of the entire isthmus is only half that of Bolivia. Central America is important for theoretical reasons. The colonial legacy made Central America resemble Mexico and Colombia. A deep-rooted hierarchy of corporate bodies, including the church, a rentier aristocracy, and merchant guilds, endowed with a range of institutional privileges, combined with an extensive network of cities and towns to create the precursors of classical oligarchic parties after independence. Indeed, during the first two decades after independence, Central America developed the rudiments of a two-party system, pitting conservatives, or *serviles*, against liberals, or *fiebres*. The partisan political arena was thus a replica of the Mexican and Colombian ones. The Central American liberals became the strongest supraregional political organization ever known in the isthmus. Like Liberalism in Mexico, Central American liberalism supplied linkages between cities and towns that otherwise had no connection.

Yet Central America fragmented into five small countries despite the fact that the territory was only a fraction of that of Mexico and of Colombia, where a party-driven process succeeded at large-scale territory consolidation. Why did nearly identical initial conditions, rooted in a colonial legacy that translated into the same partisan cleavage after independence, produce such a different outcome?

Two factors drove Central American disintegration: the emergence of a rural warlord and the availability of multiple ports. Each factor played a different role. The caudillo, Rafael Carrera, derailed the large-scale process of state formation initiated by the parties, especially the liberals led by Francisco Morazán, Carrera's nemesis. Carrera chose to consolidate his patrimonial bastion, present-day Guatemala, as an independent state. If a

Map 10.1. Central American Confederation, 1823–41

lord-driven process explains the *change* of scale in state-formation projects, the availability of ports explains why ministates became the *stable* solution. Costa Rica had four main cities, all of them along the road built in colonial times connecting both extremes of the isthmus. One of the cities in Costa Rica, Alajuela, was linked to a port along the Pacific coast. At the time, Alajuela was as important as San José, which became the capital only in 1838. Costa Rica pioneered coffee exports in Central America, and foreign trade through its own port was the fiscal pillar for sovereignty. Nicaragua had ports on both its Pacific and Atlantic coasts, and by the time of the U.S. expansion to the West (1850s), it provided the most efficient transoceanic transit route. El Salvador had since the late eighteenth century specialized in the export of indigo, a natural dyewood, and was endowed with multiple ports along its Pacific coastline. Finally, from the ports of Trujillo and Omoa in the Atlantic, Honduras could trade with Belize, the British colony that functioned as a distribution center for English manufactures. Belize's merchant community was interested in purchasing from Honduras silver and mahogany wood, which was transshipped to western Europe. The performance of the export sector in Central America in the mid-nineteenth century was clearly the poorest in Latin America. By the early nineteenth century, its main exports were indigo, cochineal (another natural dye), and small quantities of precious metals. Revenue collected in the ports of each region was barely enough to finance one level of government, that of each individual minirepublic. Sustaining a second level of government, that of the federation of the five states, was a colossal fiscal challenge. Most of the time, most of the ministates were reluctant to share the revenues of their own ports. The isolated expressions of fiscal generosity toward Central American integration in the late 1820s became even less frequent in the 1830s and extinguished in the 1840s.

Carrera broke the state of the Central America Federation and created the successor state of present-day Guatemala. Ports in the other four minirepublics made the divided political geography of present-day Central America irreversible.

Four Central American Futures
in the 1820s

Reading history backward is a ticket to causal fallacies. In the 1820s, the creation of the five minirepublics of Central America was only one among several possible outcomes, and it was certainly not the most likely one. Three alternative outcomes were viable.

The first alternative was union with Mexico. The outcome was a mere continuation of the political geography of colonial times. Union with Mexico was in fact the first response by leaders of independent Central America. In 1822, the elites of Guatemala City, which would become a key promoter of separation from the rest of Central America fifteen years later, were wholehearted supporters of the monarchic project of the Mexican general Iturbide. The elites of Guatemala City had been the traditional beneficiaries of Spanish colonial rule. Led by the Aycinena clan, they were a true aristocracy of large landowners. The program of the Mexican Empire, which was a reaction against the liberal revolt in Spain, offered the only guarantees of continued aristocratic privilege. They were the kernel of Central America's Conservative Party. The union with independent Mexico lasted only one year. It broke down together with the downfall of Iturbide as the emperor of Mexico in 1823, as analyzed in Chapter 8. If liberal forces outside Central America had not toppled Iturbide's government, the Guatemalan aristocracy would have had no reason to leave Mexico.

The second potential outcome was disintegration into dozens of microstates. This counterfactual scenario has a solid factual basis. Domingo Sarmiento, writing in 1850, in his usual provocative tone, claimed that "Central America has made a sovereign state of every village."[1] In present-day Guatemala, the East and the West were largely separate political entities for long periods. Old rivalries peaked in 1838, when the western city of Quetzaltenango created the ephemeral republic of Los Altos. Los Altos had its own port in the Pacific, its economic elites resented the power of the Guatemalan merchants, and it obtained recognition from the federal government as the "sixth state" of the union (Map 10.2). Similarly, in Nicaragua, the city of León had recurrent economic and political clashes with the city of Granada, which explains the emergence of Managua, a smaller city, as a neutral capital. The historian Jordana Dym has documented the political vitality of more than thirty cities and towns in the 1830s and 1840s.[2]

The final alternative outcome was the continuation of the federation, a unified isthmian republic as it existed between 1823 and 1839. The viability of the federation faced serious structural challenges, including mainly the lack of fiscal resources to fund the two levels of government above the municipal one, that is, state and federal personnel. Yet, in the 1850s, similar fiscal challenges were not less threatening for the Colombian federation and the Argentine confederation (present-day Argentina minus the wealthy Buenos Aires). In both cases, union prevailed. The fall of the Central American Federation is a direct result of a sequence involving two major political movements: (a) the radical liberal reform launched in the late 1820s, which included a frontal attack against the Catholic Church and the introduction of a flat personal tax, and (b) the antiliberal peasant rebellion in the densely populated area of La Montaña in Guatemala in 1837.

As all things political, none of the smaller components in the sequence, from the preludes of the radical reform to the success of the popular reac-

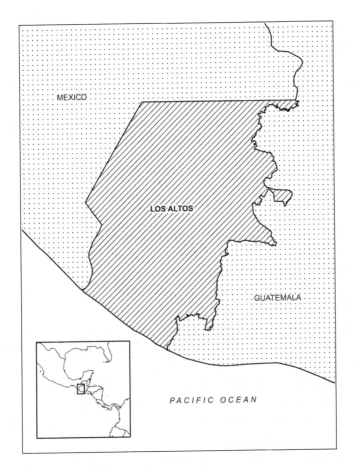

Map 10.2. Los Altos, 1838–40

tion, were inevitable. A fragile chain of events involving curious twists of fortune runs through them. Radical reform would have been avoided had a moderate liberal leader become president in the first decade after independence. Such a leader was available: José Cecilio del Valle. He was highly respected by the oligarchy and had a large popular following. Bad luck twice prevented him from becoming president. He won the elections in 1825 and 1834. In 1825, a last-minute conspiracy by a few members of the congress caused the congress to rule that the popular vote was not decisive enough. Congress selected the runner-up. In 1834, del Valle's victory against a radical incumbent was so resounding that no amount of postelection maneuvering could undermine it. But del Valle, already ill during the electoral campaign, died only weeks before inauguration. Likewise, radical reform would not have provoked an angry reaction by the indigenous and mestizo population had Guatemala not been hit by an epidemic of cholera morbus in 1837. Conservative priests manipulated the health crisis to make thousands of parishioners believe that it was divine punishment for liberal heresy.

Carrera, the Lord

Carrera was a unique lord in the history of Latin America. He was the only caudillo to reach the pinnacle of power whose original source of authority was not participation in the wars of independence or land ownership. Carrera was a *ladino*, and he was no exception to the strong correlation between mixed blood and poverty. Born in Guatemala City, lack of opportunity pushed him to try his luck in the hill district of Mita, where he transitioned from swineherd to janitor of a rural parish. Carrera was illiterate, but the priest took him as a protégé, provided the rudiments of an education, and helped him marry into a family that owned a small farm. His rise to political power was meteoric. He moved from the bottom to the top between 1835 and 1840, when he was only twenty-six years old. His stay in power was perpetual. He died in office in 1865.

A chief source of Carrera's power was his personal charisma. No theory properly accounts for charisma. Yet charisma was necessary but not sufficient in Carrera's trajectory. Carrera's *rise* to power combines structural causes, the stratification of Guatemala's society since colonial times, and historical ones, for it belonged in a sequence of peasant reaction against the liberal experiment to radically reengineer Central America's society in the 1830s. Carreras's *perpetuation* in power was a purely political phenomenon, rooted in his ability to hold together a coalition that united the most privileged members of the Guatemalan aristocracy and the vast majority of poor peasants. For the peasant component of the coalition, Carrera was a savior, the "son of God," who restored the ancestral economic and cultural lifestyle, threatened by liberal privatization of communal land (*ejidos*), modernization of the justice system, and secularization of education. The Guatemalan peasantry had practiced subsistence agriculture since time immemorial, and Carrera's abolition of the poll tax introduced by the liberals, which peasants failed to distinguish from the hated indigenous contribution of colonial times, caused a small but perceptible improvement in the material welfare of the common folk. A modest economic investment yielded enormous political gains. The popularity of Carrera's measures earned him permanent support among the largest constituency in the land.

Guatemalan aristocrats, the other component of Carrera's coalition, initially obtained from Carrera a darker but crucial benefit, the guarantee that the indigenous rebellion against liberal reform would not get out of hand and make the aristocracy its next political victim. Carrera had the authority to transform peasant unrest into destructive class warfare. In a display of extraordinary political realism, the aristocracy did not think twice about courting the favor of Carrera. From their perspective, Carrera was the undisputed leader of a large-scale protection racket. Carrera did not miss the opportunity to offer the aristocracy his services as a necessary gendarme. He protected the aristocracy from irreparable damage that he could inflict with a simple command to his peasant army. Over time, the deal between Carrera and the aristocracy improved for both sides, as Carrera's private wealth expanded to make his new economic interests indistinguishable from those of the old aristocracy. If Carrera did not become a social member of the aristocracy, it was because he had a political business to attend to, the continued support of the popular classes, and because no amount of property could erase the mark of his humble origins. The aristocracy, especially the Aycinena clan, had been exiled by the liberals, but through Carrera, it regained formal positions of power, in government, church, and university. It contributed key technical expertise to Carrera's policy making. A social rival of the peasants in colonial times, the old aristocracy helped Carrera build a hegemony that was conservative and popular at the same time.

The next subsection documents each of the periods in the rise of Carrera as the dominant lord of Guatemala and the parallel collapse of the Central American union. The analytical focus is on the coalitional dynamics driving the failure of large-scale state formation and the success of small-scale state formation.

Collapse of Central America, Rise of Guatemala

Liberal Reform: 1829-36. Very much as the independence of Mexico gained critical support from a conservative faction that abhorred the liberal revolution in Spain of 1820, Central America's independence from Mexico was embraced by the Guatemalan aristocracy after the defeat of the Mexican emperor Iturbide at the hands of republican forces in 1823. Regime change in Spain caused Mexican independence, and regime change in Mexico caused Central American independence.

Yet liberal threats to the aristocracy of Guatemala City were not only Mexican. In a few years, they developed inside the isthmus itself, especially in the city of San Salvador. Liberals of San Salvador, supported by indigo farmers who resented the monopolistic policies of the Guatemala merchant guild (*consulado*), built a multiregion political movement to abolish the legacy of colonial institutions. Liberals rejected corporate privileges and immunities, which favored the military, large import-export merchants, the clergy, and the faculty of the University of San Carlos in Guatemala City. They campaigned against the power of the church and colonial taxes, including the tithe (a property tax earmarked to support the church) and the indigenous contribution. Liberals also opposed collective property rights, which included communal indigenous land (*ejidos*) but especially the rural estate in the hands of the church. Liberals pursued the economic and social modernization of Central America through the privatization of land; the creation of a large market of free and mobile labor, unrestricted by ties to communal land and subsistence agriculture; secular education; infrastructure development; and immigration of high-skilled workers, a prerequisite of which was religious toleration to make Central America inviting to Protestant communities.

Together with a program, liberals had purely political ambitions. Central American liberals were educated minorities, in general from secondary cities, who had been excluded from the circles of colonial power in Guatemala City. The continuation of colonial institutions prevented them from occupying influential political offices. Liberals wanted to transform society because the prevailing institutions of land and labor, of Hispanic and pre-Hispanic origins, prevented the emergence of a class of entrepreneurial citizens who would appreciate the value of the liberal program. The Guatemalan Catholic Church in particular was held responsible for conservative hegemony by spreading a version of Catholicism that made challenges to traditional lifestyles, including deep-rooted social hierarchies, inconceivable.

In 1826, under the leadership of Francisco Morazán, a loose coalition of liberal politicians from El Salvador and Honduras revolted against the first government of the Central American Federation, presided over by the conservative elite of Guatemala City. A three-year civil war followed. Liberals won, despite the fact that the government had the economic support of the *consulado*, control of the inchoate Central American army, and the church's blessing. Morazán became president of Central America in 1830, but it was Mariano Gálvez, the new liberal governor of Guatemala beginning in 1831, who launched the most radical and comprehensive liberal reform. He aimed at liquidating the power of the church and the *consulado*. Although ideological motivations played a part, Gálvez's incentives were largely political. He would not be able to consolidate support for his position and program if the institutional strongholds of conservative loyalty retained veto power.

The speed and scope of Gálvez's political action were overwhelming. No other country in Latin America was at the time undertaking a liberal reform of similar magnitude. Gálvez exiled conservative leaders, including the Aycinena clan and the archbishop of Guatemala. He confiscated church property and privatized large tracts of land in the eastern lowlands for future colonization by English and German farmers. He secularized birth, marriage, and death and introduced legal divorce. The University of San Carlos, run by the church, was closed. Hundreds of schools under government control were planned. Corporate immunities benefiting generals, bishops, and the aristocracy were eliminated. The end of the *fueros* was only one part of a complete overhaul of the judicial system. The cornerstone of the reform was the Livingston Code, including trial by jury. The code was designed in Louisiana, but the state legislature considered that it was ahead of its time and decided not to implement it. Central American liberals, by contrast, wanted to believe that their society was ready for it.

The power of the *consulado*, which in addition to fixing prices was responsible for local public works, was seriously undermined. The traditional merchant houses of Guatemala lost their commercial monopolies. Tariffs on imports were drastically reduced. The colonial taxes were abolished.

Yet, to build infrastructure, an obsession shared by Morazán and Gálvez, who were right about the need to improve transportation in order to foster tropical exports, liberals introduced a two-dollar personal tax and mandated the contribution of labor for building roads.

From Local Protest to General Rebellion: 1837. In the mid-1830s, the liberals could stop worrying about the enemy they had feared the most: the colonial aristocracy. Yet the same package of reforms that weakened the privileged minority provoked the unstoppable resistance of the lower classes. The personal tax was the undoing of liberal reform and government. Quantitatively small, the tax forced a qualitative change in the peasant lifestyle. To meet their obligations, peasants had no option but to abandon subsistence agriculture and find jobs in the open market, especially in the farms of cochineal, the leading export during the liberal government. If they could not pay the tax, they were sent to prison.

Three additional circumstances turned peasant resentment into open rebellion in 1837, the annus horribilis for Central American liberals. The first was the support of priests. The list of the church's grievances was long. Many parishes were closed, the church's control of civil affairs was curtailed, ecclesiastical property was confiscated, and colonization plans brought the specter of religious contamination through Protestant settlers. Although the Archdiocese of Guatemala City suffered the biggest losses, it was the priests of rural villages, direct witnesses of the peasants' anger at what seemed the reimposition of the colonial contribution, who mobilized parishioners and cemented a reactionary coalition. Liberals miscalculated the damage of the poll taxes and were overoptimistic about the speed at which infrastructure development would translate into an improvement in overall material welfare, but their most serious mistake was to underestimate the influence of the priests of rural communities. An American observer left valuable ethnographic evidence: "Besides officiating in all the services of the church, visiting the sick, and burying the dead, my worthy host [a typical rural priest] was looked up to by every Indian in the village as a counselor, friend, and father. The door of the convent was always open, and Indians were constantly resorting to him. . . . And he was the right hand of the alcalde."[3]

Second, a cholera outbreak in Belize entered the eastern section of Guatemala in 1837. Peasant communities panicked. The church blamed liberalism. When state officials brought medications, local priests forced them to drink the whole contents of the bottles to prove it was not poison. The officials died of an overdose. The event was taken as confirmation that liberals were planning the extermination of the peasant population.

Finally there was Carrera. Among the many measures taken by Gálvez to prevent the spread of cholera, he quarantined several villages and created patrols to enforce the policy. Carrera was placed at the head of the patrol of the Mataquescuintla village. Empowering Carrera proved suicidal for liberals in the long run. Yet it was not a mistake at the time. No one could have guessed the repercussions of Carrera's intervention. Carrera had gained local influence by helping peasants who had been jailed for tax delinquency to regain freedom.[4] In 1837, Carrera used the power delegated by the government to join a peasant protest in the nearby village of Santa Rosa. The protest was fading, but Carrera's military talent, physical force, and courage turned defeat into victory. It was Carrera's baptism as a charismatic leader.

Carrera, who was barely literate when he entered politics, provided a sophisticated interpretation of the small folk's reaction to liberal policies, with a comparative assessment of gradual reform versus shock therapy. He was less critical of the contents of the reform than of the manner in which it was introduced: "When attempts are made suddenly to attack and change the customs of the people, it provokes in them such emotion that, no matter how sound the intention of those who seek to change their traditional ways and institutions, they rise in protest."[5] Carrera made no mention of his own ambitions for power. Yet, if they did not cause the rebellion, they were fundamental for its success.

The Santa Rosa rebellion placed Carrera in command of two thousand improvised soldiers. Carrera's army excelled at plundering and terrorizing, and at various junctures, it was indistinguishable from a large-scale banditry gang. However, personal ambition and advice from the priests prompted Carrera to gradually reshape his army. In only six months after the outbreak of the rebellion, Carrera embraced a political agenda that was much larger than the protection of his village.

In October 1837, Carrera issued a six-item manifesto of his antiliberal rebellion. Three clauses must have been inspired by conservative ideologues, working through the rural priests who had Carrera's ear. They urged the government to bring back the Guatemalan archbishop and restore the power of the church, to provide amnesty for the leaders exiled since 1829, and to abolish the Livingston Code. From the perspective of the peasants' material life, the key point of the manifesto was the abolition of the poll tax. The last two clauses were eminently political: protection of persons and property, and respect for Carrera's orders under the pain of execution. Perhaps because of their apparent simplicity, the two political clauses have not received major interpretive attention from historians. Yet, for all important political actors at the time, especially the conservatives, the two clauses combined to convey the unambiguous message that Carrera was in a position either to destroy or to protect private property. The offer was to accept Carrera's political leadership or see Carrera turn his army into a predatory Behemoth.

In the final months of 1837, the Aycinena clan and the dioceses of Guatemala conspired to make a deal with Carrera. They accepted the rural caudillo's leadership and decided to support his bid for power. Only such an arrangement explains a new proclamation in which Carrera demanded the abolition of the law of marriage and divorce and the termination of the English colonization contracts.

Civil War and Collapse: 1837–40. Gálvez responded to the rebellion with repression. Despite scoring important military victories, Gálvez failed. Liberal victories had two counterproductive consequences. They taught Carrera how to hide, regroup, and initiate guerrilla warfare. Because of the brutality of Gálvez's methods, which included scorched-earth policies in sanctuary villages, they also helped Carrera to increase the ranks of his followers. When liberal troops were defeated in open combat or assaulted by guerrilla patrols, a priority for Carrera was to steal the enemy's arsenal in order to grow military capabilities. His campaign was launched with only a dozen old rifles. Machetes, house knives, and improvised lances were the bulk of the original arsenal.

Carrera retaliated with terrorism. In early 1838, he invaded Guatemala City with four thousand peasants. Carrera allowed his men to get drunk before the attack and loot the city. Peasants came prepared with large sisal bags. The Guatemalan elite panicked. Foreigners spoke of "hordes" threatening civilization. Liberal authorities tried everything to avoid a bloodbath. Carrera showed not only the strength of his army but also that he was still a hybrid of extortionary bandit and political rebel. Carrera demobilized his army after being paid $1,000 for himself and $10,000 for his troops. He also earned an appointment as general commander of the Mita district, with the rank of lieutenant-colonel. A sign of liberal desperation was the supply of an undefined number of weapons to Carrera, a short-term patch that risked long-term catastrophe.

With Carrera demobilized, liberals in Guatemala resumed the attack against the church. Either liberals again underestimated the likelihood that Carrera's peasant army would retaliate, or they wanted the conflict to escalate so that Morazán, the Central American president, would be forced to get involved. Carrera rebelled again in mid-1838, and Morazán recruited a large army from the entire isthmus. A duopoly of violence emerged in Central America. Each army was willing to destroy the enemy or be destroyed trying. For a year, Morazán won almost every battle. His army was able to dismantle Carrera's mobile military camp several times. Morazán committed atrocities, including the decapitation of Carrera's father-in-law, an innocent man who had repeatedly tried to dissuade Carrera from his military adventures. Atrocities sent the message that the fight had reached a point of no return.

Throughout 1838, Carrera fully embraced guerrilla tactics. Carrera's guerrillas, clearly inferior in open battle, eventually outlasted the regular army, which was underfunded and untrained in counterinsurgency. According to the British consul, the superiority of Carrera's organization rested on a simple secret: "A man who has a patch of maize corn growing, and which does not require his care for two or three weeks, instead of remaining at home decides upon joining Carrera, on the chance of picking up some sort of booty. . . . If he likes his company and the service, he prolongs his [participation in Carrera's army]."[6]

By 1839, the liberal army was exhausted. Carrera did not miss his opportunity. He invaded Guatemala City for the second time. After crushing the liberal bastion of Los Altos, Carrera became the informal ruler of Guatemala, although not of Central America. His first two measures were to appoint guerrilla leaders, including his brother Sotero, into high-ranking army positions and to free the peasants from the poll tax.

Morazán tried to reconquer Guatemala City. This time Carrera's army was ready for open combat. In April 1840, Carrera and Morazán engaged in the final battle. Carrera won after a bloodshed. Central American liberalism died, and the Central American Federation collapsed with it.

From Large-Scale State-Breaking to Small-Scale State-Making. After the rise of Carrera in Guatemala, two related factors made the breakdown of the Central American Federation irreversible. The first was the availability of multiple ports in Central America. The second was the consolidation of a caudillo bastion within the confines of present-day Guatemala.

Each of the regions that became a country had its own port; the port was the key source of government revenues, and since the inception of the Central American union, regions had been reluctant to share revenues with the federal authorities. According to the institutional design of the union, the federal government was to be financed through customs revenues. Yet it was local authorities who appointed officials at the customhouses. Governors of each state were in direct control of the flow of revenues from foreign trade. Throughout the 1830s, governors consistently failed to meet the deadline for sending the money to the capital. A federal complaint followed, and an informal negotiation settled the matter, usually with meager results for the federal treasury. Liberal federal authorities tolerated recurrent breaches of the fiscal pact because they expected that the gradual modernization of the economy and the expansion of foreign trade would eventually generate enough revenues for both levels of government, state and federal. They did not contemplate the extraordinary expenditures required to face the Mita rebellion of 1837 and Carrera's warlordism in its aftermath.

Urged to fund an army capable of defeating Carrera's guerrillas, in 1838 Morazán decided that customs officials should be appointed by the federal government. The response was generalized rejection. All the states decided to secede, except for Guatemala, which was the only region exposed to Carrera's threat. Allegedly, secession was temporary. In fact, it became permanent. After separation, the expected growth of revenues would only make the most prosperous ministates less willing to rebuild the union. For wealthier ministates, union would most likely involve subsidizing poorer regions or funding a federal government that had no clear agenda for providing a supraregional public good that the individual states could not produce themselves. They did not need a large army to protect the economy. Given the enclave nature of the export sector in each ministate, the development of local infrastructure was more urgent than a trans-isthmian system of transportation.

In contrast to the other four states, Guatemala could have possibly created some incentives for reunification. Because of the size of its economy and population, if Guatemala had made the decision to contribute the largest share of a supraregional public good—an extensive system of primary schools, a more aggressive commercial diplomatic service, a reliable police force—the other states might have also participated. Yet, under the rule of a lord, Guatemala was unwilling to lead a new attempt at large-scale state formation.

The main reason Carrera chose to form Guatemala and did not seek unification with other states is that he preferred to reign supreme in a small country than risk political contestation in a larger political arena. His original power base was the support of the peasant villages of the Guatemalan highlands, which remained the fundamental pillar of his coalition during his twenty-five years of rule. He developed a precise knowledge of what it took to cultivate their loyalty. The only political alchemy needed was to obtain the support of the traditional aristocracy of Guatemala City. Originally, he made them an offer they could not refuse: protection from the hordes that only Carrera controlled. Over time, Carrera discovered that the methods and means for successful patronage of peasant communities were perfectly compatible with the economic and cultural agenda of the traditional Guatemalan aristocracy.

The material life of peasants improved thanks to the elimination of the poll tax and the restoration of communal lands. Such improvement did not prevent large merchants and landowners, the Aycinena clan and associates, from increasing their profits. Carrera himself became a large landowner. His will listed five haciendas and a small mine. As his wealth grew, so did his identification with the economic interests of the aristocracy. The core business was cochineal production and the importation of textiles and hardware. The production and commercialization of cochineal did not have special demands of labor, which was mobilized through multiple contractual forms, including wages, debt peonage, and sharecropping. Peasants could largely maintain their traditional economic lifestyle, based on semisubsistence agriculture, and, if they so wished, find the time to work for the commercialized sector.

The cultural agenda of the peasants and the aristocracy, thanks to generations of catechization, was virtually identical. The powers of the church and the rural priests were fully restored. Old colonial political institutions were revived, like the position of *corregidor*, a district supervisor. Under Carrera's rule, the *corregidor* in rural districts worked in close collaboration with the priest to make sure food and water and sacraments and spiritual services were in adequate supply.

In addition to small-scale state formation, the only change brought about by Carrera in relation to colonial times was *ladino* participation in political office. One of his brothers became a *corregidor* of a rural district, and another one became a high-ranked military officer. Dozens of his followers obtained positions in the military and civil administration. Yet, except for liberals, there was room for everybody in Guatemala. The Aycinena clan recovered control of the key positions. They were Carrera's financial advisers, bishops, diplomats, and university deans.

Merging with any combination of the states to the south would require Carrera to drastically alter the composition of his coalition. Moreover, the outcomes of the coalitional change were highly uncertain. Patronage worked with the indigenous communities of the Guatemalan highlands. Carrera had no idea how to incorporate the less deferential *ladino* population of Honduras, and he certainly did not want to expose himself to the pressure of new economic interest groups, like the indigo producers of El Salvador.

The Collapse of (Gran) Colombia and Páez's Venezuela

Overview

Gran Colombia was Bolívar's large-scale project of state formation. In addition to present-day Colombia, it included Panama, Venezuela, and Ecuador (Map 9.1). Gran Colombia was three times the size of France. Bolívar predicted that a big country covering all northern South America would fulfill crucial military and diplomatic goals. Union would allow resource-pooling for the creation of a larger army to defeat a common enemy. Independence would probably not have happened, and certainly would not have occurred as early as 1821 (the Battle of Carabobo), if Bolívar had not been able to draw manpower and supplies from a vast area. Also, a large country, by commanding more respect around the world, would find it easier to obtain international recognition and financial aid. Bolívar was again right. Gran Colombia earned recognition from the United States in 1822 and the United Kingdom in 1825. Additionally, English bankers extended a loan of $30 million, one of the largest issues of sovereign debt at the time. Bolívar wanted the money to build infrastructure and relaunch the export economy of the region, which suffered great losses during the wars.

Once the Spaniards were defeated, Bolívar's army became the dominant military force in northern South America. It successfully monopolized violence from Caracas to Quito. Bolívar quickly transitioned from empire-breaker to state-maker. Bolívar's army was the organizational core of the Gran Colombian state.

Bolívar held together his army for almost a decade after independence, a remarkable achievement given that he was abroad half the time, fighting royalists in Peru and Upper Peru. Yet Gran Colombia fragmented into three splinter states, Colombia (plus Panama), Venezuela, and Ecuador. Why could Bolívar's unified army not prevent the collapse of Gran Colombia?

All three splinter states combined city-ports and interior economies. Ecuador was the simplest combination: the port of Guayaquil on the Pacific coast and the more populated highlands centered on Quito. Colombia was the most complex combination, for it included two alternative Atlantic city-ports, one entrepôt in Panama, and two large, dynamic interiors: Antioquia, an enclave of prosperity based on alluvial gold mining, and Cundinamarca, the most densely populated area, which hosted the capital, Bogotá. In contrast to Colombia, where the most prosperous regions were distant from the ports, in Venezuela the most important economic region at the time of independence was the immediate hinterland of the Caribbean coast, a fertile plantation belt around Caracas, which in the eighteenth century grew tobacco, sugar, and especially cacao. Venezuela included another large agroeconomic region, the vast plains known as the Llanos in the Southwest, the most productive cattle-ranching area in all northern South America.

The Venezuelan Llanos had an indirect but decisive impact on the fragmentation of Bolívar's Gran Colombia. The Llanos were the incubator of rural warlords, like the Pampas in Argentina.

One of the *llanero* warlords, Antonio Páez, became the leader of the secession movement that broke apart Gran Colombia. In contrast to Carrera,

Páez was a hero of the revolutionary wars. He was an indispensable part of Bolívar's army. Yet, in contrast to other lieutenants of Bolívar, most notably Marshal Antonio Sucre, Páez was not a professional soldier. Economic and political conditions in the Llanos made Páez the prototypical patrimonial ruler. He made a meteoric transition from rural bandit to guerrilla leader during the first five years of the wars of independence (1809–14), which were followed by an equally impressive transformation into independence hero (1816–22).

Páez also became a major landowner. He profited from Gran Colombia's policy of rewarding achievements in the battlefield with extensive land grants. Land was as important an economic asset as it was a source of political power. Rural workers were the lord's clients. And clients, especially in cattle-ranching areas, which required a range of equestrian skills, were easily mobilized for predation, protection, or rebellion, depending on the political needs of the lord. Like Santa Anna in Mexico and Rosas and Urquiza in Argentina, Páez became an unbeatable expert in the use of economic wealth to accumulate political power and vice versa.

In the second half of the 1820s, Páez faced the opportunity to leverage his patrimonial power to achieve political supremacy. Yet a necessary prior step was to remove Venezuela from Gran Colombia. In Gran Colombia, Páez had to accept the authority of Bolívar and compete with politicians in Bogotá for the president's favor. By contrast, the truncated territory of Venezuela could become his personal bastion. Páez led Venezuela to secession so as to demarcate the area within which he could be the undisputed sovereign.

The trajectory of Páez and Venezuela provides an acid test for the theory of latecomer state formation. No Latin American leader resembled the state-making warrior of early modern western Europe as much as Páez did (excluding Paraguay's Gaspar de Francia, who in effect built a warrior state). Yet the moment he became president of independent Venezuela, Páez fully embraced the trade-led strategy of state formation. Foreign trade and co-optation of local potentates were the mutually reinforcing pillars of the creation of modern Venezuela.

The Three Futures of Venezuela
in 1820–40

Venezuela was only one possible outcome of three potential ones in 1820–40. The other two potential outcomes were the persistence of Gran Colombia and, after the collapse of Gran Colombia, the subdivision of Venezuela itself into two halves.

In the mid-1820s, Bolívar's power seemed inextinguishable. Few people imagined that his authority or the territorial integrity of Gran Colombia, his main creation, could be challenged. The undoing of Gran Colombia was an eminently political phenomenon, and Bolívar planted the seeds of it. Bolívar made two errors. Only the first error was a forced one. War against Spain required large-scale military mobilization, which in turn forced independence leaders, from Mexico to Buenos Aires, to recruit local bosses who could provide in short order entire contingents of soldiers. The Llanos were a large reservoir of military power. Leaders of cattle-rustling bands found in the wars of independence a chance to transition from outlaws to revolutionary captains. Pressed to improvise an enormous army, Bolívar empowered dozens of *llanero* leaders. Following the iron law of warlord mobilization, the most ambitious *llaneros* would eventually make a bid for political autonomy and challenge Bolívar's authority. Recruiting Páez was a forced error. But it was not enough to provoke the collapse of Gran Colombia.

After the wars of independence, Bolívar made an avoidable error. Skeptical of power sharing, Bolívar imposed a unitarian formula of territorial governance in Gran Colombia. The formula backfired in Venezuela. Bolívar's formula gave the military potentates of the Llanos the opportunity to form a retaliatory alliance with the economic plutocracy of the coastal region around Caracas. In sharp contrast to northern Brazil or Yucatán, which agreed to join a larger state in exchange for central assistance in repressing slave revolts, the plantation owners of the Venezuelan coast resented Bogotá's abolition measures. They also feared that Gran Colombia's commercial policies would hurt their distinct interest in low tariffs for English manufactures and the need to invest revenues in rebuilding the Venezuelan economy. Gran Colombia could have remained united if Bolívar had not undermined his own territorial project by imposing an unsuitable formula of territorial governance. A confederation formula, granting home rule to Venezuela, would have neutralized sources of unrest and prevented the secessionist alliance between Caracas and the Llanos.

The creation of Venezuela as a successor state was not the only alternative to the fragmentation of Gran Colombia. Venezuela itself could have broken up. Military mobilization empowered several caudillos, and most of them aspired to turn their bastions into independent states. In the early 1830s,

shortly after Páez's secession, José Tadeo Monagás, another warlord, revolted. He was the strongman of the eastern section of Venezuela, which
included the old provinces of Barcelona and Cumaná near the Orinoco delta.
Yet Páez did not make with Monagás the mistake that Bolivar had made with
him. Páez negotiated with Monagás. Páez promised not to interfere with
Monagás's local hegemony, and Monagás learned that he had a chance to replace Páez as the president of Venezuela one day. In sum, to understand
state formation in Venezuela, it is necessary to explain not only why Gran
Colombia fragmented but also why Venezuela did not.

Páez, the Lord

When the war of independence broke out, Páez's "only asset was his age":
he was twenty years old.[7] John Lynch's provocative statement is right in that
Páez, in contrast to Rosas of Buenos Aires, was born poor, so much so
that because of the lack of a formal education, he was illiterate until he
was almost thirty-five. Yet youth was not Páez's only attribute. He had
extraordinary physical strength and was a highly skilled cowboy. The two
attributes—no more than an exotic curiosity in a statesman of an advanced
society in the twenty-first century—were essential in the Venezuelan Llanos
of the early nineteenth century, a cattle-ranching frontier where the line dividing legal from illegal activities was thin and porous. Wealthy and poor
llaneros alike crossed and recrossed the line at will in search of subsistence,
security, and, with the favor of luck and talent, wealth. At age seventeen, Páez
killed a man. By remaining in his native Barinas, he risked prison. The Llanos offered a sanctuary.

The Llanos housed the society most closely resembling the Hobbesian
state of nature in South America. *Llaneros* were not atomized but organized
in bands. Force, skill, courage, reliability, and charisma made Páez a natural leader. When Bolívar launched his revolution, Páez was the head of a band
of two hundred *llaneros*. In addition to youth and talent, then, Páez also had
a substantial following. He was ready to transition from bandit to guerrilla,
which is what kept the revolution alive after Bolívar's initial failures. Páez's
baptism as a warlord occurred in late 1816. In the Apure, near the border with
Colombia, a battalion of patriot soldiers was surrounded by Spanish forces.
They mutinied to have the captain replaced by Páez. Patriots felt that only
Páez could provide protection. Páez delivered. Since 1810, Páez had become

an expert in patronage. He promised appointment as captains to rural leaders who contributed parties of forty *llaneros* and employment to families fleeing from Spanish attack. Páez always kept his word.

Páez became an independence hero in 1821. His cavalry made a decisive contribution to the victory of Carabobo. Still in the battlefield, Bolívar promoted Páez to the rank of general. Páez then seconded Bolívar in his march to Caracas, where the Spaniards offered no resistance. To complete the liberation of Caracas, Bolívar delegated to Páez the siege of Puerto Cabello, where royalist forces had taken refuge (some one hundred miles from Caracas). Páez delivered again. In twelve years, Páez moved from cattle peon to bandit to guerrilla fighter to republican hero.

Without landownership, Páez could not have become a *llanero* lord. Páez's performance in the battlefield entitled him to land grants. Aware of the extraordinary synergy between landownership and political power in the 1820s, Páez did not waste a second to acquire both cattle-ranching haciendas in the Llanos and plantations on the coast. Naturally, Páez cared about profit. Yet he prioritized the fact that land allowed him to build a reliable clientele of peons and a large reserve of horses, the two vital inputs in future bids for power. "At San Pablo near Calabozo Páez established an immense *hato*, where he ruled as a sovereign and lived like a *llanero*, still an expert rider and cowboy."[8] The San Pablo ranch was in fact a kinglet. Its perimeter was forty leagues. The economic dynamism of Venezuela was not in the interior Llanos but in the plantations near the coast. In Maracay, in the green valleys of Aragua, some fifty miles southeast of Caracas, Páez acquired a large cacao and sugar estate. By the late 1820s, Páez had purchased another ten large rural estates, was employing over three hundred families, and owned thousands of cattle and horses. Páez built a colossal fortune, which is impossible to account for only as a consequence of military rewards. Following the unwritten handbook of the patrimonial ruler, Páez used his political position to propel himself to the very top of the economic ladder.

Collapse of Gran Colombia, Rise of Venezuela

State-Breaking: 1826–30. In April 1826, Páez faced his first political challenge. It provoked him into secession. He was accused of abuse of power by the authorities of Valencia, a town one hundred miles southeast of Caracas.

The allegation, most likely truthful, was that Páez used threats to coerce recruits into the local militia. The issue escalated. Civilian authorities in Bogotá, in an attempt to teach military veterans a lesson, recalled Páez to Gran
Colombia's capital for interrogation. They obviously did not know the risks.
It took about two weeks for Páez to mobilize followers into a protest against
centralism. Páez responded to a threat against his person with a threat against
a large-scale state. The issue escalated to the very top. Bolívar, still in the
battlefields of Upper Peru, was forced to make a quick visit to Caracas. Much
more knowledgeable of what could and could not be done with his unruly
lieutenants, Bolívar pardoned Páez and confirmed him as the top political
authority within Venezuela, to the dismay of Vice President Santander and
his liberal clique in Bogotá. Bolívar realized that his options were to appease
Páez or risk the dissolution of Gran Colombia. The full saga, from Páez's sedition to Bolívar's amnesty, became known as La Cosiata, an expression
popularized by an Italian theater actor to refer to "little things" that de-
serve no attention—if they had only known that it was the beginning of
the end of Bolívar's career and of Gran Colombia. Bolívar understood the
danger as no other:

> Páez is the most ambitious and vain man in the world: he has no
> desire to obey, only to command; it pains him to see me above
> him in the political hierarchy; he does not even recognize his own
> incompetence, so blinded is he by pride and ignorance. He will
> always be an instrument of his advisers and a mere enforcer of
> decisions that are not his own. I regard him as the most danger-
> ous man for Colombia, for he has means of action, determination,
> and prestige among the *llaneros*, who are our Cossacks; and
> whenever he wishes he can secure the support of the people
> and of the blacks and *zambos* [mixed bloods]. This is my great
> fear, which I have confided to few people and now disclose in
> confidence.[9]

It was during the first five years after independence that Páez produced
his own "primitive accumulation of power." In addition to the various land
acquisitions, Páez obtained exclusive rights to supply meat to the army,
bought the building of Puerto Cabello's customhouse and rented it to the

government, and dispatched soldiers on the official payroll to his ranches in order to secure them from banditry.

In the meantime, Bolívar expelled the last royalist forces from Latin America. When he returned to Bogotá to reassume the presidency of Gran Colombia, he found himself besieged. He faced the twin threats of the Santanderista liberal protoparty in Bogotá, which wanted to place effective constitutional checks on Bolívar's power, and of the plantation plutocracy of Caracas and some Venezuelan military heroes, Páez included, who demanded that the unitarian formula of governance be replaced by a confederal one. The civilians of Bogotá were a more immediate danger than the warlords of the Llanos. The Santanderistas plotted the assassination of Bolívar. He escaped from the ambush thanks to a warning from his mistress.

Bolívar upped the ante. He assumed dictatorial powers, willing to play an all-or-nothing political game against his detractors. He lost. Gran Colombia collapsed in 1829 when Páez headed a secessionist coalition from Caracas. Exhausted by almost two decades of constant wars in almost every corner of Spanish South America, Bolívar died only a year later, his soul blackened both by political betrayal and by the tough lesson from a social reality that was much more resistant to change than he had originally thought. The coalition of Páez included two dominant interests: his own political ambitions to form an independent bastion and the economic preferences of the network of plantation owners of Venezuela's Northeast, who feared the loss of capital (slaves) caused by the abolition policies issued in Bogotá.

State-Making: 1830–46. As a state-maker, Páez transitioned from warlord to merchant—a lion turned vegetarian. Páez did not forget that the source of his power was military force. Yet, once he secured violence monopolization within the borders of Venezuela—in part as the commander of the official army and in part as the patron of a large network of minor caudillos and rural workers—he fully embraced trade-led state formation. It was not a psychological turn. It was a rational response to the incentives of the world economy. He supplied protection of property rights to the plantation plutocracy and turned potentially state-breaking caudillos into state-taking collaborators through the commitment not to interfere with their local business.

During the foundational year of 1830, Páez spent more time setting up his ranches, getting himself involved in clearing the land and branding the cattle, than in the presidential office. Páez wanted to lead by example and to encourage the Venezuelan soldiers "from the commander in chief to the simple private, to consider the country no longer in need of their services as defenders but as cultivators."[10] According to Lynch, "The Páez years were a paradise for proprietors. Laws and their enforcement were invariably biased in favor of property, and it was virtually impossible for a peon to appeal against his *patrón*. The political links between magistrates and landowners were too close to permit impartial administration of justice; local judges . . . tended to classify all rural poor as *jornaleros* and thereby subject to oppressive police laws."[11]

The transformation of Páez from war-maker to market-maker is impressive by the Darwinian standards of the bellicist path of state formation in early modern western Europe. If Páez, whose initial accumulation of political capital was purely based on military skills, made Venezuela a "paradise" for the exporters of cacao and coffee instead of a war machine, no other statemaker in Latin America could possibly have had an incentive to do so. As president, Páez actually pursued all the forbidden actions in the handbook of war-led state formation. He reduced the size of the army, he co-opted patrimonial powers, and he willingly accepted a subordinate position in the world's geopolitical hierarchy.

In his autobiography, Páez left unbeatable evidence of the priorities of a mid-nineteenth-century state-maker in Latin America: "The entire military force of the Republic consisted of eight hundred men, because security rested on public opinion. The money that could have been spent on maintaining a regular army was allocated to improving education, opening roads, improving ports, and constructing public buildings; to encouraging immigrants and civilizing miserable Indians; to paying the state debt and enhancing our internal credit."[12] The notion that order in Venezuela was based on consensus ("public opinion") has an important element of self-propaganda. What is undeniable is that, faced with a budget constraint, Páez pursued the provision of growth-enhancing class goods rather than military expansion. An illiterate man, who initiated a military career in 1810 through physical force and riding skills, twenty years later had already gained a sophisticated understanding of the need for peace to attract foreign investments and the need for foreign investments to boost tropical exports. Serving the interests of the plantation elites, of which he had become a prominent member, made him not only wealthier but also more powerful, as revenues from foreign trade would help him build an extensive network of patronage. Páez obviously had the brains to understand the mechanics of trade-led state formation. Yet the signals provided by international commerce were not hard to read.

It was not public opinion in the classical liberal sense that sustained Páez's power. But it was not force either. It was a mixture of charisma, much of it hard-earned through heroic action during independence, and massive doses of patronage and bargaining, especially with rival caudillos. The eastern section of Venezuela was the bastion of another prestigious caudillo, José Tadeo Monagás. He too aspired to supremacy. He could achieve it either by seceding from western Venezuela and creating his own bastion or by challenging Páez for control of the entire Venezuelan arena. He threatened both. Yet, for almost fifteen years, Páez and Monagás found amicable solutions to their problems. Páez incorporated Monagás and his bastion, but he did not transform it. Páez promoted Monagás through the administration, let him be the strongman to the east of the plantation belt, and promised that one day he could become president too. The contrast with war-led state formation could not be sharper. The evidence for trade-led state formation, which deliberately eschewed state building, could hardly be stronger.

It was the provision of class goods that consolidated the Venezuelan state. The key to consolidation was the dynamism of the export sector resulting from the strict enforcement of property rights, the harsh application of antivagrancy laws, and the associated availability of foreign credit.

The Breakdown of the Peru-Bolivian Confederation and Castilla's Peru
Overview

The Peru-Bolivian Confederation was an ephemeral political entity (Map 10.3). It lasted only three years (1836–39), a small fraction of the life span of the Central American Federation and Gran Colombia. Yet the historical, economic, and even cultural foundations of the union were much more solid than those in every other failed large state and also than those in some successful states like Argentina.

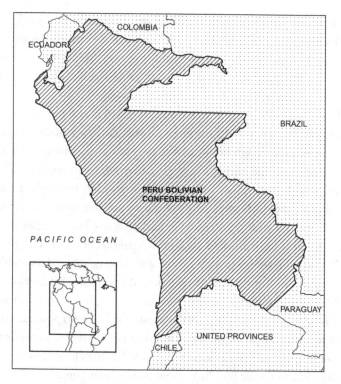

Map 10.3. Peru-Bolivian Confederation, 1836–39

Before the conquest, Cuzco in southern Peru was the center of the Inca Empire, which extended from the center of present-day Ecuador to the north of present-day Argentina. Inca settlements and tributary communities occupied a strip along the Andean range, about three thousand kilometers long from Quito to Tucumán, and three hundred kilometers wide in Cuzco. The northern section of present-day Bolivia was the first belt around the Inca core. The Titicaca lake and its surrounding plateau, today divided between Peru and Bolivia, were a single topographic and demographic region.

For the Spanish *conquistadores*, Peru and Bolivia, then called Upper Peru, were also a single region. The region was home to the two most valued economic resources from the perspective of the Spanish Crown: gigantic silver mines and abundant indigenous labor. The mines in Cerro de Pasco (Peru) and Potosí (Upper Peru), exploited under the *mita* system of forced indigenous labor, were responsible for at least a third of the wealth that made Spain a world empire. Only with the Bourbon reforms was the Upper Peru separated from the Viceroyalty of Peru. In 1776, Upper Peru was attached to Buenos Aires, then a marginal port, to subsidize its role as a barrier against Portuguese and English incursions. When independence movements began in 1810, then, the separation of Peru and Upper Peru was a very recent phenomenon. Colonial and precolonial history made Peru and Bolivia a single entity.

The leaders of Peruvian and Bolivian independence were Venezuelan generals, Bolívar and Sucre. Both of them masterminded the project of the "Federation of the Andes," which would unite Gran Colombia, Peru, and Bolivia. In 1826, Bolívar and Sucre alone commanded the necessary military prestige to lead the joint army of the three countries.

The Peru-Bolivian Confederation was the creation of one of the few fully professional lieutenants of Bolívar, the Bolivian general Andrés de Santa Cruz. Santa Cruz served first as president of Peru by orders of Bolívar (1827) and then was chosen president of Bolivia (1829–39).

Internal economic linkages in the Peru-Bolivian Confederation were neither abundant nor particularly strong. Nevertheless, they provided a more solid basis of union than those of the majority of successful states. Silver mines were the most important asset of both constituent parts of the confederation. A large country was more attractive for the badly needed foreign investments required to refit the mines after the tremendous damage during the wars of independence.

Paradoxically, the economic basis for the union of Bolivia and Peru was stronger than the linkages between Peru's own regions. Peru included two areas with opposite economic policy preferences. Northern Peru was protectionist, whereas southern Peru favored free trade. The protectionist coalition of northern Peru consisted of the monopolistic merchants from the Lima guild, a true ethnic and economic aristocracy, and a substantial class of semiurban artisans. Both southern Peru and Bolivia preferred free trade, unrestricted international navigation of the coast, and especially the liberty of foreign boats to call in ports other than Callao, the port of Lima. The vast majority of the population of southern Peru and Bolivia practiced subsistence agriculture, but they were able to produce considerable surpluses of wool and nitrates. Bolivia had its own port on the Pacific coast, Cobija. Yet access to

Cobija from the Bolivian plateau was almost as expensive as access to the more distant port of Buenos Aires because it required a challenging journey by mule train across the Atacama Desert. The best economic solution for the Bolivian plateau was to ship its output through the Arica port of southern Peru. The trade route between Potosí or Cochabamba in Bolivia and Arica in Peru was in itself a sufficient basis for the creation of a common economic area.

As analyzed in Part 1, nations were much more recent creations than states in Latin America. They could not have been agents of state formation. Yet, from independence, Peru and Bolivia have hosted two distinct nations, the Quechua and the Aymara. Each of the two nations extended over both countries. Peru and Bolivia have stronger cultural bonds than any pair of countries in South America, as well as than some individual countries like Argentina or Colombia. In sum, historical, economic, and cultural factors provided a comparatively strong basis for the union between Peru and Bolivia.

The collapse of the Peru-Bolivian Confederation is the only case of state failure in which an international war played a significant role. Chile invaded Lima and defeated Santa Cruz precisely because the confederation was a respectable political project. Yet Chile's victory would not have been so decisive if it had not received the collaboration of Peruvian warlords opposed to Santa Cruz. Each of Bolivar's military heirs in Peru and Bolivia wanted union and peace, but only if he could suppress the influence of the rest. The Peruvian general Ramón Castilla played simultaneously the role of state-breaker in relation to the Peru-Bolivian Confederation and of state-maker in relation to present-day Peru.

The defeat of Santa Cruz and the collapse of the Peru-Bolivian Confederation was followed by more failure in Bolivia, but in Peru it was followed by successful state formation under the rule of Castilla. Castilla proved to be an able statesman, but fortune played a bigger role than individual talent did. He assumed the presidency of Peru exactly when the English demand for fertilizers boomed. The guano that accumulated for centuries on the islands off the Peruvian coast happened to be the most powerful fertilizer in the world. Chile, with the help of a lord, destroyed the Peru-Bolivian Confederation. The lord, with the help of guano, made Peru.

The Four Perus in the 1830s

In addition to the creation of present-day Peru, three alternative trajectories are conceivable. The first one is the stabilization of the Peru-Bolivian Confederation. The other two counterfactual trajectories depend on the division of Peru between its northern and southern halves. Each half could have become an independent country (second trajectory), or the southern half could have joined Bolivia (third trajectory).

The obvious factor that needs to be removed from history for the survival of the Peru-Bolivian Confederation is Chile's victory at the Battle of Yungay (1839). Yungay would have not occurred if Chile itself had not been an exceptional case of precocious state formation in Latin America. Having Chile as a neighbor was bad luck for a Bolivarian project in the greater Peru area. Even keeping the strong state of Chile in the scene, Yungay could still have been avoided if the relations between the newly created confederation and Chile had taken a different tone at some point before 1838. To prevent Chile's attack, Santa Cruz should have adopted a less hostile commercial policy toward the port of Valparaíso. Valparaíso was the port of Chile's Central Valley, including the capital, Santiago. In less than two decades of independent life, Valparaíso became a major international entrepôt. Between 1810 and 1850, the Strait of Magellan was the most frequent connection between the Atlantic and Pacific Oceans (Nicaragua started to provide passage only in 1850). As a consequence, Valparaíso was the preferred port of call for ships traveling from western Europe to any port on the Pacific coast of the Americas up to San Francisco, as well as for ships coming from the Far East to cities in the southern Atlantic, like Buenos Aires and Rio de Janeiro. Besides, Valparaíso served the considerable need of imports and exports of Chile's Central Valley. Santa Cruz rightly thought that the ports of his confederation should be able to take a larger piece of the traffic along the Pacific coast. To accelerate the process, he decreed an extra import fee on goods delivered by ships that had previously called at Valparaíso. It was a tariff war, not to protect domestic industry but to promote the use of Peru-Bolivian ports. A more gradual competition against Valparaíso would have eased the tensions and prevented the war. Yet defeat at Yungay could have been avoided even after the war was initiated. The confederation was an especially poor military match for Chile because some of the Peruvian warlords fought for the enemy. Internal rivals of Santa Cruz provided Chile with crucial logistical and informational advantages.

If Peru did not become part of a larger confederation, it did not fragment either. Separation between North and South was a viable trajectory for two reasons. First, the two sections had a deep disagreement about trade policies, and any warlord could have profited from the economic conflict to make either section his personal bastion. Second, the southern section had strong economic linkages with Bolivia. The Bolivian plateau and the port of Arica in southern Peru formed a natural common economic area, which the passage of time would have made only stronger. The creation of two independent countries out of the fragmentation of Peru is a viable counterfactual, but the merger of southern Peru and Bolivia is an even more viable one. Unified Peru already had a weak fiscal basis, so an independent southern Peru, poorer than the North, would have needed a partner to be viable. Bolivia's exportable surplus of wool and minerals provided hard currency to finance imports, which would have had to pay duties at the customhouse of Arica, thus expanding the fiscal basis of the union with southern Peru and reducing the per capita costs of financing public goods.

Peru was neither absorbed by a larger union nor divided into different countries. Guano and the lord who happened to be in power when the international price of guano boomed explain territory consolidation in Peru.

Castilla, the Lord

Castilla's origins were as undistinguished as those of Carrera or Páez. Born in 1797 into a poor family, his best chance at upward social mobility was enrollment in the royalist army. At the age of twenty, he experienced a major defeat in Chacabuco, the decisive battle in the liberation of Chile (1817). Sent to jail in Buenos Aires, Castilla escaped. Back in Peru, he deserted the Spanish army to join Bolívar's forces. In the early 1820s, the theater of war was confined to Peru, the last bastion of Spanish resistance. In Ayacucho, the battle that put an effective end to colonial rule (1824), Castilla excelled, showing the marks of a true hero. He risked death to keep the charge against the enemy when his superiors were considering retreat. He was promoted by Sucre to the position of lieutenant.

Immediately after independence, Peru fell into two decades of unmitigated political chaos. Demobilized independence warlords competed for power, and no one was able to prevail. Marxist analysts will look in vain for deeper causes of conflict in the socioeconomic structure. The situation was Hobbesian rather than Marxist. As in Venezuela, Bolivia, and Argentina, the main legacy of independence was warlordism. The only relevant cleavages were those dividing former generals, who had roughly equal access to the means of destruction—the arsenal and manpower assigned to them during the joint intervention of Bolívar and San Martín.

Castilla was not a main contender in the 1830s. Aristocratic and mestizo generals alike, including Agustín Gamarra, Luis José de Orbegoso, Pedro Pablo Bermúdez, and Felipe Salaverry, engaged in violent but indecisive battles for supremacy. Given enough time, one of them would have prevailed. By the mid-1830s, forces seemed to be coalescing around two rivals, Gamarra and Obregoso. They had reached the status of supercaudillos. Lacking vast expanses of cattle-ranching land like the Venezuelan Llanos and the Argentine Pampas, which were a second source of power accumulation for caudillos aspiring to supremacy, the rivalry between Gamarra and Obregoso was purely military. What was distinctive about Gamarra was his ambition to conquer Bolivia. Obregoso in principle aspired to control only northern Peru, where he courted the favor of the economic aristocracy of Lima. In the early 1830s, Castilla decided to tie his destiny to that of Gamarra. Gamarra seemed the safest bet. He was in command of the most powerful military force and was the most popular political leader.

The year 1835 was a turning point in the Hobbesian arena of Peru. Gamarra made a deal with Bolivian president Santa Cruz to join forces against Obregoso. But Obregoso responded by offering Santa Cruz better terms. In exchange for protection against Gamarra, Obregoso committed to let Santa Cruz become the president of a united Peru-Bolivian Confederation. Santa Cruz did not think twice and forgot about Gamarra. His Bolivian army would be the pivotal force turning the scale in Peru's military stalemate.

The formation of the Peru-Bolivian Confederation found Castilla in the losing camp. Gamarra and Castilla were forced into exile in Chile. In Santiago, they offered their services to Diego Portales. Portales was not the Chilean president. He was much more powerful than the president. Portales was the kingmaker and held four out of five ministerial posts. Portales could not tolerate Santa Cruz's bid to replace Valparaíso as the leading entrepôt of the South American Pacific. With the help of Gamarra and Castilla, Portales prepared a "Liberation Expedition." It failed in its first attempt. People opposed to the war assassinated Portales. Yet the military campaign against the Peru-Bolivian Confederation continued, as if the death of its architect had given lieutenants new strength to pursue the fight. The second attempt succeeded. The Peru-Bolivian Confederation collapsed. But it was Gamarra, not Castilla, who was the leader of the hour in "restored" Peru. In the hubris of victory, Gamarra revived his ambition to conquer Bolivia. He tried and was killed in the attempt. The path to power for Castilla was cleared.

State-Making in Peru:
The Ordinary Caudillo in Extraordinary Times

In 1841, Peru exported the first substantial amount of guano. Since then, guano prices would only rise and produce a veritable economic boom. As with many big developments in Latin America, the origins of the guano boom lay outside Peru. In Great Britain, after centuries of depleting the nutrients of the pastureland, agriculture faced the option of adopting fertilizers or disappearing gradually. The boom in the price of guano reflected British farmers' decision to survive. No country in nineteenth-century Latin America received the windfall that Peru did. Yet, for government revenues, the windfall was not automatic. As a consequence, between 1839 and 1845, internal strife resumed.

The death of Gamarra, instead of propelling the career of his ally Castilla, tempted his old foes, now led by Miguel Ignacio de Vivanco, the military leader of Lima's aristocracy. Unfortunately for Vivanco but fortunately for Castilla, the revenues of the guano boom had not yet reached the torrential levels that they would in the late 1840s. The boom caught Peru by surprise, and the government's first response was to lease the guano islands to a private businessman, Francisco Quirós. The rental price of the islands was only a fraction of the income obtained by Quirós. Hence, Vivanco did not have enough money to inflict a decisive defeat on the heirs of Gamarra, the most prominent of whom was Castilla.

In 1845, in what seemed to be yet another transitory change of names in power, Castilla became president. But Castilla would last. Not only did he become the first Peruvian president to complete the term (1845–51), but he would become president again three years after the completion of the first term; his new tenure, combining a temporary and a constitutional period, would be longer (1855–62). The secret of Castilla's stabilization of power was a change in the deal brokered between the Peruvian government and the private interests in the guano sector. The government switched from leasing contracts, which secured only 5 percent of guano profits, to consignment arrangements, by which it hired the service of private firms to extract and sell the guano in exchange for a fixed fee. The government's payment covered the costs of production and a small commission. The government rehired Quirós but, in order to introduce some competition, gave the English firm of Anthony Gibbs a piece of the action.

Under the new arrangement, government revenues boomed. Castilla used them wisely. He pursued trade-led state formation and thereby stabilized presidential power, a radical novelty in independent Peru. All kinds of class goods and some genuinely public goods were financed through the guano revenues. Steam navigation, then limited to the Valparaíso-Callao route, was extended to Panama. The first railroad was built, connecting Lima and Callao. A regular service of mail and telegraph was established. A splendid building was constructed to host Lima's city market, which helped relocate hundreds of dispersed street vendors.

The most telling symptom of fiscal abundance occurred in 1854, when the indigenous tax was definitively abolished. As in Central America, the first independent governments of Peru experimented with the elimination of the tax, only to realize that it was the last barrier against total bankruptcy. In Guatemala, Carrera needed a large-scale peasant rebellion to abolish the tax, and in the process, he caused the collapse of the Central American Federation. In Peru, the guano made possible abolition without rebellion. It also gave Castilla an instant winning lottery ticket in the game of Peruvian politics. Guano turned Castilla from an ordinary warlord into a hegemonic ruler. And Castilla used the guano to consolidate modern Peru.

Conclusion

THIS IS THE END OF A LONG ROAD. It has covered two continents, fifty critical years in Latin American history, the creation of ten countries, and the failure of almost twenty. It is time to take stock and look at what lies ahead. This concluding chapter is divided into three sections. The first section summarizes the key arguments. The second highlights four contributions to the social sciences. Two are relevant for state theory and can be combined in the notion that the state has fewer functions but more institutions than is customarily acknowledged. The other two contributions are specific recommendations for the study of state formation and state building in Latin America. The third section proposes a new research agenda that turns from the causes of Latin America's political geography (the subject of Part 2) to its effects. Nineteenth-century state formation hides a master key to understanding some of the most pressing issues in contemporary Latin America, including low-quality democracies and economic backwardness.

Summation
State Formation against State Building:
Latin America and Western Europe Compared

Forming a state is not the same as building state capacity. State formation involves essentially two processes: territory consolidation and violence monopolization. Building state capacity, or state building for short, involves the expansion of the government's ability to supply public goods in a fiscally efficient and territorially even fashion. The literature has tended to see state formation and state building as synonymous or concomitant processes.

The central message of Part 1 of the book is that some paths of state formation do not lead to state building, and a subset of them create durable obstacles to it. The only region where state formation and state building advanced in tandem was western Europe in the early modern period, the crucible of first-generation modern states. Political scientists, sociologists, and historians who study state origins in early modern western Europe have for decades acknowledged that the pioneer process of state formation cannot be repeated in other parts of the world. Yet the development of a general theory of state formation and state building has proved elusive.

Contrasts in outcomes between the pioneer cases and the latecomer experiences have not been described with sufficient analytical precision, a shortcoming that has prevented the identification of the sources of variation. Differences between western Europe and other regions are often considered too large to be tractable. Theories of state formation in western Europe have given up the ambition of expanding the universe of cases to which they apply by implicitly adopting a large but usually vague number of scope conditions. Often, the scope conditions themselves are ill defined.

Seeking to build a general theory, the first part of this book drew a sharp distinction between outcomes in the modal cases of western Europe and Latin America and opened the black box of the scope conditions implicit in the canon of state-formation approaches. The Americas is the region that gave birth to the second generation of modern states. In Latin America, the contrast with western Europe with regard to final outcome is enormous. Proper analytical tools can describe the contrast in a productive way for scientific progress. Latin America succeeded at state formation but failed at state building because the former was incompatible with the latter. In both western Europe and Latin America, most centers of state formation consolidated national territories by incorporating peripheral areas. In the process of periphery incorporation, western Europe eliminated a vast array of local patrimonial oligarchies, whereas Latin America revitalized patrimonial bastions through economic subsidies, institutional immunities, and political privileges. Peripheral patrimonial rulers did more than survive state formation in Latin America. They formed a political network that came to occupy the full territorial extension of the emerging state. Latin American states were born with a built-in propensity to become large-scale patronage machines.

The conditions under which state formation occurs should not be relegated to the muddy terrain of idiosyncratic, area-specific forces. Whether state formation will be decoupled from state building crucially depends on the international environment, which can be differentiated along two dimensions. From a geopolitical perspective, the most consequential contrast is whether the world is an anarchical society or is structured as a hierarchy topped by undisputed superpowers. In economic terms, the big difference is between cases that initiated and completed state formation under feudalism and mercantilism and those that began state formation when free-trade capitalism was already a global phenomenon. The international conditions surrounding state formation in western Europe and Latin America stand in opposite analytical quadrants of the two-dimensional space. *Pioneer* state formation can in fact be seen as the joint process of territory consolidation and violence monopolization when no other modern state had formed yet and when feudalism was the dominant mode of production and mercantilism the typical foreign economic policy. England, France, Prussia, Spain, and Sweden were unambiguous pioneers of state formation. In sharp contrast, the Latin American experience of state formation, which took place during the critical decades of the mid-nineteenth century, was initiated in a world already populated by at least a dozen modern states, in the context of a well-defined geopolitical hierarchy, at the pinnacle of which were Great Britain and France. Additionally, the process was simultaneous with the first global expansion of free-trade capitalism. State formation under the aegis of world superpowers and market capitalism is the purest form of *latecomer* state formation. Pioneer state formation is war-led state formation. Latecomer state formation is trade-led state formation.

The connection between initial international conditions and final outcomes is straightforward. In the pioneer cases, Darwinian geopolitical pressures presented state-formation centers with a drastic choice: form states and build capacity at the same time or perish at the hands of powerful neighbors. In the latecomer cases of Latin America, state-formation centers did not need to build efficient administrations. Both the *Pax Britannica* and global capitalism provided the incentives and resources to form states that were trade machines rather than war machines. State-formation elites in Latin America were able to derive torrential flows of revenue by creating a propitious business environment for the export sector. To initiate a virtuous circle between state formation and international trade, all they needed to do was to provide a modicum of pacification, which essentially meant preventing predatory attacks from backward oligarchies.

State-formation elites in Latin America did not need to worry about international wars. Most of their neighbors were also pursuing foreign trade rather than territorial expansion, and in the rare case of a boundary dispute, the western European superpowers were available as international referees, a mechanism of conflict resolution conspicuously absent in the pioneer cases. Able to derive fiscal resources from foreign trade and exempted from geopolitical pressures, the centers of state formation in Latin America incorporated peripheral areas but did not transform their patrimonial rulers. Periphery transformation was both unnecessary and counterproductive. In the pioneer cases of western Europe, incorporation without transformation was a death sentence. In the latecomer cases of Latin America, on the contrary, incorporation without transformation was the most expedient strategy to join world capitalism. It allowed Latin American state-makers to take advantage of the window of opportunity opened by the surge in the international demand for primary commodities caused by the Industrial Revolution. If Latin American state-formation elites had followed the example of the pioneers and embarked on the eradication of patrimonial bastions, long civil wars would have followed, and the opportunities of international commerce would have evaporated. Patrimonial bastions were too poor compared to the export sector to justify efforts at state building. In exchange for peace, they demanded what at the time were minor concessions, including small subsidies, noninterference with local affairs, and representation quotas in national legislatures. Aggregated across the array of peripheral areas incorporated by each country and growing over time, the original concessions became insurmountable obstacles to state capacity.

Size and Timing of Violence Monopolization: Variations within Latin America

If the distinction between state formation and state building is key to understanding the contrast between western Europe and Latin America, the analysis of variations *within* Latin America requires the disaggregation of state formation into its two basic components: (a) territory consolidation and (b) violence monopolization. Along the first dimension, Latin American states showed large variations in country size, which is a proxy for the number and diversity of regions combined in a single state. The pioneer states in western Europe became roughly equivalent in size once their territories consolidated. Along the second dimension, a subset of countries in Latin America experienced a major temporal delay in the monopolization of violence after territory consolidation. The gap was always the source of protracted conflict, as a duopoly of violence pushed rival parties into a semipermanent state of civil war.

Part 2 of the book focused on these variations in the size of the territory consolidated and the timing of violence monopolization within Latin America. To account for them, a complementary approach to the same state-formation elites analyzed in Part 1 was introduced. Instead of viewing state-formation agents solely as market-makers—perfect representatives of the economic interests of the export sector—they were viewed also as *polity-makers*. Polity-makers pursued a professional agenda that, although compatible with export-led growth, was autonomous from the economic elites. They resorted to distinctly political instruments to achieve their goals. To explain the strategies of polity-makers, the focus shifted from international to domestic structures.

Three classes of agent, the *port*, the *party*, and the *lord*, set in motion distinct subpaths within the modal trade-led pattern that characterized Latin American state formation. Each agent can be seen as a distinct combination of similarities and differences in relation to the warrior in the baseline European model. When facing the incorporation of recalcitrant peripheries, a key instrument of state formation for all three agents was the formula of territorial governance, which could be confederal, federal, or unitarian.

All three kinds of agent, seeking to reach and remain at the pinnacle of political power, chose the size of the territory and adjusted the formula of territorial governance in order to maximize coalitional support. Choosing the size of a country involves momentous decisions about including and excluding regions. Yet such momentous decisions were made in service of a conventional goal: survival as a professional politician. The "conventionalization" of motives behind territory consolidation is Latin America's distinct contribution to modern processes of state formation. It can be contrasted with the "extraordinary" politics of state formation in western Europe. In western Europe, geopolitical survival trumped all other motivations during territory consolidation. Western European state-makers could not afford the

luxury of calculating whether a newly incorporated periphery would provide extra coalitional support. All adjacent regions were useful annexations
because their human and physical resources were badly needed for battle.
Within a much less pressing geopolitical context, Latin American state-
makers picked and chose what peripheries to incorporate. In particular,
they could afford the dual luxury of excluding regions that would throw
their support to a rival elite and of including regions that, despite being a
fiscal burden, would expand their coalition. The extraordinary process
of state formation in Latin America, then, was driven by ordinary political motivations.

State formation in Latin America created a few territorial colossuses
several times larger than the largest western European country. All big countries were created through a port-driven or a party-driven process. Argentina and Brazil, the largest countries in Latin America, were formed by
political entrepreneurs who brokered a master deal by which the port got the
necessary political conditions and economic instruments for export-led
growth and a vast array of backward peripheries obtained a share of political power and economic prosperity. Lords, on the other hand, created small
or, at most, medium-sized countries. Lords chose the size that was coterminous with the spatial extension of the network of dependent clients. Lords
in particular were responsible for the breakdown of large-scale projects of
state formation, like the United Provinces of the River Plate (union of Argentina, Paraguay, and Uruguay), Gran Colombia (Colombia, Venezuela, Ecuador, and Panama), the Peru-Bolivian Confederation, and the Federation
of Central America.

The party-driven path is distinctive in that it creates a major temporal
gap between border demarcation and violence monopolization. In the first
decades after independence, partisan competition induced rival parties to
search for allies outside their own locality. Unintentionally, party formation
created political linkages among otherwise disjointed regions. Party formation preceded, and caused, territory consolidation in Mexico, Colombia, and
Uruguay. After stabilizing the political arena, the rival parties remained hybrid political organizations, half electoral machines and half partisan armies.
The resulting duopoly of violence caused civil war, open or latent. It took
decades of human and material destruction for one party to inflict a decisive
victory on the other, as with the case of Mexico, or for both parties to find a

mutually agreeable mechanism of power sharing, as happened in Colombia and Uruguay.

Contributions

State Theory

The creation of Latin American countries produced *less* than state building but *more* than state formation. The persistent deficit in state building, as reflected in the chronic lack of capacity or incentives of Latin American governments to provide public goods, challenges the conventional wisdom about the state's fundamental interests and actions. The main lesson of comparative state formation in Latin America is twofold: state theory should be purged from *functionalist biases*, which are still present even in the most sophisticated studies of state authority; and, instead, it should adopt an *institutional perspective* as a necessary complement. In other words, state theory needs fewer functions and more institutions. On the one hand, the fact that Latin American state formation was uncoupled from state building gives new credit to the old but buried Weberian claim that states perform *no specific function*. On the other, the fact that states in Latin America were not the only outcomes of state formation, which also included the creation of macropolitical institutions like the formula of territorial governance, undermines the dominant sequential vision of political development. According to this vision, states emerge first, and then, in a subsequent phase, political institutions follow. States and key macropolitical institutions are *joint creations* of the state-formation process. In this section, the recommendation of a state theory with "fewer functions" will be justified first. Then the promise of a state theory with "more institutions" will be explored.

Fewer Functions. According to James C. Scott, "projects of administrative, economic, and cultural standardization are hard-wired into the architecture of the modern state itself."[1] Can Scott be wrong? The *Oxford English Dictionary* defines "hard-wiring" as "mak[ing] a function a permanent feature in a computer by means of permanently connected circuits, so that it cannot be altered by software."[2] Scott's exquisite work on authority is not precisely a representative sample of conventional theories of the state. Yet the fact that even Scott sees the state as being "hard-wired" for "standardization"—itself a prelude for more intense functions of central domination—shows how deeply rooted some key assumptions about the nature of the state are across the social sciences, policy circles, and public opinion. Scott's standardization strongly overlaps with classical Weberian claims about "bureaucratization," the nearly forgotten concept of "state penetration" developed by the first theorists of political sequencing, and the more recent notion of "capacity building" as popularized by Francis Fukuyama.[3]

Political arguments that assume that states have "functions," especially if the functions are viewed as permanent, universal, or "hard-wired," are wrong. Scott's statement is the twenty-first-century version of a fundamental claim advanced by an influential lineage of political analysis that traces back to Otto Hintze in comparative politics and Hans Morgenthau in international relations. The claim is that states are always and everywhere "territory-maximizers." Territory maximization means two things: to make the area under the state's control as large as possible and to make the control over the state's area as intense as possible. The former involves "geographic expansion," whereas the latter involves "capacity building." A sophisticated version of the claim combines both meanings by portraying the state's maximization problem as one focused on producing the optimal balance between extension and intensity of territorial power. Territory maximization is constrained only by the capacity of foreign powers and domestic economic classes.

Part 1 of this book shows that no state project is universal, permanent, or "hard-wired." State-makers in Latin America were emphatically not territory maximizers. They did not care about the physical size of the national political arena, nor did they worry about "standardizing" institutions across the state's territory. In Latin America, state formation was not only decoupled from state building. It also created persistent and strong obstacles to the development of state capacities. The claim that "standardization" is "hard-wired into the architecture of the modern state itself" is a mistaken generalization. Low capacity was a birth defect of Latin American states, and, if anything, it was an obstacle to the supposedly "hard-wired" standardization. Proximate causes of state weakness in Latin America can be divided into two groups: bureaucracies that lack the fiscal and human capital to develop infrastructural power and politicians who are unwilling to use public office to provide public goods instead of securing partisan or private benefits. When new politicians emerge with an explicit agenda to change old habits, they encounter anemic bureaucracies that cannot rise to the challenge, or more frequently, they discover that electoral survival and everyday governability requires clientelism and patrimonialism to persist.

Both proximate causes, the lack of bureaucratic power and the absence of political will, have deep historical roots. They were shaped during the critical decades of state formation in the mid-nineteenth century, when commerce rather than war drove the creation of Latin American countries. Profiting from a boom in international trade was much less demanding with regard to capacity building than securing international sovereignty was. The consequence was a second-generation state born without the functionality of the first generation.

The criticism of the modern state's allegedly universal instincts—including territory maximization and political standardization—should be more radical. Paradoxically, a radical criticism requires a return to Weber's basic definition of the state. Pointing out that "security maximization," "penetration," and "bureaucratization" are not universal functions of the state is a necessary clarification, but it is not enough. States may perform no function at all and still be states. More precisely, the state cannot be defined by any specific function. The key stylized fact in Weber's conceptualization of the state is that there is no single goal—from warfare preparation to welfare expansion, from the support of arts and sports to the incubation of scientific and industrial conglomerates—that at least some state has not performed at some point in time. And vice versa: there is no single goal that all states have pursued all the time.

The conclusion for Weber was a minirevolution in concept formation. States cannot be defined by their goals. They can be defined only by the specific means by which they pursue whatever goals any particular government might want to pursue. The means that defines the state is the territorial monopoly of violence. Other than that, no universal attribute, much less function, is shared by all states.

More Institutions. In the analysis of pathways in Latin America, state-formation agents, whether ports, parties, or lords, were depicted as polity-makers. To achieve territorial consolidation, they bargained with state-takers and state-breakers. In the bargain, state-formation elites made concessions that created a range of complementary macropolitical institutions, most formal and some informal. The additional institutional package was an integral part of the very process of state formation—no institutional concessions, no state. States and institutions are *joint* creations. A "polity" is the entity that combines, on the one hand, the attributes of the state—a consolidated territory and the monopoly of violence within it—and, on the other, the package of additional institutions required for state formation to be successful. In Latin America, the package included the formula of territorial governance, rules of power sharing, political parties, and patronage arrangements.

In Argentina, Brazil, and Mexico, the three territorial colossuses, as well as in Colombia, a fundamental institution was the *formula of territorial governance*. The formula was the master political institution for making the emerging territorial union agreeable to all the regions that would become the subnational units in the new state, including both the center and the peripheries. Argentina and Mexico would never have formed if the center had not agreed to federalism. Even cases of state failure, like Gran Colombia and the Central American Federation, highlight the effects of the formula. Gran Colombia could have remained united had Bolívar not insisted on imposing a unitarian formula and instead agreed to a power-sharing arrangement between Caracas and Bogotá. The Central American Confederation would have survived if, rather than experimenting with a loose confederal formula, it had attempted a federal union that allocated more power to the central state.

In the three cases of party-driven state formation—Mexico, Colombia, and Uruguay—parties were pre-state organizations without which territorial consolidation would have not occurred. Moreover, since in Colombia and Uruguay territory consolidation was followed by a *duopoly of violence*, a peaceful polity emerged only when the two dominant parties agreed to a formula of power sharing. Coincidentally, the formula was minority representation through the "incomplete vote," a deviant form of proportional representation. Mexico did not need proportional representation because one party defeated the other in a decisive civil war.

In all cases where state-breaking or state-taking lords were an active part of the state-formation process, another component of the additional package was the arrangement by which the center—a port, a lord, or a party's central oligarchy—committed to concessions reinforcing patrimonial bastions in the peripheries. Concessions included economic subsidies, political devolution, or a combination of both. Patrimonial arrangements became part of the polity. Key to state formation, they were an obstacle to state building.

Adding the institutional arrangements that make possible territory consolidation and violence monopolization provides new insight into the contrast between western Europe and Latin America. The Venn diagram in figure 11.1 represents the comparison of outcomes resulting from war-led state formation in western Europe and trade-led state formation in Latin America. The intersection of the two sets is the state-formation *core*, territory consolidation and violence monopolization. In western Europe, state formation was part of a process that also included state building. In Latin America, state building was excluded, but key macropolitical institutions were joint creations.[4]

Latin American Political Development

This book makes one contribution to classical debates on Latin American political development and another to recent scholarship on variations in state capacities within the region.

State Formation as a Critical Juncture. The first contribution is that state formation was the master critical juncture in Latin American history. This contribution has two aspects. First, it provides a new periodization that locates the birth of Latin American states—and the emergence of Latin American modern political geography—in 1845–75. The implication of the new periodization is that the transition from independence to state was not *automatic*. Quite the contrary, independence opened a number of possible developmental paths, each providing every country in present-day Latin America with a number of viable alternatives. Alternatives could have either fragmented the country into smaller states or subsumed it into a larger territorial unit. The period of Independence (1808–25) was followed by a period of Failure (1825–45), and the period of Failure was marked by warlordism, secessionism, failed projects of territorial conglomeration, and border fluidity. The open-ended nature of the Failure period, with its viable counterfactual states—some of which were only a few political contingencies away

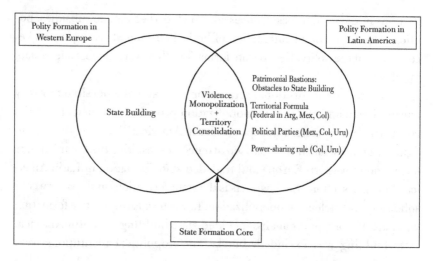

Figure 11.1. Polity formation in western Europe and Latin America

from becoming a permanent reality—should radically change how the history of individual countries is told. For good political reasons, which naturally have nothing to do with analytical rigor, national historiographies are narratives strongly biased by "retrospective determinism": in the mild version, Argentina, Brazil, Colombia, Guatemala, Mexico, Peru, and Venezuela are nearly inexorable outcomes of the independence wars; in the severe versions, which uniformly dominate high school textbooks, the countries were already "actors," usually nations, at the moment of independence and went to war to add political sovereignty to the preexisting sociological entity. Nations did not exist in Latin America in 1810. Moreover, they did not exist in the mid-nineteenth century. The agents of state formation were pre- or subnational actors: ports, parties, and lords. Their motivation was power maximization rather than cultural identity. Nations, together with national historiographies, were created decades after state formation was completed.

The second aspect of considering state formation a foundational period is that the creation of Latin America's political geography in the mid-nineteenth century becomes a possible root cause of several structural problems in the region—including political dysfunctionality and economic backwardness (discussed in the last section of this chapter). A key lesson from the book is that the study of Latin American politics and society has most likely attributed too much weight to colonialism and its legacies. Colonial political units in Spanish America were four viceroyalties. In Portuguese America, they were about a dozen captaincies. The modern political geography of Latin America could not be more different from the colonial map. Even if Portuguese America is taken as a single political unit, the colonial jurisdiction did not exempt mid-nineteenth-century Brazil from the most severe secessionist crises, which could have created a radically different political geography.

The joint effect of the periods of Independence and Failure was an irreversible erosion of the colonial legacy. The independence process in Spanish America was in fact revolutionary. It destroyed the vast majority of the social, economic, and political institutions implanted by Spain. During the period of Failure, warlordism further undermined the residual colonial legacy. Warlords were an unintended but powerful force unleashed by Spanish American revolutionary leaders. Their actions wiped out the borders of colonial units. They created minisovereignties. They opened the region to a range of new possibilities with regard to territorial combinations.

In the mid-nineteenth century, politics in Latin America was essentially about dealing with two novelties: on the one hand, the ruralization of power caused by the independence process (the legacy of the Failure period, as analyzed in Chapter 2); on the other, the globalization of free-trade capitalism under the *Pax Britannica* (discussed in Chapter 3 as a Commercial Revolution). For Díaz in Mexico, Mitre in Argentina, Páez in Venezuela, and Pedro II in Brazil, rural warlords, elections, and international commodity prices were much more pressing issues than were old colonial structures, most of which were already extinct.

The colonial legacy in Latin America should be deemphasized but not ignored. In the process of state formation, the colonial legacy did have a distinct impact on the party-driven process, one of the three pathways of territory consolidation. Regions that generated more institution building under the rule of the Iberian metropolises, like present-day Mexico, Central America, Colombia, Peru, and coastal Brazil, shared a cluster of five attributes on the eve of independence: a dense network of cities, a rentier aristocracy, a strong church, large contingents of repressed labor, and a robust system of corporate privileges (from monopolistic rights to judicial immunities). Clear connections are discernible between the level of institutional development during the colony and the emergence of a Conservative-versus-Liberal cleavage after independence. Yet the Conservative/Liberal cleavage was neither a sufficient nor a necessary condition for party-driven state formation. The cleavage played a role in state formation only in Mexico and Colombia. In Mexico, the rivalry was about whether colonial privilege should be preserved. In Colombia, it was about how fast colonial privilege should disappear. In Peru and Central America, the nascent Conservative/Liberal cleavage was erased by rural lords, political conflict morphed into a civil war between virtually identical protection rackets, and eventually one of the warlords gained undisputed supremacy. In Uruguay, the third case of party-driven state formation, parties emerged not as a response to colonial institutions, which were virtually nonexistent, but as rival factions of the independence army. Hence, the impact of the colonial legacy on the process of state formation exists, but it is tenuous and limited to two cases (Mexico and Colombia).

State Building in Latin America. Scholarship on state capacity in Latin America will benefit from a focus on state formation. Divergences in the state-formation process explain big variations in capacity, like the one that separates the French state from the Ecuadorean one. Low capacity in Latin America is the durable legacy of the three variants of trade-led state formation. In the port-led and party-led variants, the center incorporates patrimonial peripheries but does not transform them. In the lord-led variant, the center itself is patrimonial. Work on variations in state capacity in Latin America has explained small differences in capacity, like the one that separates Chile from Peru. Explanations of small variations between cases are important, but their value can be enhanced if put in proper comparative and historical perspective. Higher state capacity in individual Latin American cases has to be understood as a deviation or an exception from a general pattern of state weakness. Several authors rightly highlight that Chile has the most capable state in the region. Yet the main source of Chile's capacity is not social structure, institutional design, or elite ideology. The main source is that Chile, in its formation, incorporated no patrimonial peripheries. Along this dimension, Chile is not different from Uruguay and Costa Rica. It is useful to view the three cases as exceptions to the general pattern caused by the absence of periphery incorporation. They are the only small countries that were not formed by rural lords. In other words, the centers in Chile, Uruguay, and Costa Rica were not patrimonial, and they had no patrimonial peripheries to incorporate.

Relatedly, the very process by which a country was created in the mid-nineteenth century has constrained the success of twentieth-century state-building projects. Political scientists who overlook how the countries they study were formed miss an important source of the political and economic dynamics within them. In most Latin American cases, state formation was decoupled from state building. Hence, when well-intentioned politicians initiate efforts at state building, they repeatedly find that the legacy of state formation has set strong limits as to how much can be done. The limits are rooted in the specific combination of regions that was consolidated during state formation and the institutional concessions to peripheral rulers, including the formula of territorial governance, that made the combination possible.

A New Research Agenda: The Political and Economic Effects of Latin America's Political Geography

To the best of my knowledge, this is the first book focusing on the *causes* of Latin America's modern political geography. What about the *effects?* They are political and economic.

Political Effects

The "low quality" of Latin American democracies has inspired some of the most vibrant research agendas. Guillermo O'Donnell's last essays have been the source of fundamental ideas about how to approach the study of Latin American political institutions, formal and informal, national and subnational. Research has largely confirmed the existence of two major deficits in Latin America's democracies. One is the recurrence of episodes of presidential concentration of power at the expense of the other branches of government. Presidential concentration makes the policy-making process less *representative*, as legislators of opposition parties are deprived of a meaningful voice. It also makes the process less *transparent*, as weak courts cannot monitor the behavior of presidents, who thereby face few obstacles to using public power for partisan or private gain. The other deficit is the high incidence of subnational authoritarianism. Since the return of democracy in the 1980s, with few exceptions, presidents in Latin America have not abolished political competition at the national level. Yet, at the subnational level, many governors have done so. In Argentina and Mexico, a robust fact is the discrepancy between the democratic score of the national political regime and the average score of democracy across subnational regimes.[5] The latter is substantially lower due to persistence of provincial hegemonies, wherein the governor undermines the opposition by deploying a range of strategies, including intimidation of independent journalists, co-optation of provincial judges, and large doses of clientelistic control, usually financed with central resources that the governor obtains in exchange for electoral and coalitional favors.

This book suggests that "low quality" is less an attribute of the regime than of the state. In fact, it would only be a small exaggeration to claim that Latin American democracies are of the highest quality possible *given* the strong constraints imposed by the patrimonial nature of the state they inherited from the nineteenth century and the dysfunctionality of many territorial combinations. Presidential concentration is often a response to economic and fiscal crises. Such crises are largely a reflection of the fact that the state is a large-scale patronage machine. Chronic deficits and resource misallocations are permanent state features. Presidential concentrations are roughly as frequent as *presidential bankruptcies*, major episodes of ungovernability in which the president abandons office when faced with intractable problems. From the Andean countries to Argentina and Brazil, ungovernability derives from states that do not have the capacity to provide the public goods expected by the electorate: water, safety, transportation, health, and monetary stability.

Provincial authoritarianisms are not "enclaves," as some extreme versions of the subnational comparative method would portray them. The survival of nondemocratic governors depends on the exchange of mutual favors with the federal government. They are part of a larger system, not an isolated, self-contained entity. As shown by Edward Gibson's pioneering work, authoritarian provinces contribute "peripheral support" to electoral and governing coalitions pursuing large-scale policy change.[6] Such coalitions are unimaginable outside the peculiar internal political geography that characterizes countries like Argentina, Brazil, and Mexico. From their very foundations, large countries in Latin America combined a few dynamic centers with a vast array of patrimonial bastions. The territorial formula reinforced their local power and granted them a share of national power.

Subnational authoritarian rule, coupled with patrimonial provincial administration, seems a natural consequence.

A promising area of new research is the study of long-term trajectories of peripheral patrimonialism and the impact on national politics. Over the course of 150 years, peripheral patrimonial bastions adapted to changing circumstances, including the rise of mass politics in the metropolitan center, various forms of economic adjustment, and commodity booms. How did patrimonial reproduction happen? It seems safe to adopt the assumption that peripheral patrimonialism never lost its political appeal to the center. It is an inexpensive source of support. Research should then focus on how the exchange between central rulers and peripheral political elites evolved over time.

Economic Effects

In Latin America, income per capita, the standard measure of material prosperity, is five times higher than in tropical Africa but five times lower than in the advanced economies of the North Atlantic. If we applied the economists' distinction between geography and politics as opposite fundamental factors of long-run development, a simple but powerful picture about what causes explain what part of the variation would emerge. Geography would explain why Latin American economies are ahead of the African ones, whereas politics would explain why they are behind those of the United States and western Europe. All relevant geographic factors in South America, including proportion of fertile land, number of navigable rivers, and disease environment, are far superior to those in Africa. By contrast, political factors, including state capacity, types and stability of public institutions, viable political coalitions, and social and economic policies, are far inferior to those in western Europe and North America.

What the picture based on the geography-versus-politics distinction misses is the crucial role of a hybrid combination, namely, *political geography*. Some countries in South America could have followed the economic path that Australia and New Zealand initiated in the mid-nineteenth century. Such a path was not followed because of the way in which national boundaries were demarcated, or what this book has defined as *territory consolidation*. The path had two key legacies: on the one hand, the creation of three territorial colossuses, Argentina, Brazil, and Mexico, that were *dysfunctional combinations of subnational economies*; on the other, the emergence of smaller countries that were not powerful enough to become the engine of development for Latin America as a whole. Even though some small countries originally had viable economies, as was the case of Chile and Uruguay, they were in fact hurt by the dysfunctional economic nature of their giant neighbors.

The national territories of Argentina and Brazil in particular included vast economic areas for which international trade promised enormous material rewards. The Pampa Húmeda of Argentina (similar to the American Midwest in size and natural productivity) and the Paraíba Valley in Brazil (the undisputed world leader in coffee production) would under most circumstances be sources of growth with enough power to create a prosperous continent. However, both subnational regions were united in the same country with a larger backward periphery that thwarted the path toward prosperity.

The interaction between the regional economies within each country can be characterized as *anti-Pareto*. Depending on the results of territory consolidation, the political geography of a country will determine whether the component regions hold a *Pareto relation* among them (they all benefit), a *parasitic relation* (some benefit at the expense of others), or an *anti-Pareto relation* (all lose). No theory has predicted the emergence of countries as perverse, anti-Pareto combinations, let alone explored its effects. In the anti-Pareto countries, the periphery, through political means, including institutionally protected transfers of rents for local patronage, becomes an insurmountable burden for the development of the center. The center, through unintended economic mechanisms, including the "Dutch Disease," prevents the peripheries from finding a comparative advantage that would help them upgrade their development chances.[7]

A dysfunctional territorial configuration not only caused the failure of Argentina and Brazil to fulfill their takeoff potential as individual countries. Because of their continental influence, the dysfunctional colossuses also contributed to the underdevelopment of all South America. If Argentina and Brazil did not become Australia, Chile and Uruguay did not become New Zealand. Both Chile and Uruguay had similarly productive core areas, the Central Valley and the agricultural hinterland of the Montevideo city-port, respectively. However, these areas were too small compared to the Argentine Pampas or the Brazilian Paraíba Valley to play the role of South

American dynamo. Eventually the small economies, especially Uruguay, suffered from recurrent economic crises that originated in their giant neighbors. Regional economies outside the Southern Cone of South America lacked the natural endowments with which to initiate sustained economic growth. Hence, two specific subnational economies, the Argentine and Brazilian peripheries, had extraordinary repercussions. Their perverse effects scaled up from a purely local dimension to a continental one. They stalled the two national economies with the potential to lead the entire region toward sustained economic development.

An imaginary South American country combining the Argentine Pampa Húmeda, the entire territory of Uruguay, and the state of Rio Grande do Sul in Brazil—all three were world leaders in the production of cereals and cattle—would have been an economic powerhouse similar to Australia, and it would be free from the drag of a backward periphery. That area is a natural topographic region, the landmass corresponding to the River Plate basin. The Australia of South America, although fictional, illustrates how important borders and the associated composition of national economies are for long-term development. The fact that large countries in South America are economically dysfunctional combinations of subnational units and the fact that small countries lack the factor endowments to change the developmental fate of the continent are both a direct outcome of territory consolidation during state formation.

The common wisdom in political science, economics, and history is that Latin America's relative backwardness can be traced either to *colonial rule* prior to the 1800s (extractive institutions created for the benefit of Spanish and Portuguese conquerors) or to the rise of *mass politics* in the 1940s (dysfunctional institutions created in the context of labor mobilization). By focusing on state formation in 1845–75, this book has offered a complementary perspective that emphasizes a chronologically intermediate historical source of economic backwardness. A number of key institutional and economic malfunctions can be traced to the process of state formation. Chances to change the long-term economic and institutional course of Latin America were never as high as they were in the mid-nineteenth century, but they had already vanished by the early twentieth century.

The long-term economic effects of Latin America's political geography are the subject of my next book.

Notes

Introduction

1. Alexander Gerschenkron, *Economic Backwardness in Historical Perspective* (Cambridge, MA: Harvard University Press, 1962), 5–30.
2. Guillermo O'Donnell, "On the State, Democratization and Some Conceptual Problems: A Latin American View with Glances at Some Postcommunist Countries," *World Development* 21, no. 8 (1993): 1355–69.
3. Reinhard Bendix, *Nation-Building and Citizenship: Studies of Our Changing Social Order* (1964; repr., Berkeley: University of California Press, 1977), 16, 249, 411.
4. Charles Tilly, "Reflections on the History of European State-Making," in *The Formation of National States in Western Europe*, ed. Charles Tilly (Princeton, NJ: Princeton University Press, 1975), 14–15; Tilly, *Coercion, Capital, and European States, AD 990–1990* (Cambridge, MA: Blackwell, 1990), 33.
5. Foundational statements are Antonio Annino, "Soberanías en Lucha," in *De los Imperios a las Naciones: Iberoamérica*, ed. Antonio Annino, Luis Castro Leiva, and François-Xavier Guerra (Zaragoza: IberCaja, 1994), 269–92; and José Chiaramonte, *Nación y Estado en Iberoamérica* (Buenos Aires: Sudamericana, 2004).
6. Roderick Barman, *Brazil: The Forging of a Nation, 1798–1852* (Stanford, CA: Stanford University Press, 1994).
7. Jordana Dym, *From Sovereign Villages to National States: City, State, and Federation in Central America, 1759–1839* (Albuquerque: University of New Mexico Press, 2006).
8. For the large number of contingencies that caused the failure of the Central American union, see Thomas Karnes, *The Failure of Union: Central America, 1824–1960* (Chapel Hill: University of North Carolina Press, 1961), esp. chap. 4.

Chapter 1. A Theory of Latecomer State Formation

1. Max Weber, *Economy and Society: An Outline of Interpretive Sociology* (Berkeley: University of California Press, 1978), 1028–29.
2. Charles Tilly, *Coercion, Capital, and European States, AD 990–1992* (Cambridge, MA: Blackwell, 1992), 103–6.

3. Michael Mann, "The Autonomous Power of the State: Its Origins, Mechanisms and Results," *European Journal of Sociology / Archives Européennes de Sociologie* 25, no. 2 (1984): 185–213.

4. Guillermo O'Donnell, "On the State, Democratization and Some Conceptual Problems: A Latin American View with Glances at Some Postcommunist Countries," *World Development* 21, no. 8 (1993): 1355–69.

5. Africa contains the largest number of "weak states." Yet the insightful literature on Africa also tends to conflate state formation and state building. Deficits in violence monopolization and deficits in infrastructural capacity are customarily presented as part of the same syndrome. See Robert H. Jackson, and Carl G. Rosberg, "Why Africa's Weak States Persist: The Empirical and the Juridical in Statehood," *World Politics* 35, no. 1 (1982): 1–24; and Jeffrey Herbst, *States and Power in Africa: Comparative Lessons in Authority and Control* (Princeton, NJ: Princeton University Press, 2000).

6. Nonterritorial political organizations had many forms. A typology does not exist, but an inductive list includes (a) settings in which cultural (church) and political power are not separated (theocracies), so that members of the faith have political obligations irrespective of their physical location; (b) political centers dominating hinterlands with nonpermanent, ill-defined borders; (c) empires, which nominally claim sovereignty over the known world but de facto exert it over a continent or subcontinent; (d) political units made of fragments of noncontiguous territories; (e) "states" that are not surrounded by other states.

7. Hendrik Spruyt, "War, Trade, and State Formation," in *Oxford Handbook of Comparative Politics*, ed. Carles Boix and Susan Stokes (New York: Oxford University Press, 2007), 211–35.

8. Max Weber, *General Economic History* (New Brunswick, NJ: Transaction, 1981), 320.

9. Michael Roberts, "The Military Revolution, 1560–1660," in *Essays in Swedish History* (London: Weidenfeld and Nicolson, 1967), 195–225.

10. Richard Bean, "War and the Birth of the Nation State," *Journal of Economic History* 33, no. 1 (1973): 203–21; William H. McNeill, *The Pursuit of Power: Technology, Armed Force, and Society since AD 1000* (Chicago: University of Chicago Press, 1982); Jeremy Black, *A Military Revolution? Military Change and European Society, 1550–1800* (London: Macmillan, 1991); Clifford J. Rogers, *The Military Revolution Debate* (New York: Routledge, 2018).

11. Geoffrey Parker, *The Military Revolution: Military Innovation and the Rise of the West, 1500–1800* (Cambridge: Cambridge University Press, 1996); Christopher Duffy, *Siege Warfare: The Fortress in The Early Modern World, 1494–1660* (New York: Routledge, 2013).

12. Samuel E. Finer, "State- and Nation-Building in Europe: The Role of the Military," in *The Formation of National States in Western Europe*, ed. Charles Tilly (Princeton, NJ: Princeton University Press, 1975), 84–163.

13. Brian Downing, *The Military Revolution and Political Change: Origins of Democracy and Autocracy in Early Modern Europe* (Princeton, NJ: Princeton University Press, 1993).

14. Specialists in international relations would prefer the term "hegemony" over "hierarchy." Yet, since this is a book in comparative politics, I will refrain from using the word "hegemony" because in the subfield, it is associated with Gramscian notions of social class power. Similarly, I use the word "geopolitics" to refer to military competition among territorially defined sovereign units, although in international relations, it has a more specific meaning, which includes attributes derived from the interaction between politics and geography. Daniel Deudney, "Geopolitics as Theory: Historical Security Materialism," *European Journal of International Relations* 6, no. 1 (2000): 77–107.

15. Friedrich Engels, *The Origin of the Family, Private Property and the State* (London: Penguin, 2010); the quote is from Karl Marx and Friedrich Engels, *The Communist Manifesto* (New York: International Publishers, 1948), 11.

16. For Anderson, the modern state is "a redeployed and recharged apparatus of feudal domination, designed to clamp the peasant masses back into their traditional social position," and state formation is "a displacement of the politico-legal coercion upwards towards a centralized militarized summit—the Absolutist state." Perry Anderson, *Lineages of the Absolutist State* (London: Verso Books, 1979), 18.

17. Ibid., 197.

18. Ibid., 32.

19. The concept of public good has a long and fruitful tradition in economics. It refers to goods that are nonexcludable (e.g., public parks) and nonrivalrous (knowledge of calculus). Contrary to the public good, the club good is excludable. Only members of the club—those who financed the good through fees— can enjoy its benefits (private golf courses). I define "class good" as a deviant type of club good. Its exclusive beneficiaries are the members of the class, as occurs with the club goods, but it is the nonmembers of the class who pay for it (e.g., a railroad connecting a mine and the port, which is financed not by the mine owner but by the general public).

20. Miguel Ángel Centeno, *Blood and Debt: War and the Nation-State in Latin America* (University Park: Pennsylvania State University Press, 2002); Fernando López-Alves, *State Formation and Democracy in Latin America, 1810–1900* (Durham, NC: Duke University Press, 2000); Marcus J. Kurtz, *Latin American State Building in Comparative Perspective* (Cambridge: Cambridge University Press, 2013); Ryan Saylor, *State Building in Boom Times: Commodities and Coalitions in Latin America and Africa* (Oxford: Oxford University Press, 2014); Hillel David Soifer, *State Building in Latin America* (Cambridge: Cambridge University Press, 2015).

21. Centeno, *Blood and Debt*, 127–30.
22. Saylor, *State Building in Boom Times*, 14–21.
23. Soifer, *State Building in Latin America*, 46–58.
24. For a general statement, see Kurtz, *Latin American State Building*, 37–39; and for servile labor being inimical to state building in Peru, see 77–79.
25. See Jackson and Rosberg, "Why Africa's Weak States Persist"; and Herbst, *States and Power in Africa*.
26. Otto Hintze, "Military Organization and the Organization of the State," in *The Historical Essays of Otto Hintze*, ed. Felix Gilbert (Oxford: Oxford University Press, 1975), 181.
27. The most persuasive statement is Downing, *Military Revolution*.

Chapter 2. Independence and State Failure, 1808–45

1. This study relies on a large bibliography, which is organized and commented on in "Bibliographic Appendix to *Latecomer State Formation*," available at the author's Google Scholar page. A key reference for economic issues is Victor Bulmer-Thomas, John Henry Coatsworth, and Roberto Cortés Conde, ed., *The Cambridge Economic History of Latin America*, vol. 1 (Cambridge: Cambridge University Press, 2006). For political aspects, see Tulio Halperín Donghi, *The Contemporary History of Latin America* (Durham, NC: Duke University Press, 1993), parts 2 and 3.
2. In postcolonial Latin American, "institutions were designed to safeguard the interests of the new ruling class." John Lynch, *Caudillos in Spanish America, 1800–1850* (Oxford: Oxford University Press, 1992), 155.
3. Memorandum by Castlereagh, 1 May 1807, in *Correspondence, Dispatches and Other Papers of Viscount Castlereagh*, ed. Marquess of Londonderry, vol. 8, no. 12 (London: Murray, 1848–53), 321.
4. Augustus Granville Stapleton, *George Canning and His Times* (London: Parker, 1859), 411.
5. Juan Bautista Alberdi, *Estudios Económicos*, vol. 1 (Buenos Aires: Imprenta Europea, 1895), 116 (emphasis added).
6. The only exceptions were the captaincies of Chile within the Viceroyalty of Peru and Guatemala within the Viceroyalty of Mexico, which covered most of present-day Central America and Chiapas.
7. For the River Plate context, "To secure [men and supplies in the interior], Buenos Aires had to delegate authority to local officials and militias who made the war effort their own but who identified with the province rather than the capital." Lynch, *Caudillos in Spanish America*, 155.
8. It was during these years of delegated authority in the service of the revolutionary government that men like Facundo Quiroga, already powerful landowners, acquired military and political credentials and became "señores de horca

y cuchillo" (lords of the gallows and knives). David Peña, *Juan Facundo Quiroga* (Buenos Aires: Hyspamerica, 1971), 59–69.

9. According to Lynch, caudillo followers "preyed upon local estancias and rich merchants, seizing crops, cattle, and other property." Lynch, *Caudillos in Spanish America*, 37.

10. Simón Bolívar, "Message to the Constituent Congress of Colombia, 20 January 1830," in *Proclamas y Discursos del Libertador*, ed. Vicente Lecuna (Caracas: Del Comercio, 1939), 398.

11. Robert H. Bates, John Henry Coatsworth, and Jeffrey G. Williamson, "Lost Decades: Postindependence Performance in Latin America and Africa," *Journal of Economic History* 67, no. 4 (2007): 917–43.

12. For a general overview, see Antonio Annino, "Soberanías en Lucha," in *De los Imperios a las Naciones: Iberoamérica* (Zaragoza: IberCaja, 1994), 269–92; for Central America, see Jordana Dym, *From Sovereign Villages to National States: City, State, and Federation in Central America, 1759–1839* (Albuquerque: University of New Mexico Press, 2006); for the territory of present-day Argentina and Uruguay, see José Carlos Chiaramonte, *Ciudades, Provincias, Estados: Orígenes de la Nación Argentina (1800–1846)* (Buenos Aires: Espasa-Calpe, 1997).

13. For warlordism in Upper Peru (Bolivia), see René Danilo Arze Aguirre, *Participación Popular en la Independencia de Bolivia* (La Paz: Organización de Estados Americanos, 1979), 165–67, 197–203.

14. Tulio Halperín Donghi, *The Aftermath of Revolution in Latin America* (New York: Harper and Row, 1973); see also Frank Safford, "Politics, Ideology and Society," in *The Cambridge History of Latin America*, ed. Leslie Bethell, vol. 3 (Cambridge: Cambridge University Press, 1985), 377.

15. Claudio Véliz, "Continuidades y Rupturas en la Historia Chilena: Otra Hipótesis sobre la Crisis Chilena de 1973," *Estudios Públicos* 12 (1983): 44.

16. John Lynch, "Bolívar and the Caudillos," *Hispanic American Historical Review* 63, no. 1 (1983): 3–35.

17. In Venezuela, livestock decreased from 4.8 million head of cattle in 1812 to 256,000 in 1822 and increased to only 2 million in 1839. Augustin Codazzi, *Resumen de la Geografía de Venezuela*, vol. 1 (Paris: Fournier, 1944), 178–81.

18. Alejandra Irigoin, "Macroeconomic Aspects of Spanish American Independence: The Effects of Fiscal and Currency Fragmentation, 1800s–1860s" (Working Paper 03-45, Universidad Carlos III de Madrid, 2003); Leandro Prados de la Escosura, "The Economic Consequences of Independence in Latin America," in *The Cambridge Economic History of Latin America*, ed. Victor Bulmer-Thomas, John Henry Coatsworth, and Roberto Cortés Conde, vol. 1 (Cambridge: Cambridge University Press, 2006), 463–504.

19. Paul Eliot Gootenberg, *Between Silver and Guano: Commercial Policy and the State in Postindependence Peru* (Princeton, NJ: Princeton University Press, 2014), 101.

Chapter 3. The Triumph of Trade-Led
State Formation, 1845–75

1. This study relies on a large bibliography, which is organized and commented on in "Bibliographic Appendix to *Latecomer State Formation*," available at the author's Google Scholar page. Two key references are Tulio Halperín Donghi, *The Contemporary History of Latin America* (London: Macmillan, 1993), part 4; and David Bushnell and Neill Macaulay, *The Emergence of Latin America in the Nineteenth Century* (Oxford: Oxford University Press, 1994).

2. Tulio Halperín Donghi, "Economy and Society in Post-Independence Spanish America," in *The Cambridge History of Latin America*, ed. Leslie Bethell, vol. 3 (Cambridge: Cambridge University Press, 1985), 330.

3. Victor Bulmer-Thomas, *The Economic History of Latin America since Independence*, 2nd ed. (Cambridge: Cambridge University Press, 2003), 38, 53, 72.

4. Luis Bértola and Jeffrey G. Williamson, "Globalization in Latin America before 1940," in *The Cambridge Economic History of Latin America*, ed. Victor Bulmer-Thomas, John Henry Coatsworth, and Roberto Cortés Conde, vol. 1 (Cambridge: Cambridge University Press, 2006), 16.

5. Charles Knickerbocker Harley, "Ocean Freight Rates and Productivity, 1740–1913: The Primacy of Mechanical Invention Reaffirmed," *Journal of Economic History* 48 (1988): 853, fig. 1.

6. William Summerhill, "The Development of Infrastructure," in Bulmer-Thomas, Coatsworth, and Cortés Conde, *Cambridge Economic History of Latin America*, vol. 1, 297.

7. Ibid., 298.

8. Ibid.

9. The taxonomy of warlords is fully developed in Chapter 4.

10. Ariel de la Fuente, *Children of Facundo: Caudillo and Gaucho Insurgency during the Argentine State Formation Process (La Rioja, 1853–1870)* (Durham, NC: Duke University Press, 2000).

11. Friedrich Katz, "Mexico: Restored Republic and Porfiriato, 1867–1910," in *The Cambridge History of Latin America, 1870–1930*, ed. Leslie Bethell, vol. 5 (Cambridge: Cambridge University Press, 1986), 7.

12. James Fred Rippy, *British Investments in Latin America, 1822–1949: A Case Study in the Operations of Private Enterprise in Retarded Regions* (Hamden, CT: Archon Books, 1966), 28.

13. Bartolomé Mitre, "El Capital Inglés: Discurso del 7 de Marzo de 1861," in *Colección de Obras y Escritores y Oradores de la República Argentina*, ed. Adolfo Lamarque, vol. 1 (Buenos Aires: Imprenta Coni, 1875), 212.

14. Bulmer-Thomas, *Economic History of Latin America*, 14–17, 43.

15. For centuries, birds were attracted to the islands by abundant fish. The absence of rain along the Peruvian coastline meant that the guano that accumulated on

the islands did not lose its chemical composition, which has an exceptionally high concentration of nitrogen.

16. Amaro Cavalcanti, *Resenha Financeira do Ex-Império do Brasil em 1889* (Rio de Janeiro: Imprensa Nacional, 1900), 330.

17. In the words of one of the best economic historians of Latin America, "After a quarter century (1826–49) of stagnation in foreign trade, the decade of the 1850s marked a decisive economic and fiscal inflection for many *nations*, as exports expanded rapidly in Brazil, Chile, Peru, Buenos Aires, Colombia, and Central America. This first export boom lasted from mid-century until approximately 1873." Few of the political units in the list were states at the time—much less "nations." It was the emergence of states that in part made the export booms possible, and that is why the 1850s are not only an economic inflection point but also, and more crucially, a political one. Carlos Marichal, "Money, Taxes, and Finance," in Bulmer-Thomas, Coatsworth, and Cortés Conde, *Cambridge Economic History of Latin America*, vol. 1, 449.

18. Roque Sáenz Peña, "Programa de Gobierno," *Ateneo: Revista Mensual Ilustrada* 10 (1910): 16–17.

Chapter 4. A Politician-Centered Approach to State Formation

1. See Maps 9.1, 10.1, and 10.3.

2. As noted in Part 1, Chile and Paraguay are the only cases that skipped the Failure period between Independence and State Formation. The Uruguayan case is studied in detail in Chapter 9. Panama seceded from Colombia in 1903.

3. Alberto Alesina and Enrico Spolaore, *The Size of Nations* (Cambridge, MA: MIT Press, 2005).

4. The rudiments of the Marxist approach to state formation can be traced to Friedrich Engels, *The Origin of the Family, Private Property and the State* (London: Penguin, 2010). Yet the theory presented here borrows directly from Perry Anderson, *Lineages of the Absolutist State* (London: Verso Books, 1979).

5. See Charles Tilly, "War Making and State Making as Organized Crime," in *Bringing the State Back In*, ed. Peter Evans, Dietrich Rueschemeyer, and Theda Skocpol (New York: Cambridge University Press, 1985), 169–90. Although Tilly does not quote Weber, the Weberian inspiration of his text is obvious. See Max Weber, *Economy and Society* (Berkeley: University of California, 1978), 901–40.

6. Suggestively, in Weber's presentation of his theory of state formation, the formation of parties (together with classes and status groups) requires the context of an established state. Party formation is introduced as a logical corollary to state formation, taking place in a subsequent temporal phase. Weber, *Economy and Society*, 926. Similarly, Giovanni Sartori's definition of "party," an organization that mobilizes voter support to gain control of the state, and

his reconstruction of parties' origins in Europe, assumes an already existing state. Sartori, *Parties and Party Systems: A Framework for Analysis* (New York: Cambridge University Press, 1976), 60–64.

Chapter 5. Before Argentina

1. This study relies on a large bibliography, which is organized and commented on in "Bibliographic Appendix to *Latecomer State Formation*," available at the author's Google Scholar page. A key reference is Tulio Halperín Donghi, *De la Revolución de Independencia a la Confederación Rosista* (Buenos Aires: Paidós, 2000).

2. John Lynch, *Caudillos in Spanish America, 1800–1850* (Oxford: Oxford University Press, 1992), 39–40.

3. Carlos Alberto Silva, *El Poder Legislativo de la Nación Argentina* (Buenos Aires: Congreso de la Nación, 1938), 276–77.

4. Rosas's choice in Córdoba, Commander Manuel López, ruled for fifteen years. In 1834, Rosas also displaced San Juan's governor Martín Yanzón, accused of being unitarian, and contributed to the rise of Nazario Benavídez, who ruled the province for twenty years.

5. Entre Ríos became a major player: population grew from thirty thousand to forty-eight thousand in the 1830–50 period. In 1850, it had seventeen *saladeros*, six million cows, and two million sheep.

6. Juan Carlos Garavaglia, "Rentas, Deuda Pública y Construcción Estatal: La Confederación Argentina, 1852–1861," *Desarrollo Económico* 50, no. 198 (2010): 223–48.

7. Albert O. Hirschman, *The Strategy of Economic Development* (New Haven, CT: Yale University Press, 1958).

8. Liberalism in this context promoted free trade in economic affairs and the substitution of the rule of "Big Men," caudillos, by the rule of law in public affairs. Liberalism was essentially a dual political innovation in relation to caudillo rule: competitive politics, even if contenders were rival factions within the urban oligarchy, and civil liberties.

9. Derqui to Mitre, 30 Oct. 1860, in *Archivo del General Mitre*, vol. 7 (Buenos Aires: Biblioteca de la Nación, 1911–13), 30.

Chapter 6. Port-Driven State Formation in Argentina

1. Three state-formation projects were also formed to challenge Buenos Aires: Artigas's Liga de los Pueblos Libres, Paz's Liga del Interior, and Urquiza's Confederación.

2. Bartolome Mitre, "La República del Río de la Plata," *El Nacional*, 9 Dec. 1856, 1–2.

3. Even sophisticated accounts rely on Mitre's personality to some degree. The pioneer work is Rodolfo Rivarola, *Mitre: Una Década de Su Vida Política, 1852–1862* (Buenos Aires: Revista Argentina de Ciencias Políticas, 1921), 6.

4. Jonathan C Brown, *A Socioeconomic History of Argentina, 1776–1860* (New York: Cambridge University Press, 1979).

5. The following account is based on Roy Hora, *Historia Económica de la Argentina* (Buenos Aires: Siglo Veintiuno Editores, 2010); and Hilda Sábato, *Capitalismo y Ganadería en Buenos Aires: La Fiebre del Lanar, 1850–1890* (Buenos Aires: Editorial Sudamericana, 1989).

6. This channel has been suggested by Ricardo M. Ortíz, *Historia Económica de la Argentina* (Buenos Aires: Editorial Raigal, 1955), 255–67.

7. For Mitre's vision about the linkage between economic development and state formation, see Bartolomé Mitre, "El Capital Inglés: Discurso del 7 de Marzo de 1861," in *Colección de Obras y Escritores y Oradores de la República Argentina*, ed. Adolfo Lamarque, vol. 1 (Buenos Aires: Imprenta Coni, 1875), 197–202.

8. For an exquisite account of the rise of the professional politician by a Mitre contemporary, see Juan Bautista Alberdi, *Escritos Póstumos*, vol. 5 (Buenos Aires: Monkes, 1897), 260.

9. *Porteño* refers to people and interests of the city-port of Buenos Aires.

10. These are the so-called *elites letradas*, which had dominated the administration under colonial rule but were suddenly displaced from their positions in the wake of independence and the ensuing "ruralization of power." Tulio Halperín Donghi, *The Aftermath of Revolution in Latin America* (New York: Harper and Row, 1973).

11. Edward Thornton to Lord John Russell, 14 Mar. 1861, U.K. Foreign Office (FO), 6/232.

12. Natalio Botana, *El Orden Conservador: La Política Argentina entre 1880 y 1916* (Buenos Aires: Sudamericana, 1977).

13. Carlos D'Amico, *Buenos Aires, Sus Hombres, Su Política (1860–1890)* (Buenos Aires: Editorial Americana, 1952), 134.

14. Isidoro J. Ruiz Moreno, *El Misterio de Pavón: Las Operaciones Militares y Sus Consecuencias Políticas* (Buenos Aires: Claridad, 2005).

15. Martín Ruiz Moreno, *La Presidencia del Dr. Santiago Derqui y la Batalla de Pavón*, vol. 2 (Buenos Aires: Roldán, 1913), 181.

16. Mariano de Vedia y Mitre, *Historia de la Unidad Nacional* (Buenos Aires: Secretaría Cultura, 1952), 481.

17. Thornton to Russell, 22 Sept. 1861, FO 6/234.

18. Manuel Navarro to unknown soldier, 30 Sept. 1861, folder 118, Archivo General de la Nación, Archivo Urquiza, Buenos Aires (AGN-AU).

19. Pascual Rosas to Justo José de Urquiza, 19 Sept. 1861, folder 118, AGN-AU.

20. Isidoro Ruiz Moreno, "El Litoral Después de Pavón," in *Pavón y la Crisis de la Confederación*, ed. Equipos de Investigación Histórica (Buenos Aires, 1965), 329.

21. Ibid., 340.

22. Thornton to Russell, 1 Oct. 1861, FO 6/234.

23. Carlos Creus, 29 Sept. 1861, in *Informes Españoles sobre Argentina*, ed. Isidoro J. Ruiz Moreno (Buenos Aires: Universidad del Museo Social Argentino, 1993), 245–46.

24. Fermín Chávez, *Vida del Chacho* (Buenos Aires: Theoría, 1962), 140–41.

25. Thornton to Russell, 23 Oct. 1861, FO 6/234.

26. Ocampo, Obligado, and de la Riestra to Mitre, 13 Oct. 1861, in *Archivo del General Mitre* (*AdGM*), vol. 10 (Buenos Aires: Biblioteca de la Nación, 1911–13), 13–15.

27. Ocampo, Obligado, and de la Riestra to Mitre, 18 Oct. 1861, in *AdGM*, vol. 10, 17–19.

28. Obligado to Mitre, 19 Oct. 1861, in *AdGM*, vol. 8, 129.

29. De la Riestra to Mitre, 25 Oct. 1861, in *AdGM*, vol. 8, 175–76.

30. *Tribuna*, October 23, 1861, 1.

31. Mitre to Sarmiento, 19 Oct. 1861, document 1807, folder 14, Archivo Museo Histórico Sarmiento, Buenos Aires.

32. Mitre to Ocampo, Obligado, and de la Riestra, 29 Oct. 1861, in *AdGM*, vol. 10, 28–30.

33. Gelly y Obes to Ocampo, 20 Oct. 1861, in *AdGM*, vol. 9, 262.

34. Thornton to Russell, 20 Nov. 1961, FO 6/234.

35. Obligado to Mitre, 18 Nov. 1861, in *AdGM*, vol. 8, 139.

36. Ocampo to Mitre, 18 Nov. 1861, in *AdGM*, vol. 8, 270–71.

37. Mitre to Sarmiento, 15 Nov. 1861, in *AdGM*, vol. 8, 269–70.

38. Thornton to Russell, 20 Nov. 1961, FO 6/234.

39. Mitre to Ocampo, 19 Nov. 1861, in *AdGM*, vol. 8, 272–73.

40. Mitre to Paunero, 19 Nov. 1861, letter 9165, Museo Mitre, Buenos Aires.

41. Gelly y Obes to Ocampo, 23 Nov. 1861, in *AdGM*, vol. 9, 277.

42. Régulo Martínez to Sarmiento, Rosario, 15 Jan. 1862, Archivo Museo Histórico Sarmiento, Buenos Aires.

43. Mitre to Ocampo, 3 Dec. 1861, in *AdGM*, vol. 8, 276–77.

44. Mitre to Ocampo, 25 Dec. 1861, in *AdGM*, vol. 8, 281–82 (emphasis added).

45. Thomas Joseph Hutchinson, *Buenos Ayres and Argentine Gleanings* (London: Stanford, 1865), 162 (emphasis added).

46. Mitre to Paz, 22 Jan. 1862, Museo Mitre, Buenos Aires.

47. Gelly y Obes to Ocampo, 22 Jan. 1862, in *AdGM*, vol. 9, 78.

48. Mitre to Urquiza, 24 Jan. 1862, in *AdGM*, vol. 10, 122.

Chapter 7. Port-Driven State Formation in Brazil

1. Liberato de Castro Carreira, *Historia Financeira e Orçamentaria do Imperio do Brazil desde a Sua Fundação: Precedida de Alguns Apontamentos acerca da Sua Independencia* (Rio de Janeiro: Imprensa Nacional, 1889), 98, 116–17.

2. This study relies on a large bibliography, which is organized and commented on in "Bibliographic Appendix to *Latecomer State Formation*," available at the author's Google Scholar page. The general vision of nineteenth-century Brazil underlying this chapter was heavily shaped by two works: Roderick Barman, *Brazil: The Forging of a Nation, 1798–1852* (Stanford, CA: Stanford University Press, 1994); and Jeffrey D. Needell, *The Party of Order: The Conservatives, the State, and Slavery in the Brazilian Monarchy, 1831–1871* (Stanford, CA: Stanford University Press, 2006).

3. *Fluminense* is the demonym for the people and traditions originating in Rio de Janeiro.

4. Richard Graham, *Patronage and Politics in Nineteenth-Century Brazil* (Stanford, CA: Stanford University Press, 1994).

5. João Manuel Pereira Silva, "Documento No. 10," in appendix to *Historia do Brazil de 1831 á 1840: Governos Regenciaes durante a Menoridade* (Rio de Janeiro: Dias da Silva Jr. Editores, 1878), 15.

6. "O que mais me assusta é o Rio Grande. . . . Vai me parecendo inevitável a separação da província." Diogo Feijo to Marquês de Barbacena, in António Augusto de Aguiar, *Vida do Marquez de Barbacena* (Rio de Janeiro: Imprensa Nacional, 1896), 906–7.

7. *Anais da Câmara*, vol. 1 (Rio de Janeiro, 1836), 71. The original expression is more vivid: Brazil will be "despedaçado em diferentes estados."

8. William Gore Ouseley to Lord Palmerston, 18 Sept. 1939, U.K. Foreign Office, 13/154, quoted in Barman, *Brazil*, 200.

9. See Louis-Constant-Alexandre de Suzannet, *Souvenirs de Voyages: Les Provinces du Caucase, L'empire du Brésil* (Paris: G.-A. Dentu, 1846), 446–47.

10. Benjamin Constant, *Principes de Politique Applicables à Tous les Gouvernements Représentatifs et Particulièrement à la Constitution Actuelle de la France* (Paris: Eymery, 1815), 35.

11. Theophilo Ottoni, *Circular aos Eleitores de Minas Geraes* (Rio de Janeiro: Correio Mercantil de M. Barreto, Filhos, 1860), 16.

12. Joaquim Nabuco, *Um Estadista do Imperio: Nabuco de Araujo: Sua Vida, Suas Opiniões, Sua Época por Seu Filho Joaquim Nabuco* (Rio de Janeiro and Paris: H. Garnier 1899), 28. I am translating "exaltados" as "radicals."

13. Barman, *Brazil*, 174–75.

14. Needell, *Party of Order*, 53–55.

15. For Honório's intervention, see ibid., 49.

16. Otávio Tarquínio de Sousa, *História dos Fundadores do Império do Brasil*, vol. 3 (Brasília: Edições do Senado Federal, 2015), 173.

17. Ibid., 191.

18. The province of Rio de Janeiro was detached from the royal court through the 1834 reforms. The court's jurisdiction was the "neutral" municipality of the city of Rio de Janeiro. The capital of the province of Rio de Janeiro became Niterói, right across Guanabara Bay.

19. Walter Spalding, *A Epopeia Farroupilha* (Rio de Janeiro: Biblioteca do Exército Editora, 1963).

20. For the most persuasive argument rooting the persistence of the Brazilian state in the benefits the political class derived from it as a large-scale patronage machine, see Richard Graham, "Formando una Nación en el Brasil del Siglo XIX," in *Inventando la Nación: Iberoamérica Siglo XIX*, ed. Antonio Annino and François-Xavier Guerra (México City: Fondo de Cultura Económica, 2003), 629–53.

Chapter 8. Party-Driven State Formation in Mexico

1. David Bushnell and Neill Macaulay, *The Emergence of Latin America in the Nineteenth Century* (Oxford: Oxford University Press, 1994), 55.

2. The dollar was modeled after the Mexican silver peso, so one peso equals one dollar.

3. This study relies on a large bibliography, which is organized and commented on in "Bibliographic Appendix to *Latecomer State Formation*," available at the author's Google Scholar page. A key reference is Brian R. Hamnett, *A Concise History of Mexico* (Cambridge: Cambridge University Press, 2006).

4. Ibid., 113–76; Bushnell and Macaulay, *Emergence of Latin America*, chap. 4.

5. Josefina Zoraida Vázquez, "De la Difícil Constitución de un Estado: México, 1821–1854," in *La Fundación del Estado Mexicano, 1821–1855: Interpretaciones de la Historia de México*, ed. Josefina Zoraida Vázquez (México City: Nueva Imagen, 1994), 9.

6. Barbara A. Tenenbaum, *The Politics of Penury: Debt and Taxes in Mexico, 1821–1856* (Albuquerque: University of New Mexico Press, 1986).

7. When Rio de Janeiro, Lima, and Buenos Aires had barely reached the mark of fifty thousand dwellers, México City had already tripled the number. Guadalajara, Guanajuato, Puebla, and Querétaro were as large as Lima and Rio de Janeiro.

8. Lucas Alamán, *Historia de México*, vol. 5 (Mexico: Imprenta Victoriano Agüeros, 1885), 523.

9. For Iturbide's fall, see Nettie Lee Benson, "The Plan of Casa Mata," *Hispanic American Historical Review* 25 (February 1945): 45–56; and Jan Bazant, "Mexico from Independence to 1867," in *The Cambridge History of Latin America*, ed. Leslie Bethell, vol. 3 (Cambridge: Cambridge University Press, 1985), 426–28.

10. The Scottish Rite lodge was in part sponsored by the British minister to Mexico Henry G. Ward.

11. It was more confederal in that Mexican states had more sources of revenue than the U.S. states did. Additionally, Mexican states had equal weight in the election of the executive. It was less liberal in that no bill of individual rights was included and several customary corporate privileges were not explicitly abolished.

12. Bazant, "Mexico from Independence," 449.

13. Bushnell and Macaulay, *Emergence of Latin America*, 72.

14. I am translating Supremo Poder Conservador as "Supreme *Moderating* Branch" in order to avoid confusion between "conservative" as a partisan label and "conservative" as a constitutional term.

15. The interpretation that Santa Anna manipulated the liberal menace to blackmail the church is most clearly presented by Bazant, "Mexico from Independence," 439.

16. Ibid., 453.

17. Bushnell and Macaulay, *Emergence of Latin America*, 196–97.

18. Although liberals knew the risks of military reaction by the conservatives, they did not make war preparations. They improvised an army as the conflict unfolded. Liberal victory reveals the weakness of the official army.

Chapter 9. Party-Driven State Formation in Comparative Perspective

1. This study relies on a large bibliography, which is organized and commented on in "Bibliographic Appendix to *Latecomer State Formation*," available at the author's Google Scholar page. A key reference is Frank Safford and Marco Palacios, *Colombia: Fragmented Land, Divided Society* (Oxford: Oxford University Press, 2001).

2. Zamira Díaz de Zuluaga, *Oro, Sociedad y Economía: El Sistema Colonial en la Gobernación de Popayán, 1533–1733* (Bogotá: Banco de la República, 1994).

3. David Bushnell, *The Santander Regime in Gran Colombia* (Westport, CT: Greenwood, 1970), 58–75.

4. The history of party formation that follows draws on two convergent sources: Frank Safford and Marco Palacios, *Colombia: Fragmented Land, Divided Society* (Oxford: Oxford University Press, 2001), 134–56; and Helen Delpar, *Red against Blue: The Liberal Party in Colombian Politics, 1863–1899* (Tuscaloosa: University of Alabama Press, 2010).

5. Frank Safford, "Social Aspects of Politics in Nineteenth-Century Spanish America: New Granada, 1825–1850," *Journal of Social History* 5, no. 3 (1972): 344–70.

6. A wonderful source on the artisans' disappointment is Ambrosio López, *El Desengaño (o Confidencias de Ambrosio López, Primer Director de la Sociedad de Artesanos de Bogotá, Denominada Hoi Sociedad Democratica)* (Bogotá: Imprenta de Espinosa, 1851).

7. Carlos Real de Azúa, *Historia y Política en el Uruguay* (Montevideo: Editorial Cal y Canto, 1997), 56–59.

8. Juan A. Oddone, "The Formation of Modern Uruguay, c. 1870–1930," in *The Cambridge History of Latin America*, ed. Leslie Bethell, vol. 5 (Cambridge: Cambridge University Press, 1986), 454.

9. Juan P. Barrán, *Apogeo y Crisis del Uruguay Pastoril y Caudillesco: 1839–1875* (Montevideo: Ediciones de la Banda Oriental, 1979).

10. Oddone, "The Formation of Modern Uruguay," 455.

11. Hernán Brienza, *Urquiza, el Salvaje: El Traidor que Constituyó la Nación* (Buenos Aires: Aguilar, 2017), chap. 3.

12. Carlos Real de Azúa, *El Patriciado Uruguayo* (Montevideo: Asir, 1961), 77–98.

13. Javier Gallardo, "Las Ideas Republicanas en los Orígenes de la Democracia Uruguaya," *Araucaria: Revista Iberoamericana de Filosofía, Política y Humanidades* 9, no. 1 (2003): 3–44; Gerardo Caetano, "Genealogías de la Política Uruguaya Moderna: Disputas y Balances entre Liberalismo, Republicanismo y Democracia en el Siglo XIX," *Claves: Revista de Historia* 2, no. 2 (2016): 111–43.

14. The indelible rural marks of Uruguayan politics are most persuasively presented in Fernando López-Alves, "Between the Economy and the Polity in the River Plate: Uruguay, 1811–1890" (Occasional Papers, Institute of Latin American Studies, University of London, 1993), 1–97.

15. Carlos Calderón Reyes, *Anales del Senado* (1898), 105–6.

16. Rafael Uribe Uribe, *Anales de la Cámara de Representantes* (1898), 386.

17. Ibid., 389–90.

18. Carlos Martínez Silva, "La Vieja Iniquidad," in *Repertorio Colombiano* (Bogotá, 1896), 161–69.

19. Report by Benjamín Herrera (Liberal), Felipe Angulo (Conservative), and Gerardo Pulecio (Reyista), *Anales de la Asamblea Nacional* (1905), 73.

20. Julio H. Palacio, *Historia de Mi Vida* (Bogotá: Camacho Roldan, 1942), 249, 290.

21. Pedro Navarro, *El Parlamento en Pijama* (Bogotá: Talleres Mundo al Día, 1935), 15–16.

22. José Espalter, *El Problema Nacional* (Montevideo: Imprenta Tribuna Popular, 1905), 59–60.

Chapter 10. Lord-Driven State Formation

1. Domingo F. Sarmiento, *Argirópolis* (1850; repr., Villa María, Argentina: Eduvim, 2012).

2. Jordana Dym, *From Sovereign Villages to National States: City, State, and Federation in Central America, 1759–1839* (Albuquerque: University of New Mexico Press, 2006).

3. John Stephens, *Incidents of Travel in Central America*, vol. 1 (New York City: Harper, 1848), 134.

4. Rafael Carrera, *Memorias 1837 á 1840* (Guatemala: Ignacio Solís, 1979), 18.

5. Ibid., 15.

6. Frederick Chatfield to Lord Palmerston, San Salvador, 16 Aug. 1838, PRO, U.K. Foreign Office, 15/20.
7. John Lynch, *Caudillos in Spanish America, 1800–1850* (Oxford: Oxford University Press, 1992), 276.
8. Ibid., 283.
9. Luis Peru de Lacroix, *Diario de Bucaramanga* (Paris: Ollendorff, 1912), 71–72.
10. Robert Ker Porter, *Ker Porter's Caracas Diary*, ed. Walter Dupouy (Caracas: Arte, 1966), 679.
11. Lynch, *Caudillos in Spanish America*, 291.
12. José Antonio Páez, *Autobiografía*, vol. 2 (New York: Ponce de León), 303.

Conclusion

1. James C. Scott, *The Art of Not Being Governed: An Anarchist History of Upland Southeast Asia* (New Haven, CT: Yale University Press, 2009), 4.
2. *Oxford English Dictionary Online*, s.v. "hard-wiring," accessed May 2020, https://www-oed-com.proxy1.library.jhu.edu/view/Entry/393643?rskey =KYoTnQ&result=1#eid.
3. For state penetration, see Joseph LaPalombara and Myron Weiner, "The Origin and Development of Political Parties," in *Political Parties and Political Development*, ed. Joseph LaPalombara and Myron Weiner (Princeton, NJ: Princeton University Press, 1966), 20–21. For capacity building, Francis Fukuyama, *State Building: Governance and World Order in the Twenty-First Century* (Ithaca, NY: Cornell University Press, 2004).
4. Literature on western European state formation has also acknowledged a number of institutions that were jointly created with territorial consolidation. A classical source is Otto Hintze, *The Historical Essays of Otto Hintze*, ed. Felix Gilbert (Oxford: Oxford University Press, 1975); for a more recent source, see Daniel Ziblatt, *Structuring the State* (Princeton, NJ: Princeton University Press, 2006).
5. Agustina Giraudy, *Democrats and Autocrats: Pathways of Subnational Undemocratic Regime Continuity within Democratic Countries* (New York: Oxford University Press, 2015).
6. See Edward L. Gibson, "The Populist Road to Market Reform: Policy and Electoral Coalitions in Mexico and Argentina," *World Politics* 49, no. 3 (1997): 339–70; and Edward L. Gibson and Ernesto Calvo, "Federalism and Low-Maintenance Constituencies: Territorial Dimensions of Economic Reform in Argentina," *Studies in Comparative International Development* 35, no. 3 (2000): 32–55.
7. The Dutch Disease occurs when foreign sales from the leading export sector cause currency overvaluation, which makes the other sectors less competitive.

Index

Note: Page numbers in italics refer to figures and maps. Numbers in bold refer to tables.